COSMIC BEGINNINGS AND
HUMAN ENDS

COSMIC BEGINNINGS AND HUMAN ENDS

Where Science and Religion Meet

EDITED BY

Clifford N. Matthews

Roy Abraham Varghese

Open ✹ Court

Chicago and La Salle, Illinois

"Science at the Crossroads" by George Bugliarello is based upon the paper he delivered to Sigma Xi, the Scientific Research Society, at the Sigma Xi Forum in San Francisco, 1993.

Grateful acknowledgement is made for permission to reprint the following:

"Creation Stories, Religious and Atheistic" by John Leslie appeared originally in *Philosophy of Religion* 34:65–77. © 1993 Kluwer Academic Publishers.

"A Search for Beliefs to Live by Consistent with Science" by Roger W. Sperry appeared originally in *Zygon: Journal of Religion and Science*, volume 26, number 2 (June 1991): 237–58. © 1991 by the Joint Publication Board of *Zygon*.

"The Origin of Consciousness" by Richard G. Swinburne appeared originally in *Origin and Evolution of the Universe: Evidence for Design?*, J.M. Robson, ed. (Montreal: McGill-Queen's University Press, 1987). © 1987 McGill-Queen's University Press.

• • • • • • • • • •

Library of Congress Cataloging-in-Publication Data

Cosmic beginnings and human ends : where science and religion meet / edited by Clifford N. Matthews, Roy Abraham Varghese.
    p.   cm.
    Includes bibliographical references and index.
    ISBN 0-8126-9269-1.—ISBN 0-8126-9270-5 (pbk.)
    1. Religion and science—Congresses. 2. Cosmogony—Congresses. 3. Cosmology—Congresses. I. Matthews, Clifford N., 1921–
II. Varghese, Roy Abraham.
    BL241. C588 1994
    291.1' 75—dc20   94-23845
                                     CIP

• • • • • • • • • •

CONTENTS

PREFACE

Cosmic Beginnings and Human Ends was the title of a symposium on science and religion held in Chicago at the 1993 Parliament of the World's Religions, a convocation that celebrated the centenary of the original Parliament. The significance of this theme for the Parliament as a whole can hardly be exaggerated in view of the enormous impact of modern science on all aspects of twentieth century life, particularly religion. It is our hope that the presentations were of value not simply in terms of the relation of science to religion but also for the light shed on the nature of the world revealed by modern science. Perhaps, to quote Thomas Berry's remark at the Parliament, "The story of the universe is the only thing that can bring the religions of the world together"—at least in the sense of providing a common point of reference.

In this anthology we publish the papers presented by the various participants in these sessions along with articles by other scholars who have helped set the agenda in the contemporary discussion on cosmic beginnings and human ends. As one might expect from the title, the contributions to this collection range from presentations by scientists at the forefront of research into the beginnings of matter, life, and mind, to studies by philosophers and theologians noted for their inquiries into the nature of science and the destiny of *Homo sapiens.* Diversity in philosophical perspective, religious affiliation, and academic discipline is the hallmark of this anthology as it was of the Parliament itself.

The scientists included in this volume need little introduction to the student of modern science. Edward "Rocky" Kolb is among those at the leading edge of modern cosmology noted for his ability to convey the excitement of his subject to the lay reader. Cyril Ponnamperuma, a pioneer in origin of life studies, continues to stimulate worldwide interest in this new field of investigation. Among the other scientist contributors, Lynn Margulis is renowned for her ideas on symbiosis and Gaia; James Shapiro, for opening up new thinking about bacteria; George Sudarshan, for his provocative work on faster-than-light tachyons; and Nobel-laureate Roger Sperry, for his revealing experiments on the emergent properties of the brain. Theologian Mary Hunt and psychologist Alice Dan present feminist perspectives on the science/society interface, while ethical concerns raised by modern science and technology are addressed by scientist-theologian Rustum Roy, by engineer-philosopher George Bugliarello, and by the interdisciplinary humanist Kenneth Vaux.

Three leading philosophers of science have made a significant addition to this anthology: Ian Barbour, with his philosophical analysis of theories of the origin of the universe; John Leslie, noted for his work on the anthropic principle, with a comparative study of religious and atheistic pictures of creation; and Richard Swinburne, with an inquiry into the origin of consciousness in the light of evolutionary theory. Also contributing in a philosophic vein is the author and journalist Timothy Ferris, who has been exceptionally successful in explaining developments in modern science to the general public through his writings and television productions.

Two influential Eastern visions of reality are represented in the papers by John Dobson (Advaita Vedanta) and Hsing-Tsung Huang (the Tao), while Raimon Panikkar compares directly phenomenological aspects of science and Christianity. We are especially pleased to have an Introduction by Jim Kenney, Program Chair of the Parliament; without his practical help and day-by-day encouragement throughout the months of planning, there would have been no Symposium. This Preface, of course, was written by the Editors, who have also taken the opportunity to write overviews touching on many of the ideas presented in the following pages. Editing has been kept to a minimum in order to preserve the unique styles and formats of each contributor.

The papers are generally followed by a section with answers from the authors to three key questions posed by the editors specifically for this volume:

1 What are your views on cosmic beginnings, particularly with reference to the origin of the universe, of life, and of *Homo sapiens?*
2 What are your views on human ends, especially as this relates to the framework of cosmic beginnings?
3 What do you think should be the relationship between religion and science?

Regarding the last question, we are reminded that the original scientific revolution represented a break with the inflexible rationalism of classical Greece, which had little use for empirical observation and experimental verification. We appear today to be at the center of a second revolution, this time a reaction against the rationalistic straitjackets imposed by certain kinds of scientific thought. It seems the religions of the world may have a unique opportunity to contribute to the paradigms now emerging from the extremes of positivism and relativism. To be taken seriously, their insights must be tempered by respect for the reductionist and integrative modes of operation that have always characterized the scientific enterprise. In the same spirit, science must be open to the efforts of religion to establish values in the world of facts. This anthology, we hope, will lend impetus to the new dialogue between modern science and the religions of the world.

During the compilation of this volume we were deeply saddened to hear that Roger Sperry had died of a heart attack in Pasadena, California, on April 17, 1994. Despite a disease that robbed him of mobility for many years, Professor Sperry remained intellectually active until his last days, concentrating in his later work on the relationship between mind and consciousness and ethical values.

With his wife Norma he took a keen interest in the events of the Parliament. Eager to contribute to *Cosmic Beginnings and Human Ends,* his last letter to us, dated March 17, began:

> *Just a quick afterthought: considering the circumstances it occurs to me that you might prefer to use the enclosed "personalized account of the beliefs I live by as a scientist and how I arrived at them."*

Of course we are more than pleased to have the opportunity to reprint this eloquent account of "A Search for Beliefs to Live by Consistent with Science" from a man who made titanic contributions to neurobiology and who I heard described at a recent memorial observance as a superb teacher, a wonderful and generous colleague, and a dear friend. His willingness to take philosophical questions seriously, with their many ethical implications, can only be an encouragement to others to share his concerns about science and human values.

INTRODUCTION

· · · · · · · · · ·

Jim Kenney

Jim Kenney is the co-founder and Executive Director of Common Ground, an adult educational organization and study center in greater Chicago which offers a wide range of programs focusing on the great cultural, religious, philosophical, and spiritual traditions of the world. Program Chair for the Parliament of the World's Religions, he was responsible for planning and organizing the many events that took place in Chicago from 28 August–4 September 1993. A well-known lecturer and consultant on multicultural topics, he is the co-editor, with Ron Miller, of *The Fireball and the Lotus: Emerging Spirituality from Ancient Roots.*

· · · · · · · · · ·

It was simply the most extraordinary interfaith event of all time. Over 7,000 participants, including 1,000 presenters—religious and spiritual leaders as well as scholars and experts on a wide variety of subjects—gathered in the early fall of 1993 at Chicago's Palmer House Hilton for eight days of lectures, seminars, performances, concerts, interreligious dialogue, conversation, and fellowship. The occasion was the Parliament of the World's Religions, the result of five years of intensive planning, consultation, and ground-breaking interfaith cooperation, organized under the auspices of the Council for a Parliament of the World's Religions.

The Parliament was first conceived as a centennial celebration of the 1893 World's Parliament of Religions—one of several "congresses" which took place during Chicago's Columbian Exposition celebrating "A Century of Progress." Once planning was underway, however, it became clear that the 1993 event would far surpass the original. Hundreds of the world's most revered, influential, and engaged religious and spiritual leaders attended, along with thousands of believers from nearly every faith and walk of life. The depth and variety of interfaith participation alone would have guaranteed that the Parliament would have enormous significance, but there was more.

From the beginning, the Council was determined that the

1

gathering should address the range of critical issues which confront us all at this vital juncture in human history. To this end, scholars and scientists, cosmologists and ecologists, researchers and theoreticians were invited to come to Chicago to join in the discussion of the role of religion in the future of the planetary community.

The planning process itself was a journey through largely uncharted territory. As I look back on it, it seems that those of us who gathered on a June day in 1988 and began to dream about the possibilities were often sustained by our naiveté. Had we known how complex and how daunting the real task would become, we might never have begun. Somehow, though, the tortuous planning process gave life to a rich and vibrant interfaith eco-system. (That metaphor seems particularly appropriate, since each part of the overall design helped to inform and enliven every other.)

As Program Chair for the event, I'm happy to say that the 1993 Parliament in many ways went beyond my hopes. It took form as a wonderful gathering of concerned and engaged women and men from virtually every faith tradition, every culture, and every discipline. The energy and enthusiasm which one encountered in the corridors (and, perhaps especially, in the crowded elevators) gave genuine testimony to the transformative power of interfaith and interdisciplinary encounter and dialogue.

Without question, one of the most provocative and fruitful dimensions of the Parliament program was the Symposium on Science and Religion, "Cosmic Beginnings and Human Ends." It offered participants a unique opportunity to reflect upon the interaction of religion with science and technology as humankind approaches the threshold of the twenty-first century. The Symposium consisted of a series of thematically linked presentations by distinguished members of the international scientific community, addressing key areas in which scientific and technological developments are raising issues of direct concern to the world's religious communities. Underlying these presentations were fundamental questions concerning life on earth and in the universe. This book grows out of that remarkable series of conversations.

Over the course of several days, participants in the Symposium were challenged to rethink familiar notions—some long-cherished—about the universe and life itself. There was no lack of intriguing questions, and most had profound relevance for the renewed dialogue between science and religion. Why is there something, rather than nothing? Why is there a universe at all? Does life exist throughout the cosmos? How does mind interact with nature? Do mythic elements in the very structure of human consciousness play a role in the construction of our scientific world view? How do traditional eastern and western philosophical and religious concepts bear on our interpretation of discoveries in the sciences? How are we to understand and to model existence, reality, change, and permanence? What are the theological implications of "Big Bang" cosmology? Has sexism plagued science as it has theology? How are we to understand the implications of the slow but steady convergence of the world's religions in the light of globalizing modern technology? And what is the likely future of the compact between science and society and the encounter between science and religion?

I'm personally delighted to have been asked to contribute an Introduction to this collection of essays. There are, in my view, few undertakings more vital than the rejoining of the all but abandoned dialogue between science and applied technology, on the one hand, and religion, theology, and spirituality, on the other.

A good friend once asked me, "How many people do you think lived through the Renaissance?" I've never forgotten his question. He wasn't inquiring about population figures, but about the essence of the time. How many people knew then that they were living in an age of revolution? How many woke each morning eager to find out "how is the Renaissance coming along?" How many simply went about their daily tasks blissfully unaware of the new world taking shape around them? Who responded to the opportunity and the challenge? Who exulted?

The situation that confronts us today is similar in many ways. We live in an era of revolutionary transformation and yet we are often so preoccupied with simply "coping" that we fail to notice dramatic changes in the fundamental rhythms of life and thought. Gradually, however, we may be beginning to awaken. Our concern for the issues of the modern era expresses a growing awareness of the realities which challenge the human community. Ironically enough, the despair we sometimes feel may be a sign of growth. If we are dismayed at the mess we seem to have made of things, it may be because we are beginning to understand. Perhaps the step from lamentation to commitment will prove shorter than we might have imagined.

One thing at least seems certain: when future historians

gather to mull over the complex weave and texture of their past, they will spend a great deal of time and energy trying to come to terms with the late twentieth century. They will reflect and wonder, but their central question may very well be: "What was it like to live in such an extraordinary time?"

Black holes? Quantum jumps? Strange Attractors? Synthetic RNA? What's happened to science? What's become of reality? Do we inhabit a comfortable and familiar "machine universe" or an incomprehensible mystery whose every happenchance fits somehow into a larger scheme? How do we ordinary mortals begin to comprehend the implications for our own lives and our own choices? I'm reminded of a cartoon that appeared in *The New Yorker* some years ago. It's a party scene and one *bon vivant* is saying to another, "I have the greatest respect for reality, but I don't let it interfere with my life."

It's been some thirty years since the philosopher Thomas Kuhn, in his landmark work *The Structure of Scientific Revolutions*, described the progress of science as marked by periods dominated by more or less fixed sets of assumptions but occasionally punctuated by non-cumulative breaks with tradition or with "the norm." Kuhn used the term "paradigm shift" to denote the relatively abrupt departure from prevailing theoretical models, predispositions, experimental protocols, and preeminent hypotheses and the entry into a radically new scientific view of reality.

A paradigm is a pattern or structure of belief and understanding which consists of a network of associated ideas, concepts, ways of speaking, assumptions, beliefs, attitudes, values, songs, and stories which come together to influence the way one sees the world. Just as rose-colored glasses filter the light which reaches the wearer, paradigms (as sets of notions about what is 'good', 'true', 'possible', etc.) influence our experience of the world and our reaction to it. As the futurist Jay Ogilvy puts it, "Paradigms are like models, moods, myths, or metaphors." The mood swing has clearly begun, and paradigm shift may prove to be the most significant development of the modern era.

Models or paradigms are of vital importance for human experience and understanding. They condition our patterns of response to the world of everyday experience, to each other, and to the unseen universe. A culture necessarily depends upon a net of assumptions so interwoven that to challenge one strand is to threaten the entire structure. As a result, a real paradigm shift eventually touches and transforms every phase of the life of the individual or the society in which it takes place. Religion and science are perhaps more immediately and more deeply affected than any other dimensions of culture.

The concept of paradigm shift has taken on a figurative life that Kuhn certainly did not anticipate. We hear the term bandied about these days—and rather uncritically—in the most unlikely contexts. It's become part of the language of New Age culture and has even surfaced recently in some of the hipper blandishments of Madison Avenue. But the not-so-simple fact is that we *are* living in an age of shifting paradigms.

Not since the Copernicans and Newtonians leveled the medieval scholastic establishment has a comparable transformation of the human view of the universe taken place. In Europe, four hundred and fifty years ago, it was utterly obvious to most thinking persons that the daily flow of events depended on divine will. Whether that will was ordered or whimsical, whether it could be cajoled or influenced by human act or by prayer, was left to the theologians to puzzle out. The Scientific Revolution changed all that. Western civilization came in time to accept the mechanistic paradigm—the complex structure of rational models predicated on the concept of materialism and the notion of a "clockwork" universe.

It is that mechanistic-materialistic, reductionistic, and eminently commonsensical world view which is today gradually being subsumed under a newer overarching scheme. Twentieth-century science, with physics in the lead, has come to question and even to reject many of the basic conceptions of reality which have served us so well since Copernicus first dared to suggest that the Earth was not the fixed center of the universe.

A provocative recent book by physicists Paul Davies and John Gribbin puts the latest paradigm jump in perspective. *The Matter Myth: Dramatic Discoveries That Challenge Our Understanding of Physical Reality* offers a panoramic view of the career of the new science, and the authors say without hesitation:

> The paradigm shift that we are now living through is a shift away from reductionism and toward holism; it is as profound as any paradigm shift in the history of science.

That contention is borne out in the essays assembled here.

"Reality," says Walter Truett Anderson (in the title of his

recent book), "isn't what it used to be." True enough. Anderson's work addresses the emergence of the postmodern mindset. Moderns deal in absolutes and revel in certainties. Postmoderns, on the other hand, know too much to be very certain about anything but the quest itself. Science has provided the postmodern world with its most essential riddles.

We live in a time of transition from mechanistic and reductionistic models of experience (concerned almost exclusively with the analysis of the moving parts of the whole) to models which may be characterized as holistic, or even "organic" (concerned with the description of the behavior of entire systems). The most central fact of the modern paradigm shift is the rediscovery of the interdependence of all existence. Its characteristic theme is the convergence of what had seemed to an earlier age to be impossibly disparate and unrelated dimensions of reality and modes of human experience.

When Thomas Kuhn coined the term "paradigm shift," he was particularly fascinated with the sweeping transformation of European culture which was brought about by the last great shift, the sixteenth-century Copernican Revolution. The discovery by the great Polish astronomer Nikolas Copernicus that the Earth was not the fixed center of the universe demolished the comfortable fabric of medieval presuppositions. In time, it led to the Scientific Revolution (and the "earthshaking" contributions of Galileo, Kepler, and Newton) and contributed to the end of the long-unchallenged cultural domination of the Church. The power of the new paradigm lay in its compelling argument that the universe was a reasonable place, that is, that its movements, its patterns, and its changes were shaped not by divine whimsy but by the rational (and discoverable) principles which governed every element and every event of existence.

In a way, the Copernican Revolution had what one might call a centrifugal character. It dislodged Earth from its supposed fixity at the center of the universe and sent it hurling off to join the other "planets" (from the Greek, "wanderers") in their meanderings around the sun. Perhaps, as we shall see, it's not too much to suggest that the paradigm shift which is now underway has something of a centripetal feel: instead of being thrown out into the vastness of the cosmos (and that must have been the way it felt to many in the sixteenth century), we find ourselves drawn inexorably toward a center.

Like the Copernican ferment, the modern stirring which can already be felt in so many disciplines and areas of experience is in a sense a reflection of developments in our understanding of the physical world. Put as simply as possible, it derives in part from increasing evidence of the radical interdependence of the elements of existence, elements which were once believed to be only occasionally interconnected. Physicist David Bohm comments on the implications of the two great edifices of modern physics, relativity theory and quantum mechanics:

> One is led to a new notion of unbroken wholeness which denies the classical idea of the analyzability of the world into separately and independently existing parts. . . . We have reversed the usual classical notion that the independent 'elementary parts' of the world are the fundamental reality, and that the various systems are merely particular contingent forms and arrangements of these parts. Rather, we say that the inseparable quantum interconnectedness of the whole universe is the fundamental reality, and that relatively independently behaving parts are merely particular and contingent forms within the whole.

The new scientific understanding which has taken shape over the last several decades involves a fundamental shift from emphasis on the individual parts of a given system to an inquiry into the dynamic processes which shape and structure the whole. While the new paradigm certainly does not demand that we discard the extremely useful and important structural-mechanical model, it focuses our attention on the systems themselves and on the processes which underlie the familiar structures. Once attention has shifted from parts to wholes, powerful new questions must be posed about the dynamic and interdependent character of those all-embracing processes.

And as the scientific enterprise takes up questions of this sort, its relevance to the sphere of religious inquiry becomes clearer. There can be little doubt that the long estrangement of the estates of religion, philosophy, and science has played a major role in the modern breakdown of traditional models for understanding. But there is reason for hope. The emergence of interdependence as a central theme in late twentieth-century science and the new ideas and approaches which animate the discussions comprising this volume may well bring about a new and revitalized encounter between the traditional estates. Over sixty years ago, the Nobel Prize-winning, Austrian physicist Wolfgang Pauli observed that:

> It was precisely the idea of an objective world running its course in time and space according to strict causal laws that produced a sharp clash between science and the spiritual formulations of the various religions. If science goes beyond this strict view—and it has done just that with relativity theory and is likely to go even further with quantum theory—then the relationship between science and the contents religions try to express must change once again. Perhaps science, by revealing the existence of new relationships during the past thirty years, may have lent our thought much greater depth.

In the Rinzai tradition of Zen Buddhism, a *koan* is a riddle, puzzle, or paradox which becomes a subject for meditative contemplation—e.g., "What is the sound of one hand clapping?" The seeker's *koan* is his or her key. What is the modern *koan?* One could argue that it's to be found in the continuing scientific and religious meditation on the nature of reality and in the themes which resonate there. Reality may not be what it used to be, but it gets more interesting with every paradigm shift.

· · · · · · · · · ·
Science and Religion at the Threshold of Space, Time, Life, and Consciousness

1 What are your views on cosmic beginnings, particularly with reference to the origin of the universe, of life, and of *Homo sapiens?*

As a non-scientist, I am of course unable properly to weigh the evidence which is advanced in support of Big Bang cosmology, but I am persuaded that the preponderance of scientific opinion supports that theory and the concomitant expansionary model of the universe. As a longtime student of the relationship between science and religion, I am captivated by the elegance of the developing theory and by its mythic and symbolic quality.

It is at the same time a powerful testimony to the power of the human mind and will and a daunting reminder of the limits of knowing. Thus far we have, most experts believe, peered back to within 10^{-43} seconds of the first breath of time and space. We may yet move even closer. But there is no likelihood that we will ever unlock the secrets of the singularity from which the Big Bang may have pulsed forth. That inscrutable "point" represents not only the threshold of space and time but also the threshold of mystery.

In the beginning was the unknowable. There followed the point-instant that birthed the universe. And then—100,000 years into the process?—there was light.

2 What are your views on human ends, especially as this relates to the framework of cosmic beginnings?

The essential theme of religious, philosophical, spiritual, and cultural discussions of "human ends" has always been *vision*, or the lack thereof. That is, in its quest for significance, humankind has consistently sought a vision of its place in some larger scheme of things. That vision need not, of course, be theocentric. Indeed, many thinkers (e.g., the French philosophers Jean-Paul Sartre and Albert Camus) have insisted that the very meaninglessness of the chaotic cosmos is the only certainty and that human "ends" can only be grounded in the moment of authentic choice. Some voices have emphasized the role of a personal and—to some degree— knowable God as the constant source of meaning and direction in human existence. Others speak of a God who has set the universe in motion and "absconded," leaving humankind to determine its own course. Still others deny the existence of a creator while affirming the inherent human potential for meaningful existence and even "enlightenment."

Whatever one's view, it is increasingly clear that the search for understanding of the beginnings of cosmic reality is, in the last half of the troubled twentieth century, energized by more than the desire to know. As we inquire into the first fractions of the first second or struggle to comprehend the first stirrings of life itself, we are in a sense desperate to understand something more about our place, our purpose, our proper ends.

As we move tantalizingly closer to a limited but coherent vision of cosmic beginnings and life's origins, we cannot help but ponder—consciously or unconsciously—the most ancient mystery of all: Why are we?

3 What do you think should be the relationship between religion and science?

I am convinced that the alienation which is so characteristic of the modern (or postmodern?) experience is in no small measure due to the estrangement, at the very threshold of the modern era, of the estates of religion, philosophy, and science. But, just perhaps, that estrangement is diminishing.

The more elegant our scientific models become, the more

mysterious is their import. It is at the threshold of space, time, life, and consciousness that the conversation between religion and science is most enriching.

I am convinced that religious discourse uninformed by the scientific enterprise is often bankrupt. But scientific inquiry ignores the great religious and philosophical questions at its peril.

1

Images of Enlightenment: A Mandala for Science

Clifford N. Matthews

Clifford N. Matthews was born in Hong Kong in 1921. His early education was interrupted by his experience as a prisoner-of-war there and in Japan from 1941 to 1945. After the war he completed his undergraduate studies in England at the University of London and then moved to the United States for graduate work in chemistry at Yale University. After several years in industry, mostly at Monsanto carrying out fundamental chemical research, he became in 1969 a professor of chemistry at the University of Illinois at Chicago, where his research on cosmochemistry and the origin of life led him to use the unifying theme of cosmic evolution in all his teaching activities. As emeritus professor since 1992, he continues to work on his controversial cyanide model for the simultaneous origin of proteins and nucleic acids.

Abstract

To help in defining today's scientific world view, we construct here a mandala—a diagram of the structure of human consciousness—arising from fundamental underlying concepts of science concerned with matter, life, and mind. Its mythic elements include the well-known ouroboros, DNA, and yin-yang symbols, combined to represent a universe we see as participatory, transcendent, and open.

Mandalas East and West

Mandala, the Sanskrit word for circle, is defined in the *Random House Dictionary of the English Language* as

1 a schematized representation of the cosmos, chiefly characterized by a concentric configuration of geometric shapes, each of which contains an image of a deity or an attribute of a deity;
2 (in Jungian psychology) a symbol representing the effort to reunify the self.

Most familiar to us are the colorful works of art on cloth or paper that we see as visual scriptures of Buddhism, illustrating the

FIGURE 1.   *Mandala of Kalachakra.*

FIGURE 2.   *A modern mandala.*

teachings arising from the Buddha's profound understanding of human nature. In conjunction with the Parliament of the World's Religions, a most intriguing event was the construction in Chicago's Field Museum of the sand mandala of Kalachakra by Tibetan monks from the Namgyal Monastery of Dharamsala, India. Colored grains of sand were patiently sifted into elaborate patterns and symbols rich in meanings that have been developed and handed down in unbroken lineage since the time of the Buddha over 2500 years ago. Only in recent years has this ceremony of building and dismantling been performed outside Asia, thanks mainly to the initiative of the present Dalai Lama who sees Kalachakra—the Wheel of Time—as "a vehicle for attaining world peace."

Mandalas found in other cultures might include such western manifestations as Navajo sand paintings, Aztec stone calendars, and the stained glass windows of Gothic cathedrals. Contemplating these devotional artifacts of the past makes one aware how changed we are from our worshipping ancestors. However devout we may be, we have come to realize that science, rather than religion, is the shaping cultural force of our time, affecting the way we live, the way we see, the way we think. If indeed "scientists are the shamans and wizards, the wonderworkers and myth-givers of today," as suggested by John Updike, can their revelations be expressed as a mandala, a visual embodiment of reason? Let's try, beginning by identifying key images and symbols that define certain critical periods in western intellectual history. Five sets of figures are displayed in the following pages, each accompanied by a collection of quotations and ruminations that lead step-by-step to the design of a mandala for science.

· · · · · · · · · ·

Divine Symmetry

Around the time of the Buddha's awakening, another path to enlightenment was opening up, this time based on a continuing examination of nature itself. Lovers of wisdom—philosophers— living on the islands and mainland of the eastern Mediterranean began to investigate nature's laws separately from any specific consideration of religion. Most influential was the introduction and development of mathematics by the Pythagorean brotherhood, true believers in the mathematical (and musical) harmony of nature. It took only 150 years for the startling announcement of Pythagoras—"All things are numbers"—to become the legen-

FIGURE 3. *The five regular solids of Pythagoras and Plato. From Johannes Kepler,* Harmony of the World *(1619).*

FIGURE 4. *Cosmos.*

dary motto of Plato's Academy: "Let no one ignorant of mathematics enter here."

Once again, as in the Far East, the circle and the sphere became dominant cosmic images. The cosmos was seen as spherical because the sphere is the most homogeneous of shapes: circular motion of its components most befitted reason and intelligence. The same argument was applied to the world around us consisting entirely of the four elements of Empedocles: earth, water, air, and fire. For Plato and his star pupil Aristotle, these elements just had to be directly related to the regular polyhedra beloved by the Pythagoreans for the beauty and simplicity of their symmetry. Only five such shapes can be constructed, as was proved later by Euclid. Each can be inscribed into a sphere so that their corners lie on the sphere's surface. Each can also circumscribe a sphere that touches the center of every face. The five Platonic solids can thus be regarded as approximations to the one figure possessing perfect symmetry—the sphere—just as our world, in Plato's view, is but a shadow of the true, underlying reality of things—the ideal. With his mystical appreciation of geometry, Plato saw fire in the tetrahedron, air in the octahedron, earth in the hexahedron (the cube), and water in the icosahedron. Each of these four polygons has surfaces consisting of triangles and squares. The fifth is different, however, being made up of pentagons. This quintessence was ascribed to a mysterious ether, the substance of the heavenly bodies above. Down here on Earth, primary physical qualities such as heat, cold, moisture, and dryness must have resulted from particular combinations of the other four elements, an idea that was later adopted by practising alchemists, mostly Arabic, investigating transformations of matter.

Aristotle went on to teach that Earth was at the center of the cosmos, unmoved and unmoving, surrounded by concentric spheres of water, air, and fire that could interact with each other. Then came the heavenly spheres, crystalline and invisible, where the moon, Mercury, Venus, the Sun, Mars, Jupiter, Saturn and the firmament of fixed stars resided separately. Above these was the sphere of the *primum mobile*, the prime mover or driving force of the whole system, moving with infinite speed. Beyond lay a fiery outer sphere, the Empyrean, the unmoved mover that was the cause of all this activity. In medieval times the unmoved mover became God, perceived by some mystics as an intelligent sphere with center everywhere and circumference nowhere. For two

FIGURE 5. *Human measurement according to Vitruvius.*

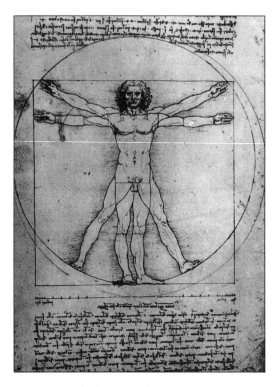

FIGURE 6. *Leonardo da Vinci's figure of man, after Vitruvius.*

thousand years belief in such a cosmos—absolute, divine, eternal —was central to western civilization. Only when this heritage of classical Greece was challenged by observation and experiment could a new world come into being.

· · · · · · · · ·

Human Designs

At the center of the *School of Athens* fresco in the Vatican we find Aristotle debating with a white-bearded Plato, whom Raphael had portrayed with the features of Leonardo da Vinci. This may have been to acknowledge the debt owed by the Renaissance not only to Aristotle but also to his mentor Plato, whose rediscovered manuscripts were being eagerly read by the intellectuals of Florence. What an honor for Leonardo! And for Plato too! Yet we know how different from each other these two geniuses really were: Plato, the ultimate conservative who warned against "the prison house of sight" and indeed of all the senses, and Leonardo, whose unpublished notebooks contained the seeds of the future expressed in precise drawings and pregnant phrases such as the observation that "the eye, which is called the window of the soul, is the chief means whereby the understanding may most fully and abundantly appreciate the infinite works of nature."

We see Leonardo's images everywhere. In Chicago in December of 1993, I was fortunate enough to catch a wonderful stage performance of *The Notebooks of Leonardo da Vinci*. Conceived by Mary Zimmerman, every word of text and lyrics was taken from the writings of the master. Under her direction, eight actor/ dancers in enchanting settings conveyed the boundless curiosity and intellectual passion of this incredibly versatile artist, architect, musician, scientist, inventor, and engineer who signed himself *Leonardo da Vinci, disciple of experiment.* It seems Leonardo himself was fond of spectacle and created many allegorical, theatrical entertainments for his patrons. I believe he would have applauded this special event.

As it happened I had just returned from a conference in Italy on the origin of life. Passing through the international airport in Rome named after Leonardo da Vinci, I noticed in its lobby a larger-than-life three-dimensional wooden version of his well-known image of a human body enclosed in a square and circle. The original drawing in brown ink is, of course, only the size of this page. I had seen it in all its modest power a year or so earlier in Washington at the exhibition entitled *Circa 1492: Art in the Age of*

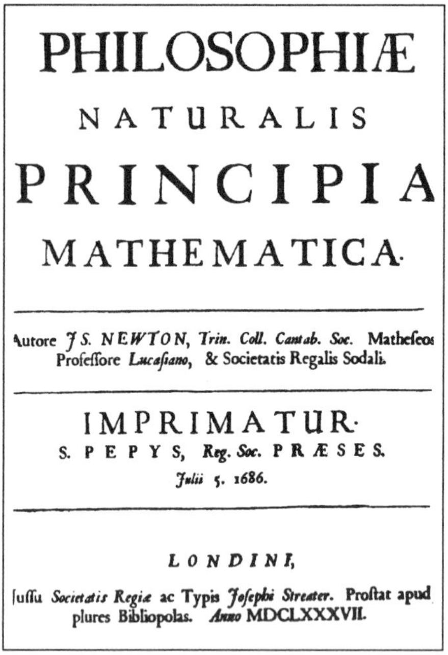

PHILOSOPHIÆ

N A T U R A L I S

P R I N C I P I A

MATHEMATICA·

Autore *J* S. *NEWTON, Trin. Coll. Cantab. Soc.* Mathefeos
Profeffore *Lucafiano,* & Societatis Regalis Sodali.

IMPRIMATUR·
S. P E P Y S, *Reg. Soc.* P R Æ S E S.
Julii 5. 1686.

L O N D I N I,

Juſſu *Societatis Regiæ* ac Typis *Jofephi Streater.* Proſtat apud
plures Bibliopolas. *Anno* MDCLXXXVII.

FIGURE 7.

I do not know what I may appear to the world; but to myself I seem to have been only like a boy, playing on the seashore, and diverting myself now and then finding a smoother pebble or prettier shell than the ordinary, while the great ocean of truth lay all undiscovered before me.

—Isaac Newton

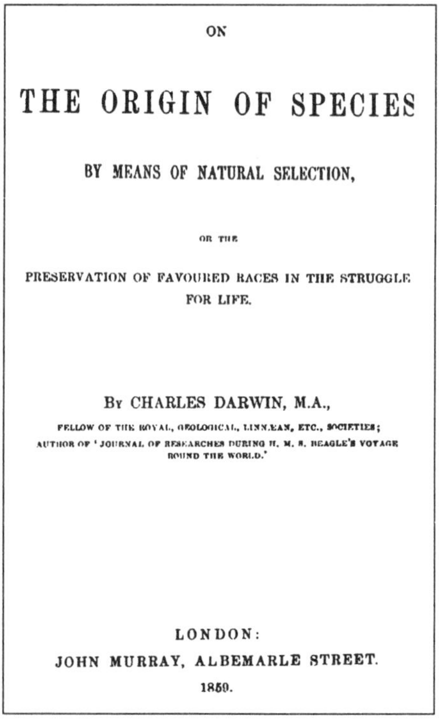

ON

THE ORIGIN OF SPECIES

BY MEANS OF NATURAL SELECTION,

OR THE

PRESERVATION OF FAVOURED RACES IN THE STRUGGLE
FOR LIFE.

By CHARLES DARWIN, M.A.,

FELLOW OF THE ROYAL, GEOLOGICAL, LINNÆAN, ETC., SOCIETIES;
AUTHOR OF ' JOURNAL OF RESEARCHES DURING H. M. S. BEAGLE'S VOYAGE
ROUND THE WORLD.'

LONDON:
JOHN MURRAY, ALBEMARLE STREET.
1859.

FIGURE 8.

There is grandeur in this view of life, with its several powers, having been originally breathed by the Creator into a few forms or into one; and that, whilst this planet has gone cycling on according to the fixed laws of gravity, from so simple a beginning endless forms most beautiful and most wonderful have been and are being evolved.

—Charles Darwin

Exploration, where an enlarged copy also served as a striking poster for the show. Leonardo's remark that "Each man is an image of the world" may help to explain the universal appeal of this emblem combining the new humanism with neoplatonism. First propounded by Vitruvius, a scholarly architect in the Rome of Augustus Caesar, it aims to show that the human body is so proportioned that it can be incorporated into the perfect shapes of circle and square—Heaven and Earth—beloved of Pythagoras and Plato. Vitruvius managed an exact fit of the three components but only by distorting the human figure, which seems to me to be under considerable strain. In Leonardo's more truthful version, however, based on close observation of actual torsos, we see that this perfect arrangement is not really possible. The outstretched body can fit exactly into either of the two shapes but not when the square is circumscribed by the circle. Using mind and hand and eye, Leonardo had inadvertently shown for the first time that the ideal symmetry of Plato was not demanded by nature.

· · · · · · · · · ·

The Unexpected Universe

Investigating the world around us by theory, experiment, and observation soon became the hallmark of post–da Vinci Europe. Specific beliefs of Aristotle were first toppled by the achievements in astronomy and physics of Copernicus, Brahe, Kepler, Galileo, and Newton. More difficult, it seems, was the denial of the divine symmetry taught by Plato. "I undertake to prove that God, in creating the universe and regulating the order of the cosmos, had in view the five regular bodies of geometry as known since the days of Pythagoras and Plato," wrote Kepler in the preface to his first book, *The Mystery of the Cosmos.* Ironically, his attempts to make cosmological use of these symmetrical figures proved fruitless, and instead he became the reluctant iconoclast who showed that the planetary orbits were not circular but elliptical. For Galileo, that staunch Copernican, this oval pathway was unacceptable, given his view of nature as "a grand book written in the language of mathematics; its characters are triangles, circles, and other geometrical figures." It remained for Newton to rationalize the seminal discoveries of his predecessors so that a dynamic open universe could now replace the closed world of the ancients. Perhaps most revolutionary was the dawning realization of the significance of nature's asymmetry, for in the words of Richard Goodwin," to strip humanity of its focal position in an eternal

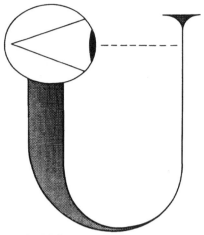

A true science of life must let infinity in . . .

—Arthur Koestler

But infinities are only theoretical and terminate
in the limit
of the solitary
I.

—Roald Hoffmann
(from his poem
"To What End"
in *The Metamict State*)

FIGURE 9.
The universe is a self-excited circuit. As it expands, cools, and develops, it gives rise to observer participancy. Observer participancy gives what we call tangible reality to the universe.

—John Archibald Wheeler

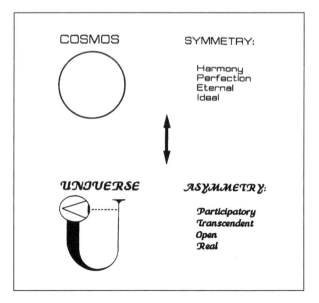

COSMOS

SYMMETRY:

Harmony
Perfection
Eternal
Ideal

UNIVERSE

ASYMMETRY:

Participatory
Transcendent
Open
Real

FIGURE 10.   *The Essential Tension.*

symmetry and to place it on a tiny circling globe carelessly lodged in endless space was not exile but liberation."

No wonder Sir Isaac Newton became the first hero-scientist, one who established the very style of modern physical science employing advanced mathematics to develop increasingly sophisticated concepts of matter and energy. As described by Arthur Koestler in *The Sleepwalkers*, "In one of the most reckless and sweeping generalizations in the history of thought, Newton filled the entire space of the universe with interlocking forces of attraction issuing from all particles of matter and acting on all particles of matter, across the boundless abysses of darkness." Later, Charles Darwin's theory of evolution by natural selection made us aware for the first time that no living thing was created ready made. Instead, all living forms have a family history and are related by common descent, "one of those half dozen shattering ideas that science has developed to overturn past hopes and assumptions, and to enlighten our current thoughts" according to Stephen Jay Gould. Closer to our era, Albert Einstein's theories of relativity showed not only that matter and energy are equivalent but also that space and time are one and that curved spacetime can account for the presence of gravity, Newton's pervasive force which "dictates the motion of our planets, the rhythm of the tides, the fall of a stone, the float of an astronaut, and the expansion of the universe." On the microcosmic scale—what is the world made of?—Max Planck's discovery that energy can exist as particles—quanta—and as waves enabled Niels Bohr and others to develop the fundamental ideas underlying that other great generalization of science, that everything within and around us, down here and up there, consists of atoms of which a hundred or so varieties—our modern elements—are known. With admiration, we recall that the Ionian philosophers opposed by Plato and Aristotle had anticipated many of these ideas, particularly Democritus, who believed that "nothing exists but atoms and the void," and Heraclitus, with his paradoxical thesis that "the only permanent thing in nature is change."

Broken Symmetry

Taken together, these wide-ranging discoveries concerning space, time, matter, energy, and life give us a world that is not a collection of things but a network of relations in which causality and determinism are replaced by probability and chance. We see,

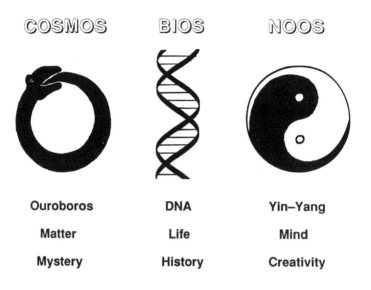

FIGURE 11.   *Universal Asymmetric Symbols.*

Two versions in English of the closing lines of the first stanza of the
Tao Te Ching:

Yet mystery and manifestations
arise from the same source
This source is called darkness.

Darkness within darkness.
The gateway to all understanding.
                    —Stephen Mitchell

The core and the surface
Are essentially the same.
Words making them seem different
Only to express appearance.
If name is needed, wonder names them both.
From wonder into wonder
Existence opens.
                    —Witter Bynner

too, with Karl Popper that "the cosmos bears the imprint of our mind" and that "all science is cosmology."

Consider the striking U-shaped symbol (Figure 9, page 20) designed by John Archibald Wheeler, who worked closely with Einstein and Bohr and is still one of the most original theoretical physicists of our time. Starting small with the Big Bang and the synthesis of hydrogen atoms (facing page; see the papers in this volume by Edward Kolb and George Sudarshan), the universe expands with the formation in galaxies of stars and planets, followed by the appearance of life (see the papers by Cyril Ponnamperuma, by James Shapiro, and by Lynn Margulis and Michael Dolan). Observer participation eventually sets in (Figure 10, page 20; see the paper by Timothy Ferris) and in turn determines what we can say about even the earliest days of the universe. No longer are we mere observers; instead, we take part in the defining of reality (see the paper by Roger Sperry).

The outcome is a universe perhaps best described as participatory, transcendent, and open: participatory as explained above, but also because "each one of us, and all of us, are truly and literally a little bit of stardust," as William Fowler noted when accepting a Nobel Prize in 1983 for his contributions to cosmochemistry; transcendent, in that we know that any whole is more than the sum of its parts; and open, we sense, to possibilities "infinite in all directions," to use the title of Freeman Dyson's eloquent volume celebrating the diversity of our world and ourselves.

Most surprising is the continuing discovery in nature of principles of asymmetry operating at all levels of organization. As pointed out by John Barrow and Joseph Silk in *The Left Hand of Creation*, "one of the most extraordinary things about our universe is that although it often appears, at first sight, to be perfectly symmetric, closer examination invariably reveals that the symmetry is not quite exact. The universe is almost, but not quite uniform over its largest expanses; elementary particles are almost but not quite the same as those that are their mirror images; protons are almost but not quite, stable . . . We invariably find that tiny breaches in the perfect pattern we might have expected to find are the cogs of a glittering mechanism at the center of things, and are one of the reasons our very existence is possible . . . This tale of broken symmetries extends from the beginning of time to the here and now."

Broken symmetry, of course, implies the shadowy presence of

symmetry. In our everyday encounters with art, science, and religion, it seems we equate symmetry with stability and asymmetry with the ability to undergo change. Within us, then, there is an essential tension arising from our attempts, conscious or unconscious, to relate the asymmetric real universe we live in— participatory, transcendent, open—to an ideally symmetric cosmos ruled by principles of harmony, perfection, and the eternal. Perhaps, as Vaclav Havel suggested on receiving the Philadelphia Liberty Medal at Independence Hall on July 4, 1994, "the only real hope of people today is . . . a renewal of our certainty that we are rooted in the Earth and, at the same time, the cosmos. This awareness endows us with the capacity for self-transcendence."

. . . .

Underlying Realities

Examining Wheeler's diagram of existence viewed as a self-synthesizing system makes us ask what special properties of matter, life, and mind give rise to our unexpected universe? We might gain some insight into this question by considering those familiar symbols known as ouroboros, DNA, and yin-yang.

Ouroboros is defined in the new *Encyclopædia Britannica* (15th Edition) as the "emblematic serpent of ancient Egypt and Greece represented with its tail in its mouth continually devouring itself and being reborn from itself. A Gnostic and alchemical symbol, ouroboros expresses the unity of all things, material and spiritual, which never disappear but perpetually change form in an eternal cycle of destruction and re-creation." Like Wheeler's figure, it is an entity self-generating and self-sustaining, with built-in principles of self-organization. It represents our universe of change, of cycles rather than circles. It raises questions of beginnings and ends and leads us from the rational to the mystical, where, with Wittgenstein, we puzzle over "not how the world is, but that it is." (See the discussions by Ian Barbour and Roy Varghese.) Ouroboros points to the connection between the microcosm of the atom, the macrocosm of the heavens, and everything in between.

"The spiral structure of DNA has become the most vivid image of science in the last years," observed Jacob Bronowski in *The Ascent of Man*. Deservedly, too, for according to J.D. Bernal "the double helix is the greatest and most comprehensive idea in all science." The unravelling of its molecular structure by James Watson and Francis Crick in 1953 immediately made rational much of biology, including the theory of evolution, by supplying for cells and genes a copying process that is almost, but not quite, perfect. Mistakes will happen, which is why we are here, together with so many other species. The double helix, then, would be a most appropriate symbol for life and its history on our planet.

"One Yin and one Yang go to make the Tao" says the *Book of Changes*, the *I-Ching* (see the paper by Hsing-Tsung Huang). It is significant that the yin-yang symbol pointing to the complementary forces of nature in ancient Chinese philosophy was adopted by Niels Bohr, the father of the atom, for his family coat of arms, which was also graced by a legend in Latin meaning "opposites are complementary." Seeing this profoundly simple design always makes me think of the left and right hemispheres of the brain, shown experimentally by neuroscientist Roger Sperry to be complementary spheres of consciousness, with linear thinking and analysis dominant in the left brain, spatial awareness and synthesis in the right. In his Nobel acceptance speech in 1981, Professor Sperry went on to propose that in our universe "although the causal forces at the lower quantal, atomic, molecular levels in the infrastructure continue to operate in full force as usual, they are enveloped, encompassed, overwhelmed, superseded, supervened, and outclassed by the new causal properties that emerge in the whole" (see the paper by Roger Sperry). It would seem that the yin-yang representation could well stand for mind in all its creativity.

Overall, these universal symbols can be seen to parallel the domains of *cosmos, bios,* and *noos* which today we see as three stages of evolution.

· · · · · · · · · ·

A Mandala for Science

Now we are in a position to construct a mandala combining the unidirectional loop of ouroboros, representing matter and mystery; the open-ended double helix of DNA, representing life and history; and the yin-yang circle of oneness, representing mind and creativity. Note that each of these pulsating symbols is asymmetric and that, to quote Freeman Dyson again, "every time a symmetry is broken, new levels of diversity and creativity become possible. It may be that the nature of our universe and the nature of life are such that this process of diversification will have no end." Within this simple design we can see the emergence of the new sciences of chaos and complexity.

For background we can use a square divided by color into four

One aim of the physical sciences has been to give an exact picture of the material world. One achievement of physics in the twentieth century has been to prove that that aim is unattainable . . .

There is no absolute knowledge. And those who claim it, whether scientists or dogmatists, open the door to tragedy. All information is imperfect. We have to treat it with humility. That is the human condition . . .

—Jacob Bronowski
in *The Ascent of Man*

Imperfection, rather than perfection . . . is more in keeping with human nature.

—Rita Levi-Montalcini
in *In Praise of Imperfection*

FIGURE 12.   *A Mandala for Science.*

We are free on earth
 because of cloudiness,
 because of error,
 bec ause of marvelous limitation . . .

—Saul Bellow
in *Humboldt's Gift*

different sections (see the back cover of this volume) representing the elements of old—earth, water, air, fire—as well as the four quantum numbers that define today's atoms. And for a motto I would choose the following sentence I was delighted to come across in Saul Bellow's novel *Humboldt's Gift:*

We are free on earth because of cloudiness,
because of error,
because of marvelous limitation . . .

There is, indeed, an inevitable cloudiness about matter, as noted by Werner Heisenberg when he wrote that "by getting to smaller and smaller units we do not come to units that are fundamental or indivisible. We do reach a point where division has no meaning." He added further that "the common division of the world into subject and object, inner world and outer world, body and soul, is no longer valid." Concerning life's history and the need for error, we recall Lewis Thomas's conclusion that "the capacity to blunder is the real miracle of DNA. Without this special attribute, we would still be anaerobic bacteria. . . ." And regarding creativity and our mind's limits, we hear Igor Stravinsky saying "well, limits are precisely what I need and am looking for in everything I compose. The limits generate the form."

Such remarks bring to mind the prescient words of Democritus, reiterated in our time by Jacques Monod, that "everything existing in the universe is the fruit of chance and necessity" (see the paper by Ian Barbour). Within these bounds, though, we are free . . . free to express our creativity, satisfy our curiosity, and, above all, experience community. In our evolving universe— participatory, transcendent, open—we come to terms daily with the ultimate mystery of existence through our creative activities in art, science, and religion that produce the metaphors, models, and myths by which we live.

We see that there are no final truths nor universal keys to salvation. Acknowledging the award of a Nobel Prize in Physics in 1954 for his insight into the role of probability in atomic modelling, Max Born spoke for many when he concluded, "this loosening of thinking seems to me to be the greatest blessing which modern science has given us—for the belief in a single truth and in being the possessor thereof is the root cause of all the evil in the world." What message could be more appropriate for a Parliament of the World's Religions?

· · · · · · · · · ·
Acknowledgments

I thank Magdalen Matthews for help with the design of the mandala and the writing of this paper; Sandra Matthews, Chris Matthews, Eugene Falk and Tom Falk for stimulating comments; and Pat Ratajczyk for invaluable secretarial assistance with the planning of the Symposium and the preparation of this volume.

· · · · · · · · · ·
Background Reading

Barry Bryant, *The Wheel of Time Sand Mandala* (San Francisco: Harper Collins, 1992).

José and Miriam Arguelles, *Mandalas* (Boulder and London: Shambhala, 1972).

George Sarton, *A History of Science, Volumes 1 and 2* (New York: Norton, 1970).

Thomas Goldstein, *Dawn of Modern Science* (Boston: Houghton Mifflin, 1980).

Martin Kemp and Jane Roberts, *Leonardo da Vinci* (New Haven and London: Yale, 1989).

Arthur Koestler, *The Sleepwalkers* (New York: Grosset and Dunlap, 1959).

J. D. Bernal, *Science in History* (Cambridge, Mass.: MIT Press, 1971).

Colin Ronan, *Science: Its History and Development among the World's Cultures* (New York: Facts on File, 1982).

Karl Popper, *The Open Society and Its Enemies*, 5th Ed. (Princeton, N.J.: Princeton University Press, 1971).

Jacob Bronowski, *The Ascent of Man* (Boston: Little, Brown, 1973).

Richard Goodwin, *The American Condition* (New York: Doubleday, 1974).

Werner Heisenberg, *Physics and Beyond* (New York: Harper, 1971).

Jacques Monod, *Chance and Necessity* (New York: Knopf, 1971).

Max Born, *My Life* (New York: Scribner's, 1978).

Lewis Thomas, *The Medusa and the Snail* (New York: Bantam/Viking, 1979).

Stephen Jay Gould, *The Flamingo's Smile* (New York and London: Norton, 1985).

Richard Dawkins, *The Blind Watchmaker* (New York and London: Norton, 1986).

Connie Barlow, ed., *From Gaia to Selfish Genes* (Cambridge, Mass.: MIT Press, 1991).

————, *Evolution Extended* (Cambridge, Mass.: MIT Press, 1994).

John Updike, *Roger's Version* (New York: Knopf, 1985).

————, *Odd Jobs* (New York: Knopf, 1991).

Martin Gardner, *The New Ambidextrous Universe, Revised Edition* (San Francisco: Freeman, 1990).

Douglas Hofstadter, *Gödel, Escher, Bach* (New York: Vintage, 1980).

John Barrow and Joseph Silk, *The Left Hand of Creation* (New York: Basic Books, 1983).

Paul Davies, *The Cosmic Blueprint* (New York: Simon and Schuster, 1988).

Freeman Dyson, *Infinite in all Directions* (New York: Harper and Row, 1988).

Rita Levi-Montalcini, *In Praise of Imperfection* (New York: Basic Books, 1988).

Timothy Ferris, *The Mind's Sky* (New York: Bantam, 1992).

Timothy Ferris, Ed., *The World Treasury of Physics, Astronomy, and Mathematics* (New York: Little Brown, 1991).

Angela Tilby, *Soul: God, Self, and the New Cosmology* (New York: Doubleday, 1992).

Roald Hoffmann and Vivian Torrance, *Chemistry Imagined: Reflections on Science* (Washington, D.C. and London: Smithsonian, 1993).

John Archibald Wheeler, *A Journey into Gravity and Space Time* (New York: Scientific American Library, 1990).

————, *At Home in the Universe* (Woodbury, N. Y.: American Institute of Physics, 1994).

Vaclav Havel, "The End of the Modern Era" (Op-Ed page, *New York Times*, March 1, 1992).

————, "The New Measure of Man" (Op-Ed page, *New York Times*, July 8, 1994).

James Gleick, *Chaos: Making a New Science* (New York: Viking, 1987).

. . . .
A Continuing Probe into the Mystery of Order

Science

• an endless search for unity in nature
• a continuing probe into the mystery of order
• a wandering dialogue with the unknown

is in our time achieving a new universality through the revelation that life may be an inherent property of matter arising by continuous processes of

• chemical evolution
• biological evolution
• cultural evolution

making possible today our re-entry into Nature, here on Earth and in the cosmos as a whole.

In our evolving universe

• participatory
• transcendent
• open

we come to terms daily with the ultimate mystery of existence through our creative activities in

- art
- science
- religion

that produce the

- metaphors
- models
- myths

by which we live.

2
Science and Genesis

· · · · · · · · · ·

Timothy Ferris

Timothy Ferris is the author of seven books, among them *The Mind's Sky, Coming of Age in the Milky Way,* and *Galaxies,* and of more than one hundred articles and reviews. He has twice been awarded the American Institute of Physics Prize and has twice received the American Association for the Advancement of Science writing award, once each in the print and broadcast categories. He wrote and narrated *The Creation of the Universe,* an award-winning PBS television special, and produced the Voyager phonograph record, an artifact of human civilization containing music, sounds of Earth, and encoded photographs launched aboard the Voyager interstellar spacecraft.

A graduate of Northwestern University, Professor Ferris has taught astronomy, science writing, and the history and philosophy of science at the California Institute of Technology, the University of Southern California, and the City University of New York. Currently he is on the faculty of the University of California, Berkeley, where he teaches Journalism, English, and Astronomy.

· · · · · · · · · ·

Abstract

The standard cosmological model permits investigation of cosmic history back to within a fraction of a second after the commencement of the "Big Bang." But it also implies the existence of previously undiscerned limitations on what can be known about the origin of the universe. The Heisenberg indeterminacy principle may have blurred information about the history of the early universe. The possible domination of the infant cosmos by spacetime foam could have tangled spacetime vectors like a ball of yarn. If inflation occurred, ballooning the universe to enormous dimensions, it may also have stretched out information about early times too much for it to be read by any observer at the present epoch. It is urged that investigation of these and related views is facilitated by adopting an approach in which the universe is viewed as based, not on spacetime, matter, and energy, but on information.

The past few decades have seen a change in the relationship between scientific ideas about the origin of the universe and those we associate with religion, theology, and philosophy. Traditionally, scientists had little to say about genesis, while theologians and philosophers were more willing to speculate about this

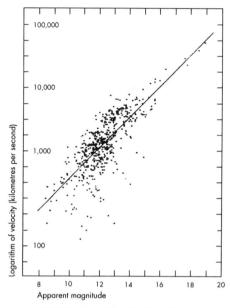

FIGURE 1.   *The Hubble diagram.*

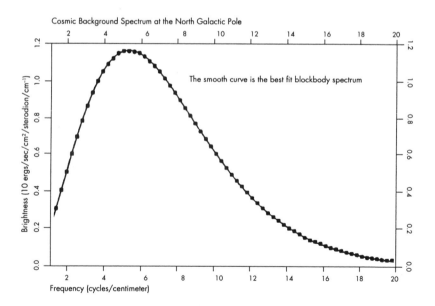

FIGURE 2.   *The blackbody curve of the cosmic microwave background radiation. From J. C. Mather, et al., "A Preliminary Measurement of the Cosmic Microwave Background Spectrum by the* Cosmic Background Explorer (COBE) *Satellite," Ap. J. 354 (10 May 1990): L37–L40.*

ancient riddle. One reason for the distinction is that scientists typically analyze a problem by first constructing a set of prior conditions and then working out the consequences: such an approach clearly is untenable when it comes to the origin of the universe, since here, uniquely, the initial conditions are what one is trying to solve for. Nevertheless, scientific cosmology has now begun to break with tradition and investigate the question of what went on at—or at least very close to—the beginning of time.

My intent is to discuss a few of the ways in which contemporary science approaches the question of the origin of the universe, with emphasis on mechanisms that may place absolute limits on inquiry. Specifically, I'm going to discuss first, the expansion and evolution of the universe; second, the physics of the early universe; and third, the relationship between mind and universe, specifically the prospect for basing a philosophy of science not on space and time or matter and energy but on information.

The Big Bang Theory

By "Big Bang Theory" I mean what is sometimes called the "hot" Big Bang theory. It asserts that the universe is expanding, that it began in a state of high density and therefore presumably of high energy—that's the "hot" part—and that the geometry of the universe can be adequately described by the General Theory of Relativity for epochs after the first 10^{-43} second.[1]

The Hubble diagram (see Figure 1, facing page) presents the fundamental data on which astronomical theories about the expansion of the universe are based. The vertical axis in the diagram displays redshifts observed in the spectra of starlight coming from distant galaxies. The only fully consistent explanation of the redshift is that it represents a Doppler shift caused by velocity—i.e., that the universe is expanding and that the redshifts are produced by the velocities of galaxies rushing apart from one another owing to cosmic expansion. The horizontal axis is the apparent brightness of the galaxies, which is taken as a rough indicator of their distances from us. Brightness is only an approximate indication of galactic distances, since galaxies differ considerably in their intrinsic luminosities: this is thought to account for most of the scatter in the Hubble diagram. Notwithstanding this noise in the signal, one can see the basic relationship: the further away we look in the universe the more rapidly we find that galaxies are receding.

It's important to keep in mind that the expansion of the universe, as portrayed in the standard model based on Einstein's General Theory of Relativity, is an expansion of space itself. It's not a matter of galaxies rushing through static space. To explain this I need to say something about relativity.

In the general theory of relativity, the universe is mapped on a spacetime continuum, and the topography of the spacetime continuum is said to be altered in proximity to matter. To put this another way, we take light rays as our fiduciaries for straight lines, find that the paths of light rays are bent when they pass near massive objects like stars, and deduce that matter warps space. (The bending of light rays was first observed in the vicinity of the sun during the solar eclipse of May 29, 1919, and has since been verified in a wide variety of circumstances.)[2] It follows that if the overall density of stars and other forms of matter is sufficiently high, cosmic spacetime is "closed." A closed universe would have a shape comparable to that of a four-dimensional sphere with all observers located on its surface. Our situation in such a cosmos would resemble our situation on the surface of the earth. We would be surrounded by a finite but unbounded plenum of space, through which one could travel indefinitely in any direction and never come to an edge.

Relativity theory mandates that cosmic space cannot be static but must be either expanding or contracting. The theory is indifferent as to which of these alternatives actually pertains, but since we observe redshifts rather than blueshifts in the spectra of distant galaxies, we conclude that the universe we live in is expanding rather than contracting. To return to the analogy of the spacetime continuum as comparable to the two-dimensional surface of the earth, imagine that the earth were expanding, at a rate such that it doubled in size during the next hour. That would mean that this room, for instance, would after one hour be twice the size that it was at the beginning. Looking around the room, you would find that every person was slowly moving away from you. The farther a particular individual was from you to start with, the faster he would be receding. Someone sitting three feet away would move only three feet in the next hour, while those sitting thirty feet away would move ten times faster, at a velocity of thirty feet per hour, and so forth. If we went outside we'd see the same sort of thing. Towns nearby would be moving at slow velocities but more distant cities would be moving more rapidly, at velocities directly proportional to their distances. And this is just what is observed when astronomers study the distant galaxies.

In addition to the Hubble relation, two other important sets of evidence support the Big Bang theory. These are the cosmic element abundance and the existence and spectrum of the cosmic microwave background.

The abundance of the light elements helium and lithium observed in the stars and nebulae is just about what we would expect if those atoms were forged by thermonuclear processes in the Big Bang. A hot Big Bang resembles a nuclear explosion in that lots of protons would have fused together in the Big Bang to form nuclei of helium and lithium atoms. One can calculate the nuclear physics of the Big Bang and come up with specific predictions. These calculations predict that about a quarter of all the stuff in the universe today should be helium if indeed there was a Big Bang. And that's about what is observed: contemporary observations put the helium abundance at 22%–26% of all visible matter.

The existence of a cosmic microwave background radiation—CMB for short—was also predicted by researchers, early in the history of Big Bang theory. According to the standard model the CMB consists of photons that were released when the universe was about a million years old, at which point the primordial material had thinned out enough so that light could travel freely through space. (It's like a clearing of a mist, if you like.) The idea is that if the Big Bang theory were correct, the universe as a whole should to this day be suffused with photons released in the initial flash of light. The original prediction was forgotten—there was no such thing as microwave radio astronomy at the time—but in 1965, radio astronomers using a microwave receiver accidently detected the background radiation.

Just as predicted, the CMB is observed to be isotropic—that is, it has pretty much the same intensity in all sectors of the sky—and its spectrum describes a "black body" curve with an intensity of roughly three degrees Kelvin. (Current measurements yield a value of 2.735 ±0.060°K.) Figure 2 (page 32), which illustrates the black body curve of the CMB, constitutes what must be one of the most extraordinary confirmations of theory by observation in the whole history of science. The unbroken line is the theoretical prediction of the spectrum of the CMB—photons released in the early universe and still producing a dull background glow all over the universe. The boxes represent observa-

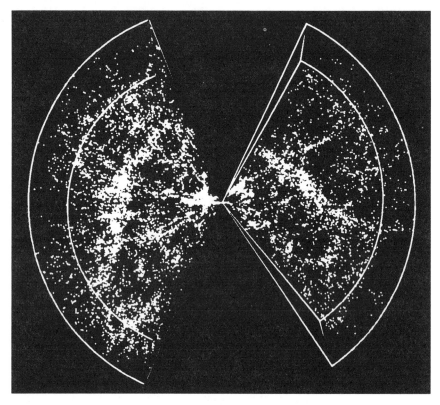

FIGURE 3. *Map prepared by Margaret Geller and John Huchra, showing the distribution of visible matter in the universe.*

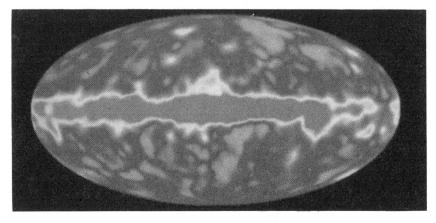

FIGURE 4. *Map provided by the COBE satellite showing traces of incipient large-scale structure in the cosmic microwave background radiation.*

tions made with the help of a special satellite that was built and launched solely to explore this background radiation. It's called the cosmic background explorer, or COBE. As you can see, every box in this plot of COBE data falls on the predicted line. You can't get much better verification than that.

The Big Bang theory also predicts that structure should be found in the CMB. This prediction too was tested by the COBE satellite, by pushing its detectors to their limits. To understand the observational test, we need first to look at a little of what is known about the large-scale structure of the universe—that is, how matter is distributed across cosmic space.

A map put together by Margaret Geller and her colleagues at Harvard (see Figure 3, facing page) shows the largest known structures defined by visible matter in the universe. Each dot is a galaxy. The map cuts a slice through redshift space, meaning that the distances of the galaxies are plotted solely from their redshifts. One can readily see that galaxies are not arrayed homogeneously on this scale but in what look like bubbles. Galaxies are found on the walls of the bubbles, with gigantic spaces—"voids"—in between. Each void measures a little under three hundred million light years in diameter.

If, as is thought, gravity is the sole force that gathers matter together on these vast scales, then for structures this big to be around today, inhomogeneities—lumps—must have been present in the matter distribution of the universe back when the CMB photons were released. If so, such structure should be visible in the CMB. So the COBE satellite was put to work to see if indeed traces of incipient large-scale structure could be identified in the cosmic background radiation. The result was an all-sky map of the CMB (Figure 4, facing page). The dark band across the center of the sky is where dust and gas in our own galaxy obscures our view of the wider universe. Were there no lumps in the matter of the early universe, the rest of the sky would look bald and smooth. Instead, COBE detected the lily pad structures seen in this plot. They are isophotes—i.e., they represent lines of comparable brightness. The theoretical interpretation is that the distribution of matter in the early universe was somewhat inhomogeneous, as theory requires. Because their greater gravitational attraction retards the escaping photons, the denser areas appear a bit less bright than the more thinned-out areas. This effect produces the patterns seen in the COBE plot.

The spectrum of the inhomogeneities confirms a specific

theoretical picture, called the gravitational instability model, that was promulgated more than twenty years ago by Edward Harrison in the U.S. and Yakov Zeldovich in the U.S.S.R.[3] For the benefit of those among my journalist colleagues who not long ago were writing stories declaring that the Big Bang theory was all but dead owing to the large-scale structure problem, let me compare the prediction of the Harrison-Zeldovich theory with the spectrum as observed by COBE. The quantity referred to as $\Delta T/T$ is the difference between the hotter and the cooler areas in the CMB, which as I've said is taken as evidence of the extent to which the distribution of matter in the early universe was inhomogeneous:

$$\text{Theoretical prediction: } \Delta T/T < 10^{-5}$$
$$\text{COBE observation: } \Delta T/T\ 5.5 \times 10^{-6}$$

In the world of astrophysics, where error bars of plus or minus one in the exponent are not uncommon, that's right in the same ballpark. So COBE's message is that the Big Bang theory in general—and the gravitational instability picture more specifically—appear to be in healthy shape.

If we step back and look at what the Big Bang scenario has contributed to our world view in the broadest possible terms, we are presented with an evolutionary picture of cosmic history. That picture looks something like this:

Time (ABT)	Noteworthy Events
0–1 second	Origin of space and time
10^{-6} sec–3 min 42 sec	Hydrogen, helium nuclei form
10^6 years	Photon decoupling; origin of cosmic microwave background
$<10^9$ years	Galaxies, stars form
18×10^9 years	Council for a Parliament of the World's Religions meets

From the standpoint of high-energy physics, the earliest part of this timeline is the most interesting part. When people ask why we should build big accelerators like the superconducting super collider—which, sadly, it now appears we are not going to build—one answer is that research conducted using colliders can help us understand how the early universe evolved. There's even a new and promising field called quantum cosmology, which is concerned, among other things, with how the structure of the universe might have been influenced by quantum flux events. These are random, subatomic level fluctuations that, much magnified by an extremely rapid early expansion of the universe, may have generated the structure seen in the COBE map.

Another very appealing fruit of the collaboration between particle physicists and cosmologists lies in the prospect of arriving at a unified theory of particle interactions. Such a theory might reveal that a single force ruled the universe at the onset of time. Some theorists hypothesize that the universe began in a state of perfect symmetry and evolved via symmetry-breaking events. That's a big subject; here I'll just note that all physics can be described as the study of symmetry and that the ubiquity of symmetry in nature may be a strong clue that symmetry holds clues to the secret of genesis.

A third prospective gift of particle physics to cosmology has to do with resolving the dark matter issue. When studying the dynamics of the universe locally, one finds evidence that most of the matter in our galaxy and elsewhere emits little or no light. Ninety to ninety-five percent of the matter in the universe is not bright but dark. What's it made of? It could be dim stars or black holes or any number of big things, but if the dark matter is made of small things, the theoretical physicists are standing by with a list of observed or theoretical particles that could do the job. If the supersymmetry theories are correct, there's literally an infinite number of gravitationally interacting particles available, and it just becomes a question of which variety God or nature selected to play the role of dark matter.

· · · · · · · · · ·

The Origin of the Universe

I'd like to discuss three considerations that relate to the investigation of the origin of the universe. The first is the Heisenberg uncertainty (I prefer the term "indeterminacy") principle. The second is the inflationary hypothesis. The third is the multiple universe conjecture. As you can infer from my use of the words "principle," "hypothesis," and "conjecture," these three considerations are listed in order of ascending speculation. The indeterminacy principle is as firm as anything in science—indeed it may be *the* basic principle of physics. Inflation is a hypothesis. The multiple universe idea is a conjecture, albeit a very interesting one.

To start with the Heisenberg indeterminacy principle:

Indeterminacy, it is worth remembering, has always been with us. Long before the advent of quantum physics, scientists understood that all experimental data contain uncertainties. They included "error bars" in their published papers showing how much uncertainty they estimated the data to contain. But they assumed that it was theoretically possible to eliminate uncertainties altogether, or reduce them to an arbitrarily small quantity.

This assumption turned out to be false, for several reasons. On the classical level it's false in that some things—indeed most things—are too complex to be predicted. The behavior of anyone in this room for the next second is an example. The positions of all the molecules in the Orion nebula is another. Such systems are simply too complicated for anyone to gather the data and compute all the variables: we could forge all the silicon on Earth into a computer chip and we'd still not have enough processing power to do the job. So even in the classical paradigm, absolute predictive exactitude is possible only for the simplest systems, such as those involving just a few atoms.

But the Heisenberg indeterminacy principle shows us that absolute certainty is impossible on the atomic level as well. The Heisenberg equation looks like this:

$$\Delta X \Delta \rho = \hbar/2.$$

The deltas mean uncertainty; X represents the position of a particle; ρ is the particle's momentum (meaning in what direction the particle is moving and how fast); and $\hbar$ is Planck's constant, the basic unit of all quantum physics. The equation tells us that not only matter and energy but knowledge itself is quantized. There is in other words a fundamental unit—a quantum—of information. Predictions cannot be made more precisely than the limits set by this essential graininess of knowledge.

For most purposes Heisenberg indeterminacy is important only on the subatomic scale. But in the very early universe nearly everything of importance *was* subatomic. So the Heisenberg principle may limit how much we can know about the origin of the universe. If we go back to the very beginning—prior to the first 10^{-43} second—we enter what's called the Planck epoch. During the Planck epoch the energy density was so high that every quantum of matter/energy generated enough gravitational force to significantly distort spacetime. Owing to these distortions, cosmic geometry originally may have been fragmented into what is called spacetime foam.

To describe spacetime foam, imagine that we're aboard the Space Shuttle, looking down at the sea. From such a distance, the ocean looks flat, which is how space looks to us on the level of human perception. But if we were adrift in a lifeboat on the surface, we'd see that the ocean is actually choppy and that bits of it break off as foam and fly off into the breeze and so forth. That's what spacetime foam presumably would look like if we could observe down to the Planck scale.[4] (Which we can't: we'd be seeing things much smaller than a single wave of light, which is impossible.)

In an early universe fraught with spacetime foam, indeterminacy could have wiped out all records of what came before. This would be the case not only for space but also (because it's a space*time* foam) for time. My point is that, if the universe emerged from spacetime foam, the arrow of time may have been lost. In that case the question of what went on before that time ceases to have meaning.

So the Heisenberg indeterminacy principle confronts us with at least two limitations on our ability to obtain information about the very early universe: first, a blurring of information due to the indeterminate behavior of particles; and second, even earlier in cosmic history, an indecipherable tangle of spacetime foam.

Another potential limitation on our knowledge of genesis arises from the inflationary hypothesis. This hypothesis says that the universe expanded very fast—much faster than the speed of light—for a brief but significant moment during the first second of time. If inflation occurred, the universe is, as Ed Sullivan liked to say, "really big"—much bigger than the classical Big Bang universe. The diagram on page 42 (Figure 5), based on one drawn by the cosmologist Andrei Linde at Stanford University, illustrates the inflationary timeline. The bottom line shows the classic Big Bang expansion rate. The upper lines show three possible inflationary rates of expansion. The exponent near the center describes the factor by which the universe ballooned, owing to inflation, during the first 10^{-35} of a second. Note that it reads ten to the tenth to the eighth! I'd never seen such a number until Professor Linde showed it to me, whereupon I asked one of the stupidest questions in my life. "In what units is that figure expressed?" I inquired. "Is it megaparsecs, or Hubble radii of the universe, or what?"

Linde laughed and said, "Well, you know, when you're dealing with ten to the tenth to the eighth, it really doesn't matter

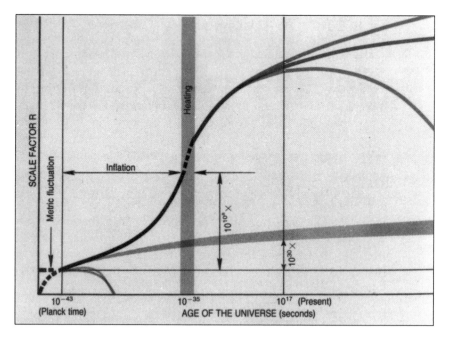

FIGURE 5.   *Diagram illustrating the inflationary timeline. Adapted from Linde.*

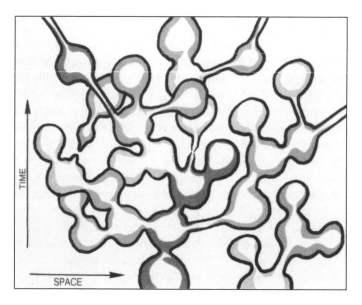

FIGURE 6.   *Drawing that illustrates the concept of multiple universes nucleating from earlier universes. Adapted from Linde.*

what the unit is." The inflationary universe expanded a *lot*. It's *really* big.

Inflation is popular among cosmologists these days, because it solves several problems that previously afflicted the Big Bang theory. It explains, for one thing, why cosmic spacetime, though it must have *some* overall ("global") curvature, is found observationally to be almost exactly flat. (You may recall that cosmologists have been unable to predict the future of the universe. The reason is that the fate of the universe—whether it will expand forever or will ultimately collapse—is a function of the global curvature of spacetime, which evidently is so gentle as to be indistinguishable from flat spacetime within the error bars imposed by the best instruments attached to the largest telescopes in the world.) The inflationary paradigm *predicts* that spacetime will be almost perfectly flat throughout the observable universe. An inflationary universe is so large that even if globally spherical it will appear to be flat within the tiny part of it that can as yet be observed by us or anybody else.

To appreciate this point, consider that any observer's visible universe is limited by the amount of time that has passed since the beginning of time. The universe is estimated to be roughly eighteen billion years old. Therefore we can see only those things that lie within eighteen billion light years of Earth; news of events taking place farther away has not yet had time to reach us. The part of the universe within that radius is called the *observable* universe. If, say, the universe is shaped like a (four-dimensional) sphere, we can detect its sphericity only if we have a large enough sample. And we don't. To detect the shape of an inflated cosmos is as difficult as trying to deduce the sphericity of the earth from a sample of farmland only one millimeter square.

Why might this limit our ability to investigate the origin of the universe? To borrow a metaphor from Professor Linde, imagine that information about the very early universe was written across the fabric of spacetime. No matter how small the writing, inflation would have stretched it out so that the message got too big to read. Each observer could detect only a small part of one letter, and consequently none could piece together the message. In such a picture the secret of cosmic origin, even if globally decipherable, is locally *in*decipherable. So inflation may in that sense have erased information about creation. One consolation is that, since the radius of the observable universe is expanding at the velocity of light, more and more of the message should keep coming into view, to be read, perhaps, by our distant descendants.

To sum up, if the Heisenberg principle represents blurring of information, and if quantum spacetime foam resembles a tangled ball of yarn that loses the direction of time and the dimensions of space, then the inflationary epoch is like silly putty, stretching out the message to the point that it may be impossible to read it.

A final perspective on the issue of cosmic origins has to do with the issue of infinite regression. Here again I am drawing on the work of Linde and other investigators.[5]

The inflationary hypothesis fits well with the notion that the universe began in Planckian spacetime foam. That's because there are reasonable theoretical grounds for believing that some of the bubbles that form in spacetime foam can inflate to create new universes. Alan Guth of MIT has investigated this question, and he finds that if you were to concentrate a lot of energy on a small point in a vacuum you might very well be able to create a universe in—or from—your laboratory. Nobody's likely to do it soon, as the technology does not exist, but it just might be possible. Even with adequate technology it would be hard to get a National Science Foundation grant to run the experiment, because you probably could not verify your results. Suppose you ran the experiment and succeeded: all you'd see is a little "poof" of x-rays, just as if you'd made a miniature black hole that existed for a moment and then evaporated. You might dive into the black hole—or, as we say in academia, send a graduate student in—to observe whether in fact you'd made a universe on the other side, but even if the graduate student survived the passage, the new universe would have a new set of physical laws, generated at random, and the daring student would be highly unlikely to survive in such a universe. And even if he *did* survive, and flourished, and made a decent living for a change, the graduate could send no information back. That's the definition of another universe—a region from which information cannot be conveyed to our universe.

The significance of this line of thought therefore resides less in the prospect of our making new universes in a laboratory than in the notion that new universes might be originating out of the spacetime foam of our universe today. In such a scenario there are many universes—perhaps infinitely many—of which ours is one. The drawing by Professor Linde on page 42 (Figure 6) illustrates the concept of multiple universes nucleating from earlier universes. In this scenario, solving the riddle of genesis becomes as difficult as asking, amid a tangle of vines in a rain forest, what properly is to be called the point of origin of any one vine.

. . . .

Mind and Universe

Here as in much of modern cosmology the concepts of space and time, though indubitably useful, become rather limited. That's one reason I favor a view of science as information-theoretical, by which I mean that one regards scientific cosmology as being based not on space and time and matter and energy but on information. Its horizons are then defined by what can be inferred from the sum of all actual and potential data of observation. (Inflation and the multiple-universe models I've been discussing would fall within the horizon of cosmology because evidence that would confirm them—e.g., traces of the spacetime umbilical connecting ours to its progenitor universe—should eventually crawl over the horizon of the observable universe, albeit in the distant future.) The information-theoretical picture—"IT" for short—tends to eliminate the pane of glass that otherwise separates us from the universe under study: We are *in* the universe, in that it is defined in terms of information reaching us.

"IT" draws on the Copenhagen interpretation of quantum theory—the assertion that, as Niels Bohr put it, no phenomenon *is* a phenomenon until it is an *observed* phenomenon. The question then arises: how can we talk of the origin of the universe, an event no observer could have witnessed? Among possible answers to this excellent question are these:

1 More may be observable than we think. The cosmic microwave background originated when the universe was only
   one million years old, yet astronomers all over the world are
   observing it today. The cosmic neutrino background, theoretically observable though as yet undetected, would date
   from a much earlier time. So one must be careful in ruling
   out phenomena on grounds that they cannot be detected.
   Doctoral degrees are being awarded today on the basis of
   observations undreamed of forty years ago.

2 It may be possible to modify or abandon the Copenhagen
   interpretation. James Hartle, Stephen Hawking, and others
   have been doing very promising work on the question of
   redefining observership to make more sense in quantum
   models of the early universe. (Interestingly, this approach,

called the "many worlds" or "many histories" version of quantum physics, implies the existence of infinite numbers of universes *within* our universe.)

3 Perhaps one can imagine some sort of "cosmic consciousness" capable of observing phenomena beyond the limits set by laws of nature pertinent in our universe. Some theologians' speculations on God resemble this insight, though I see no compelling reason that if, say, the universe came to be regarded as a single, sentient entity, that entity would necessarily be identified with a religious deity. As religion is the subject of this conference, however, I should mention the old and respected—if unscientific—idea that God solves the observership issue. This point is enunciated with admirable succinctness in a well-worn verse:

> There once was a man who said, 'God
> Must think it exceedingly odd
> If he finds that this tree
> Continues to be
> When there is no one about in the quad.'

> 'Dear sir, your astonishment's odd
> I am always about in the quad
> And that's why the tree
> Will continue to be
> Since observed by,
> Yours faithfully, God.'

Lately we've all heard a certain amount of grumbling from scientists and philosophers who assert that theories like supersymmetry, quantum cosmology, and cosmic inflation have got so far away from the province of experimental test as to have fled the arena of science altogether. I don't think that's the case. It's true that one must demand of any potentially valid theory that it be vulnerable to disproof at the hands of experiment, but historically speaking many excellent theories were conceived of well before they could be tested. General relativity is being tested today with lasers and space probes and spheres designed for release by the Space Shuttle and by many other methods that could not have been imagined when Einstein composed the theory in 1916. Few would urge that we pledge allegiance to theories that have no hope of being checked for centuries to come, but neither can we be certain what experimental tests may be possible in the future. Moreover, a challenging theory can light the way to the creation of innovative experiments.

So permit me to broadcast a modest advertisement for keeping an open mind. In coming to terms with the vast scale of the galaxies and the tiny scale of the atom, researchers have been obliged to alter many of their commonsensical ideas of how nature works. It could hardly have been otherwise, given our evolutionary history as parochial residents in one small planet. Yet many philosophical arguments continue to be burdened by an unwillingness, on the part of some thinkers, to evince a comparable intellectual flexibility. Too often, philosophical discussions about cosmology are conducted by sticking an old label on a new idea and then critiquing the label. This approach is inherently static. It assumes that all of the necessary tools are already in our tool kit, so that all we require of a new scientific idea is that it produce fresh data that can be fit with an appropriate term. Some of this is of course unavoidable: As Bohr often insisted, even quantum physics must ultimately be reportable in terms of classical concepts, which is to say that if one is to swing from vine to vine one had better not let go of the first vine until confident of grasping the second. But much of academic philosophy, insofar as I can tell, consists of hanging on to the first vine until all progress has been halted. This sort of discourse suffers from what Bohr on his deathbed called "a lack of a sense that there is something yet to be learned."

It seems to me that we have a lot left to learn and that we ought not simply categorize everything that science adduces as scientific and assume that outside of science we already have all the requisite concepts to assess everything that comes from science. Specifically I'd like to close with a cautionary word about the concept of *beauty* in nature and scientific theory.

Scientific theories can be regarded not only as logical or illogical but also as beautiful or ugly. Many theorists have taken such a view; the notoriously reticent Paul Dirac went so far as to assert that "it is more important to have beauty in one's equations than to have them fit experiment."[6] But in evaluating new theories it's worth remembering that many revolutionary scientific ideas taken for granted today did not at first strike people as beautiful. The sun-centered universe of Copernicus was criticized, and rightly so, for being as cumbersome and inaccurate as the earth-centered Ptolemaic universe it was meant to replace. General relativity was criticized as overly elaborate. (It *is* elaborate, but not overly so). Einstein himself found at least one of the fundamental assumptions of quantum physics to be philosophically repugnant: that was the indeterminacy principle. Today we see beauty in all these theories and in many others that once seemed ungainly and brash.

A good theory may be beautiful, but more to the point it's creative, in the sense that a good work of art is creative. By virtue of its originality it challenges us to change our way of looking at things, and one of the things that can change is our sense of what is beautiful. What matters at the outset is not that people immediately find a new creation to be aesthetically pleasing—indeed, artists are often reminded by their teachers that praise can trap an artist—but that people respond to it. They may respond with anger or disgust, as audiences did, say, to the premiere of Stravinsky's *Rite of Spring*, or they may be enthusiastic. But the emblem of potential success in a creative idea is reaction, not necessarily favorable reaction.

As cosmology advances we may find that many of its ideas conflict with our conception of the beauty of the universe. If so, good. That means that the cosmologists are doing their job, which is to bring our benighted species into a more comprehending relationship with the vast universe. My plea to the philosophers is that they avoid getting tied up in the assumption that sound cosmological theories must be beautiful *as viewed by the lights of our prior conceptions.* Many religious thinkers feel that the universe is beautiful because God made it that way, but it took our species a long time to appreciate the beauty of our own planet—its mountains and trees and rivers, orangutans and beetles—and I should be surprised if the real beauty of the naked architecture of the cold and uncaring universe were to be appreciated overnight. A mission of art, science, and religion alike is to teach us to see the beauty in everything that's true, not just in what also happens to be pretty.

Humorists are in the same frame-busting business, as witnessed for example by this assault, in an old Monty Python skit, on religious sentimentalism:

> All things dull and ugly,
> All creatures short and squat,
> All things rude and nasty,
> The Lord God made the lot.

The ugly and the uninspiring are all part of the universe, too, and are all of infinite value.

· · · · · · · · · ·

Questions From the Audience

Can you say a few more words about the idea of basing science on information theory?

All scientific concepts answer to the data of observation. Space, time, causation—all these concepts are useful only so long as they answer to the data. I therefore suggest that information is more fundamental than are concepts *based* on information. If you take this to heart in cosmology, the cosmic horizon comes to be defined in terms of potentially obtainable information. The observable universe would then consist of all obtainable information, though of course we would continue to use derived models based on spacetime and so forth. Viewed in these terms, what is expanding in an expanding universe is not just space but the plenum of potential information. In a recent book (*The Mind's Sky*) I have sought to demonstrate how an information-theoretical approach may prove efficacious in other arenas of science, evolutionary biology for one.

Would you care to comment on the anthropic principle?

The anthropic principle entered science primarily through work done by James Dickey at Princeton some years ago. More recently it has been discussed by many researchers. It is the subject of a noteworthy book, *The Anthropic Cosmological Principle* by John Barrow and Frank Tipler (Oxford University Press, 1986). Briefly stated, the anthropic principle asserts that certain aspects of the universe can be "explained" by the fact that there are living observers in the universe. If, for instance, the gravitational constant were much higher than it is, the expansion of the universe would have halted when the universe was young: in that case the universe would have been just a little bubble that subsided into spacetime foam before life had a chance to evolve. And if the gravitational constant were much lower, the universe would have expanded as a gas, the galaxies wouldn't have formed, and there may have been no abodes for life. Proponents of the anthropic principle thereby "explain" the gravitational constant by noting that if it were much different, we wouldn't be here to wonder why it has the value that it does. And they account for some of the other laws of nature in similar fashion.

Within the framework of classical cosmology, I dispute the anthropic principle on several grounds, starting with what I see as its pernicious tendency to discourage scientific inquiry. At its worst the anthropic principle resembles the beerhall tune: "We're here because we're here because we're here because we're here." That is to say that the principle may be merely circular: if one can explain away things by using it, one is discouraged from looking for more substantial reasons. One might find that the gravitational constant attained its value as the result of a random symmetry-breaking event: this explanation seems to me to have greater power than the one proffered by the anthropic principle, which if relied upon exclusively might discourage the sort of hard work that might uncover the deeper explicatum.

However, the multiple-universe conjecture puts some meat on these bones. If indeed you entertain the hypothesis that there are many universes, each with different physical laws, then it makes sense to expect that some can harbor life and others cannot. This view strikes me as reasonable and as not discouraging further inquiry into the ongoing question of what happened, historically, in the evolution of *our* universe.

Would you please elaborate on what you were saying about beauty?

Beauty can indeed help guide scientists toward sound scientific theories, keeping in mind that the modifier "scientific" means testable by experiment and observation. But several fields of contemporary science now deal with regimes so far removed from our customary experience as to severely try our received notions of the beautiful. So my point is that in philosophical dialogues generally, and particularly where aesthetics is concerned, we should try to keep an open mind. That means resisting the temptation to clutch at a set of data or a particular theory and run home with that, proclaiming it sound in that it fits one's preconceptions. One needs sometimes to alter one's conceptions as a result of what the data and theories teach us. A scientist with good taste knows what Robert Baden-Powell used to try to teach the Boy Scouts—how in going through one's backpack one should keep the essential and discard everything else.

You said that a religious person might attribute the beauty and order of nature to God's handiwork. But what about Buddhism, which is a religion that does not postulate the existence of God? Not all religious persons believe in God.

Agreed. My point was that a religious individual *might* attribute natural order to God, not that every religious person believes in God.

Do you think it possible, as artists and scientists sometimes assert, to genuinely be at one with the universe?

Yes.

• • • • • • • • • •

Notes

1. This last assertion is pretty ambitious, in that 10^{-43} second is an extremely short period of time. The flash of a camera's strobelight takes less of a fraction of time out of the whole history of the universe than 10^{-43} second takes out of a second. Yet the Big Bang theory claims to be able to account for everything that has happened since that first brief moment. "Interesting if true, and interesting anyway," as Dr. Johnson used to say.

2. Arthur Stanley Eddington, Frank Watson Dyson, and Charles Davidson, "A Determination of the Deflection of Light by the Sun's Gravitational Field. . . ." *Philosophical Transactions of the Royal Society (London)*, 220 (1920): 291–333.

3. E. R. Harrison, "Fluctuations at the Threshold of Classical Cosmology." *Phys. Rev. D.* 1 (1970) 2727; Zeldovich, Ya. B., "A Hypothesis, Unifying the Structure and the Entropy of the Universe." *Mon. Not. R. Astr. Soc.* 160 (1972): 1P.

4. I have adapted this metaphor from one employed by John Archibald Wheeler.

5. See, for example, Andre Linde, *Inflation and Quantum Cosmology* (New York: Academic Press, 1990); also, "The Self-Reproducing Inflationary Universe," *Scientific American*, November 1994, 48.

6. P. A. M. Dirac, "The Evolution of the Physicist's Picture of Nature," *Scientific American*, May 1963, 47.

• • • • • • • • • •

The Ballooning of a Bubble of Spacetime Foam

1 What are your views on cosmic beginnings, particularly with reference to the origin of the universe, of life, and of *Homo sapiens*?

I speculate that the universe will in the twenty-first century come to be viewed as having originated in the ballooning of a bubble of spacetime foam and that the foam will be presumed to have belonged to the spacetime of a previous universe that itself originated the same way. The constants of nature may have sprung from random symmetry-breaking events early in the evolution of our bubble. This hypothesis will be difficult but not impossible to test insofar as our universe is concerned. Whether anything could be discerned as to the architecture of the putative prior universe raises questions of quantum theory, unified theory, and information theory that we do not yet know how to pose. Quite possibly the existence of a precursor universe will prove impossible to prove or disprove, in which case that aspect of the theory could rightly be dismissed as extrascientific.

2 What are your views on human ends, especially as this relates to the framework of cosmic beginnings?

Notwithstanding some thoughtful inquiries into this question, notably by Freeman Dyson and Frank Tipler, I expect that little or nothing is understood about the long-term future of the universe. The extrapolation of the second law of thermodynamics to proclaim the ultimate "heat death" of the universe, though widely accepted among cosmologists, depends upon the assumption that the universe is rightly to be regarded as a closed system, which may or may not be true. And even if the universe is a closed system, the role played by quantum flux in the early universe, which we see written across the sky today in the gigantic metaclusters and voids, virtually insures that some parts of the universe will remain warmer than others indefinitely—a situation that would enable work to be done for a very long time. So this I regard as an open question.

3 What do you think should be the relationship between religion and science?

That they need not be at war is obvious. Anti-scientific attitudes among religious fundamentalists and anti-religious attitudes among scientists—or should I say believers in scientism, the assertion that science has a patent on truth—usually spring from ignorance and can be attenuated by education. In support of this opinion I cite two sets of evidence: first, that the creationists who oppose Darwinian evolution are as a group far less well educated than are their better educated believers, and second, that those scientists who most loudly dismiss religion tend as a group to be the ones with the least theological study behind them. There are of course exceptions to these rules.

That said, I see no necessity of "unifying" science with religion. In my view the beauty of human thought, past, present, and future, resembles that of a garden, not a granite monolith. Hell would be a universal parliament in which everyone agreed about everything.

I would associate myself with the opinion stated by Joseph Needham, which he in turn ascribed to his teacher, the Oxford scholar R. G. Collingwood. There are, Collingwood advised Needham, five forms of human experience: religion, science, history, philosophy, and aesthetics. "If you are tone deaf to one of them, you are in trouble," Needham said recently. "I don't think there is any necessity to reconcile them" (in Marguerite Holloway, "The Builder of Bridges," *Scientific American*, May 1992, 56).

3

The Big Bang Origin of the Universe

Edward W. Kolb

Edward W. Kolb is head of the NASA/Fermilab Astrophysics Group at Fermi National Accelerator Laboratory in Batavia, Illinois. He is also a member of the faculty of the University of Chicago, where he is Professor of Astronomy and Astrophysics, a Professor in the College, and a member of the Enrico Fermi Institute. Born in New Orleans in 1951, he received a Ph.D. in theoretical physics from the University of Texas in 1978. His postdoctoral research was performed at the California Institute of Technology and Los Alamos National Laboratory, where he was the J. Robert Oppenheimer Research Fellow. He was the deputy group leader of the Theoretical Astrophysics Group at Los Alamos before coming to Fermilab in 1983 to start the astrophysics group. His field of research is the application of high-energy physics to the study of the very early universe. In addition, he is deeply concerned with science education—he likes to share the mysteries of the universe with students and teachers at all levels.

Abstract

Some highlights of the Big Bang model for the origin and evolution of the universe are discussed. The observational foundations of the expanding-universe model are reviewed, as well as the basis of the Big Bang model in the laws of physics. It is shown how the connection with high-energy physics, which studies the smallest objects in the universe, allows us to understand the largest things in the universe. Some of the physical conditions in the very early universe, such as the age and the temperature, are considered. Finally, the discussion closes with some speculations about events which might have occurred earlier than one second into the life of the universe.

A gaze into the dark night sky evokes some of the deepest of questions about our universe. How big, how old? Where is the edge, the center? What is beyond? What occurred before the Bang? Every culture has asked these questions and has employed people expert in such matters to provide answers.

In the twentieth century, the study of such questions form a scientific discipline known as cosmology. The word "cosmology" is derived from the Greek κόσμος (*cosmos*). In this context κόσμος does not mean enormous or immense. Rather, it is the Greek word for *order*. Cosmologists attempt to bring some order to our view of the universe.

Modern cosmologists use physical law as the tool for understanding an apparently complex and mysterious universe. The strategy is straightforward: learn the laws of physics by performing laboratory experiments, and explain the observed universe on the basis of these laws. The outcome of this effort is a *model* of the universe. The twentieth century model of the universe is known as *the Big Bang Model.*

Before discussing the Big Bang model, it is useful to understand exactly why it is necessary to have a model in hand when confronting the universe. The first reason is the sheer enormity of the number of objects in the universe. On a clear night on a mountain away from city lights, about 2500 stars, one moon, and five planets are visible to the unaided eye. With a good pair of binoculars, and enough patience to examine the entire sky, over 160,000 stars can be seen. If the mountaintop happens to have an observatory on it, photographic plates at the focus of a moderate-sized telescope could image over 17 million stars if enough time were taken to survey the entire sky.

If the observatory happens to house a telescope with a six-meter mirror, say Mount Palomar Observatory outside of San Diego, California, then with modern electronic detectors substituted for photographic plates, it is possible to image many more than a billion stars in the visible part of the sky. Of course the large telescopes would reveal more than merely the stars in our own galaxy, the Milky Way; with large telescopes one begins to see external galaxies, quasars, and so forth, objects outside of our galaxy.

All objects in the universe are interesting and beautiful in their own right, but not all objects have equal potential to lead to a greater appreciation of nature. Without a model, all of the thousands of points of light on the photograph look alike. But with a model, we are able to grasp the significance of the fact that some of the marks on the picture look like extended smudges: they are galaxies external to our own. With a model we also discover that one of the objects in the box at the top of the picture is peculiar (see Figure 1, page 58). When we blow up the region of the box and study it in still finer detail (Figure 2, page 58), we notice that one of the dots (not the largest and not the smallest) is also a source of radiation in the long-wavelength, radio region of the electromagnetic spectrum. When we study that particular object even more closely we find that although it looks like a dim star, it is at an enormous distance from us. In fact that one dot, known by the un-romantic name of 3C273, was the first quasar discovered. It was identified as a quasar in 1962 by Maarten Schmidt, but its image had appeared on photographs like this for decades and was seen in radio surveys of the sky. In fact, it is not all that dim and can be seen with a small telescope of an amateur astronomer as a faint blue star.

The story of the discovery of something as fundamental as quasars demonstrates that just the ability to see something does not naturally lead to an understanding of its significance. Only with the aid of a cosmological model is it possible to sort through the bewildering mass of information and to identify the points of light that might be special. The story illustrates that the secrets of nature are not easily elucidated. Sadly for the astronomer, nature does not provide arrows in the sky pointing to the interesting objects; they must be ferreted out by hard work. It also raises the question of what other small dots on the picture are the keys to unlock the mysteries of the universe. Astronomers are haunted with the thought that discoveries are before their eyes, but they are too blind to see them.

The second reason that a model of the universe is crucial is that there are not many things we can learn about the universe. This statement may seem puzzling in light of the fact that we have just seen that there are so many objects in the universe. However, there is simply not much information we can obtain directly about any one object. For instance, observing a bright object with the unaided eye, we can determine its color, its apparent brightness, its apparent angular size, and its position relative to other objects in the sky. Of course we can also determine any change in these observables. This is not very much information with which to put together a model of the universe. Telescopes and other modern instruments generally do not lead to qualitatively different information, they mostly enable us to refine and quantify the types of measurements we can make with our eyes. We need a model to make the most of the meager information we can acquire.

Any scientific model of the universe must be grounded in

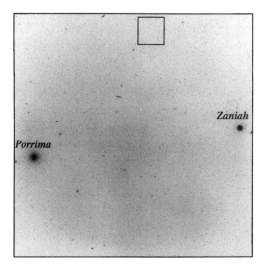

FIGURE 1. *A region of the sky in the Virgo constellation observed by Caltech astronomers using the Mount Palomar Observatory. The star on the left is Porrima and the star on the right is Zaniah. The picture was taken in 1955 with a one-hour exposure at the focus of a 70-inch telescope.*

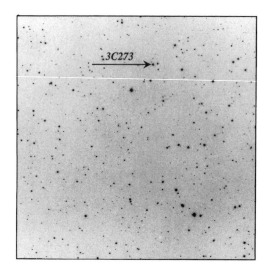

FIGURE 2. *A blow-up of the region of the sky denoted by the box in the previous photograph. The region indicated by the arrow is the first quasar discovered, 3C273, the 273rd entry in the 3rd Cambridge catalog of celestial sources of radio emission.*

physical law. The idea of using physical laws to explain the universe did not arise until sometime in the seventeenth century. I don't know who the first person was to try this revolutionary approach, but perhaps the most successful was Isaac Newton. Everyone has heard that Newton "discovered" gravity. More precisely, Newton discovered the law of gravity—the gravitational force between two objects is proportional to the product of their masses and inversely proportional to the square of the distance between them. The discovery of this law was a triumph of genius. Newton made a further discovery, an even greater one than the discovery of the law of gravity. He discovered the "universality" of gravity. Newton realized that the force responsible for an apple falling on his head was the same force responsible for the movement of the moon about the earth and the planets about the sun. Gravity is a "universal" phenomenon. Newton discovered that the forces responsible for the motion of the planets are capable of human comprehension and that they can be studied in terrestrial laboratories; an example of what we can see is the connection between the Inner Space of the laboratory and the Outer Space of the cosmos. With a single sweep of genius, Newton freed celestial mechanics from the impression that crystal spheres, mechanical gears, and other sundry devices moved the planets. Is there anyone who can fail to appreciate the simplicity and beauty of the Newtonian view of the solar system? To those who say Newton removed the hand of God from the heavens, I say he replaced a toilsome hand of brute force with an elegant hand of beauty.

Cosmology has an important place in our culture. Many of the things we cherish and value (e.g., art, literature, poetry, religion, music, etc.) are in some way manifestations of our struggle for an answer to the question "what is our place in the universe?"; cosmology attempts to answer a yet more fundamental question, "what *is* the universe?" Throughout history the answer to the second question has influenced our attempts to answer the first question. Cosmology serves as a canvas upon which we paint a vision of our place in the universe as, for instance, Newton's realization that the forces of the heavens are comprehensible led to the dawn of the Age of Reason.

The task before the modern cosmologist is the same faced by Newton: understand the laws of physics and apply them to the universe. The laws of physics will be our guide as we develop a model for the origin of the universe.

. . . .

Building Blocks of the Universe

What is the universe made of? A simple answer might be that the universe is made of three things: 1) matter, 2) energy in the form of radiation, and 3) space. Cosmology connects the three, and it is impossible to study one without the others. Let us take each in turn.

1) *Matter.* Cosmology is the study of the origin and large-scale structure of the universe. Here, "large" refers to scales larger than a galaxy. The distance from the earth to the sun is about 10^{13} centimeters (cm). It takes light about eight minutes to travel from the Sun to Earth. The next nearest star, α-Centauri, is about 10^{18}cm, or three light-years, away. Our solar system is about 30,000 light-years from the center of our galaxy. Our entire galaxy of more than 100 billion stars is 100,000 light-years in diameter. Yet these scales are "small" to a cosmologist. The distances studied by cosmologists are so large that the basic unit of distance for cosmologists is a *megaparsec*, which is three million light-years, or 10^{24}cm. A megaparsec (Mpc) is the typical distance between galaxies.

What does matter look like? How is it distributed in space? To the naked eye, matter is in the form of stars. The stars we see with the unaided eye are all in our own galaxy. Only a sharp eye can see the fuzzy form of a few nearby external galaxies. Our estimate of the size of the universe did not increase gradually with time, but rather grew by great leaps as instruments and technology improved and allowed us to see further. In the early decades of this century, Edwin Hubble discovered that our Milky Way "island universe" was only one of countless galaxies in the universe. Our galaxy is not the largest, brightest, oldest, or youngest galaxy.

Galaxies are basic building blocks for cosmologists. Some astronomers spend their lives observing galaxies and classifying them by their type (spiral, elliptical, irregular, and so forth). Since the stars we see in the universe are in galaxies, a cosmological model must explain why there are galaxies and why they take the shapes and sizes they do.

If galaxies are the basic things in the universe, how are they distributed in space? In the past few years a new picture has begun to emerge. It is slowly becoming clear that galaxies are not spread completely at random throughout the universe; some seem to be grouped into still larger objects known as clusters. Even clusters of galaxies may be part of larger groups known as superclusters. There is also evidence for giant voids in the universe, regions free of any visible galaxies. These voids seem to form enormous bubbles 30 Mpc across surrounded by a thin film of galaxies. We are able now to see only the vague outlines of these structures, a hundred megaparsecs in size, containing thousands of galaxies.

Galaxies do not appear to be spread in a completely random way in the universe; nevertheless the distribution of galaxies does seem to be approximately smooth on scales larger than a dozen megaparsecs, and the distribution becomes smoother on larger scales. The large structures discussed above are impressed on an otherwise smooth distribution of galaxies. Eventually, we must understand the origin of the structure (clusters, superclusters, bubbles, and so forth), but first we must understand the smoothness of the universe. To study the irregularities and ignore the smooth background would be like studying waves while ignoring the ocean.

Thus, the most important lesson to be learned from observations of matter is that it is homogeneous (the same at every point) and isotropic (the same in every direction). If the universe is smooth on large scales, then there is no special place, no boundary, no center.

We can be a little more specific about the nature of matter; we can observe its chemical composition. Since cosmologists study the universe on the grand scale, we cannot be concerned with the individual characteristics of all 109 elements in the periodic table. We deal with a simplified periodic table of only three elements, hydrogen, helium, and metals. Hydrogen and helium have mass numbers 1 and 4; anything with a mass number larger than 4 is called a metal (the mass number of an element is simply the total number of protons and neutrons in the nucleus of the atom). Most of the universe, about 75% by mass, is made of hydrogen. About 24% is helium, and metals comprise less than 1%. All the elements so important for life (calcium, oxygen, nitrogen, iron, and so on) are but an incidental contamination in a universe of hydrogen and helium. We believe that hydrogen and helium were made in the first minutes of the Big Bang. Billions of years later, the first stars formed from the primordial hydrogen and helium, processed the primordial fuel to metals by nuclear reactions, then exploded and enriched the interstellar medium with "metals." The next generation of stars coalesced with some metals from the debris of the first generation, processed them further, exploded, and further enriched the interstellar medium. In a real sense we are all star material. Any atom in our bodies other than hydrogen or helium was once part of a star!

This is the first example of a feature of the universe that we encounter again and again—*change*. The universe is constantly changing, evolving, developing. Modern cosmology has rejected the eighteenth and nineteenth century picture of a static, infinite universe.

Although stars are in galaxies, there is no certainty that all matter is in stars. In fact there is evidence that most of the mass of a galaxy is *not* in the form of stars. There seems to be a large amount of *dark matter* in galaxies. There is more mass than can be accounted for by the stars. This extra matter is not visible, hence the name dark matter. Not only is dark matter found in galaxies, but it is found on larger scales as well. The nature of the dark matter is uncertain, we only know that it does not "shine" in any part of the electromagnetic spectrum. There is reason to believe that dark matter is not composed of ordinary matter made of neutrons, protons, and electrons, but rather is composed of some undiscovered weakly-interacting massive particle. The possibility that the nature of most of the mass of the universe still awaits discovery is a sobering thought.

2) *Radiation*. A view of the sky, day or night, suggests that the universe is awash in electromagnetic radiation—light. Visible light occupies only a small fraction of the spectrum of electromagnetic radiation, special only because it is the part to which our eyes are sensitive. The visible electromagnetic radiation may seem important to us, but it is an insignificant fraction of the total electromagnetic radiation in the universe.

Most of the radiation in the universe is not in visible wavelengths, but rather in the invisible microwave region of the spectrum. In 1964, with a Bell Laboratories microwave antenna in Crawford Hill, New Jersey, Arno Penzias and Robert Wilson discovered that our universe has about 400 photons per cubic centimeter with wavelength of about 1 millimeter (the wavelength of radiation in your microwave oven is somewhat longer, a few centimeters). If your eyes were sensitive to these microwave photons, they would "see" about 10^{10} photons per second pass through them.

The microwave background radiation permeates all of space. Even in the recesses of intergalactic space, there are 400 microwave photons in every cubic centimeter. These photons form a thermal background of 2.73 degrees Kelvin, or −454 degrees Fahrenheit. The thermal nature of the microwave background implies that the universe was once hot and dense enough for matter to ionize and interact with the radiation. This occurred some 14 billion years ago when the universe was only about 260,000 years old.

The microwave background provides further evidence for the smoothness of the universe. The radiation reaches us from all directions, and the detected flux is the same from all directions to better than one part in a thousand. This isotropy of the microwave background tells us that 260,000 years after the Bang when the microwave photons last scattered, the universe was *very* smooth.

A small departure from perfect isotropy is caused by the motion of our galaxy with respect to the rest frame of the microwave background radiation at a velocity of 600 km/sec (1.4 million miles/hour). This velocity causes the radiation coming to us from one region of the sky to appear hotter than the average temperature by about one part in a thousand. If one removes this effect and studies the microwave background even more carefully, at about thirty parts per million a pattern of temperature fluctuations emerges, and we see that there are regions of the universe that are slightly hotter or slightly colder than other regions. Here "slightly" means about thirty parts per million—an incredibly small effect. Although the effect is small, it is believed that this pattern of hot and cold spots was impressed upon the structure of the universe in the very earliest moments of the Big Bang and that the pattern is related to the small inhomogeneities in the distribution of matter that eventually grew to become galaxies, clusters, voids, and all the large-scale structures of the universe.

Although the 400 microwave photons per cubic centimeter are more numerous than the nucleons (neutrons and protons have a present average number density of about 10^{-7} per cubic centimeter), the rest mass of the nucleons is so much greater than the average energy of the photons that today the universe is matter dominated, i.e., the mass density of the nucleons dominates the energy density of the photons.

3) *Space.* The homogeneity and isotropy of matter and radia-

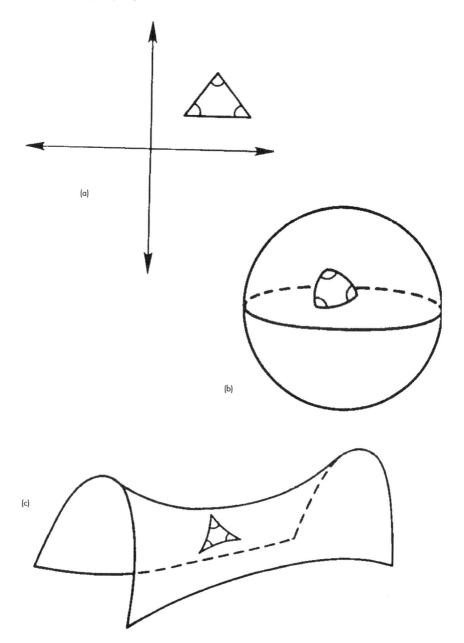

FIGURE 3. *Space can be flat with infinite volume (a), positively curved with finite volume (b), or negatively curved with infinite volume (c). In the three cases the sum of the interior angles of a triangle are exactly 180°, greater than 180°, or less than 180°, respectively.*

tion must be reflected by the homogeneity and isotropy of space. The homogeneity and isotropy of the universe is so important that it has been elevated to the status of a principle, known as *the Cosmological Principle*, which states that there is no unique or special place in the universe.

The fact that there is no special point in space actually tells us something about the shape of the universe. Let's start with an easy example: one spatial dimension. An infinite straight line is the simplest example of a space that has no special point. Every point on a straight line is equivalent. It is possible to define a coordinate system on the line and call one point the origin, but clearly there is nothing special about that point since any point could have been chosen as the origin without loss of generality. The straight line is an infinite space that is unbounded. There is no "edge" to the line, it goes on forever. Another example of a one-dimensional space that has no special point is a circle. A circle is a one-dimensional space that, like the line, is unbounded, but unlike the line has finite length ($2\pi R$, where R is the radius of the circle). An unbounded space can have finite "volume" if it is curved back on itself. Although the circle is a one-dimensional space, it is most easily visualized by drawing it on a two-dimensional flat space.

Examples of two-dimensional spaces with no special point are also familiar—the infinite plane and the surface of the earth. The infinite plane has infinite area and is unbounded. There is no edge, no center. The surface of the earth is an example of a space known as a 2-sphere (see Figure 3). It is unbounded, but it has finite volume. If you walk in any one direction on the earth, you eventually return to your point of origin, but you never encounter an edge. There is also no special point on the surface of the earth, at least not in the geometrical sense. The surface of the earth has finite area ($4\pi R^2$, where R is the radius of the earth), because it is a curved space. We can prove it is curved in constructing a triangle by picking three points on the surface, connecting them by the shortest paths, and measuring the sum of the interior angles of the triangle. The sum of the interior angles will not be $180°$, but will be greater than $180°$. Although the surface of the earth is a two-dimensional space (any point can be specified by two coordinates, e.g., latitude and longitude), we picture the 2-sphere by embedding it in a three-dimensional flat space, and in projection it can be drawn on a flat two-dimensional space, as shown in Figure 3 (facing page).

There is no problem visualizing an unbounded, flat universe

with 3 spatial dimensions. Such a universe has no edge, it goes on forever. It has no center, every point is equivalent. It is also possible that our universe has spatial curvature and has the geometry of a 3-sphere. Just as the circle (1-sphere) and the surface of the earth (2-sphere), the 3-sphere has no boundary, has no special point, and has finite volume ($2\pi^2R^3$). Note that the volume is *not* $4\pi R^3/3$: that is the volume of a solid body that has a center and an edge. The 3-sphere must be visualized by embedding it in four flat dimensions, and such visualization requires imagination.

There is another possibility for the geometry of the universe. Space may be curved in the opposite sense of the 3-sphere. Such a space is, of course, unbounded. It has infinite volume. To visualize this space, it is necessary to embed it in a flat space of seven dimensions.

In principle, it is possible to measure directly the curvature and determine the shape of the universe. In practice, it is not so easy. If space is "curved" like the 3-sphere, the radius of curvature is greater than 10^{28} centimeters, or 10^{23} miles. The answer to the question of the center of the universe is simple—there is none. Neither is there an edge to the universe, even though the universe may have finite volume. If the universe is curved like a 3-sphere, then if you look out far enough into the universe, you might see the back of your head!

Whatever the geometry of the universe, it is expanding, as was discovered in 1929 by Edwin Hubble. This greatest discovery of twentieth century astronomy was made by studying the spectra from distant galaxies.

Everyone knows that if light is passed through a prism, "white" light is separated into a spectrum consisting of different colors. If an element is heated until it glows, and that light passes through a prism, the colors present in the spectrum are a signature of that element. A spectroscopist can examine the spectrum and determine exactly what element is responsible for the light. A typical spectrum will consist of a series of lines of different colors. The different colors of the spectrum correspond to light of different wavelength. The longer the wavelength, the redder the light.

It was known before Hubble that the spectra from distant galaxies were not quite identical to laboratory spectra. If the spectrum from a distant galaxy was examined in detail, it was found that the wavelength of each line in the spectrum was slightly longer (redder) than the wavelength measured on earth (see Figure 4, page 68). Hubble discovered the connection between the amount of this red shift and the distance to the galaxy; he noticed that the red shift of the lines increased in direct proportion to the distance to the galaxy.

The red shift of light waves can be understood by an analogy with the Doppler shift of sound waves. If a wave source, say sound waves from an airplane, is approaching the observer, the detected wavelength will be shorter. If the source is receding from the observer, the detected wavelength will be longer. This leads to the sense that the sound of an approaching airplane is different than the sound of a receding airplane. The linear increase of the wavelength of light with distance to the galaxy can be understood as due to the fact that the distant galaxy is receding. The more distant a galaxy, the faster its recessional velocity.

If all the galaxies are receding from us, does that make us the center of an explosion? The answer is No! The expansion of the universe is not an explosion of matter into empty space but rather the creation of space! Let us illustrate the expansion of the universe by a loaf of raisin bread. Imagine the raisins as galaxies, and the intervening bread as space. As the bread is baked, the distance between the raisins increases because space is expanding. Now simply imagine an infinite loaf of raisin bread. The distance between any two raisins increases as the bread is baked. In the infinite loaf there is no center and no edge. Every raisin "sees" every other raisin receding from it, just as an astronomer on a galaxy 500 Mpc from us would see the Milky Way receding.

The study of the building blocks of the universe has led to two important conclusions. The first, the Cosmological Principle, resulted from the revolution which Copernicus initiated. The second, the expansion of the universe, was discovered in 1929 and was completely unanticipated. The expansion of the universe is yet another indication that the universe is not static; the universe is dynamic, it is expanding, evolving, changing.

The Cosmological Principle has profound implications. Whatever our place in the universe, it is not in a special location. Copernicus proved that the earth is not the center of the solar system. We now know that the solar system is not the center of our galaxy, and our galaxy is not the center of the universe. Our galaxy is not even at rest with respect to the microwave background radiation. Perhaps dark matter is the inevitable culmination of the Copernican revolution: not only do we not occupy a

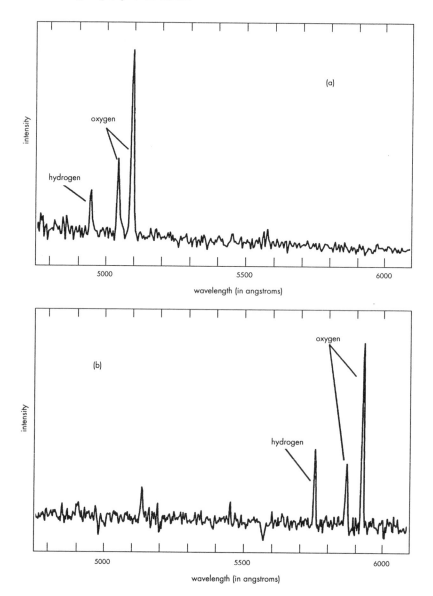

FIGURE 4. *(a) is the spectrum from a galaxy 110 Mpc distant, while (b) is the spectrum from a galaxy 1100 Mpc away. Notice that the repeated pattern of two oxygen lines and one hydrogen line, but at different wavelengths. The laboratory wavelength of the hydrogen line is 4861Å (1Å = 10⁻⁸cm). For the nearby galaxy, the observed wavelength is 4950Å, while for the more distant galaxy the wavelength appears to be 5755Å. (Data courtesy of Richard Kron.)*

special place in the solar system, the galaxy, or the universe, but the neutrons, protons, and electrons that make up our body are but a small part of the total mass of the universe, and most of the mass is invisible to us.

The discovery of the expansion of the universe illustrates how deeply rooted our view of the universe is. In 1905, Albert Einstein examined the results of his calculations and realized that space and time were connected and that the view of space and time held for millennia must be modified. In 1915, Einstein examined the results of further calculations and realized that space was curved and that the view of geometry maintained since the time of Euclid must be modified. In 1917, Einstein examined the applications of his beautiful equations to cosmology and realized that his equations predicted that the universe was expanding or contracting. But Einstein was educated in the nineteenth century with the cosmological view that the universe is infinite and static. A man who could modify his view of space and time to conform to his equations, and modify his view of geometry to agree with his equations, could not change his view of the universe. Einstein did not predict that the universe is expanding but rather butchered his beautiful equations to conform to his view of the universe. Later, when Hubble discovered the expansion, Einstein regretted modifying his equations and referred to it as the "biggest blunder of my life." If the imagination of a man like Einstein was bound by his view of the universe, how is ours prejudiced?

The idea that we do not live in a special place in the universe has upset a lot of people. Giordano Bruno was burned at the stake in Campo di Fiori in Rome in February 1600 for espousing such an idea. However, the idea remains, it was not scattered to the wind with Bruno's ashes. In my opinion, people become upset upon hearing that we do not live in a special place in the universe because they confuse the fact that we do not occupy a special place with the statement that we are not special. I think that location is not special, but what makes us special is that on a small planet orbiting an insignificant star on the outer arms of a typical spiral galaxy, we look up into the immense cosmos, in awe but not in fear, and boldly attempt to comprehend it.

· · · · · · · · · ·

The Big Bang

The universe is expanding and is full of radiation. These two facts are the cornerstones of the Big Bang. If the distance between points in the universe is increasing, in the past the distance was smaller and the universe was denser. Just as a gas cools upon expansion and heats upon compression, the temperature of the universe changes. The universe is expanding and cooling. When the universe was denser, it was also hotter. Earlier epochs in the history of the universe were hotter and denser. Let us denote as $t = 0$, the time of the Big Bang, when the temperature and density were infinite.

In order to understand the present state of the universe, we must understand the origins of the universe. What hope do we have of trying to understand what the universe was like 14 billion years ago? Well, we can follow the lead of Newton and take physical law as our guide. After all, in the seventeenth century it may have been asked of Newton what hope he had of understanding the motion of distant planets. Extrapolation of knowledge over great time and distance is possible if we understand the nature of physical law under the conditions encountered. Where the physics is simple, or at least understood, predictions can be made. For instance, the temperature on Mars next week can be predicted with greater precision than the temperature in Cleveland. Although Mars is distant, the physics of Martian weather is not complicated by the turbulence of an atmosphere as on Earth.

History of the Universe

Epoch	Age	Size	Temperataure
now	14 billion years	1	2.73 K
earth forms	9 billion years	0.34	3.67 K
oldest quasars	1 billion years	0.2	13.6 K
comfort zone	12.5 million years	0.009	295 K
hotter than hell	3.3 million years	0.004	718 K
atoms melt	260,000 years	0.0007	3,850 K
radiation era	31,200 years	0.0002	15,800 K
nuclei melt	1 second	10^{-10}	10^{10} K
nucleons melt	10^{-4} seconds	10^{-12}	10^{12} K
weak unity	10^{-10} seconds	10^{-16}	10^{16} K
grand unity	10^{-35} seconds	10^{-28}	10^{28} K
super unity	10^{-43} seconds	10^{-32}	10^{32} K
singularity	0	0	infinite

TABLE 1: Some interesting developments in the history of the universe. The distance between any two points in the universe is proportional to size. For instance, a point that is 100 Mpc away today was only 20 Mpc away at the time of the formation of the oldest visible quasars.

A brief history of the universe is given in Table 1. Let us journey back in time to see what the universe was like. The temperature in our 14 billion year old universe is now 2.73 K (-454 F). In order to illustrate the expansion of the universe, let us pick a radio source known by the unromantic name of 3C84.0, which is at a present distance of 100 Mpc, as a reference.

When Earth formed some 5 billion years ago, the universe was already 9 billion years old and the temperature was 3.67 K. The universe was somewhat denser; 3C84.0 was at a distance of 34 Mpc. The universe at this time closely resembled the universe we observe today.

Quasars are the most distant (hence the oldest) astrophysical objects we observe. The light we now observe from the most distant quasar was emitted some 13 billion years ago when the universe was only a billion years old and had a temperature of 13.6 K. The distance to our reference source (although the source probably had not formed yet) was a mere 20 Mpc. Quasars probably signify the earliest epoch of galaxy formation.

Prior to the quasar epoch, galaxies and stars did not exist, and the distribution of matter in the universe was very smooth. The mass density in galaxies today is about 10^{-24}g cm^{-3}, or about a million times the present average density in the universe, 10^{-29}g cm^{-3}. Before the quasar era, the regions that would eventually form galaxies had a density only a few percent larger than the average density at that time. Over billions of years, these regions of slight over-density accreted other matter by gravitational attraction and eventually grew to become the structure we observe. If the universe today is smooth on large scales, the early universe was *very* smooth on all scales. Although any tiny irregularities in the density will inexorably grow, the nature of the resulting structure depends on the amplitudes and sizes of the irregularities. We must study the universe at even earlier epochs to learn the nature of the irregularities.

The temperature of the universe was a comfortable 295 K (72 F) when the universe was about 12.5 million years old. The temperature of the universe was hot enough to boil water (although no oxygen was present to form H_2O) 9 million years after the Bang and cold enough to freeze water 14 million years after the Bang. (There is no cosmological significance to the comfort zone.)

Earlier than about 3.3 million years after the Bang, the universe was really hot. In fact, it was hotter than hell (assuming that the temperature of hell is less than the boiling point of brimstone, 718 K). At that time the distance to our reference galaxy (at least the matter that would eventually form our reference galaxy) was only 0.4 Mpc.

A temperature of 3,850 K marks an important cosmological event. When the temperature was higher than this, the universe was so hot that the hydrogen and helium present fell apart and became ionized. Before this era, the universe was a plasma of nuclei and electrons. This era was 260,000 years after the Bang, nearly 14 billion years ago. It was at this time that the microwave photons last interacted with the matter. The microwave background is a direct probe of the universe at this time.

The universe at the time of ionization was so dense that our reference source that is today 100 Mpc distant was then only 70,000 parsecs distant. Recall that our galaxy is 100,000 parsecs in size. Although the universe at this early era was hot and dense compared to the present state of the universe, the density and temperature is not extreme by laboratory standards. The average density of matter at ionization was a mere 10^{-19}g cm^{-3} or 10^{19} times less dense than water. A temperature of 15,800 K is routinely obtained in plasma physics laboratories. We have a complete understanding of physical law under these conditions, and it is with confidence that we can speak of the universe at this time.

Although the energy density of the radiation in the universe is today much smaller than the mass density of matter, earlier than 31,200 years after the Bang the density of radiation was larger. In the very early universe, matter played a negligible role in the dynamics of expansion.

The next important era encountered in the journey to the beginning of the universe is the era of primordial nucleosynthesis. When the universe was hotter than 10^{10} (10 billion) K, any nuclei present would have melted to their constituent particles, neutrons and protons. In this era the density of matter was still not very high, about 3.6 g cm^{-3}. The energy of the particles present was high by normal experience but is routinely reproduced today in nuclear physics laboratories. Since we understand the structure of matter under these conditions of density and temperature, we expect to make reasonable predictions about the state of the universe in this era.

One of the predictions we can make has to do with the chemical composition of the universe after primordial nucleosynthesis. If we start with an expanding universe of neutrons and protons at 10^{10}K, about three minutes later the neutrons and protons will be cooked into nuclei that are 76% hydrogen and 24% helium, exactly the proportions needed. (This is another example of the Inner Space/Outer Space connection.) If the universe expanded more slowly than predicted, a smaller fraction of helium would have resulted; a slightly faster expansion would have resulted in too much helium. There is an interplay between the laws of nuclear physics (Inner Space) and the law of cosmic expansion (Outer Space).

At a tenth of a millisecond (10^{-4}sec) after the Bang, the density of the universe was so high that nucleons were touching. Individual neutrons and protons did not exist, but for a brief moment the universe was as one giant nucleus. This nuclear matter density was so great that one solar mass would occupy a sphere of 14 kilometers, and the mass of a galaxy would be contained in a sphere smaller than the sun. The physics of nuclear matter is difficult, but many of its most important properties can be calculated with the aid of quantum mechanics and the calculations checked by laboratory experiments.

Before the nuclear density era, the universe was so hot and dense that individual neutrons and protons could not exist as such but melted into their constituent particles, quarks and gluons. The universe before 10^{-4}sec was a primordial soup of elementary particles: leptons (electrons, muons, taus, neutrinos) and hadrons (quarks and gluons).

How can we hope to understand the universe a microsecond after the Bang? Every day, in a handful of particle accelerators throughout the world, scientists accelerate protons or electrons to tremendous energies and collide them. In these collisions we can recreate for a brief moment the conditions that have not existed in the universe for 14 billion years. By studying the properties of elementary particles we can gain insight into the origin of the universe in the same way laboratory experiments of the seventeenth century measured the gravitational force and led to insight into the motion of the planets.

The highest-energy collisions we can study in the laboratory have an energy equivalent to 10^{12} electron volts, or 10^{16}K. This was the temperature of the universe about 10^{-10}sec after the Bang. At this point our direct knowledge of the properties of matter ends, and hence we are able only to speculate about the universe at earlier times.

This energy is at the threshold of what we think should be an important transition in the history of the universe. At temperatures above about 10^{16}K, the universe is predicted to have more symmetry than it does today. At high temperature there is a true unification of the weak and electromagnetic interactions. The universe should have undergone a phase transition around 10^{-16}sec into its history. The transition to weak unity, the unification of the weak and electromagnetic interactions, is perhaps just the last event in a series of unification transitions.

Many particle physicists feel that the four fundamental forces (electromagnetic, strong, weak, and gravitational) are unified at some extremely high energy. If this is so, the universe should have undergone a series of phase transitions, starting at 10^{-43}sec when the "super" symmetry between the gravitational force and the other forces was lost. Then, at 10^{-35}sec the "grand" symmetry between the strong and electroweak forces was lost. Finally at 10^{-10}sec the weak force split from the electromagnetic force.

There are many interesting and exotic phenomena that are predicted to occur in these phase transitions. Cosmic strings, domain walls, magnetic monopoles, cosmic inflation, origin of density inhomogeneities, even the origin of the universe at 10^{-43}sec. Clearly the grand and super unity transitions are beyond the reach of accelerators in the near future.

. . . .

Conclusions

There is a simple, beautiful picture of the universe based upon the Big Bang model. We have direct evidence, in the form of primordial hydrogen and helium, for the structure of the universe over the last 14 billion years, starting 1 second after the Bang. We can use the Inner Space/Outer Space connection and apply the knowledge we learn in the laboratory to extend our knowledge about the universe back to 10^{-10}sec after the Bang. We seem to be on the verge of understanding a crucial transition in the universe, the weak unity transition.

Where should we stop? If we have a consistent picture of the universe for the last 14 billion years, back to a second after the Bang, is that enough? No, I think we will never stop asking fundamental questions about the universe.

I often wonder what people in the next century will think of our attempts to understand the very early universe. Will they look upon our ideas of grand and super unification with the same amusement with which we look upon the efforts of previous centuries, and think them naïve? However they judge our scientific efforts, I believe that they will not judge us lacking in boldness and imagination in attacking problems once thought to lie outside the realm of human comprehension.

. . . .

Something Wonderful in Humanity

1 What are your views on cosmic beginnings, particularly with reference to the origin of the universe, of life, and of Homo sapiens?

The Big Bang cosmological model is central to my view of the origin of the universe. We have very firm evidence as to conditions in the universe as early as one second after the Bang. Based upon the known laws of physics, we can make a sensible extrapolation back to about a millionth of a millionth of a second after the Bang. Extrapolation to earlier times requires assuming we know the laws of physics on distance scales smaller than we have directly probed by experiment. Nevertheless, if we do make such an extrapolation, we find a conceptual barrier at a time known as the Planck time. If the Planck time is expressed in seconds, it would be a decimal point, followed by 43 zeros before a 1. We do not have any idea what the universe was like earlier than the Planck time, because for time intervals this small, there is quantum uncertainty in exactly what is meant by time.

One attractive possibility about quantum aspects at the Planck time is that it allows the possibility that the universe emerged as a result of a "quantum tunnelling event," which means that it spontaneously appeared from nothing. (Here "nothing" means no matter, no radiation, no space, and no time—only the laws of physics.) If this is true, then the appearance of a universe is an inevitable result of the laws of Nature.

I prefer to leave questions regarding the origins of life and of *Homo sapiens* to others. As a cosmologist interested in the early universe, things that happened on our little planet billions of years after the Bang do not interest me as much.

2 What are your views on human ends, especially as this relates to the framework of cosmic beginnings?

I do not regard life on our planet as very significant in the context of the entire universe. Life on this planet will certainly come to a halt some five billion years from now when our sun has exhausted its supply of hydrogen and enters a red giant phase of stellar evolution. Perhaps the best we can hope for is that some of the atoms in our bodies will be recycled in the interstellar medium for some future generation of stars and planetary systems.

3 What do you think should be the relationship between religion and science?

I do not believe that a conflict is inevitable. Freedom of human enquiry should be a fundamental tenet of any religion. Just as science can never prove or disprove the existence of God, scientific fact will never be the result of revealed truth but can only be arrived at after long, hard effort in the traditional methods of science. You will not discover God by looking through a telescope any more than you will advance science by prayer for divine inspiration.

We should cherish both religion and science as manifestations of something wonderful in humanity, the desire for knowledge. As Galileo said, "I do not believe that the same God who has endowed us with reason, intellect, and sense, has intended us to forego their use."

4

Beyond Immutability:
The Birth and Death of Elementary Particles

E. C. G. Sudarshan

Enackal Chandy George Sudarshan is Professor of Physics at the University of Texas, Austin. From 1970 to 1991 he directed the Center for Particle Physics there, following academic years at Syracuse University, the University of Rochester, and Harvard University. Born in Kerala, India, he began his scientific studies in Madras and conducted research at the Tata Institute in Bombay. Since 1971 he has also been a Senior Professor at the Centre for Theoretical Studies, Bangalore. He was Director of the Institute for Mathematical Sciences in Madras from 1984 to 1991. In addition to publishing numerous scientific papers, he is the co-author of several volumes on particle theory. In that field he is best known for his seminal work on tachyons, particles that move faster than light.

Abstract

Elementary particles—atoms and their components—are not immutable but undergo birth and death, production and decay. By considering them to be different states of a substratum—the quantized field—we discuss here the phenomena of identity in change.

Introduction

A natural development of physics is to go beyond particles as immutable to particles undergoing the birth and death of production and decay. In this context we must consider a substratum of which the presence of the particle and the absence of the particle are merely distinct states of this substratum. This substratum is the quantized field. We may need states of not one but many particles to describe spontaneous decay. The laws of birth and death derived from quantum mechanical principles involving transition amplitudes is inherently statistical.

The need to go beyond the obvious to find the substratum reminds me of the verse from Ramayana:

rāmam daśaratham viddhi
mām viddhi janakātmajām.

(When one transcends limitations of perception, time is recognized as a chariot; but one whose perception is limited cognizes progenitor and offspring.)

· · · · · · · · · ·

Laws of Motion

The physical universe around and within us is constantly changing, yet there are permanent aspects to it. When the heavens change we recognize that much of the change is motion: the relative positions change. We see this on the terrestrial scale too. Automobiles and people move, birds fly, and flags flutter in the wind. It is then the identity in change: the abstract entity that takes on different positions that is the subject of study of the physical discipline of mechanics. Modern physics traces to Galileo and Newton the precise formulation of the principles of mechanics. In Newton's hands the mathematical formulation became adequate to treat the motion of heavenly bodies, the tides in the sea, and the falling apple, as well as a host of other phenomena like the propagation of sound in a gas.

The equation of motion states

$$\frac{dp}{dt} = F$$

where the lefthand side of the equation is the rate of change of momentum of the particle, while the righthand side is the force acting on the particle. When there are a number of particles, the mutual interactions of the particles obey the principle of action and reaction and are equal and opposite.

The grand design of mechanics, however, seemed to be leaving out chemical changes as well as dissipative processes. In the first, the material itself undergoes a chemical change, a change in species so that we can no longer consider the changes to be due to motion. For simple dissipative processes like friction or viscosity, one appealed to the existence of subunits, the "particles" which changed the nature of their collective motion into more disorderly motion and which manifested as a dissipative process. Here we may recognize the enigma of the Second Law of Thermodynamics, the propensity of disorder developing spontaneously and thus providing an arrow of time, from order to disorder.

A quantitative measure of the disorder is given by the

thermodynamic quantity of "entropy." The Second Law of Thermodynamics may be formulated as the tendency of entropy to increase with time, while the First Law states that the energy remains constant.

Chemical changes could be brought under the scheme of a physics of permanent matter changing its configuration by invoking the atomic theory. The Greeks had the notion of atoms as indivisible permanent objects which constituted the observed matter. For each kind of matter there was a different kind of atom. But with this we still do not have an understanding of chemical change. It is better to use the older *Vaiśeṣika* doctrine of atoms with qualities and the possibility of forming two or three atom complexes. This theory was reinvented by Dalton in a quantitative form. The chemical compounds could now be seen as various combinations of a few elementary atoms. In a chemical reaction the atoms could change associations, dissociate, or recombine.

The burning of carbon to produce carbon dioxide is given by the chemical equation

$$C + O_2 \rightarrow CO_2,$$

while the combination of hydrogen and oxygen to form water is given by

$$2H_2 + O_2 \rightarrow 2H_2O.$$

Sodium combines with chlorine from hydrochloric acid to create sodium chloride and then release hydrogen:

$$2Na + 2HCl \rightarrow 2NaCl + H_2.$$

The precipitation of calcium carbonate from calcium chloride mixed with carbonic acid:

$$HCO_3 + CaCl \rightarrow CaCO_3 + HCl.$$

In all these chemical equations we see that the atomic specificity is preserved but their associations are changed.

If we are willing to enlarge the notion of the configuration of a physical system to include the state of association between atoms, we could consider the laws of chemical processes to be part of the equations of motion of physical systems. The atoms now become the elementary objects of the theoretical framework.

· · · · · · · · · ·

Emission of Light by Atoms: Decay of Excited Atoms

But atoms have other properties. They emit and absorb light. For example, the excited atom of a hydrogen atom deexcites with the emission of a light quantum γ

$$A^* \rightarrow A + \gamma$$

and equally well excites by absorption of light:

$$A + \gamma \rightarrow A^*.$$

The states of the system thus include the vacuum (no particles), atom, atom + one light quantum, atom + two light quanta, and so forth. Since the light wave that is emitted or absorbed has a wavelength several hundred times the size of the atom, the light is not inside the atom after it is absorbed or before it is emitted. Instead, we have a changed state of the atom and an excited state with more energy than the ground state of the atom. The absorption of light by atoms is therefore of a different kind of process from a chemical change, where the atoms remain intact but only change their associations. But many mechanical attributes are preserved under the transitions: the energy, the momentum, and the angular momentum for instance. What is preserved in the transitions are not the constituents but only such attributes. If we want to include these transitions also in our enlarged framework of "motion," we must consider the ground-state atom *plus* light on the one hand and the excited atom on the other as both states of a single system. This single system is not an atom, but a more abstract object which has these different kinds of states.

· · · · · · · · · ·

Birth and Death of Particles

In the search for deeper and deeper levels of matter, we come across a large number of particles like pions, nucleons, and strange particles which also undergo such dramatic changes. For example, nucleons are of two kinds, the positively charged "protons" and the electrically neutral "neutron." The pions come in three varieties: the positive, the neutral, and the negative. In studying their reactions we can have processes like:

$$p + \pi^- \to n + \pi^0$$
$$p + \pi^+ \to p + \pi^0 + \pi^+$$
$$p + \pi^- \to n + \pi^+ + \pi^-$$

It is useful and advantageous to consider both neutron and proton as different states of the "nucleon" and to consider the three kinds of pions as different states of the "pion."

In Newton's mechanics the equations of motion described the rates of change of position of a particle and its velocity. The object of discussion is an abstract "particle" which may take on one position and velocity or another. The particle with the attributes of position and velocity is the concrete object, but the framework discusses the abstract object. When we come to modern particle physics, we carry the level of abstraction much further to associate a family of particles as the concrete realization of an abstract particle.

· · · · · · · · ·
Decay as Change of State

Already at the level of emission and absorption of light by atoms, we see an asymmetry: an excited atom can spontaneously emit a quantum of light and go to the ground state. The excited atom "decays." Decay is a change of state: a single object is transmitted into two or more particles. This is a spontaneous transformation. The reverse transformation of recombination of the decay product can be induced under suitable conditions, thus recreating the decaying entity. Decay and creation are two aspects of the same process. New objects appear when old objects disappear.

This process can be quantified and described in a formalism where both the old and the new states enter on an equal footing. The aim of the theoretical framework would be to calculate the rate of transition into the various possible decay products.

In the realm of high-energy physics, decaying particles dominate the scene. There are only a few particles: the proton, the light quantum, the electron, and the neutrino, which are all stable. All the others decay with a time scale from a few minutes for the neutron to a millionth of a millionth second or even shorter at the other end.

The neutron decays into a proton, electron, and neutrino by a weak interaction:

$$n \rightarrow p + e^- + \widehat{\nu}$$

while the pion and the muon have decays:

$$\pi^+ \rightarrow \mu^+ + \nu_\mu$$
$$\pi^0 \rightarrow \gamma + \nu$$
$$\mu^+ \rightarrow e^+ + \nu + \widehat{\nu}_\mu$$

but not all reactions take place:

$$\mu^- \nrightarrow e^- + \gamma.$$

The lifetime, which is the time it takes for the survival probability for the particle, is approximately one-third.

The laws of decay are statistical. Given a collection of identical unstable particles within a given time interval, some of them would decay and some would not decay. Individual decays cannot be predicted, but the probability that any one particle will decay can be calculated. The method follows the application of quantum mechanics to the spontaneous alpha radioactive decays of atomic nuclei and the emission of light by excited atoms. This method gives a quantitative understanding of various decay processes and the underlying laws governing them.

· · · · · · · · · ·

Quantum Theory of Decay

Quantum theory is a mathematical model of physical processes which describes the amplitudes for various processes. These amplitudes obey equations of motion which enable us to compute them as functions of time. The growth of the amplitude for the decay products and the decline of the amplitude for the decaying object take place gradually very much like a rotating vector has one of its components increase and another decrease or as a Polaroid photograph gradually develops. In fact, the mathematical theory envisages an abstract vector in an infinite dimensional space of states gradually evolving.

Since the decay is a physical process, it is also subject to the principle of relativity. So the apparent law changes somewhat when we go to a moving frame. In fact, a moving unstable particle decays at a slower rate than the same particle at rest; and the ratio by which it gets changed is a computable universal function of the velocity with which the particle moves.

If the lifetime at rest is τ_0, the lifetime of a particle moving with the velocity v is τ related to τ_0 by the formula:

$$\tau = \left(1 - \left(\frac{v^2}{c^2}\right)\right)^{-\frac{1}{2}} \tau_0$$

where c is the velocity of light. Moving particles live longer.

It also follows that when the quantum theory is strictly applied, very frequent observations on the decaying particle can inhibit its decay. This is called the Zeno effect and has been verified by experiments in atomic physics. There are other consequences of the strict application of quantum theory to the decay amplitude. The amplitude is an analytic function of time, stemming from the existence of a lowest energy state for a generic system, which in turn is in accordance with the Second Law of Thermodynamics. This has the further consequence that for very long times the survival amplitude no longer dies down exponentially with time but dies only as an inverse power of time.

· · · · · · · · · ·

Birth of Particles

The possibility that particles can decay is compensated for by the possibility that such unstable particles can be created. The light quantum is born at the decay of the excited atom. The pions are born in high-energy nuclear collisions and subsequently decay. The charged pions decay into muons and neutrinos, and the muons decay into an electron and neutrinos. The more exotic shortlived particles of high-energy physics are born in extremely high-energy collisions between particles in a collider and live for a very short time and then decay into other particles. It is in the nature of the principles of quantum theory that if the particles can decay, they can be created and vice versa. The more interacting the particle, the more birth and death are inevitable for the particle; and hence the study of the birth and death of particles is a good way to study its interaction with other particles.

· · · · · · · · · ·

Role of Birth and Death in Nucleogenesis

The processes of the birth and death of particles play a very important role in the observed processes. The spontaneous emission and induced absorption of light by atoms is responsible for bodies glowing as their temperatures rise; when a body is properly isolated, the light in its vicinity per unit volume rises as the fourth power of its absolute temperature independent of the specific nature of the material. But this equilibrium state is brought about by the decay of excited atoms and the birth of the excitations by interaction with the light. X-rays are produced by high-energy electrons suddenly decelerating and emitting short wavelength "light." When primordial matter undergoes nucleosynthesis, the higher atomic number elements are brought about by capture and radioactive decay in collusion.

Our understanding of the forces between particles is in terms of "virtual particle exchange" between them. Nucleons exchange pions or gluons between them; these virtual particles emerge from one particle and merge into the other. This birth and death of the exchanged quantum then serves to produce a force between the source and the absorber. This idea has been so fruitful that we tend to view all forces between particles as due to such processes.

· · · · · · · · · ·

Cosmology and the Laws of Interaction

In all these stages we have acted as if the properties of the particle (which is born and which dies) and its interaction with the other particles are fixed once and for all. Modern cosmology proposes extreme conditions of energy density and temperature in early stages of the universe and even at the present time in the interiors of very dense heavenly objects. In such situations the properties of the particles may change. In particular, massive particles could become massless, and the interactions they mediate may become stronger. This interface between cosmology and particle physics is an extremely fertile field for new results and possible clues to the nature of matter itself.

Birth and death of elementary particles is an interplay of the harmonious evolution of the physical state and of the incompatible observational criteria we put on. It is a challenge to us to proceed beyond habitual perception of the superficial and look for a deeper structure.

· · · · · · · · · ·

It Is Not Possible to Separate Initial Conditions and Physical Laws

1 What are your views on cosmic beginnings, particularly with reference to the origin of the universe, of life, and of Homo sapiens?

To the extent that we consider the physical universe, we have a plausible theory of its cosmic beginning. Since the cosmos is unique, it is not possible to separate initial conditions and physical laws. A certain act of faith is needed in devising such a model. While the origin of life itself has not been demonstrated, replication, mutation, and evolution of species are well established. It is another leap of induction to include (human) awareness as just another aspect of evolution. As for me, I keep an open mind on each of these three crucial acts of faith.

2 What are your views on human ends, especially as this relates to the framework of cosmic beginnings?

Cosmic beginning and evolution are not contrary to physical law but, rather, adapt to it. So do human ends. We cannot legislate or dictate to bring about a desired human event but may do so in accordance with natural law. So human ends are to be brought about by selectively enlisting natural laws of human/human and human/non-human interactions. We choose our course but "go with the flow."

3 What do you think should be the relationship between religion and science?

In my experience religion and science are both experiential and theoretical. In theory, other people's experiential knowledge can be used, but ultimately each person has to make direct verification. Science deals with public knowledge, while religion includes private (personal) knowledge. In both cases the results are communicable but only to those who share a certain common framework; science does not need religion to validate it, nor does religion need to be validated by science. But when they speak about the same domain of experience, they should agree.

5

From Mystery to Mystery

Eric D. Carlson

Eric D. Carlson is astronomer at the Adler Planetarium in Chicago, Illinois, where he teaches, writes scripts for the Planetarium's Sky Show presentations, and coordinates adult course programs.

Speaking as an astronomer I find the current Big Bang "standard model" to be a satisfying fit to the observations we have obtained so far. We see a tiniest seedling of spacetime balloon in an instant into a universe far larger than we can hope ever to observe. We see it fill instantaneously and everywhere with light and particles. We see it expand and cool and give birth to numberless galaxies of stars. And we see stars explode and seed the atoms of life throughout the galaxies. We see our own Sun and planet form, single-celled life jumping into formation soon after our Earth enshawls itself with cool oceans. We see life enriching the air with oxygen, multicelled organisms growing, cosmic impacts rupturing and stirring the mix of life forms. Out of it all a simian consciousness brews forth language and tools, music and art, telescopes and relativity—and at last a "standard model" of the universe.

Some think we have thus "explained" the universe with our magic show of knowledge. But far from "explaining" it or the emergence of life and consciousness, our model reveals a process so vast, so complex, and so startling in its configurations that we can only marvel at the radical mystery of it glimpsed at every turn and at every scale—from the "dancing point" electrons to expanses of space beyond our ability to measure. Our finest equations and models we fling across the face of this Great Mystery (as Native Americans prefer to call it). Yet ultimately our equations only deepen the mystery, for they cry to us, "Why do the fundamental interplays of energy and mass and space and time happen as they do and not some other way? What keeps them the same through vast times? Why are the 'commonplace' but inconceivably complex architectures of particles that make us up even possible at all? From what could that primordial seedling of spacetime have sprung? If we were to know whence it came, then from what did *that* spring?''

What we have is a story of the universe we can see and imagine, set within an ultimate mystery, a myth like all the preceding ones of whatever culture or religion. Except that this one is woven by all of humankind from far wider strands of experience and imagination, fed by electronic circuitries and seen through electronic eyes, and shepherded by a common scientific method. It is our ultimate personal history, tracing our individual existence beyond our families, beyond our species, beyond life, beyond the earliest galaxies, and finally beyond even the primordial fireball to the time when there was no time, the place where was no space, and there was only mystery. And is our time and place today really so different? For is not every aspect of our existence today still only mystery, ultimately, no matter how familiar it may seem?

And if science ultimately must exist in the embrace of radical mystery, what of religion? Religion, too, has its models and verbal equations and story. And it flings them across the face of the Great Mystery almost with greater deliberation than does science, for science at least has recently humbled itself to describing its models without capitalized letters. So, how then are the two different? I would say that science has successfully taken over the job of describing the mysteries of physical existence as far as possible and sincerely showing us the edges of such knowledge. Religion then remains as our way of dealing with our personal consciousness and its many mysteries, in our relationships with other consciousness (whether human or non-human, terrestrial or extraterrestrial, mundane or cosmic), and especially in how we establish our stance toward the mysteries of both the physical and the personal.

As for human ends, or human purposiveness as I'll call it—after all this highlighting of the radical mysteries of cosmic and human existence, I think of human purposiveness as our personal and collective advance into the mystery of time. The manner of this advance at the personal level is certainly a form of religion at its best. I conceive my own advance as one of projecting a plan of action based on my own conscious thought while inviting a larger kind of consciousness to co-create the newly forming present. I find it helpful to give the name of Co-creator (and yes, a capital does help!) to this larger consciousness. I prefer not to demand to know what the geographic or temporal extent of my Co-creator may be—it's alright with me whether this all occurs within my head, or extends beyond it locally in space and time, or even extends throughout all of space and time. And I prefer not to demand to know whether my Co-creator is a process or entity or whatever. As you can see, this leaves plenty of room for mystery around the edges and on the inside, too. Why not? It's more fun that way!

Who really believes they have got the Great Mystery all locked up in a box? Surely, the scientists do not, although some outsiders seem to think they do. And surely, the religions do not, although some of their insiders seem to think they do. We all function within the categories of both science and religion—we always have and we always will—there has never been a problem in doing both at the same time, as I see it. The idea of a "problem" only arises when someone in either category decides they have got the mystery, or even part of it, locked in a box—their box. Ah, how godlike indeed. But, of course, anyone else can always come along and put them and their box inside a bigger box. And so, I give you . . . an infinite regress of boxes, if you like boxes. But, then, there is always the Mystery, if you don't like boxes! Or an infinite regress of mysteries . . . if you don't like just one. And, you can always invite in a Co-creator if you like . . . or a co-creator . . . or not . . . whatever. Enjoy!

6

The Origin, Evolution, and Distribution of Life in the Universe
. . . .

Cyril Ponnamperuma

Cyril Ponnamperuma has been Professor of Chemistry and Director of the Laboratory of Chemical Evolution of the University of Maryland since 1971. His pioneering research on the origin of life, which included a close involvement with NASA on the Apollo, Viking, and Voyager missions, led to his being awarded the first A. I. Oparin Gold Medal in 1980. In 1984 he was appointed Science and Technology Advisor to the President of Sri Lanka and became Director there of the Institute of Fundamental Studies (1984–1991) and of the Arthur C. Clarke Centre for Modern Technologies (1985–1987). He is President of the Third World Foundation of North America and Director General of the Network for International Centers for Sustainable Development to be established by the Third World Academy of Sciences. In 1991 the University of Maryland honored him with the first Distinguished International Science Award for his scholarly career combined with extraordinary services to the scientific community.

. . . .
Abstract

According to the Oparin-Haldane Hypothesis of Chemical Evolution, the formation of molecules of biological significance was a necessary preamble to the emergence of life on earth. The analysis of carbonaceous chondrites has revealed the presence of these same molecules in the early samples of the solar system. Radio astronomers have discovered a vast array of organic molecules in the interstellar medium. We are thus led to the inescapable conclusion that life must be commonplace in the cosmos. Laboratory experiments help us retrace the path of chemical evolution on earth. Planetary probes search for evidence of life in our solar system. Radio signals from outer space may reveal the presence of our distant neighbors.

. . . .
The Challenge

"La silence eternel des espaces infinis m'effraie," wrote Pascal in his *Pensees*. To our ancestors, the vastness of the earth was a dominant fact controlling their thoughts and lives. A few hundred miles was almost like infinity. Great empires and cultures could flourish on the same continent knowing almost nothing of each other. Only a lifetime ago, parents waved farewell to their emigrating children in the virtual certainty that they would never meet again. But now, within one incredible generation, all this has changed. Ulysses took ten years to traverse the seas over which the modern jet speeds its way in less than an hour. But the stage that is presently opening up for the human drama may not shrink as the old one has done.

From a world that has become too small, we are moving out into one that will be forever too large, whose frontiers will recede from us almost before we reach for them. We now have instruments that can determine the energy flux in the depths of the stars. A century ago, even the greatest physicist would not have believed of the existence of such forms of energy. We now have vessels that can carry men beyond the atmosphere and to the moon and back. A generation ago such a feat belonged also to the realm of fantasy. Yet, in spite of all this knowledge, we are awed by the mystery of the universe around us. The question looms larger than ever: "Are we alone in the universe?" If we can track the radio waves from a distant galaxy, what may we not hear if we listen closely? If we stand on the alien dust of another world, what may we not stumble over as we walk?

It is an ancient dream of men that someday we might reach beyond the earth and walk on other planets and speak with those who dwell there. As early as the year A.D. 160 Lucius of Samosata wrote about voyages to the moon. The dream lay fallow for fourteen centuries until Copernicus revitalized the idea that the earth was only one among several planets revolving round the sun. Today, we wish to explore the heavens, not merely by peering through our cloudy atmosphere but by crossing the millions of miles that lie between other planets and the earth, in the way Columbus did. Five centuries ago Columbus stood on the shores of the Atlantic and gazed across the horizon stretching before him. When most people thought his quest foolish, the spirit of adventure and the urge to explore impelled him across the waves. Like Columbus, modern space explorers stand before a new horizon, but this horizon stretches almost to infinity in space and time. Like Ulysses they are urged on: "Oh, brothers, through a hundred thousand perils have ye driven to the West. Now in the brief and tiny span that still remains to you of waking life, refuse not to explore whatever lies beyond the sun." The spirit of this search is the quintessence of the new science of exobiology.

In an authoritative document, the National Academy of Sciences of the United States has set down the search for extraterrestrial life as the prime goal of space biology:

> It is not since Darwin and, before him, Copernicus, that science has had the opportunity for so great an impact on man's understanding of man. The scientific question at stake in exobiology is the most exciting, the most challenging, and most profound issue, not only of this century, but of the entire naturalistic movement that has characterized the history of western thought for over three hundred years and thought for ages before. If there is life on Mars and if we can demonstrate its independent origin, then we shall have an enlightening answer to the question of the improbability and uniqueness in the origin of life. Arising twice in a single planetary system, it must surely occur abundantly elsewhere in the staggering number of comparable planetary systems.

· · · · · · · · · ·

Evidence for Life in the Universe

Modern astronomy by its exhaustive study of galactic, stellar, and planetary evolution has come to the inescapable conclusion that life in the universe must be of common occurrence. On the basis of our sampling of galaxy populations to the limit attainable by present-day telescopes, we can readily compute that there are more than 10^{20} stars in the universe. Each one of these can maintain the photochemical reactions that are the basis of plant and animal life. Let us impose a number of restrictions in considering the stars that can support life. Suppose that because of doubling, clustering, and secondary collisions, only one star in a thousand has a planetary system. Suppose that only one out of a thousand of those stars with planetary systems has a planet at the right distance from the star to provide the water and the warmth that life requires. In our own planetary system we have two such planets. Further, let us suppose that only one out of a thousand of those stars with planets at the right distance has a planet large enough to hold an atmosphere. In our planetary system at least seven of the nine can do that. Suppose a further restriction is made, and we suggest that the right chemical composition for life to arise occurs only once in a thousand times. Assuming all these four restrictions, we come to the conclusion that there are at least a hundred million possibilities for the existence of life. This is a conservative estimate made by Harlow Shapley.

The late astronomer Su-Shu Huang has been less rigorous in his requirements for the existence of life in the universe. In considering the time scales of biological and stellar evolution, the habitable zones of a star, dynamic and other considerations, he has come to the astonishing conclusion that at least five percent of the stars in the universe must support life. This means that there are at least a hundred billion sites for the existence of life.

Harrison Brown has used the illuminacy function to estimate the number of invisible planet-like objects in the neighborhood of the sun. Taking into account the likely chemical composition of planets in relation to the composition of the main sequence stars, he has suggested that there may be about sixty objects more massive than Mars in the neighborhood of visible stars. According to him, stars, together with cold objects, may have been formed in clusters, random in size. On this basis, virtually every star should have a planetary system associated with it. The conclusion is inevitable, therefore, that the conditions feasible for life processes may be far more abundant than has been generally thought to be possible. On the basis of Harrison Brown's calculations, there must be at least a hundred billion planetary systems in our galaxy alone.

This conclusion which astronomers have reached by the rigorous analysis of scientific data was already prophetically foretold by Giordano Bruno in the sixteenth century:

> Sky, universe, all-embracing ether, and immeasurable space alive with movement . . . all these are of one nature. In space there are countless constellations, suns, and planets; we see only the suns because they give light; the planets remain invisible, for they are small and dark. There are also numberless earths circling around their suns, no worse and no less than this globe of ours. For no reasonable mind can assume that heavenly bodies which may be far more magnificent than ours would not bear upon them creatures similar or even superior to those upon our human Earth.

· · · · · · · · ·

The Search

In our search for the existence of extraterrestrial life, three possible approaches present themselves to us. First, the landing of instruments or man somewhere in the universe. With our present knowledge, this attempt would undoubtedly be restricted to our own planetary system. A second method is via radio contact with civilizations in outer space. This presupposes the existence of intelligent beings in space with a technology as advanced or even greater than our own. Thirdly, we have the experimental attack on the problem. Here life is considered an inevitable consequence of the evolution of matter. Since the laws of chemistry and physics are universal laws, the retracing in the laboratory of the path by which life appeared on earth would give strong support to our belief in its existence elsewhere in the universe.

· · · · · · · · · ·

Life on Mars

Our effort to land an instrument or eventually a scientist astronaut on a neighboring planet is primarily directed to the planet Mars. The possibility of life on Mars has often been raised. The canal-like structures on Mars and the seasonal wave of darkening across the planet have led many to believe that there must be some form of life on Mars. Some have suggested the existence of highly intelligent beings, who by incredible feats of engineering have saved for themselves the depleting water supply on the planet by building mammoth canals crisscrossing the planet. All these speculations have fired the imagination of the planetary scientist and have made him determined to find out the answer to the question, "Is there life on Mars?"

When we leave speculation aside and consider the actual conditions that exist on Mars today, we must very likely exclude the existence of advanced forms of life. However, the physical conditions are such that low forms of life, such as microorganisms, could survive on the planet. The atmosphere of Mars is made up of a small amount of carbon dioxide and a trace of water. There must be a high ultraviolet flux which reaches the surface of Mars, since the Martian atmosphere does not appear to have a built-in protection from ultraviolet light as our own earth. With this high incidence of ultraviolet radiation, Martian organisms would have to protect themselves by burrowing into the surface, or they may have evolved a mechanism compatible with the existence of a high ultraviolet flux.

Polarization data have shown that the polar caps of Mars consist of solid carbon dioxide mixed with ice. They wax and wane with the seasons. They are probably extremely thin and perhaps not more than a few centimeters in thickness. In the summer, the pole cap recedes by about thirty-five kilometers per day. As one pole cap recedes, the other is under a cloud. A dark band has been observed to follow the receding pole cap. It is this dark band which has led many to speculate on the existence of vegetation. The wave of darkening proceeds from pole to equator at the rate of about thirty-five kilometers per day during the spring and summer. It seems attractive to interpret this wave of darkening as a gradual growth of vegetation across the planet. The average temperature of Mars is considerably lower than the average temperature of the earth. However, the extremes may not be incompatible with life. The highest temperature observed during the day near the equator is about forty degrees centigrade. The night temperatures go well below zero to about minus eighty-five degrees.

The atmospheric pressure on Mars was long disputed. The recent data confirm the low estimate that it is only one one-hundredth of that of the earth. While this low pressure may not in itself be a factor which affects the survival of microorganisms, it might have an effect on the availability of water. The amount of water present on Mars is about one thousandth of that found in the earth's atmosphere. This again does not preclude the existence of micro environments in which above average accumulations of water may occur.

A very sketchy survey of the physical parameters of Mars indicates to us that, although the conditions are rigorous as compared to the earth, they are within the range in which microorganisms can survive. Indeed, laboratory experiments in which these conditions have been simulated have shown that some earth microorganisms can survive and even multiply under such conditions. Furthermore, if we consider planetary evolution, on account of the smallness of the planet Mars, the processes of chemical evolution may have proceeded very rapidly. Life may have evolved and disappeared. Visitors to Mars may be greeted by relics or fossils of a once-thriving biosphere.

To celebrate the two hundredth anniversary of the birth of our nation, two spacecraft—Viking I and Viking II—arrived on Mars in July 1976. The first pictures photographed on another planet were transmitted to earth. The red desert area of Mars was clearly visible. These were exciting moments. Several experiments of interest to the life scientists were performed. A handful of soil was analyzed for organic matter. The surprising result was that there was less than 5 parts per billion of carbon. This was a figure that was least expected considering that the moon gave us 200 parts per million. There was less carbon on Mars than on the moon. In the absence of carbon, would there be life? It is most unlikely. However, we continued the experiments in search of microbes on Mars. The gas exchange experiment, the labelled release experiment, and the pyrolytic release experiment, all simple approaches to see whether there were any viable changes on the surface of the planet due to simple forms of life, were conducted. There were some false-positives. Since there was no organic matter on Mars, further investigations led us to believe that the surface of Mars was mimicking biology. Our conclusion therefore is that the Viking missions to Mars provided no evidence for the presence of life on the red planet. Further missions to Mars may explore the ancient history of the planet and give us some information about the early history of life on that planet if it did really exist.

· · · · · · · · · ·

Intelligent Life

According to our calculations of the distribution of life in the universe, it is reasonable to assume that intelligent life must have evolved in a large number of sites. An estimate of the distribution of intelligent life in the universe made by Professor Carl Sagan of Cornell University puts the figure at a million in our own galaxy. The distance between these civilizations may be as large as a thousand light years. The separation between civilizations seems to be almost infinite by human standards.

> There is one race of men; one race of gods; both have breath of life from a single mother. But sundered power holds us divided, so that one is nothing, while for the other the brazen sky is established their sure citadel forever,

wrote Pindar in the sixth *Nemean Ode*.

Among the methods available for interstellar communication, nuclear particle radiation and electromagnetic radiation present themselves as possible methods. Nuclear particle radiation can carry information at the speed of light; while known useful nuclear particles possess far more energy than photons, their information content is very similar to that of electromagnetic radiation. Electromagnetic radiation may travel at the velocity of light with little interference to distances of a thousand light years or more.

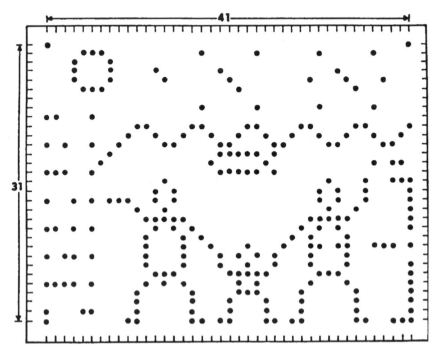

FIGURE 5. *Extraterrestrial message, arranged in 31 lines.*

TABLE 1. Composition of the Sun

Element	Percent
Hydrogen	87.0
Helium	12.9
Oxygen	0.025
Nitrogen	0.02
Carbon	0.01
Magnesium	0.003
Silicon	0.002
Iron	0.001
Sulfur	0.001
Others	0.038

If electromagnetic communication is chosen as the best method of solving the problem, the next question centers around the best wavelength at which to transmit a message. The first theoretical discussion of this was made in 1959 by Cocconi and Morrison, who suggested that of the hydrogen line at twenty-one centimeters. The sub-harmonics and harmonics of the hydrogen line frequency have also been suggested as possible candidates. One search for intelligent signals has already been made on the hydrogen line frequency. The hydrogen line at twenty-one centimeters has been considered to be the one that intelligent beings somewhere in the universe might use. This is presumably because frequencies of lower wave length will be jammed by natural radio noise. According to Professor Frank Drake, who directed Project Ozma, this monumental search for intelligent beings in the universe may be compared to meeting a friend in New York City, without making arrangements in advance about a meeting place. One does not just wander the streets looking everywhere. Instead, the most likely places to look are the places that are already familiar—Grand Central Station, for instance, or Times Square. There are similar places in every city with which most people are acquainted. This is what the radio astronomer is in search of—a Grand Central Station of the galaxy—some special frequency about which everyone in the Milky Way would know. This indeed is the emanation of the hydrogen line.

Perhaps the best place to seek for intelligent signals with our present state of knowledge seems to be to concentrate on the nearest stars. The two nearest for consideration are Tau Ceti in the constellation of Cetus and the star Epsilon Eridani in the constellation of Eridanus. Both of these are about ten light years away.

In the search conducted at the Green Bank Observatory, each day at three in the morning the telescope was pointed to Tau Ceti. When Tau Ceti set beyond the mountains, the telescope was swung to Epsilon Eridani, and the search carried on. A signal was picked up twice; the same signal each time. The discovery was exciting, but moving the antenna showed that these were actually signals from the earth and not from space. At the end of two months' endeavor, no evidence of signals from space could be found on the records. These were the first steps of the endeavor at the National Astronomical Observatory in the Project Ozma, named after the Princess Os, who lived in the mythical land of Oz. It is clear that one should not be disappointed or discouraged because the first attempts of Project Ozma to find another civilization have failed. It will take many long years with larger radio telescopes and more sensitive receivers to have a good chance of success. Let us assume that after years of futile listening, we receive a peculiar series of pulses and spaces from Epsilon Eridani (see Figure 1, page 98). The message is repeated every twenty-two hours and fifty-three minutes, apparently the length of their day. The pulses occur at separations which are integral multiples of a minimum separation. Writing ones for pulses, and filling the blanks with the appropriate numbers of zeros, we get a binary series. It consists of 1271 ones and zeros. The number 1271 is the product of two prime numbers, 31 × 41. This strongly suggests that we arrange the message in a 31 × 41 array. When we do so, putting blanks for zeros and a dot for each pulse, we get the nonrandom pattern. Apparently we are in touch with a race of erect bipeds who reproduce sexually; there is even a suggestion that they might be mammals. The crude circle and column of dots at the left suggest their sun and planetary systems. The figure is pointing to the fourth planet, evidently their home. The wavy line over the third planet indicates that it is covered with water, and the fish-like form shows that there is marine life there. The bipeds know this, so they must have space travel.

· · · · · · · · · ·

The Experimental Approach

Laboratory experiments on earth can reveal which materials and conditions available in the universe might give rise to chemical components and structural attributes of life as we know it. Earlier we noted that the retracing of the pattern by which life appeared on earth would give strong support to the theory of its existence elsewhere in the universe. This is the study of chemical evolution.

The Darwinian theory of evolution has postulated the unity of Earth's entire biosphere. According to Darwin, the higher forms of life evolved from the lower over a very extended period in the life of this planet. Fossil analysis has shown that the oldest known forms of life may be about three-and-a-half billion years old. Geochemical data tells us that Earth is about four and one-half billion years old. Life, indeed, had a beginning on this planet. A question immediately arises as to the history of our own planet between its birth four and one-half billion years ago and the emergence of life. This idea was uppermost in the mind of the physicist Tyndall, when in 1871 he wrote in his "Fragments of Science of Unscientific People,"

Darwin placed at the root of life a primordial germ, from which he conceived that the amazing richness and variety of the life now upon the earth's surface might have deduced. If this hypothesis were true, it would not be final. The human imagination would infallibly look beyond the germ and, however hopeless the attempt, would enquire into the history of its genesis. . . . A desire immediately arises to connect the present life of our planet with the past. We wish to know something of our remotest ancestry. . . . Does life belong to what we know as matter, or is it an independent principle inserted into matter at some suitable epoch, when the physical conditions became such as to permit of the development of life?

The consideration of biological evolution thus leads us logically to another form of evolution, namely, chemical evolution.

Recent biochemical discoveries have underlined the remarkable unity of living matter. In all living organisms, from the smallest microbe to the largest mammal, there are two basic molecules. Their interaction appears to result in that unique property of matter which is generally described by the word "life." These two molecules are the nucleic acids and protein. While each one of these molecules is complex in form, the units comprising them are few in number. The nucleic acid molecule consists of nucleotides strung together like beads along a chain. The nucleotides, in turn, are made up of a purine or pyrimidine base, a sugar, and a phosphate. In the protein molecule, twenty amino acids link up with one another to give the macromolecule. A study of the composition of living matter thus leads us to the inescapable conclusion that all living organisms must have had some common chemical ancestry. A form of evolution purely chemical in nature must of necessity have preceded biological evolution.

Chemical evolution may be considered to have taken place in three stages: from inorganic chemistry to organic chemistry and from organic chemistry to biological chemistry. The first stage of chemical evolution perhaps began with the very origin of matter. In a series of cataclysmic reactions during the birth of our sun, the elements of the periodic table must have been formed. Almost fifteen billion years later, when our solar system was being formed, the highly reactive elements which occur in living organisms probably existed in combination with hydrogen— carbon as methane, nitrogen as ammonia, and oxygen as water.

Four-and-a-half billion years ago, when the planet Earth was being born from the primitive dust cloud, the rudimentary molecules, which were the forerunners of the complex biological polymers of today, were perhaps already in existence. Within this framework, life appears to be a special property of matter, a property which arose at a particular period in the existence of our planet and which resulted from its orderly development.

The idea of life arising from non-life, or the theory of spontaneous generation, had been accepted for centuries. One had only to accept the evidence of the senses, thought the ancients: worms from mud, maggots from decaying meat, and mice from old linen. Aristotle had propounded the doctrine of spontaneous generation in his *Metaphysics.* He had traced the generation of fireflies to morning dew and the birth of mice to moist soil. His teaching was accepted by the long line of Western thinkers who had turned to him as the final authority in matters metaphysical and physical. Newton, Harvey, Descartes, van Helmont, all accepted the idea of spontaneous generation without serious question. Even the English Jesuit John Turberville Needham could subscribe to this view, for Genesis tells not that God created plants and animals directly but that he bade the earth and waters to bring them forth. The world's literature is full of allusions to this popular belief in spontaneous generation. Virgil in his *Georgics* tells us how a swarm of bees arose from the carcass of a calf. Recall *Antony and Cleopatra,* Act II, Scene VII, where Lepidus tells Mark Anthony, "Your serpent of Egypt is bred . . . now of your mud by the operation of your sun—so is your crocodile."

The great impetus, however, to the experimental study of the origin of life began with a Russian biochemist pointing out "that there was no fundamental difference between a living organism and brute matter. The complex combination of manifestations and properties so characteristic of life must have arisen in the process of the evolution of matter." According to Oparin,

> . . . at first there were the simple solutions of organic substances whose behavior was governed by the properties of their component atoms and the arrangement of these atoms in the molecular structure. But gradually, as a result of growth, and increasing complexity of the molecules, new properties have come into being and a new colloidal chemical order was imposed on the more simple organic chemical relations. These newer properties

were determined by the spatial arrangement and mutual relationship of the molecules. In this process biological orderliness already comes into prominence.

Independently of Oparin, Haldane in 1928 had speculated on the early conditions suitable for the emergence of terrestrial life:

> When ultraviolet light acts on a mixture of water, carbon dioxide and ammonia, a variety of organic substances are made, including sugars and apparently some of the materials from which proteins are built up. Before the origin of life they must have accumulated until the primitive oceans reached the constituency of a *hot dilute soup*.

A starting point for any experimental consideration of the origin of life must turn round the question of the cosmic distribution of elements. Astronomical spectroscopy reveals that with surprising uniformity the most abundant elements in our galaxy are, in the order of rank: hydrogen, helium, oxygen, nitrogen, and carbon. Hydrogen, oxygen, nitrogen, and carbon are indeed the basic constituents of living systems. The table on the composition of the sun (page 98) illustrates the distribution of these elements very clearly. In the presence of hydrogen, carbon will be in the form of methane, oxygen as water, and nitrogen as ammonia. It is this atmosphere of water vapor, containing C, H, N, and O, which is considered in this discussion as the primitive atmosphere of the earth.

The energies available for the synthesis of organic compounds under primitive earth conditions are ultraviolet light from the sun, electric discharges, ionizing radiation, and heat. It is evident that sunlight was the principle source of energy. Photochemical reactions would have taken place in the upper atmosphere and the products transferred by convection. Next in importance as a source of energy are electric discharges such as lighting and corona discharges from pointed objects. These occur close to the earth's surface and hence would more efficiently deposit the reaction products in the primitive oceans. A certain amount of energy was also available from the disintegration of uranium, thorium, and potassium 40. While some of this energy may have been expended on the solid material (such as rocks), a certain proportion of it was available in the oceans and the atmosphere. Heat from volcanoes may also have been effective in primordial organic synthesis. In comparison to the energy from the sun and electric discharges, this was, perhaps, not too widely distributed, and its effect may have been only local on the sides of volcanoes, for example. Most of these forms of energy have been used in the laboratory for the synthesis of organic molecules. Simulation experiments have been devised to study the effect of ionizing radiation, electric discharges, heat, and ultraviolet light on the assumed early atmosphere of the earth. The analysis of the end products has often yielded, very surprisingly, the very compounds which we consider today as important for living systems.

In the experiments in our own laboratory, we have adopted the simple working hypothesis that the molecules which are fundamental now, were fundamental at the time of the origin of life. We are analyzing "the primordial soup" described by Haldane. The various forms of energy which are thought to have been present in the primitive earth have been used by us in a series of experiments. In the experiments with methane, ammonia, and water, electron irradiation was used as a convenient source of ionizing radiation simulating the K-40 on the primitive earth. The results of this investigation clearly establish adenine as a product of the irradiation of methane, ammonia, and water. It is the single largest non-volatile compound produced. The apparent preference for adenine synthesis may be related to adenine's multiple roles in biological systems. Not only is it a constituent of both the nucleic acids DNA and RNA, but it is also a unit of many important co-factors. In these and other experiments, most of the molecules necessary for life have been synthesized.

· · · · · · · · · ·

Conclusion

There is no reason to doubt that we shall rediscover, one by one, all the steps in physical and chemical evolution. We may even reproduce the intermediate steps in the laboratory. Looking back upon the biochemical understanding gained during the span of one human generation, we have the right to be quite optimistic. In contrast to unconscious nature which had to spend billions of years, conscious nature has a purpose and knows the outcome.

In *The Phenomenon of Man*, Pere Teilhard de Chardin, priest, philosopher, and scientist, has attempted to give us a comprehensive picture of the evolving universe. To him, mankind in its totality is a phenomenon which could be described and analyzed like any other phenomenon. Though for certain limited purposes it may be useful to think of phenomena as isolated statically in time, they are in point of fact never static: they are always processes or parts of a process. He speaks of complexification as an all-pervading tendency, involving the universe in all its parts in an "enroulement organique sur soi-meme." The noosphere is a new layer or membrane on the earth's surface, superimposed on the living layer or the biosphere, which in turn has evolved from the lifeless layer of inorganic material or the lithosphere.

Before the dawn of the twenty-first century, manned exploration of the solar system may tell us whether we are alone in our universe. Radio telescopes scanning the distant galaxies for intelligible messages may reveal the presence of our remote neighbors. Laboratory experiments will endeavor to retrace the path of chemical evolution and may support our belief in the existence of extraterrestrial life.

To conclude with Harlow Shapley:

> The new discoveries and developments contribute to the unfolding of a magnificent universe, . . . with our confreres on distant planets; with our fellow animals and plants of land, air and sea; with the rocks and waters of all planetary crusts and the photons and atoms that make up the stars . . . with all these we are associated in an existence and an evolution . . . and as groping philosophers and scientists we are thankful for the mysteries that still lie beyond our grasp.

· · · · · · · · · ·

References

A Review of Space Research, National Research Council Publication No. 1079, ch. 9 (Washington, DC: National Academy of Sciences, 1962).

G. Bruno, *Dialoghi Italiani*, G. Aquileccha, ed., 1958.

G. Cocconi and P. Morrison. *Nature* 1894, 844, 1959.

C. Darwin, *Life and Letters 3*, Notes of the Royal Society, London, 14, No. 1, 1959.

F. Drake, *Intelligent Life in Space* (New York: Macmillan, 1964).

J. B. S. Haldane, "The Origin of Life," *Rationalist Annual*, 148 (1928): 3–10.

S.-S. Huang, *American Scientist* 47 (1959):397.

A. I. Oparin, *Origin of Life* (New York: Dover, 1938).

C. Ponnamperuma, "Experimental Studies on the Origin of Life," *Journal of the British Interplanetary Society*, 42 (1989):397–400.

H. Shapley, *Of Stars and Men* (Boston: Beacon, 1958).

J. Tyndall, *Fragments of Science for Unscientific People* (London: Longmans, Green, 1871).

Some recent discussions on the origin of life and the search for extra-terrestrial intelligence are in:

D. Deamer and G. Fleischaker, *Origins of Life: The Central Concepts* (Boston and London: Jones & Bartlett, 1994).

F. Drake and D. Sobel, *Is Anyone Out There?* (New York: Delacorte, 1992).

M. Eigen, *Steps Towards Life* (Oxford: Oxford University Press, 1992).

H. Morowitz, *Beginnings of Cellular Life* (New Haven and London: Yale University Press, 1992).

J. W. Schopf, *Major Events in the History of Life* (Boston & London: Jones & Bartlett, 1992).

W. Sullivan, *We Are Not Alone*, Rev. Ed. (New York and London: Dutton, Penguin, 1993).

· · · · · · · · ·

Truth Is One, and a Philosopher Interprets the Facts

1 What are your views on cosmic beginnings, particularly with reference to the origin of the universe, of life, and of *Homo sapiens*?

In trying to answer this question, we have to look at two different points of view: the scientific and the philosophical. From the point of view of science, we make a judgment on our observations. From the philosophical point of view, we try to answer questions from any lead that we may have to satisfy our own aspirations, not always related to observations. Thus, the scientific evidence for the Big Bang appears to be very impressive. From the expansion of the universe, the observation of the red shift, to the recent data from COBE, for example, it is clear that this universe in which we are living had a beginning at some point. Scientifically, we conclude that our universe began about fifteen billion years ago, but we must recognize the mathematical uncertainties about that point which prevents us from finding out what may have happened before the Big Bang.

With regard to the origins of life, as a scientist who has devoted almost his entire professional life to the understanding of this study, we dare to conclude that life appears to be a result of the evolutionary process in the universe and that indeed the purpose of the universe may be life itself. No one has yet shown the beginning of life in a test tube, but the massive amount of data we have before us clearly shows that it is inevitable that the emergence of life is inherent to the universe.

As to the origin of *Homo sapiens*, we could say that this is an extension of the evolutionary process in the universe. Although there is only one example of *Homo sapiens* that we know (us), let me accent the observations that we have from the chemical and biological aspects of evolution. We will have to conclude that *Homo sapiens* is a result of this process. The most satisfying answer was perhaps the one given by the priest and philosopher Teilhard de Chardin, that in the universe the biosphere is a layer over the lithosphere, and the noossphere, or the region of the mind, is what has evolved from the biosphere.

2 What are your views on human ends, especially as this relates to the framework of cosmic beginnings?

We observe the ends as part of the physical process that we see in the universe, so that the ending is only a change of phase from a material point of view. However, the human spirit yearns to believe that something does live on. We know that the Greek philosophers gave us the phrase "panta rei," meaning "all things change." Thus, the carbon in our bodies was synthesized during the birth of a star. We are the stuff of which stars are made! Some continuity is inherent in the process of life. Whether it can be limited to what we call an individual is something which cannot be proved at the moment by our scientific observations and is only reserved to the realm of faith.

3 What do you think should be the relationship between religion and science?

I firmly believe that there should be no conflict. In other words, truth is one, and a philosopher interprets the facts; the scientist makes the observations and presents them to the philosopher. With expanding knowledge, the apparent difference that we see between religion and science will appear less than ever.

7
Science at the Crossroads

George Bugliarello

George Bugliarello, President of Polytechnic University in New York from 1973 to February 1994 and now Chancellor, is an engineer and educator with a broad background ranging from civil engineering and computer languages to biomedical engineering and fluid mechanics, and a wide experience in local, national, and international organizations. In New York he was Chairman of the Mayor's Commission on Science and Technology during the Koch administration, and he currently chairs the Metrotech Corporation for the creation of a research park that is a model for urban development. He is a past chairman of the National Science Foundation's Advisory Committee for Science and Engineering Education .and of the Board of Science and Technology for International Development of the National Academy of Sciences. A prolific author of professional papers and books, he is founder and editor of *Technology in Society—an International Journal.*

Abstract

Today, the scientific and technological enterprise is at a crossroads because of a growing imbalance between its achievements and the ability of society to use them effectively. It is urgent that we address simultaneously a number of key issues that define the crossroads: the question of progress, the question of the "end of science," the purpose of science and technology, their accountability and their need for a new compact with the rest of society, as well as the question of multicultural and multireligious influences on science, and of multidisciplinarity and the organization of science. An important underlying obstacle is the seemingly impossible chasm between science and religion as well as between science and the moral aspects of philosophy.

Today's Predicament

There can be little doubt that science—the scientific and technological enterprise—is at a crossroads.[1] Old compacts, spoken and unspoken, between science and the rest of society are questioned by a world that often has seen hopes for social progress dashed in spite of science's magnificent achievements and promise. The need for new compacts and new directions is made imperative by

109

the growing imbalance between those achievements and the ability of society to use them effectively.

When we talk of the promise of science, we must of course be clear as to who does the promising, and to whom. For instance, the Leninist-Stalinist ideology promised a better world through the application of "rational" scientific tenets. That ideology had not been shaped by scientists and engineers but by political theorists and appropriated by totalitarian leaders as an instrument of power. Tragically, scientists and engineers had to acquiesce to it in spite of the fact that the Marxist doctrine saw the concept of truth in such self-seeking, relative terms (Murphy) as to be fundamentally antithetic to science. In the West, during and after World War II and most explicitly after Sputnik, it was primarily the scientists and engineers who promised and convincingly demonstrated the military strength achievable through science. And today science and engineering have become for many the indispensable ingredients of competitiveness and job creation as an article of faith, just as the prospect for ever greater medical advances has.

Each of these promises and hopes had a valid underlying rationale and became embodied, implicitly or explicitly, in some kind of compact. But because each promise has been taken too literally or tied to a specific context, it was inevitable that each would be broken when the context was dishonest, as in the case of science under the Soviet dictatorship, or when it changed, as is the case in the United States after the Cold War.

Yet few would disagree that the potential of science and technology is greater than ever. Developments of new scientific ideas and of medical and engineering knowledge are ever more rapid and their societal consequences ever more revolutionary. Suffice it to think of molecular biology or information technology.

Hence, the peculiar nature of what has brought us to today's crossroads: the skepticism engendered by promises, however ill-defined, that have not been realized or seem no longer relevant, and at the same time the frustration of those both inside and outside science, who see the new possibilities offered by science, medicine, and engineering but have not been able to overcome the obstacles to transform them into reality. To further complicate the issue, science has become, in the eyes of some, less believable when parts of its vast establishment are self-seeking or when individual scientists bring a vested interest to a controversy. An example is the impact of the widespread criticism of self-referrals in medicine or of the loss of trust in scientists when a few of them fudge or fake their results or when they contradict each other as expert witnesses.

This is certainly not the first time that science and technology have reached a crossroads in the long path of development that originated when we emerged as a distinct species. Since the beginning of our species, our twin quests to understand and to modify nature have enabled us to transcend some of our biologically inherited or culturally evolved forms of behavior. They have created societies that complement, enhance, and at the same time constrain biology and that extend the niches of our survival in our "great drama of fighting against the unknown" (Kranzberg and Pursell). The most compelling reason for examining today's crossroads and for seeking new compacts is the fact that our transcendence of biology through social adaptation abetted by technology is far from successful (witness today's continuing violence and global environmental deterioration).

The crossroads at which we find ourselves is a crossroads of purpose, of method, of organization, of public perception and confidence, and of connection with the rest of society. It is extremely complex because never before have science and technology played so pervasive a role in human society. Neither has there ever been so urgent a need to address simultaneously so many issues and to make so many choices. These issues are not always present in the minds of all scientists, engineers, and physicians, and are not always clear in their implications to society as a whole. Let me identify some that appear to me to be among the most important:

- the question of progress, historically and prospectively
- the question of the "end of science" and the related questions of reductionism and of the redefinition of science
- the question of the purpose of science, of the direction of society, and of the reconvergence of science and belief
- the question of accountability and, with it, of the support and supervision of science and of a new compact between science and society
- the question of multicultural influences on science, now that science has become a global enterprise
- the question of the specific directions of science and of the restructuring of the scientific enterprise.

Before discussing—by necessity very briefly—each of these immense questions, let me underscore what I believe are their two fundamental and inextricably connected underpinnings: the ethical responsibility of science and the belief in the further evolution of humankind. Society is doomed if science and technology, with their overarching power, do not have a clear moral sense of their responsibility. But society, so far extended beyond the biological survival capabilities of the individual, is also doomed if it loses confidence in its ability to advance its understanding of nature and in its power to modify nature.

The Question of Progress

A belief in progress accompanied all the scientific discoveries and technical inventions made from the advent of the Encyclopedists of the eighteenth century to the eve of World War I, a faith unshaken even by the carnage of the Napoleonic wars or the American Civil War. The two World Wars and above all the nuclear weapons race shook that belief among many scientists and non-scientists alike. Science and technology came to be seen as having centuplicated the destructive tendencies of our psyche and the negative impact of our species upon the planet. That negative sense is reinforced by the ecological catastrophes in Eastern Europe, even if they occurred under regimes that held different views of the meaning of a human life.

Pessimism also has to do with science and engineering having given birth to technologies so pervasive, like autos, television, or computers, that they seem to have acquired a power of their own over those who use them and are caught in their pathologies without the possibility of escape. Kurt Vonnegut's autobiographical *Player Piano* or Kobo Abe's works are eloquent visions of people trapped by modern life.

Technologies have given us unprecedented powers, but their undisciplined and indiscriminate use has created the modern existentialist nightmares in which, as in a traffic jam, the victims are at the same time the perpetrators. Diminished as we are when we are caught in these nightmares, we find our lives at risk, economically and even physically, if we do not participate in the technologies that cause them. Such for instance is the fate of the homeless.

It is the revulsion against these historic catastrophes and these nightmares that has brought about more than anything else the loss of a sense of innocence about progress and the promise of science. Particularly disquieting is that loss among scientists.

Yet, it is obvious that without science and technology life expectancy today would be much lower—as it was at the turn of the century and as it still is in third- and fourth-world countries— and life for a large portion of humankind would be much more miserable and unproductive, if possible at all. Thus it is a moot point to blame science and technology for today's ills, particularly since not all societies share—or share to the same degree—our malaise about the future. Most recently, for instance, when visiting China, Stephen Cutcliffe observed "little disillusion with the power of science and technology," even though among some scholars there was "a certain openness to the potential shortcomings of Western Technological development" (Cutcliffe). What is not moot, however, for scientists and engineers is to try to reestablish society's belief in progress. The first step in that direction must be the restoration of confidence among scientists and technologists themselves. That cannot occur without changes in the way science in the broadest sense sees itself and its responsibility to the rest of society.

· · · · · · · · ·

The Question of the End of Science

Crucial to the issue of progress is the *deja vu* notion—restated by some today in *"épater le bourgeois"* terms—that science may be coming virtually to an end because there is little left of fundamental value to discover (e.g., Elvee).

The reduction of reality to simpler models started with Galileo and Descartes and became the methodological base of modern science. But the notion of the end of science is the most recent statement of that reductionistic dream that has made periodic reappearances since the 1600's, related to the earlier positivism of Comte, Mach, and others (Agazzi).

Today's argument must be considered very seriously. It stems from the very important pursuit of a unified theory capable of explaining the origin of mass and nature (Weinberg) and also from the absolute belief by some biologists in the finality of the Darwinian scheme of evolution (e.g., Mayr). Extreme interpretation and extrapolation of these final theories could see science as being left with only "a few loose ends" (Horgan). The importance of the question for science lies not only in the possibility that this would make science revert to a constraining and demoralizing

Aristotelian construct but also that it would keep science focused exclusively on the understanding of nature *as it is.* It can be argued that, even if a final theory were to emerge, the new frontier of science will lie in ending the separation between knowing and modifying nature. This is already happening when we modify nature in order to understand it, as the chemist does now with synthetic molecules, and when we try to understand nature in order to modify it, as the biotechnologist does with molecular biology. (It is tempting to quote what Heidegger said of one science: "Anthropology is the interpretation of man that already knows what man is and hence can never ask who he may be" [Heidegger]). The challenge of creating what is not, whether new organisms or new worlds in space, offers science not an end but an endless future.

Few scientists or engineers have debated with sufficient vigor the reductionistic argument of the end of science, although they may be viscerally opposed to it as they see the immense complexity associated with higher levels of organization. That complexity cannot be understood just in terms of the properties of the basic elements of the organization. There is a need for a broad scientific debate to address the issue and give again to science and scientists a clearer sense of their future. Otherwise the concept of the end of science, misinterpreted or put forth in hubris, can only deflect from science the brightest minds on which it relies for its advance. Repudiation of reductionism does not mean, however, that the search for unity in science should be abandoned among the great varieties and directions of scientific pursuits. As Francis Bacon underscored, quoting an old ecclesiastical statement: "in veste varietas sit, scissura non sit"—let there be variety, not schism (Bacon).

. . . .

The Question of the Purpose of Science and the Direction of Society

Science and technology have made possible today's society—a society far different from that envisioned by the Encyclopedists, by Rousseau or Hobbes, or even by our own Constitution. By enhancing beyond measure the material aspects of our society, science has profoundly affected the relation between the spiritual and the material that is fundamental to our humanity. Twentieth century culture is polarized between an exasperated quest for rationality and an irrepressible emotionalism. The first is expected to govern our actions and our technology-based society. The latter manifests itself in wars, in a search for fulfillment through religion or cults and in an aggressive, popular, and often self-indulgent post-modernism. The very visible embodiment of the polarization in today's architecture serves to remind us how much closer to art modern science was at its dawn (e.g., Siraisi). Today science and technology have become divorced from art, even though they may search for beauty in the structures of nature and in utilitarian artifacts (e.g., Hoffmann and Torrence). I believe that a reconvergence of science and art would go a long way toward the reintegration of science and culture.

But above all, in their relentless pursuits, science and technology have weakened the aspiration in our lives to something that transcends the material, to something that provided a moral coherence to previous societies, as in the Middle Ages (e.g., Cantor).

So, having defeated the grotesque scientific pieties of Marxism, and at the same time questioning the concept of progress, pragmatically as well as on religious or philosophical grounds, our society is now moving over unchartered territory, torn between the two polarities. Ironically, the adverse emotional reaction to science and technology is also a consequence of the immense production capacities that scientific technology makes available to satisfy our primitive instincts. With consumption the bellwether of well-being, society has become unable to envision and rationalize its own limits and to discipline the acquisitive urges of its members. How many pairs of shoes are enough? How many pairs of jeans? How many cars? How many appliances? Indeed, how many of us? And, is there any purpose to the relentless growth of our physical stature? Most importantly, how does one reconcile our unchecked urge to continue with the poverty of a very large portion of mankind?

Thus ours is a society truly at the crossroads—of which science's own crossroads is both the cause and the consequence. If some 500,000 years ago the utilization of fire became a key divide in human evolution, our ability today to alter our environment and our biology to a degree unimagined even in the middle of this century are an even greater divide.

At this junction the burden is squarely on scientists and engineers. Can we help provide intellectual and moral leadership to a society that cannot continue, without great peril, to be torn apart between today's polarities? Science—the scientific and technological enterprise—has caused or abetted that polarity. It must now must decide whether it has the capacity to transcend its self-imposed boundaries and help guide not only with rationality but also with passion and compassion a human society that in recent years, thanks to science and technology, has acquired a common history and a common future. This is an unprecedented challenge for a science that has derived great advantages from its interactions with government and industry but has been immensely reluctant to assume deeper responsibilities and enter the arena of politics for which it holds such revolutionary implications (e.g., Bondi). Within science itself, the very conservatism of the scientific collective mind may often discourage expression and discussion of ideas yet only imperfectly formulated. That discussion, however, is as essential today as it was at the time of Copernicus and must be fostered, if science is to transcend its traditional limits.

But politics is only one aspect of today's dilemma for science. A greater challenge is whether a way can be found to overcome the difficulties that at different times and for different reasons have created a seemingly impassable chasm between science and religion, as well as moral philosophy. From its early times humankind has believed in an afterlife. By destroying that belief without providing some equivalent comfort, science will not be able to point society toward the future unless it becomes more emotionally satisfying and better adept at communicating the passion, the joy, and the comfort of its pursuits.

Also, from time immemorial humans, both individually and in entire societies, have striven for greatness. That quest has been neither universal nor explicit. But for the first time there is through science the opportunity to offer, not to selected groups but to humankind as a whole, a new vision of greatness based on a new vision of the future of man. We scientists and engineers have the potential, if willing to reach boldly beyond the comforting fastness of science's traditional domain, to prevent today's squandering of human talent in the pursuit of a globally unsustainable consumerism. We have the potential to stimulate a new vision and a new philosophy of the law to better deal with the modifications of our biological nature, with our responsibilities to the rest of the universe as well as with the role of the human-made in our lives. And we have the potential, if united in our purpose, to move governments and religions to address the questions of the limits to population growth and of global responses to war, poverty, disease, and ignorance; in this can lie the ultimate greatness of science and of our species.

It would be extreme hubris, however, for us scientists, engineers, and physicians to believe that we can solve these problems by ourselves. But is it not moral cowardice for us not to use our resources of knowledge and know-how to propose new paradigms of the relation of the biological, the social, and the machine that will stimulate society to rethink these crucial issues?[2] And is it not also possible for us to go one step beyond, by becoming passionately involved in the required decisions and in their execution? If we choose this path, the starting point must be the conviction that it is legitimate and urgent for science to search for a new morality and for a new alliance of science and belief. That search is too important to be left to the philosophers and the theologians alone.

After many thousands of generations of humans as a distinct species, the new potentials of science project the possibility of genetic and reproductive interventions outside the barriers of traditional biology. In so doing, they strike at the core of many religious beliefs and demand a fundamental rethinking of the relation of science to religion—religion as a powerful formal social entity but also as the expression of an innate human sense of wonderment at creation, of hope beyond death, and of one's responsibility to one's self and to other humans, as well as to nature. Science can acquire a religious connotation in the measure that, on the basis of its understanding of nature, it seeks new ethical rules for humans and human society. The starting point in rethinking the relation of science to religion may be the recognition that emotions and belief are essential tools in building societies, civilizations, and cultures, just as science and technology are. Bertrand Russell's position (Russell) that science cannot decide on value problems is simply too limiting. Although it is true that such problems are outside the realm of truth and error, as he puts it, they can benefit from the involvement of scientists and technologists who are sensitive to the importance of emotion and belief and capable of accepting them in applying the results of their investigations.

The outcome to be avoided is a renewal of the "warfare of science with theology," to use White's famous expression (White). Certainly Einstein did not see science and religion as "irreconcilable antagonists" (Einstein)—yet that warfare has been much too real, making it so difficult even today in many parts of the world to address reproductive issues and the connected ecological ones. Thus, it is to be hoped that it may be possible after millennia to see again convergence of science and belief. This does not mean closing the circle for a science that was originally the instrument of and part and parcel of religion, but it means endeavoring to bring science and religions onto an openly synergistic path motivated by the common desire to enhance and elevate the human condition.

If this is the path to be chosen, it puts an enormous responsibility on science and the scientists, as it does on religion and religiosity, not to view science—as Pascal ultimately did—as antithetical to the concept of spirituality. The Soviet state was the most recent and dramatic example of the dangers of a science and technology devoid of moral compass and operating as instruments of an exclusively materialistic doctrine. The lesson is not the collapse of that state, as it is entirely conceivable that, with different leadership and better organization, it could have prevailed, just as the might of the Mongols, with their primitive but most effective military technology, prevailed in the thirteenth and fourteenth centuries over much of Asia and Europe. The lesson, rather, is the destruction of civilized forms of human existence that a science and technology unwilling or unable to take a strong moral stand engender. In our society, indifference to the plight of the cities, the poor, and the sick or to the trampling of privacy are clear signs of danger and a moral warning to our science and technology not to sit idly by.

We must note of how little help, in these issues, are the specific philosophies of science and of engineering. The crucial philosophical problem we need to address has to do with our purpose in endeavoring to understand and modify nature. Today the philosophy of science is focused far more on the concepts, paradigms, theories, and methodologies of science, than on that purpose. The philosophy of engineering, much more recent in its emergence, as of late has been drawn almost inevitably, given the urgency of the need, to the issue of the public responsibility of the engineer (Mitcham). But the central question for engineering is that of the nature and purpose of the artifact; in spite of some groundbreaking research work (e.g., Durbin), it requires much more attention. The growing field of bioethics, in considering the moral dilemmas of health care cost and access, is the one that comes perhaps closer to addressing the question of the modification of nature, albeit in the specialized context of medicine.[3]

Clearly any philosophy of those modifications, whether one deals with engineering or medicine, must address the issue of permissible future directions of the modifications. To search for what is humanly desirable demands a deep dialogue of science with belief and philosophy. The dialogue is urgent but will not occur unless it is made an integral part of the education of scientists, engineers, and physicians.

· · · · · · · · · ·

Compacts, Covenants and the Accountability of Science

The concept of a compact or, more formally, a covenant is of course not new in human history. The Ten Commandments, the Magna Charta, Hobbes's and Rousseau's social contract, and more generally the compact theory of the eighteenth century and the ensuing concept of natural rights embodied in our Constitution (e.g., Windelband) are all examples. However, the belief in a compact in force between science (broadly defined) and the rest of society is a recent one. It has its origin in the United States of World War II when science was called to help win the war. Science of course had been called to help the war effort in other nations and other conflicts as well. But only in the United States did there emerge a clear statement of the unspoken pact between science and the rest of society, as articulated by Vannevar Bush (Bush). The pact was reinforced in the post-war years by the activities of the Committee on Science and Technology established by the House of Representatives in 1959 under the stimulus of Sputnik ("Toward the Endless Frontier"). That unspoken pact has come to be viewed by many scientists in the United States as a solemn commitment by society to support science, even though never formally stated and even if its original purpose was military, while today our society faces many other challenges.

Because of this long lasting, largely unexamined and ultimately naive belief in the self-evidence of an obsolete compact that is now being invoked under very different circumstances, we scientists and engineers are shocked when the compact is questioned by the rest of society and are unprepared to propose a new one. Yet a new compact is needed. Our society cannot function and prosper without the support of a strong science base. Science in turn cannot expect to thrive and help guide society if it does not consciously and explicitly address the question of its relation to the rest of society and of its accountability.

The challenge in formulating a new compact is complex. In the first place, science must accept as legitimate the concern of society as to how science—with its immense power—keeps its own house. In turn society, in committing itself to supporting science, should not deprive science of the freedom so essential to its health and success. The genius of a compact is in preserving this delicate balance—a balance that, to paraphrase Dante's definition of the law, if preserved preserves human society, but if destroyed destroys it.

Secondly, it is evident today that a new compact must find a way to respond not only to the new needs of defense but also to the harder-to-define ones of commercial competitiveness and social progress. So much is being discussed about these needs, as not to warrant elaboration here.

In the third place, a new compact must deal with the supervision and financing of science and with conflicts of interest. Inevitably, as science comes to absorb significant portions of a nation's Gross National Product, there is bound to be an increasing demand by government and the public for strict accountability of scientific expenses. Furthermore, as research is viewed more and more as a key ingredient of competitiveness, its direction and its potential conflicts of interest become major issues. The situation is quite different from the old compact when science in the United States had substantial freedom to pursue its own goals and to police itself in what many scientists believe was a golden age. The question today is whether the science enterprise is capable of taking a hard look at itself and policing itself so as to reduce the need for outside intervention.

Fourthly, the not-always-politically-correct question should be addressed as to how science will also fulfil its responsibility to itself, as science for science's sake—science, as Francis Bacon put it, for ornament and delight, rather than exclusively for utilitarian purposes.

Lastly and most importantly, if a new compact is to be formulated, we must decide whether it should be based on an even broader sense of reciprocal responsibilities of science and society than outlined in the previous points. The first of those responsibilities is to restore a sense of hope and progress. I already suggested the importance of a new relation of science to belief. Should a new compact—indeed a new covenant—be governed also by a new set of fundamental concepts involving our relation as individuals and society to the artifacts we have created and to the rest of the nature, the environment on earth and beyond? If so, should not the covenant, in addition to providing a practical guide for the relationship among these entities, also be inspired by a new vision of how that relationship can evolve to enhance our essential humanity?

The Question of Multiculturalism

If science endeavors to establish a new ethics for itself and a new compact with the rest of society, one issue that looms large but has received scarce attention is multiculturalism. The second half of the century, after World War II, has seen an embracing of modern science by wider and wider groups of the world population. Science has become virtually universal. It is practiced, albeit with different intensity and success, in most parts of the world, and is looked upon as an instrument of progress and disenfranchisement from poverty and, much too often still, as an instrument of military power.

Scientists all over the world are engaged in what for all practical purposes is one science, Western science, even if created by the historic contributions of several cultures. Yet the cultural beliefs of the scientists—ethical, social, and religious—are obviously far from uniform. Though an extremely powerful and universal instrument, science is not wielded today with a commonality of purposes, ethical views, or sociological practices. Under these conditions, the emergence globally of a new role and a new responsibility for science becomes that much more difficult and the accountability of science to society that much more complicated. The problem is urgent and must be addressed. The issue of multiculturalism applies also inside the United States, where a substantial portion of academic researchers come from outside the dominant culture. If successfully resolved, the very challenge that the United States science establishment faces in this regard can provide a unique laboratory and model for the global community. In that model multiculturalism, rather than being submerged or ignored, could become a new powerful instrument of science.

The Question of the Specific Direction of Science, Its Organization, and Its Relation to Nature

An ever present question in science is the direction in which it will move at any given time, under the momentum of its own discoveries and achievements as well as under the influence of exogenous factors. The question becomes particularly critical today, in a period of great expansion of knowledge and great investment in science. It affects most immediately not only the scientific and technological community, but also the life of every citizen, whether one considers the issue of AIDS, of research into "orphan" diseases, of energy policies and nuclear power, or of science education.

Of all the many possible directions in which science can move, those favored by investment of resources and by the attention of the scientists are obviously more likely to advance. Given the limits to the resources available, this places a heavy burden on the scientific community to intervene in the decisions, pondering their implications not only in the narrower context of the advancement of science and technology but in the broader one of the interest of society as a whole.

The basic choices for science today—such as unmanned space exploration versus space stations, "big science" versus broad-based support of individual investigators, biology and medicine versus applied biotechnology, life sciences versus the physical sciences and engineering—are too well known to bear repeating here, even if some issues such as the support of mature sciences or of far-out independent researchers warrant more attention.[4] Rather, what needs to be underscored is the issue of whether the traditional organization and institutions of science should be modified or enhanced. For instance, would a reorganization along more flexible lines facilitate interdisciplinarity as well as disciplinary advances? Also, would a rearrangement of institutional and disciplinary boundaries facilitate a closer relation of science with the rest of society and help effect the integration of the knowing of and the modification of nature?

· · · · · · · · · ·

The Path Ahead

My purpose in this paper has been to focus, by necessity in a very brief and subjective way, on some of the enormously complex issues that have brought science to today's crossroads—and to underscore some of their implications. If we do not intend to continue with business as usual, we must make a deliberate attempt to place science, engineering, and medicine on a higher moral plane—higher not because of the authority of knowledge but because of the association of that authority with a passionate commitment to make the best use of that knowledge.

What constitutes the best use implies, of course, a value judgment. The most fundamental question at today's crossroads is whether science, *qua* science, should participate in those value judgments. Clearly a value judgment is not a scientific statement. But society's investment in science and the scientific-technological enterprise's impact on society are the results of value judgments. We scientists, and the scientific community in its ensemble, cannot disavow the fact that our knowledge and know-how are an indispensable base for the kind of difficult value judgments that our society will be called to make with increasing urgency in deciding the directions of its future. For example, should science have something to say as to whether there be limits to material growth, population growth, and consumption or to the prolongation of life at all costs, as to what should be the purpose of space exploration and travel, as to the issue of homosexuality, as to the most appropriate role of automation and hence of work in our society, or as to the allowable direction of biotechnological interventions on our own genes and on those of other species?

At this moment, by default, many of these judgments are based on irrational fears, on shortsighted self-interest, on political expedience, on inflexible religious dogma, or on economic paradigms that, even if greatly refined and multidimensional, are still the progeny of Henry Adams's *Homo oeconomicus*.

The disasters that continue to beset our globe, from the Somali famine to the burning of Los Angeles to ethnic cleansing in Europe, will be repeated and amplified unless the value judgments we make about the direction of our future are guided by a much stronger infusion of scientific knowledge. But for that to happen, sheer scientific knowledge, no matter how penetrating and capable of predicting and modeling future trends, no matter how powerfully complemented by the technological ability to modify nature, does not suffice. Would we have today so many faith healers, so many tales of the supernatural in books and movies, so many parodies of the scientist and the engineer—the scientist usually mad and the engineer a nerd—if scientific and engineering knowledge were felt to be comforting, believable, and emotionally satisfying, a knowledge to which one could both rationally and in faith entrust one's future and with which one could entertain a rich human dialogue?

Unfortunately today we scientists and engineers tend to avoid that dialogue. We talk to ourselves. We retrench behind the intimidating jargon of our trade and the professed avoidance of value judgments, and we eschew public life and the public pulpit. In the United States, with less than a handful of scientists and engineers in Congress, the direction of the country is left to lawyers and other callings that are removed from any direct experience in understanding or modifying nature. Scientists and engineers confine themselves to cautious advice to the federal government through the National Academies and other organs and are satisfied with subordinate positions of power in government. Even weaker is their position in state and local governments, where so many day-by-day decisions affecting our life are being made.

At today's crossroads it is urgent to decide whether science and technology should endeavor to pursue a new path that will give them a new moral authority and a new role in helping guide society toward a better future. The responsibility for that decision must fall in the first place on American science, as the largest and most influential single grouping of active scientists and engineers in the world—a grouping unhampered by state ideology and by religious dogma and built on the acceptance and utilization of scientists from all over the world.

· · · · · · · · · ·

Notes

1. For brevity, when warranted, I shall use the term "science" to encompass both the discovery of nature and its modification by rational means, that is by technology—engineering, medicine, and so forth. Further, although science, scientific method, and scientists are not synonymous terms, I may in a context when the distinction is not important use one for all three. The term "science" itself is one of multiple meanings—an activity and a body of knowledge, as well as the complex of individuals and organizations that do science. In their endeavors to understand and modify nature, science and engineering differentiate themselves from other efforts to understand and modify nature by the method they use, specifically, the scientific method.

2. For the sake of brevity, I have used elsewhere the term "biosoma" to describe the entity formed by the indissoluble combination of biological organism, society, and machines, i.e., artifacts (e.g., Bugliarello). The interactions among these three entities, and between them and the environment, shape our lives and, as they evolve, determine our future.

3. Medicine in its endeavor to modify a natural phenomenon (disease) is

akin to engineering; they both are based on a scientific understanding of nature but committed to modify aspects of nature.

4. It may be argued that mature disciplines in a new context can have a resurgence, as is the case of pharmaceutical botany or of railroad engineering with the TGV's *(trains grande vitesse)* and the prospects of magnetic levitation. Also, it may be argued that it is not clear whether the era of the far-out inventor not supported by a social infrastructure of agencies, foundations, study groups, or academic departments, as was initially the case with Marconi and Goddard, is necessarily over, and whether we need to pay more attention to that precious human venture capital.

• • • • • • • • •

References

Evandro Agazzi, "The Problems of Reductionism in Science," *Episteme,* Volume 18 (Dordrecht: Kluver, 1991).

Francis Bacon, "The Essay or Counsels, Civil and Moral" (Mt. Vernon, New York: Peter Pauper Press).

Hermann Bondi, "Bridging the Gulf," *Technology in Society,* Volume 4, 1992, 9–14.

George Bugliarello, "Technology and the Environment", in *Changing the Global Environment,* Botkin, Caswell, Estes, and Orio, eds. (New York: Academic Press, 1989).

Vannevar Bush, "Science, the Endless Frontier", in *A Report to the President.* (Washington, D.C.: U.S. Government Printing Office, July 1945).

Norman Cantor, *Inventing the Middle Ages* (New York: Morrow, 1991).

Stephen Cutcliffe, "Of Auto Horns, Steam Locomotives and Hydro-electric Dams," *STS Today,* November 1992, University Park, Pennsylvania.

Paul T. Durbin, *Research in Philosophy and Technology,* 12 volumes (Greenwich, Connecticut: Jai Press, 1978–1992).

Albert Einstein, *Ideas and Opinions* (New York: Bonanza Books, 1954).

Richard Q. Elvee, ed., *End of Science? Attack or Defend* (Lanham, Maryland: University Press of America, 1992).

Martin Heidegger, *The Question Concerning Technology and Other Essays,* trans. William Lovitt (New York: Harper Torchbooks, 1977).

Roald Hoffmann and Vivian Torrence, *Chemistry Imagined* (Washington, D.C.: Smithsonian Institution Press, 1993).

John Horgan, "The New Challenges," *Scientific American,* December 1992, 16–22.

Melvin Kranzberg and Carroll W. Pursell, Jr., eds., *Technology in Western Civilization,* Volume 1 (New York: Oxford University Press, 1967).

Ernst Mayr, *One Long Argument: Charles Darwin and the Genesis of Modern Evolutionary Thought* (Cambridge, Massachusetts: Harvard University Press, 1991).

Carl Mitcham, "Ethics in Engineering Research," Chapter 8 in K. S. Shrader-Frechette, *Research Ethics* (forthcoming).

Kenneth Murphy, *Retreat from Finland Station* (New York: Free Press, 1992).

Bertrand Russell, *Religion and Science* (Oxford: Oxford University Press, 1961).

Nancy G. Siraisi, *Arts and Sciences at Padua: the Studium at Padua before 1350* (Toronto: Pontifical Institute of Medieval Studies, 1973).

Toward the Endless Frontier—History of the Committee on Science and Technology, 1959–79, U.S. House of Representatives (Washington, D.C.: U.S. Government Printing Office, 1980).

Kurt Vonnegut, Jr., *Player Piano* (New York: Delacorte, 1952).

Steven Weinberg, *Dreams of a Final Theory* (New York: Pantheon, 1993).

Wilhelm Windelband, *A History of Philosophy*, 2 volumes (New York: Harper, 1958). (Reprint of 1901 translation by James W. Tufts.)

Andrew D. White, *A History of the Warfare of Science with Theology in Christendom*, 2 volumes (New York: Dover, 1960).

• • • • • • • • •

Science and Religion Should Recognize Their Reciprocal Spirituality and Purpose

1 What are your views on cosmic beginnings, particularly with reference to the origin of the universe, of life, and of Homo sapiens?

Through evolution, larger brains have made possible larger intellectual capacities. (This evolutionary increase has not always been monotonic, as presumably, for instance, some dinosaurs had larger capacities than our mammalian ancestors.) Larger intellectual capacity means greater ability to think, leading *Homo sapiens* to create theories about nature and collect data.

For the past 50,000 years or so, our biological intellectual capacity has remained constant, but our ability to understand the complexities of nature has expanded, thanks to the accumulation of a collective body of knowledge and to the creation by humans of ever more powerful machines endowed with the ability to process data and to perform a series of intelligent tasks. Thanks to these accelerating developments, we will be able to know much more about the origins of the universe than we do know now. Thus, any of today's cosmogonies must be viewed as provisory. However, a number of concepts will remain firm. Thus, we can be reasonably sure that the main outline of the evolution of life, as we envision it today, and above all of the evolution of *Homo sapiens*, will continue to hold in the future its main thrust. Yet, many of the events of which today we are ignorant or in doubt will be clarified—such as the origins of life and of the first set of genetic instructions, the process of earth's creation, or the causes of the demise of dinosaurs.

2 What are your views on human ends, especially as this relates to the framework of cosmic beginnings?

Human ends are inscrutable. I believe that human beings are a product of the trial and error process of evolution (even if we are far from completely understanding how), not of a teleological development.

However, if we accept that we are what we are, we need to ask ourselves: how can we use what we are and what we have—our intelligence, our abilities, our technology, our social instruments —to reinforce our innate biological drive to survive? How can we keep in check our destructive tendencies, now that we have the ability to destroy myriads of other species and all human life on earth? And how can we expand the concurrent drive that we have possessed since we emerged as a distinct species, to enhance intelligently, however mutated in the future, our biological reach? How, in particular, if we survive as a species, will we be able to overcome the still very distant disappearance of the earth and learn to live elsewhere?

3 What do you think should be the relationship between religion and science?

Science is about rationality. It is, in its endeavor to understand nature, the product of disciplined thinking subject to the test of logic and, as much as possible, verifiability.

Religion is about mystery and emotion—about things we cannot comprehend, from the reasons for the cosmos, if there are any, to the comforting belief in an afterlife. Religion is also a code of behavior, often associated with divine recompense or retribution.

Religion is about spirituality, but science also is endowed with its own spirituality. That spirituality is engendered by the achievements of the human mind in endeavoring to understand the structure and details of the complexity of nature and in expanding the human outreach.

The spiritualities of religion and of science, of different origin but both born our of wonderment, are where science and religion should meet, today just as in earlier human times when the priest and the scientist were one. The challenge today is to have these two products of the human intellect—religion and science—

recognize their reciprocal spirituality and purpose. Although operating on different planes and harking to different concepts of truth, religion and science need to converge toward a new conception of the future of human kind, a conception capable of overcoming the destructive aimlessness of today's psyche.

8
The Coming Clash of the Titans
. . . .
Rustum Roy

Rustum Roy is Evan Pugh Professor of the Solid State, Professor of Geochemistry, and Professor of Science, Technology, and Society at Pennsylvania State University. As one of the nation's leading materials scientists, he has had a mineral, Rustumite, named after him! His many other activities covering science policy, science education, and the science-religion interface have led to his becoming simultaneously a well-known contrarian within the United States science establishment and the father figure of the rapidly growing national and international STS movement concerned with the interaction of science, technology, and society. Reared in an activist Christian family in a pluralist culture in India, and deeply involved in many facets of United States church life, he was invited to give the centenary Hibbert Lectures in London in 1979, published later as *Experimenting with Truth.*

. . . .
Abstract

A clash of titans is in the making after a century of turmoil in which technology has become, for all practical purposes, the dominant religion, complete with its own theology, rituals, orthodoxies, and conclaves. And this emerging religious force is now about to be pitted against the old-time religious institutions—which are meanwhile slowly and reluctantly abandoning some of their old-time monopolistic claims as depositories of Truth. They seem prepared to show signs of a macro-ecumenical awareness and to adopt a radically pluralist stance, without becoming unfaithful to their historical, cultural, ethnic, spiritual roots.

. . . .
Historical: Emergence of the Technological System

Put in its most stark terms I will develop the thesis that by any existential measure, the religion with the most believers is the *religion* of technology. I will use these terms advisedly as it is important to retain these boundaries of meaning in contrast to the "fuzziness" all too much in vogue.

One can approximate my use of the term "technology" by referring back to the sense in which Jacques Ellul meant it in his masterwork titled, in French, *La technique* (in English, *The Techno-*

logical Society). Thirty years later Ellul updated his thesis under the title *The Technological System*. The "technological system" is the equivalent of a religious system like Christianity, a total system built around the Christian faith; or the Islamic system, "systems" with control of human behavior through an administrative structure, a liturgy, rituals, and embedded within, their theology—their core beliefs. We may call each of these entities the Judaeo-Christian, or the Islamic, or the Buddhist "system," because that is how they function: as interacting set of philosophy, social structures, economics, politics, and so forth I use IT for "International Technology," and this as shorthand for "the technological system," just as Christianity and Judaism are shorthand for the Christian and the Judaic systems. In the religion of technology, the vector of its development started out with the uses of technology and the practice of its disciplines. Then it worked its way inwards to influence (or condition) human behavior. It gave rise to a priestly caste which undertook the subtle adoption of the core beliefs of Western science into its "theology." In most religious systems, Buddhism, Christianity, and Islam, for examples, the vector ran in the opposite direction: their development started with a person and that person's or founder's ideas and small groups of followers which grew in time and took over control of the socio-politico-economic system.

I will show systematically that IT, the International Technology system, is in fact today a full-blown religion with its theology, a powerful priesthood, rituals, icons, and a claim to exclusive truth. Some of its claims for truth may not be completely universal, but they have the great advantage of being testable and verifiable. Effective "technologies" have of course existed for millenia, and generally experienced "scientific truths" have been accumulating for more than three centuries, starting with phenomena like Newton's laws, Maxwell's equations, with energy-mass equivalence, with the structure of the atom and finally (?) with quantum mechanics. But only following World War II and the attribution of mythic powers to the atom bomb, the quasi-canonization of its alleged creators, the particle physicists, "science" and "technology" gained the important, and to a religion indispensable, flavor of *omnipotence*. The tenuous connections that were claimed between "basic" science and technology distorted the terminology—but more on that later. For very nearly fifty years, starting with the Alamogordo nuclear test on July 16, 1945, and ending on

October 21, 1993, with the defeat of the Superconducting Supercollider, humankind has been subjected to an incessant worldwide *evangelization campaign* on behalf of this new religion of IT. This propaganda has proved devastatingly successful, partly because the established religions had not realized that they were dealing with a *system* which would provide not only a "secular, value-neutral" process to manipulate nature, but all the elements that typify a religion as well.

The Reality of IT as Religion

As evidence for my thesis, instead of using esoteric scholarly arguments, I offer here some empirical evidence of the deep penetration of the idea of technology-as-religion in the popular mind, in the form of a few cartoons that have appeared in a wide variety of publications over the last several years. Individually, these cartoons tell us truths about ourselves that are more convincing than any text, and that these truths can be told with such humor shows how far they have entered into our culture. Taken as a whole, the set seems to confirm that Americans have indeed bought into the possibility of technology functioning as a religious system. The first cartoon shows a mountain-climbing searcher of enlightenment arriving at the perch of a scientist in his lab coat, with computer, microscope, and other such paraphernalia about, while on a ledge on another mountain nearby squats a bearded guru; this cartoon explicitly shows the transfer of allegiance from the Eastern religions, fashionable in the sixties and seventies, to the "high-tech" world which had become the new "guru" of the eighties. The second, from *The New Yorker*, shows a goose-stepping platoon of lab-coated figures drilling in front of laboratory-like buildings to the tune of "Semper Fidelis," "From the cyclotron of Berkeley to the labs of M.I.T. . . . ." and indicates clearly where we think our salvation comes from: the laboratories of our universities. The quotations from *Parade* magazine that speak of science education as the *sine qua non* for success tell all Americans where to look for hope—in "science." *Omni* magazine's button distributed at the World Future Society's meeting— "The meek will inherit the earth, the rest of us will go to the stars"—speaks volumes and explicitly juxtaposes Biblical "religious meekness" to technology's triumphalism. The cover of the Lutheran student gathering's program inadvertently shows a human being trying to steer an enormous Star Trek-type vessel—

indeed a hopeless task. That this hopelessness is not yet felt by this enthusiastic human, is a perfect illustration of the religious establishment's naive view of technology. That IT can deal with ultimate matters of Life and Death is nicely capsulated by the advertisement for freezing heads from decapitated bodies. Just in case some might feel that all this is no more than circumstantial evidence of the religious nature of S/T, I add one of the very first editorials written by Daniel Koshland, editor of U.S. science's flagship publication, who pontificates:

> A Department of Science could be useful if it is devoted to untidiness and *evangelism.* It could serve as a catalytic force for increasing scientific research and generating *scientific approaches in all phases of our society* and our governmental structures. It could send out its missionaries to bring the *gospel of basic research* to the *heathen* in the *outer darkness.* For research is not only an endless frontier but a peaceful one in which the gains of one country are not made at the expense of others. The temporary technological edge achieved in one country is eventually *reflected in increased living standards for all.* (Emphasis added.)
> —from *Science* (February 8, 1985)

Sending out "missionaries" to the "heathen in the outer darkness," preaching the Gospel of Basic Research is—I can testify to it from within the sanctum sanctorum of the U.S. science establishment—an accurate reflection of the felt attitudes and commitments of a large fraction of that body, whatever they may *say* about their beliefs and values. They act from this religious stance—a dependence, a genuine belief in the propositions of science and promises, not in the God of Abraham and Moses, not in a contemporary pan-en-theist liberal Protestant view, but in International Technology.

How Did This Happen—Unannounced?

It is essential that we trace the origin of this "takeover" by this newcomer to the world of religions. It could happen because the established religious agencies were guarding the wrong entrance to their fortress. From Cardinal Bellarmine to Bishop Wilberforce to contemporary fundamentalist Christians, Muslims, and Hindus, religion has guarded its orthodoxy—its dogmas—instead of promoting orthopraxis. Among these religious tycoons the principal battlegrounds were, and remain, those areas which are the most esoteric and least relevant to the daily life of all their adherents—for example, the dogmatic accounts of cosmology and creation and evolution. For generations the frontlines in the war between science and theology were drawn around such issues. Over the centuries theology tried to adapt itself in more or less gracious ways to the new learnings from science. The significance of these apparent "concessions" or "defeats" after unnecessary battles was not lost on the populace at a deeper level. But the entire cosmology issue has been and continues to this day, in the eyes of this observer, to be a side show. Worse yet, it distracts the champions of the science-religion dialogue from the real issues and helps them waste a great deal of energy on pseudo-problems which existentially are of minor interest for most citizens. No founder of a major religion ever propounded a creation myth—only his followers have time for such trivia. The Gilgamesh, Genesis, and Big Bang/Green Dragon versions of creation would be recognized, let alone quoted, by only a minuscule percentage of ordinary citizens whether or not belonging to one of those faiths. The real and broad front, on which the real battle has been joined between the two major forces competing for the allegiance of humankind, is not that of ortho*doxy*, but of ortho*praxis*. The *religion* which directs and controls human behavior and human choices is the winner! And the winner is IT.

If one traces how the masses of Western humanity slowly but surely fell under the spell of IT, one will understand its attraction in the world today. Start if you will with Benjamin Franklin and his kite-flying experiments which led to the lightning rod. The eighteenth-century citizens of Philadelphia lived in the consciousness of "acts of God"—natural disasters—which had to be accepted as part of the divine dispensation and against which the only defense was prayer. Hence lightning rods became controversial: should churches, the bastions of the prayer defense, erect lightning rods? Eventually, one after the other of Philadelphia's church steeples was adorned with a lightning conductor, and technology had won its early, unheralded, but major symbolic victory.

Simply put, technology wins human hands, heads, and hearts because it delivers the goods it promises. The religionist may assert that these goods are only immediate, short-term gains, but these gains are precisely what builds "customer confidence." Reliable, "sensible" benefits accrue to those who "rely on" technology. I tell my large classes of Science, Technology, and

Society students the story of the "play-offs" between Elijah and the prophets of Baal (fewer than 2 or 3% of Penn State sophomores and juniors have heard of Elijah; fewer than 5–10% have any recollection of Joseph and the Pharaoh). There, right in the Bible, the side that delivered the goods—i.e., brought down the fire—won the allegiance of all. And technology has delivered to ever more hundreds of millions their most immediate needs—shelter from the elements, reliable sources of food, security, increasing comfort in many aspects of living—and that is what slowly but surely made followers of—if not believers in—the new "Way," the Way of Technology. Perhaps the most effective technologies made its converts in the area of human health, the deliverance from sickness, pain, and death. Medical "miracles" were the bestsellers and made innumerable converts to the new Way.

The stage was set for technology's stepchild, science, to join in. Science, with its own cosmology, its own downscaling of the human role in the cosmos, so radically different from the Judaeo-Christian views, soon substituted its own mysteries and icons for the traditional ones. Instead of the Virgin Mary, and the Sacred Heart, and assorted saints, science provided for our contemporaries an endless stream of icons: pictures of galaxies and pulsars and supernovae, of the details on the backside of an asteroid, of criss-crossing squiggles on a photographic plate, which to the unsuspecting billions were sold as proof that a "W particle" exists, whatever soundbite of scientific trivia was deemed sexy. A scientist pontificates (*"knows"*?) what happened in the first trillion trillionth of a second after the "beginning" of the universe. Still, all this would not have sufficed to create a new religion without the newer technologies of communication, without the broadcast technologies in particular. Printed missives by the hundreds of millions, radio and television now reaching nearly half of the five billions of humans, preach daily, boldly, subtly or subliminally, the Gospel of International Technology.

Thus was the "pyramid scheme" created, in which IT built its infrastructure of benefits delivered to large numbers of citizens, and on top of that, the superstructure of explanations, mystifications, and "beliefs." Just as once Western transportation and war technology and the commerce that followed the conquest of the colonies all paved the way for Christianization, so the advance of more elaborate technology is now paving the way for the emerging triumphant "religion of science and technology." The American empire attained the zenith of its powers in the early Sixties, on its total dominance in the spectacular modern technologies from nuclear weapons and nuclear power, from consumer electronics, radio, television, penicillin, and heart transplants to space exploration. The dominance of this "force," this still nameless worldview, or system, or religion, to which we all subscribed, liberal and conservative, capitalist and communist, rich nations and poor alike, was best caught up in a (now, almost unbelievable) paean of praise to the Godhead by the master rhetorician of American politics, Adlai Stevenson, who wrote in 1964:

> Yesterday, most of mankind could look forward only to a life that would be "nasty, brutish and short," on the verge of privation in good years, starving when the harvests failed. Now wheat pours out of our ears. We swim in milk. We are threatened with vegetable and fruit surpluses and even, in some happy years, wine gluts as well. Water, man's precious resource, will be captured from the oceans by desalinization; nuclear power promises unlimited energy; the rocket, unlimited speed; electronics, unlimited technical control. All the old locks of scarcity have been sprung, the prisons flung open. From the first stone tool to the cell which snaps a camera shutter on the far side of the moon, the stride of man's abundance is all but unimaginable—and yet it is here.
>
> This is the basic miracle of modern technology. This is why it is, in a real sense, a magic wand which gives us what we desire. Don't let us miss the miracle by underestimating this fabulous new tool. We can have what we want. This is the astonishing fact of the modern scientific and technological economy. This is the triumph we hail today. This is the new instrument of human betterment that is at our hand if we are ready to take it up.

Summing Up

I believe the facts speak for themselves and that I do not distort language too much when I say that by the end of the twentieth century the international technology system had become:

- the world's most powerful religion;
- the most rapidly growing religion;
- the only totally cross-national, cross-cultural (East-West, North-South) religion;

with its theology (albeit non-theist), its rituals, and its mysteries, from Higgs bosons and charmed quarks to brain synapses.

One could summarize in tabular form the status of this interloper among religions in the following table.

Culture-Tradition-Religion	International Technology
Provided for:	Now offers:
1. Meaning of Life	1. To explain origin of universe, life, etc., via science
2. Structure of society—laws, ethics, rules—governing everything (e.g., deity laws, keeping the sabbath, coveting)	2. To dominate the reality of every aspect. Rules, ethics, laws with exactly the opposite effect, no diety laws, no sabbath, coveting as a virtue for consumerism.
3. Help in crisis · health · death, etc	3. High-tech crisis management · health care · death, etc

· · · · · · · · · ·
The First Challenges to IT

Nothing, it would have seemed in 1965, could halt humankind's progress, its march into the future propelled by ascendant (then still national) technology.

Yet there were appearing on the horizon "clouds no bigger than a man's hand." A Pittsburgh biologist working out of her home—Rachel Carson—was penning a strange warning, *Silent Spring*. Nuclear weapons testing began to generate international protests. The massive technological power first of France, then the United States, was shown to be impotent against a village culture of twenty million Vietnamese with little technology but much spirit. A tiny bloc of Arab oil-producing nations could throw a monkey wrench into the worldwide techno-economy. In a French provincial town there appeared a prophet to challenge this "Imperial Rome"; a professor of law in Bordeaux, Jacques Ellul, starting in 1954, but continuously since, and with many allies, became a latter-day John the Baptist, pointing out the dangers inherent in the technology system. By the mid-seventies, Adlai Stevenson sounded downright quaint, if not utterly naive. What had looked like a total world sweep by IT now was caught in the sand trap of the environmental crisis, the anti-nuclear movement, and the defeat of America's high-tech war machine by a small Third World country. What had gone wrong?

What had gone wrong flowed from the fact that the benefits of technology are tangible, easily produced (or obtained) and appreciated, but at a cost which is well concealed, which always comes later, and these costs are often to be borne by other subsets of the population. Anna Harrison in a Presidential address to the AAAS put it this way:

> I suggest three premises: (1) every technological innovation, regardless of how great its positive impact on society, also has a negative impact on society; (2) the benefits and the negative impacts may be experienced by different subsets of society; and (3) the benefits and the negative impacts may be experienced in different time frames.

She has also pointed out that human choices do affect the direction technology takes, albeit, we would say, well within Ellul's limits to its own freedom:

> (1) The direction and the rate of extension of scientific knowledge are to a large degree determined by social, economic, and political factors, and (2) the direction and the rate of development of technology are to a large degree determined by social, economic, and political factors.

What had gone wrong was that the downside of any technology which is being sold to the public is *never* exposed at the beginning. To be fair, it is often still unknown. When the "wonderdrug" of agricultural technology, DDT, was discovered, no one could have known or thought about its effect on bird's eggs. When nuclear power appeared, the problems of radioactive waste were partly neglected but also partly unknown. The "cure" for an acute disease may merely make us more likely to die of a chronic one, often at much greater personal and societal cost. The automobile gave us magnificent mobility, but was not innocent in the destruction of the family and extended family, in the promotion of sexual anarchy, of contributing to massive air pollution. Vaccination and public health programs were not unconnected with our population explosion. And with zero thought of costs or consequences, serious scientists even dare talk about shipping our excess population to other planets (which ones are never specified!)

The Ultimate Faustian Bargain

International Technology Offers			
National & Personal "Security"	Health	Comfort	Riskless Adventure
Better Weapons; Arms; Financial Security, etc.	Longer lives, less pain, less disease.	Less work, more leisure, power at our fingertips.	Spectator activities from sports to drama to help us pump adrenalin into our system, sitting in our armchairs.
In Exchange It Demands			
Breaking ties to all earlier authorities: "God," tradition; family, which were the basis of security.	Less control of our own health and how we live and die.	Mobility for stability. Conformity to mass values.	Trading action for reflection. Other directedness for inner directedness.

In a less dramatic but more consequential way, humankind has struck the ultimate Faustian bargain with its own Technological Self. The table above summarizes the trade-offs it has made for the very real benefits it has gained. *In all cases, the costs are hidden by time or space from those who actually benefit.* This is why technology is a system in a "thermal run-away" condition, where as the system gets hotter, resistivity goes down, even more current flows, and the temperature rises ever faster.

What is extraordinary is why this imperial tendency, this dangerous characteristic at the basis of our techno-economy, has attracted so little commentary and criticism from our historians and philosophers. With the exception of Lewis Mumford, the understanding of the deep threat from the technology system seems to come from Asian and European scholars deeply committed to a religious value system.

Very few realize that this selfsame controversy was at the heart of the showdown between Mahatma Gandhi, father of India, and his own handpicked successor and first prime minister, Jawaharlal Nehru, which took place as India's Congress party set the course for the economic development of India. Nehru, the westernized Cantabrigian under the sway of modern science, argued explicitly for the *religion* of science and technology and for technology's autonomy in a "secular" India; Gandhi argued for the hegemony of Indian traditions to be maintained over all technologies to be established in India. The year was 1947: no one except the deepest religious thinkers had yet realized the hidden dangers of technology. Jacques Ellul first spotted the worm in the technological apple in *La Technique* (1954) in which, with amazing prescience, he argued the case that technology has escaped human control, because he drew on his deep Protestant Christian heritage. In the Sixties and Seventies, E. F. Schumacher, a Catholic layman, brother-in-law of Heisenberg and understudy of Maynard Keynes, also argued the case for conscious decentralization in his bestseller, *Small Is Beautiful—Economics as though People Mattered*. (It was Schumacher who once turned to me after I had introduced him as he was about to address a large university audience and said, "Perhaps the chairman will disagree if I were to tell this audience that I believe that Gandhi had only one true disciple—Mao Tse-tung—who was totally committed to the decentralized village economy.") Two other scholars, Ivan Illich and Raimon Panikkar, both Roman Catholic priests and scholars of the development of societies, emerged in the Seventies as critics of modern technology. A few perceptive Western scholars, like Lewis Mumford, Robert Heilbroner, and C. P. Snow, also seem to have sensed the religious dimension of the tension between technology and society.

· · · · · · · · · ·

The Shaking of the Foundations

Let me summarize my claims under four headings and comment on each.

1 *International technology levels all religions in its path and has become the functional world religion.* From the preceding sections it follows that this has occurred in much of the developed world without any confrontation and hence with very little awareness on the part of the public. In the "developing" world technology equals prosperity, and *any* tradeoff, any sacrifice of values or tradition, is eagerly offered by the leadership. (The Yeltsin Russian example is but the most abject example of rice-Christians being made or forced to convert from a socialist to a market IT economy.)

2 *All traditional religions' influence over behavior is radically weakened in world urban culture.* In our day-to-day life the truly incredible impact of global technology can be felt and tasted by the masses in the common experiences of their lives. No dietary considerations can stand in the path of the onrushing fast food giants. Of course some dedicated, orthodox adherents will resist. What is significant is that the mainstream, the center of the masses, has given in; and obviously not all change is bad. But in sexual behavior, premarital sex has become normative in the West; its acceptance has been forced on all religious cultures which opposed it, as the price of mobility and prosperity. Gay and lesbian sex, proscribed by some religions, has won great victories of acceptance, and with it emerging from the shadows of rigid religion are new forms of co-marital sex, all made *possible* first, then *common*, then *acceptable*. Whenever religions failed to evolve, to bring their dogma into line with their praxis in the real world in new situations, technology was always there offering "reality therapy."

3 *All religions' dogmatic claims have been radically weakened and have become ignored in practice.* The basic categories and terms of religious dialogue (heaven, hell, and salvation, for example) are totally empty for most born after the Sixties.

4 *The core theologies are corroded beyond patching: no official body can agree on any meaningful "definition" of terms such as God, Christ, Grace, "Satori," Avidya, Bodhisattva.* Meaningful discourse on theology is virtually impossible outside small communities which share precise meanings attached to certain words because of common experience. For the rest of the world there is an enormous range of meanings and associations for even the most central concepts of theology. Perhaps it was always thus, but the masses believed that someone knew exactly what was intended, and hence pronouncements *ex cathedra* became the commonly held core of belief. This has all but disappeared.

. . . .

The Clash of the Titans

Two parallel struggles are going on for the body, mind, heart, and soul of humankind. Ranged on one side are the forces of International Technology, which has been winning hands down in gaining adherents. They point towards uniformity in all the (mundane) aspects of life, food, clothing, entertainment, and so forth. So far the McCulture is victorious, with Disneyland as its Mecca.

On the other side, reeling from the attack are the religious traditions whose foundations have all too obviously been shaken. They do not yet realize it but they can only survive if preservation of the *diversity of cultures* becomes at least as important as preserving the diversity of animal species. Unless cultural diversity produces a more emotional, gut-level commitment, the traditional religions will not make it. And to that end the re-emphasis on localization, on community-based economies, lifestyles, values is the ally of all the religions; but the forces of these religions are curiously unaware of being simultaneously under attack and that they must make common cause if they are to have a chance to resist this new force.

· · · · · · · · · ·

Is Technology Controllable: by What?

Carl Friedrich von Weizsäcker, perhaps the only scientist of stature who also devoted much of his professional life to theology, ends his Gifford Lectures, the "History of Nature," with a hermeneutic tour-de-force on the Garden of Eden myth. The Technological System, in his view, is the natural result of humankind's "pursuit of knowledge without love":

> The scientific and technical world of modern man is the result of his daring enterprise, knowledge without love. . . . But when knowledge without love becomes the hireling of the resistance against love, then it assumes the role which in the Christian mythical imagery is the role of the devil. The serpent in paradise urges on man knowledge without love. Anti-Christ is the power in history that leads loveless knowledge into the battle of destruction against love. But it is at the same time also the power that destroys itself in its triumph. The battle is still raging. We are in the midst of it, at a post not of our choosing where we must prove ourselves.

Technology without a guidance system *must* grow in a manner which respects no particular societal or human needs or laws; the technological imperative for growth is even more intrinsically connected to its nature than is the biblical command, "Go ye and make disciples of all nations." Ellul's arguments made systematically (now for forty years) sounded strange to technophilic

American and European societies in the Sixties. Today, at least the debate is joined. Is the worldwide technological system out of human control? If not, what force is supposed to control it? Corporate good citizenship? Hardly, in a uniformly capitalist competitive era. National laws? Not in a globalized economy. The United Nations? Doubtful. Technology has no intrinsic values nor does its only master, global megacapital. What it offers even the most powerful technologically sophisticated leaders is the total illusion of "leadership in high-tech, high-paying jobs, greater security, etc." Statements such as this are not half-truths or quarter-truths. They are, in food labelling language, "artificially flavored with truth." Of course, somewhere, for a short time, some company in some country will create a small number of "high-paying jobs." The reality is that in the globalized economy no nation-state can decide where those jobs will wind up in ten years, no one can promise a longer life span, no nation-state can control the ownership of the idea, the jobs, the products.

If no community, no $10 billion corporation, no nation-state can control the destiny of a technology, what can? A religion-dominated culture? For China, under Mao, the religion of communism determined the technologies that were acceptable. Decentralism projected into the villages led to the myriad back-yard steel furnaces. They failed. Today, literally, China has 2,000 high-pressure presses to make synthetic diamonds. They are doing very well. At the MIT World Council of Churches meeting in 1979, the Muslim delegates were quite explicit: Islamic countries would only encourage and develop those technologies which fitted the framework of Islamic teachings. To no small extent the downfall of the Shah of Iran was caused by his importation, without control, of all Western technology. Native American cultures have never fitted into a modern lifestyle because of the insistence that religious traditions take precedence over short-range gains in wealth or power. In less than a decade, the Chinese giant has capitulated in large part to the seductions of the globalized economy, prosperity, and modernity for some of its people; the fate of others affirming the hegemony of religion or values over technology—as in Cuba—is still in the balance.

• • • • • • • • •

The Disarray in Traditional Religions

Of one thing there can be no doubt whatsoever. At least in the West, all centralized religious establishments are in more or less total disarray. The Roman Catholic Church in Europe and America has crumbled before our eyes in hardly thirty years. Vatican II had appeared to give it a chance to catch up to reality, but it failed because the successors of the visionary John XXIII could not face the pace of change demanded. From a world monolithic power, it is now another sect with its own peculiar emphases and heresies. In 1965, in our bestseller, *Honest Sex* (subtitled: *A Revolutionary Sex Ethics by and for Christians*), my wife and I predicted that if the Roman Catholic Church did not come to terms with sexual reality (on the spiritually trivial issues of masturbation, contraception, divorce, and so forth), it would be rejected by its own masses. Our prediction proved too conservative. The heretical fixation of this church on sexuality—most poignantly shown by the fact that a scholar like Pope John Paul II would spend a very large portion of his magnum opus encyclical "Veritatis Splendor" on these self-same issues—illustrates the degree of utter irrelevance into which establishment religion has fallen. The catastrophic decline in women religious, the backbone of the system, and the nearly equal decline in the vocations to the priesthood, are numerically accessible signs of a more widespread disintegration. In mainstream Protestantism, similar but not as catastrophic declines are visible.

I recite these data on the decline of mainline religious establishments to make two points. First, in this I find the evidence of the victory of the forces of IT—the successful pushover of religious praxis (behavior, action) by IT's much more permissive posture. Second, that not all the desertions are to secularism, or to single-minded IT worship. Indeed, a great number move to *smaller*, more esoteric (e.g., Eastern) religions or to fundamentalist Christian sects. The need for the psychological fulfillments of religion seems to be steady.

Judaism mirrors some of these trends, with Reform and (to a lesser extent) Conservative groups being increasingly assimilated and intermarried into mainstream IT followers, while Orthodox and ultra-Orthodox groups emphasizing ethnic and cultural roots do better. Where Islam is numerically strong (Pakistan, Bangladesh, Indonesia), the influence of IT has not yet been felt by the masses. In the Middle East, while large percentages have been impacted by IT, the authoritarian governments, whether of the Iranian variety or the Saudi Arabian, have not allowed enough self-expression for us to get an accurate reading of who is winning the hearts of the masses.

These two conflicting signals in the Western religions, which have been on the front lines in dealing with IT—on the one hand, obeisance to IT, on the other, retreat to more personalistic, simpler religious lifestyles—must be taken into account in looking for future trends.

Indeed the tragic failure of the major religious establishments to elucidate, develop, and update their dogmas, to make them relevant to present human experience, has led to the incredible situation where "Christian" and "Islamic" have become monopolized appellations to be avoided, for they all too frequently are misappropriated, literally stolen, to be attached as adjectival prefixes to "fundamentalisms."

Among non-western religions where the children of the Book and the Written word are not so significant, the potential for direct conflict on issues of dogma is much less. In those cultures it is directly at the point of religious practices where IT is making its impact. Whether it is at the pivotal point of equality for women, or on changes of dietary habits, IT is being felt throughout Hindu, Buddhist, Confucian, and Shinto cultures. If form and function, practice and theory, are intimately involved in the totality of these religious traditions, then they are already being co-opted from within by IT with its universal, technologically optimized practices and inherent values.

But, it may be argued, there is an enormous resurgence in fundamentalism worldwide—Jewish, Christian, and Muslim. Glass cathedrals and 10,000-member churches, television evangelists and indeed cable channels adorn the landscape. Surely religion is alive and well in today's technoculture. What interpretation can we make of this fact, in the light of our thesis? This is, precisely, an expression of the human need for the spiritual dimension of life being channelled into whatever form is available, often local, often tribal structures. These structures, I believe, will become the new pattern for living in the twenty-first century. The question is, under what belief system(s).

· · · · · · · · · ·

The Good News: The Ending of IT's Hegemony

Jesus comments in Matthew on the nature of true insightfulness, on the ability to spot from the very first signs the major trends. He talks of those who can predict rain when they see at the horizon "a cloud no bigger than a man's hand." I will identify in the following some clouds that may be bigger than a man's hand—

but which still escape the notice of the masses—that signal a major change in the power which science and technology separately exercise over humanity.

First, the end of the era of the continuous worship of Big Science and the wonderful truths to be revealed by it was signalled by the shutting down of the Superconducting Supercollider (SSC) project by Congress on October 21, 1993. Never in the foreseeable future will either money or attention ever again be focussed so narrowly on a single nation building a machine. We have passed the beginning of the end of Big Science and science hype. This does not mean some sudden cutoff of all funding, but without doubt the inexorable, slow turning off of the spigot has started. Second, the undermining of the hegemony of the United States in both military and economic realms has called into question much of the bombast and triumphalism of the post-war era, which had pushed IT to the top of the popularity charts among religions because of America's success! At a more fundamental level I represent the school of thought among senior scientists who having thought about it, have concluded that science itself is on an asymptotic approach to saturation in the satisfactions it can provide to humankind. The discoveries of really new principles—those which affect humankind—seem to have reached their peak in quantum mechanics. So very little has happened on the truly fundamental side of late, and after such great expenditures for fifty years, that really new, big discoveries become less likely every year. Science is the victim of its own success. This should not be misread as saying that science is at an end or that there is nothing more to do. There can never be an end to human curiosity; but the particular focus on nature has yielded much fruit and with so many tens of thousands of pickers, there are few things left to find. Of course, "horizontal" proliferation of knowledge, or filling in details, or refining precision to the nth place of decimals, will continue as long as society is willing to pay; but science will not be humankind's great adventure in the twenty-first century.

Likewise, although technology has pretty well saturated most of the appetites in the affluent developed world for new gadgets, in graduate classes students are unable to imagine any new function that technology can perform except "teleportation" ("beam me up, Scotty"). But there is still the great opportunity to spread this consumerism worldwide and to add gold-plating, minor frills to many existing technologies.

These rational analyses (which may, of course, be proved incorrect by history) are received by the science community with exactly the same reaction as fundamentalists accord to devoted Christian scholars who dare deny the inerrancy of the Bible while living by its spirit. During 1993 I counted in major pronouncements, such as agency heads testifying before Congress, people giving examples of the wonders which basic science has produced in the past, mainly references to "old" discoveries, i.e., before 1950. And these people, by some most unscientific extrapolation, guarantee that they will produce more, on schedule, in the future! The examples ranged from Roentgen rays (x-rays), theories of relativity, and quantum mechanics to penicillin, the transistor, and the structure of DNA. Unwittingly, they proved my case: not much seems to have come out in the last thirty or forty years. The number of scientists and the amounts of equipment, money, and effort poured worldwide into basic science in the first fifty years of the century was probably in aggregate between 1,000 and 10,000 times *smaller* than what has been spent in the last fifty years. And yet we find that not a single example of anything as fundamental has been discovered. And this is the science community's best case for continuing such work! I do not wish to disparage the beautiful details of the annual series of sharper and sharper photomontages of no-longer-existing galaxies which come out of our telescopes. My claim is much more serious: one can expect nothing else, just more detail on increasingly irrelevant topics far removed from human concern. A bigger telescope, a finer microscope, a Tev accelerator, is absolutely certain to produce only something slightly sharper or smaller, or whatever. But unless it can be found, as P. W. Bridgman, the only American Nobel laureate physicist-philosopher, has written, to be related "back at the level of the large scale events of daily life," these discoveries will end up in the dusty corner of esoterica. A very large fraction of modern basic science funded by the public to the tune of over $10 billion a year has failed that test. The death of the Superconducting Supercollider is the starting gun of the gradual or not so gradual attrition which will surely reduce that enterprise. The virtual guarantee of this prediction's being right appeared in the private sector research world in the short time period of 1992–93, during which all of the highest tech companies of the world—IBM, Dupont, AT&T—*all* decided that their "corporate basic research" labs were unnecessary and, as many of their vice-presidents have put it to me, "we have all the science we can use right now, and we have an ever-increasing supply from all over the world sitting on the shelf—why should we pay for more?" That does not mean that corporations' purpose-related research and development is stopped or even decreased but it is no longer of the "hope-in-the-sky," "something-is-sure-to-come-up" variety. It is all telestic (purposeful or utilitarian) science from now on. Another specific cause for the erosion of science's posture in society is that the priests have been caught "selling indulgences," practicing soft cheating. The Gallo and Baltimore scandals, the cases of fraud, the exaggerations of cold fusion, the funding on university overhead rates, and on and on, have certainly changed the public's trust in science.

Telestic science, applied science of all kinds, engineering, first-rate and pedestrian, all will be maintained at solid substantial levels; they may even increase here and there. But even such, technology's time for cut-back may only be a couple of decades away, because already Chernobyl, Bhopal, and Challenger have raised deep-seated doubts in the public. In the near future, the hype, the worship, the expectations, for all of science and technology will return to the more reasonable levels of the pre-bomb era.

A Vision for the Future

To match the dawn of the post-Supercollider era in science and technology, the Parliament of the World's Religions in August 1993 was a milestone on the tortured journey of humankind's different organized spiritual aspirations and desires to relate to each other. For anyone who was present at the event, what was most striking was the absolutely unanimous commitment to mutual acceptance, respect, and accommodations. Not a trace of exclusivity remained. Not one person in any speech could have recited the previous core belief of many major religious bodies. "Nulla salus extra (meam) ecclesiam." Throughout the Parliament my long-standing deduction was completely confirmed. All the discussion focussed on human behavior. Each religious body was anxious to show how to support peace, justice, sustainability, equality, using their *practices;* not one session was devoted to discuss specialized *dogmas* and differences among them.

I believe that there are here profound empirical learnings on how religious bodies should get together.

1 The first is: focus on ortho*praxis*, not ortho*doxy*. Determine the wide range of societal issues on which the major reli-

gions can agree and make this the basis for a coalescence of a transcendent value structure for all major religions. "Service" or "serving society" could become one of the key mindsets encouraged by all religions;

2 "Working together": apply this common religious value to evaluate and criticize proposed and actual interventions by IT. And in order to be able to do this, the churches themselves should encourage technological literacy and citizen science among their members in schools, colleges, and Sunday school;

3 Start a movement within each religious establishment to challenge the monistic view as being inapplicable to a whole world; and instead to adopt a radically pluralist posture towards other theologies.

. . . .

Countering the Technological Fix

By far the most potent weapon the religious bodies will have to offer will be plans and working models for a healthy future for most citizens which requires new values and new social structures, without depending on new technology. Substantial segments of the population are now sensitized to the many possible disadvantages of many techno-fixes. The table below tabulates some of the elements which could be offered as positive alternatives in a values-controlled society.

The VCT (values-controlled technology) approach always involves the larger system whenever possible. Hence, designing entire living-working habitats suitable for today's humans is the same challenge as was faced across the northeast and midwest in the middle of the nineteenth-century industrial revolution. Entire communities were designed, planned, and lived in; striking

VCT Alternatives to the "Techno-Fix"
• Churches again pioneering in socio-technological innovation (cf. Oneida, Amana)
• Decentralized smaller communities closer to countryside, nature (cf. Henry Ford)
• "Local capacity-based" production and employment
• New models (physical and social) for alternate extended families, including intergenerational groupings
• New (= old) values: frugality, simplicity, richness in relationships

examples were the Oneida and Amana communities, or in our time the Bruderhof—each based on specialized or new technologies (silverplate in one and appliances in another and toys in the third) as a source of jobs, but also on a shared communal lifestyle. The Amish communities growing in the face of IT for two hundred years offer a more esoteric but equally successful model.

Jacques Ellul has urged as his response to the present crisis policies to "repopulate the villages." Henry Ford strongly advocated that his company would buy parts from suppliers in small towns with many parks (on the banks of a river) because he felt that small town living would make the best workers.

In almost direct contradiction to the tendencies of the globalized economy we should seek to build on local capacities in raw materials, worker skills, and so forth. Lord Maynard Keynes wrote some decades ago on the importance of preserving local skills and styles and avoiding the international financial entanglements which dominate our world today:

> I sympathize, therefore, with those who would minimize, rather than those who would maximize, economic entanglement between nations. Ideas, knowledge, art, hospitality, travel—these are the things which should of their nature be international. But let goods be homespun whenever it is reasonably and conveniently possible; and, above all, let finance be primarily national.

Not only the job-base but the family structures and communal responsibilities could also reflect the diverse cultural groupings which exist. A measure of the transference of our trust from our religious values to what IT demands can be seen in the Oneida community's ability to experiment with new social patterns, including radical sexual sharing. Such systems experimentation would be nearly impossible today.

Indeed a moment's reflection will show how the present socio-psychological situation has reached an impasse. When I came to the United States in 1945, I found a fully developed liberal WASP culture. It was tolerant and reasonably permissive, but assuredly Protestant; Catholics were almost included, except for high office. Blacks were clearly second-class citizens, especially in the South, but everyone felt guilty about that. The melting-pot concept was working, and the dominant culture into which everyone—as far as possible—was melted was WASP. Today, the melting pot has been abandoned and diversity has rightly assumed the rank of a major value. We mean "diversity" presumably of cultures—ethnicity, religion, and so forth. But what does that mean? Can ten Native Americans with 900 WASPs, 50 Blacks, and 40 Hispanics, in a town of a thousand, express their culture as part of diversity? Can the Blacks or Hispanics? Clearly we need a critical mass of humans to sustain any sense of a cultural unit. My analysis of the size of stable social units, from Rhesus monkey groups (about 50) to the Pennsylvania Amish communities which merge and move (about 1000), would suggest that a viable sustainable cultural unit in modern society would number between 1,000 and 10,000. Given all the modern technologies of communication and travel, a goal for VCT social engineering could be to create systems which are diverse consisting of relatively or dominantly (of course, *not* exclusively) culturally homogeneous units. The job-base should reflect local resources and opportunities. This diverse system of linked, culturally homogeneous, "extended family" units is the kind of goal which the emerging Alliance of World Religions should be working towards. There is in fact a very, very impressive model which has emphasized all these values, except diversity. It is the Mondragon experiment in the Basque province in Spain. Mondragon is both the biggest single corporation in Spain, and the most impressive alternative technological system in the world.

· · · · · · · · · ·

An End Run around the Theological Dimension in the Encounter with IT

The emerging Alliance of World Religions will of course have its work cut out for it in reconciling the theological differences among its members. In the following I simply point the direction of my thinking on this issue. But I believe that instead of that very old and largely fruitless task (inter-religious dialogue), they address together, as members of the same Alliance of World Religions team, to a very different task—the clarification of their joint position vis-à-vis IT. The very first among these tasks is to compare and contrast the differences between the scientific/technological approaches to reality with the theological/religious counterparts. I have dealt with this question at length in my book *Experimenting with Truth* and there summarize the relevant points. The classical views of the relations between science and theology, or technology and religion, are radically different from mine, which as far as I know are unique and new.

Relations between Scientific and Religious Knowing

Classical Views

1. SCIENCE is knowledge about MATTER (material things)
   RELIGION (theology) is knowledge about SPIRIT (spiritual things)

2. SCIENCE is about the WORLD
   RELIGION (theology) is about GOD and, only derivatively, the WORLD

3. SCIENCE is knowledge about NATURE
   RELIGION (theology) is knowledge about RELATIONS among HUMANS and to GOD

4. SCIENCE is verifiable, testable, falsifiable, KNOWLEDGE
   RELIGION (theology) is KNOWLEDGE which cannot be verified but is yet significant

Contemporary (Roy's) Views

1. SCIENCE is intrinsically, fundamentally reductionist
   THEOLOGY is always wholist

2. SCIENCE is only about separate parts
   THEOLOGY is about wholes

3. SCIENCE can ONLY provide details
   THEOLOGY can only provide the big picture

4. THEOLOGY locates one on the map of life and points directions
   SCIENCE and technology provide vehicles to get there

The only developed theological basis on which the Alliance of World Religions can collectively face contemporary IT is panentheist. This awkward term describes a theology which fits perfectly the new macro-ecumenical stance of the Alliance.

Pan-En-Theism
God *Through* Everything

- Only absolute absolutism
- Only viable theos-logos in the modern world dominated by science and technology
- Lays the base for macro-ecumenism (the new federalism in religion)
- Transcendent/immanent as distinct from immanence of pantheism

---

Panentheism (which I have called a Reality Theology) has had a long, honorable heritage and tradition but has long gone incognito. John Robinson talked of "beginning at the other end" as he re-introduced panentheism into the current debate. It is Peter Berger's "inductive option," and hence it is compatible with science and technology. Many of the greatest theologians have skirted around its edges. Thus Schleiermacher wrote of the "signs and intimations of the infinite even in the most natural and common events," and William James spoke of the "reality of the unseen." The profound human dimension of a panentheist worldview was exquisitely painted in Petru Dumitriu's *Incognito*.

Panentheism is the only theological stance that can deal totally with the profound role of chance (a theme invariably avoided in all religions) as part of the reality through which we touch the transcendent. (I have dealt with this at length in my Gross Memorial Lecture.)

Panentheism is, finally, ipso facto, radically pluralist in the sense that Raimon Panikkar defines it: radical pluralism proceeds and acts as though even apparently conflicting viewpoints (authenticated in tested human experience) point back to the same reality. Hence panentheism is the key theological basis for the emerging world religions.

· · · · · · · · · ·

Summary

My thesis is that all the religions of the world are in rapid retreat, except the newest entry into the arena of religions: the worldwide science and technology system which I have dubbed IT (International Technology).

An even bolder claim is that in the early Nineties humankind rounded a corner. Science itself has saturated society with knowledge of the kind that nobody is willing to pay tens of billions for; hence, the era of science as the pre-eminent human endeavor has begun to close. Technology also has shown its dark face—in the environmental insult, the threat of nuclear war, the dissolving of traditional societies—and now as it is beginning to be seen as destroying the jobs of tens of millions in the West, humankind's servile attitude towards technology will change.

The second part of the good news is that the world's religions have entered into a new mode of relating based on praxis, not dogma. And if they can accept a radically pluralist approach to theological issues, a new day can dawn. On this basis, acting together, humankind could be led into an era where religious values guide and control all technologies to be introduced or utilized.

• • • • • • • • •

References

P. W. Bridgman, *Reflections of a Physicist* (New York: Philosophical Library, 1955).

P. Dumitriu, *Incognito* (London: Collins, 1964).

Jacques Ellul, *The Technological Society* (New York: Knopf, 1966).

Raimon Panikkar, "Religious Pluralism: The Metaphysical Challenge," in *Religious Pluralism*, L. S. Rauner, ed. (Notre Dame: Notre Dame Press, 1984), 97–115.

John A. T. Robinson, *Exploration into God* (Stanford: Stanford University Press, 1967).

Rustum Roy, *An Appropriate God for a Technological Society*, Gross Memorial Lecture, Valparaiso University (1991).

———, *Experimenting with Truth* (New York: Pergamon Press, 1981).

C. F. von Weizsäcker, *The Relevance of Science* (London: Collins, 1964).

• • • • • • • • •

Religion Gives the Map, Science the Means to Move Around

1 What are your views on cosmic beginnings, particularly with reference to the origin of the universe, of life, and of *Homo sapiens*?

The most important aspect of my thinking on this question is that it is relatively unimportant in the grand scheme of human needs, wishes, dreams, and deepest meanings.

The question of cosmic beginnings is the very last question we need to ask as our concern for our origins moves outward from our persons. Where did *I* come from starts with my genetic and immediate family lineage and my locality. Way at the end of the chain is where the cosmos comes from. It is of very little day-to-day, even year-to-year, significance, but *one* line of curiosity.

As one who teaches this topic to graduate students, I take a rather critical attitude to the imperialist posture about the *current* scientific best guess (and it is no more than that) about cosmic beginnings. I make certain that people understand the uncertainty (e.g., ±5 billion on the age) and processes associated with present scientific knowledge and that this "belief" makes no difference— by itself—to any human being.

2 What are your views on human ends, especially as this relates to the framework of cosmic beginnings?

> As I note above the connection of the purpose of humans on earth has virtually zero connection to cosmogenesis.
>
> Of course, my position on the role of humans in nature is that it is vastly, vastly more important. Humans are the "most evolved" form of animal life on this earth using our measuring criteria of awareness, consciousness, ability to alter our environment, and shape the future. But we are part of the complex web of mineral-vegetable-animal interaction called Life-on-Gaia (Logaia?) and our relationship to that—as to our fellow humans —is ideally that of the ("suffering," if necessary) *servant*.

3 What do you think should be the relationship between religion and science?

> My book on this very topic, *Experimenting with Truth*, takes a unique position (as far as I know). I aver first that the proper hierarchical parallel to religion is technology, not science; it is theology that is matched to science. Very briefly I have developed the argument in detail that science is to theology as the detail is to the grand design. Theology is like the panorama on Mount Rushmore; science can only tell us about the material which makes up the bridge on President Roosevelt's "glasses." Religion is the Bayeux tapestry, technology is the explanation of how to place the gold threads into the weaving.
>
> In brief, religion gives you the map, shows you the big picture and where you are located on it. Science and technology give you the means to move around on the map but, intrinsically, cannot help you steer, nor tell you where you are going.

9
A Distinctly Human Face
Frederick Franck

Born in Maastricht, the Netherlands, in 1909, trained in medicine in Brussels, Edinburgh, and Pittsburgh, and practicing for many years in New York City, Frederick Franck's remarkable odyssey has led to a life divided between his medical career and his true vocation as an artist and writer. His last three decades have been devoted to writing, sculpting, drawing, and tending *Pacem in Terris*, the trans-religious sanctuary he built in Warwick, New York, now open to visitors. Among the best-known of his two dozen books are *My Days with Albert Schweitzer; The Zen of Seeing; Zen Seeing, Zen Drawing; Fingers Pointing toward the Sacred;* and *To Be Human Against All Odds*.

Frederick Franck was unfortunately unable to attend the Parliament due to illness. He would have been a responder to Rustum Roy's presentation and has since submitted this response to the paper by his good friend Professor Roy.

. . . .

A most impressive but uncomfortable swelling, not of my left brain but of the left cheek, prevents me from listening as planned to what I had some reason to surmise Professor Rustum Roy was bound to say as a Parliamentarian, and in the hope to respond to it more or less adequately, I can only respond here as the artist, the unaffiliated *Homo religiosus* I happen to be. As everybody knows by now, someone who spends his days drawing, painting, sculpting, and scribbling books necessarily limps on the right side of a brain of which the left hemisphere is sadly underdeveloped. The artist's recessive left brain could never have spawned those triumphs known as science and technology, those microwave ovens, quantum physics, frozen pizzas, and that most glorious triumph of the left brain, television, which, in full color and absolutely free, teaches us twenty-four hours a day the simple and technological solution of life's most vexing problems by merely the pull of a trigger, except perhaps that problem of the magical disposal of radioactive and other toxic waste, not such a minor problem after all. One of the latest and noblest secretions of the left brain is a concept known as ecology. It was reached at a moment in which the latest triumphs of science and technology undeniably indicated the impending grand finale of the human species, whether with the big bang of bomb or the soft whisper of pollution.

Ecology, a word which a few decades ago was almost unknown, is in reality the rising into human consciousness of the radical interdependence of all phenomena in the universe and, as such, a heresy in the eye of the true believers of the idol of International Technology, which Dr. Roy correctly describes as an idolatry pretending to be a religion. The greatest sinners against ecological sanity are no doubt the transnational corporations, who defensively developed the art of ecolalia (my neologism) with the help of the highest paid public relations virtuosi Madison Avenue has to offer. Ecolalia, a variant of glossolalia—that "gift of tongues," defined as non-meaningful speech, associated with certain schizophrenias but also with various religious sects—now resonates through auditoriums worldwide to whitewash the giants of the petroleum, paper, and agricultural industries, and so forth, and to justify their desecration of the earth, their waste of irreplaceable resources, and their pollution of oceans, rivers, and the atmosphere.

In your paper, I presume, you speak of the modern Science which spawned Technology (until the roles were reversed) as being closer to a life-threatening pathology than to the universal valid criteria of Truth/Reality it has pretended to be, more or less, since Copernicus in 1543 published "On the Revolutions of the Heavenly Spheres," where people who had seen the world in terms of miracle and mystery, after a series of cataclysms, began to turn their world of I-Thou relationships in a new worldview of I-It relatedness. This view reached its summit in Descartes, to whom the universe became a mindlessly gyrating machinery of which we and all other living things were the miniaturized replicas. We had become objectified, even auto-objectified strangers to ourselves, "individual non-persons" destined to be further quantified into code numbers, until—in tyrannies and democratic societies almost alike—the inner life of these code numbers became ignored as non-existent and their only relevancy left was in their tabulation as voters and their categorization as consumers of products of Science/Technology stretching from frozen pizzas to Rolex Oysters. "Toys'R Us" has become "Us'R Toys." Whose toys?—the toys of a technology running amuck, the props of the pseudo-religion of Science/Technology. Half a century ago Erich

Fromm and George Orwell saw the connections between fascism and the objectification of the individual, the radical separation of feeling and reason. Science/Technology is part and parcel of this Machiavellian separation which makes it proclaim the axiom that all the catastrophes that science and technology cause can be rectified by more of the same.

All I have said here would point at some absolute pessimism, were it not for recent proofs of discernment between sane, "symbiotic" technology as an alternative to the suicidally insane, "antagonistic" science and technology which brought us to the brink. E. F. Schumacher was one of the prophets of this metanoia. In my "Science, Technology, and Society" talk a few months ago, I pointed to three random revolutionary examples of "sane," responsible technology, in shrill contrast with such megascience extravaganzas as Supercolliders and Laser Interferometer Gravitation stuff. They were: John Todd's Center for the Restoration of Water in Falmouth, Massachusetts, and his "Living Machines" that restore hopelessly polluted effluent into potable water; Julius Hensel's offsetting of the ravages of acid rain by sprinkling crushed rock on the de-mineralized soil of Austrian forests; and the restoration and rehabilitation of landmark buildings in New York, scheduled for replacement by steel and glass "sick" buildings, into ecologically sound human environments (Audubon Society, National Resources Defense Council).

What these projects share is their distinctly human face, their motivation by human values. Ninety percent of the species that once populated the earth have become extinct. If we are to have a chance to remain among the ten percent surviving for a while, we need the maximally sane technologies in which specific human values overcome our pre-human atavisms, outfitted as they are with the immense know-how-without-wisdom which has brought us to this dead end. A Parliament of Religions worthy of its title should, in our present predicament, focus less on the relationships between the various religious traditions than on what they undoubtedly have in common: *the religious orientation to existence as such*, as being ultimately Meaningful, as having that sacred Meaning we can only ignore and deny under penalty of megadeath at short notice. It is indeed a matter of restoring Raimon Panikkar's "Cosmotheandric" connection. It is a matter not of a religious revival but of its opposite: a religious renaissance.

10

Tao, Modern Science, and Human Destiny

Hsing-Tsung Huang

H. T. Huang is a biochemist who retired recently as Program Director, Biochemistry, at the National Science Foundation in Washington. He was brought up in Malacca, now part of Malaysia, in a Chinese Christian family and received his advanced scientific education in Hong Kong, England, and the United States, where he conducted research in industry from 1951 to 1975. During World War II his travels in China with Joseph Needham started a friendship and collaboration that continues to this day with the writing of *History of Fermentations, Food Science and Nutrition* that will become part of Volume 6 of Needham's monumental *Science and Civilization in China.* Currently he is a Deputy Director of the Needham Research Institute in Cambridge, England.

Abstract

Tao is a basic philosophical and religious concept in Chinese culture. It is often translated as "the Way," but it may also be taken as Ultimate Reality or the Order of Nature. In this paper we shall first introduce the philosophy of Taoism, especially those aspects that are relevant to discoveries in modern science. Secondly, we shall discuss modern discoveries in physics and show that our scientific concepts of matter and energy are remarkably consonant with Taoist ideas of Ultimate Reality. Thirdly, we shall review the affinity between our current understanding of the evolution of life on earth and Taoist concepts of the interaction between opposites, yin and yang, life and death, and so forth as a normal function in the Order of Nature. Finally, we shall see how some of the basic ideas in Taoism bear an astonishing resemblance to aspects of the Christian faith. In conclusion, we shall attempt to indicate how some of the ideas surveyed may serve as a guide to human behavior.

Confucianism and Taoism

Most westerners are aware of the fact that there were two major currents of thought in ancient China, Confucianism and Taoism. Each school was later elevated to the status of a religion or quasi-religion.[1] Their founders, Confucius and Lao-tzu, lived at about 500 BC. Their teachings were disseminated, discussed, and

159

debated on among other schools of philosophy for centuries until 136 BC, when Confucianism was adopted as the official dogma of the Empire. Since then Confucianism has remained the moral and philosophical underpinning of the structure of Chinese society and its system of government. The influence of Confucianism on China is perhaps even greater than that of Christianity on modern Europe. In later years, Confucianism was also adopted by other countries in East Asia, namely Japan, Korea, and Vietnam. Even today, Confucianism remains so strong in East Asia that Confucian ethics have often been credited as a major factor in sustaining the rapid economic growth which the so-called "four little tigers" of the Pacific Rim, i.e., South Korea, Taiwan, Hong Kong, and Singapore, have enjoyed in recent years.

At first glance it would seem obvious that, of the two indigenous Chinese religions, Confucianism was the one that had by far the greater impact on the course of Chinese history. But the influence of Taoism can easily be underestimated. It is well known that while officials in Chinese history have always towed the Confucian line, artists, writers, and poets have usually preferred the teachings of Lao-tzu. Indeed, as Lin Yutang has wryly observed, "when writers and poets became officials, they liked Confucious openly, but Lao-tzu and Chuang-tzu (Taoism's best known exponents) secretly."[2] Why is this so? Lin has tried to explain the situation.[3]

> Confucian philosophy is a philosophy of social order, and order is seldom exciting; it deals with human relationships, and preoccupation with human relationships of the workaday world is apt to dull one's senses to the spiritual yearnings and imaginative flights of which the human' soul is capable. Confucians worship culture and reason; Taoists reject them in favor of nature and intuition.

Indeed, the affinity to nature in Taoist thought has led the eminent Chinese philosopher Fêng Yu-lan to say, "Taoism is the only system of mysticism which the world has ever seen that is not profoundly anti-scientific."[4] But mysticism is, after all, an integral element in a religious experience. Thus, it seems to me that Taoist philosophy might serve as a link between the world view of modern science and that of a mainstream religion, such as Christianity.

What I wish to explore in this paper is how Taoist philosophy relates to modern science on the one hand and to Christianity on the other. As a scientist, a Christian, and an inheritor of the cultural traditions of China, this exercise may be regarded as an attempt to bring a degree of ecumenism to the pluralistic influences that have shaped my own life. I shall proceed in four stages:

1 Introduce the philosophy of Taoism, especially those aspects that are relevant to discoveries in modern science.
2 Discuss modern discoveries in physics in the light of Taoist ideas of the Ultimate Reality.
3 Compare modern discoveries in biology with Taoist ideas of nature and the order of nature.
4 Compare basic ideas in Taoism with aspects of the Christian faith, and ascertain how they might influence human destiny.

What is Taoist philosophy? For an answer we need to look at the writings that Lao-tzu, the founder of Taoism, and Chuang-tzu, its chief expositor, have left us, in particular, the *Tao Te Ching* of Lao-tzu.

Tao Te Ching

Little is known about the author of the *Tao Te Ching*, the bible of Taoism. Legend has it that it was written by Lao-tzu (literally, "old master" or "venerable teacher"), an older contemporary of Confucius, who lived from 551 to 479 BC. Lao-tzu was the keeper of the archives at the capital. It is said that his fame was such that Confucious paid a special visit to him to ask for his advice on ceremonial rites. Perplexed but impressed by Lao-tzu's comments, he told his pupils after the visit, "This day I have seen Lao-tzu, who is perhaps like a dragon."[5] Eventually, saddened by human perversity, Lao-tzu rode away on a water buffalo beyond the Great Wall into retirement. But at the gate, the warden prevailed upon him to record for posterity the principles of his teaching. This he did in eighty-one verses, comprising about 5,500 characters, which have come down to us as the *Tao Te Ching*.

In spite of its small size, the *Tao Te Ching* has had the most profound influence on Chinese science, medicine, art, literature, philosophy, and religion. It is a wonderful work, poetic, mystical, paradoxical, yet full of power and charm. It has been translated many times into western languages. (In 1948, Lin Yutang knew of at least nine translations in German and twelve in English. In 1963, D. C. Lau counted over thirty versions in English and lamented that, "unfortunately, it cannot be said that it [i.e., the *Tao*

Te Ching] has been best served by its numerous translators, as the nature of the work attracted many whose enthusiasm for Eastern mysticism far outstripped their acquaintance with Chinese thought or even with Chinese language."[6] Just picking up a new translation whenever I see one in my neighborhood bookstore, I myself have accumulated fourteen English versions of the *Tao Te Ching*. These are shown in Table 1.)

TABLE 1. Some English Translations of the *Tao Te Ching*

Translator	Title	Translation of	
		TAO	TE
James Legge 1891	*Tao Te Ching*	Tao	Attribute of Tao
Suzuki & Carus 1913	*The Canon of Reason and Virtue*	Reason	Virtue
C. H. Mackintosh 1926	*Tao* (a rendering into English verse)	Way	Virtue
Arthur Waley 1930's	*The Way and its Power*	Way	Power
Witter Bynner 1944	*The Way of Life*	Existence	Fitness
Lin Yutang 1948	*The Wisdom of Laotse*	Tao	Character
R. B. Blakney 1955	*The Way of Life*	Way	Virtue
John C. H. Wu 1961	*Tao Te Ching*	Tao	Virtue
F. J. MacHovec 1962	*The Book of Tao*	Tao	Teh
D. C. Lau 1963	*Tao Te Ching*	Way	Virtue
Feng & English 1972	*Tao Te Ching*	Tao	Goodness
C. Y. Chang 1975	*Tao: A New Way of Thinking*	Tao	Attainment
S. Mitchell 1988	*Tao Te Ching*	Tao	Power, goodness
R. G. Henricks 1989	*Te Tao Ching*	Way	Virtue

Even from such an incomplete list, it is obvious that no definitive rendition of the *Tao Te Ching* in English has yet appeared. Perhaps there will never be one that will please every reader. The task of extracting the meaning of a Chinese character and expressing it in an equivalent word in English is often fraught with ambiguities. For example, consider the translation of the word *Tao*. On this list Tao is rendered variously as Way, Reason, Existence, or else it is simply left untranslated. In other connections Tao has also been interpreted as Nature, Ultimate Reality, Truth, God, the Absolute, etc. (Similarly, *Te* has been translated as Virtue, Attribute of Tao, Power, Fitness, Character, Attainment, Integrity, Honor, Wisdom, and Goodness. *Ching* simply means a sacred book or canon). For our purpose it is probably best to leave the word Tao untranslated, as several of the translators have done. Thus, in this paper we shall simply refer to Lao-tzu's book as the *Tao Te Ching*. The last item on this list, the rendition by R. G. Henricks, deserves a special comment.[7] In contrast to all the other versions, the title of the work is *Te Tao Ching* rather than *Tao Te Ching*. This translation is based on two manuscripts written on silk discovered in 1973 in a Han tomb at Ma-wang-tui, dated at about 160 BC. In these manuscripts the traditional chapters 38–81 (those dealing with *Te*) form the first part of the folio, while chapters 1–37 (those dealing with *Tao*) appear as the second part. So the work is appropriately titled *Te Tao Ching*. In spite of the reversed order of the *Tao* and *Te* sections, there is a remarkable agreement between the 160 BC silk manuscripts and the traditional text that has been handed down from the Han to the present day.

Next in importance to the *Tao Te Ching* is the *Chuang-tzu* of Master Chuang Chou, who lived from 369 to 286 BC. His relationship to Lao-tzu has often been compared to that of Saint Paul to Jesus. Chuang-tzu has been much admired by scholars for the beauty of his writing as well as for the appeal of his philosophy. The noted American sinologist H. G. Creel says, "The *Chuang-tzu* is in my estimation the finest philosophical work known to me, in any language."[8] The *Chuang-tzu* has been translated into English by Legge, Giles, Burton Watson, Lin Yutang (in part), and others. I shall occasionally refer to the *Chuang-tzu* to bolster and amplify some of the ideas expressed in the *Tao Te Ching*.

If we look at the character for Tao in Chinese, we see that it consists of two parts (Figure 1, page 164), the radical for "head," *shou*, and the radical for "moving on," *ch'o*. Thus, literally, the two together suggest a *going ahead*, a *way* or *path*. Since "way" can also denote a means to reach an end, in the sense of completing a task or solving a problem, it can be interpreted as a *method*. A method has to be *explained* in "rational speech" or *word*, which is reminiscent of the Greek *logos*. All these terms have been used to

FIGURE 1.   *The Two Parts of the Character* Tao.

denote Tao, particularly Way. But what does the *Tao Te Ching* itself say about the nature of Tao?

The opening chapter of the *Tao Te Ching* declares:

The Tao that can be told,	*Tao k'o Tao,*
Is not the eternal Tao.	*fei ch'ang Tao*
The Name that can be named	*Ming k'o Ming,*
Is not the eternal Name.	*fei ch'ang Ming.*

The nameless is the origin of heaven and earth.
The named is the **mother** of ten thousand things.
Free from desire, you realize the Tao's wonder;
Caught in desire, you see only its manifestations.
Yet the two spring from the same source, and differ only in
    name.
This source is called Mystery,
Mystery within Mystery,
The gateway to all understanding.
        —(Mitchell, Feng-English, mod.[9])

I have included the original Chinese text (in Romanized form) of the first two lines, which means literally,

The *Tao* that can be *taoed* is not the eternal *Tao.*
The Name that can be named is not the eternal Name.

That is to say, Tao, just like "name," can be used both as a noun and as a verb. This stresses that Tao can be dynamic as well as static, an idea that we will return to later. For now, we can say that Tao is the eternal or ultimate reality. It cannot be named or defined in words. Its origin is a mystery. The concept is further developed in Chapter 4, the Character of Tao:

Tao is like an empty bowl:
Use will not fill it up.
Fathomless, it is the origin of all things.
It blunts all sharp edges,
It unties all tangles,
It harmonizes all lights,
It settles the dust.
Hidden in the deeps,
It seems to exist forever.
I do not know whose child it is,
An image of what existed before "God"?
        —(Wu, Lin, Lau, mod.)

Tao is the origin of all things and existed even before the formation of the universe (Heaven-and-Earth) and the advent of living things. This view is further amplified in Chapter 25, Four Eternal Models:

> There was something nebulous that existed before Heaven and Earth.
> Silent; infinite; standing alone; never changing.
> It is everywhere, ever present and in motion.
> It is the **Mother** of all.
> I do not know its name. I style it **Tao.**
> If I must name it, I call it Great.
> Great means never-ending;
> Never-ending means far-reaching;
> Far-reaching means returning.
> Thus, Tao is great;
> Heaven is great;
> Earth is great;
> And Man is also great.
> There are four supremes in the universe; man is one of them.
> Man follows the ways of the earth,
> The earth follows the ways of the universe;
> The universe follows the ways of Tao, and
> Tao follows the ways of its own nature.
>
> —(MacHovec, Lin, mod.)

The Chinese word for Nature is *tzu jan,* meaning that which spontaneously exists or occurs. Thus, everything in the universe should in the end follow the Tao or the Order of Nature. But while all things, including life, owe their origin to Tao, it does not seek to dominate them. In other words, the Order of Nature is not a forced order, the result of laws which we are compelled to obey by the threat of punishment. This is shown in Chapter 34, Tao Flows Everywhere:

> The Great Tao flows everywhere. It may go left or right.
> All things depend on it for life. It does not turn away from them.
> It does its work, but it makes no claim for itself.
> It clothes and feeds all, but does not lord it over them.
> Always without desires, it may be called "the Little."
> All things return to it, yet it does not lord it over them;
> Thus, it may be called "the Great."

Therefore, the sage never strives himself for the Great,
And thereby the Great is achieved.

—(Chan, Wu, mod.[10])

Thus, Tao is the course, the flow, the drift, the order or process of Nature as well as Nature itself. All things in Nature are unified by the presence of Tao. All things in Nature, even opposites, are merely polar aspects of the same reality. Therefore, every thing or every event is only what it is in relation to all other things or events. This idea is expressed in Chapter 2, Rise of Relative Opposites:

When the people see some things as beautiful,
Other things become ugly.
When the people see some things as good,
Other things become bad.
Being and non-being give rise to each other.
Difficult and easy complement each other.
Long and short measure each other.
High and low define each other.
Voice and sound harmonize each other.
Before and after follow each other.
Therefore the Master manages without action,
Teaches without words.
Things arise and she lets them come.
She supports but does not possess them.
She nurtures them yet exacts no gratitude.
When her work is done, she forgets it.
That is why it lasts forever.

—(Mitchell, Lin, Wu, Lau, mod.)

Thus, we can say that Tao is the Ultimate Reality. It is everywhere. It was already present before the beginning of the universe (Heaven-and-Earth). It is expressed as the flow or order of Nature. Two attributes are particularly pertinent in the consideration of Tao and Physics.

1 Tao is a mystery. It cannot be defined in words. Indeed, the Master teaches it without words. "It is felt but not conceived, intuited but not categorized, divined but not explained."[11]

2 Tao encompasses everything. Thus, Nature is a unified entity. Polar opposites are aspects of the same reality. Every thing or event is only discernible as it relates to every other thing or event.

Let us now see how these ideas stand up to the discoveries of modern Physics.

· · · · · · · · · ·

Tao and Physics

Physics is the scientific study of matter and energy against a background of space and time. These are the measurable entities of the universe. All the objects we see around us are composed of matter. We see them because our eyes can sense the light that emanates from them. Light is a form of energy. We are aware of matter and energy wherever we are. At the beginning of the twentieth century, physicists were quite confident about the nature of both entities. Matter is composed of particles, atoms, and molecules; light is a form of electromagnetic radiation. Most nineteenth century physicists would agree with Isaac Newton's seventeenth century view of how God created the material world.[12]

> It seemed probable to me that God in the beginning formed matter in solid, massy, hard, impenetrable, movable particles, of such sizes and figures, and with such other properties, and in such proportion to space, as most conduced to the end for which He formed them; and that these primitive particles, being solids, are incomparably harder than any bodies compounded of them; even so very hard, as never to wear or break in pieces; no ordinary power being able to divide what God himself made one in the first creation.

These solid particles, or aggregates thereof, move about in space and time according to the laws of gravitation. Newton invented a new mathematics, the differential calculus, to put the behavior of gravitational force in precise mathematical terms. The success of the application of Newtonian mechanics in astronomy and to the motion of fluids and vibration of elastic bodies reinforces the notion that the universe is causal and determinate. The philosophical basis of this determinism is that the observer is a separate and independent being who has no effect on the observed phenomenon. Space and time are absolute entities. Thus, the world can be described objectively, without ever having to consider the presence of the human observer.

Newtonian mechanics, however, was unable to explain the electric and magnetic forces discovered in the nineteenth century.

The work of Michael Faraday and Clerk Maxwell resulted in the formulation of electrodynamics, which defines light as a rapidly alternating electromagnetic field traveling through space as waves. Today we know that x-rays, light, microwaves, and radiowaves are all electromagnetic waves, differing only in the frequency of their oscillation.

At the beginning of the twentieth century, physicists had two successful theories to explain the physical world: Newtonian mechanics and Maxwell's electrodynamics. But by the end of the first third of the twentieth century, the situation had changed dramatically. "Two separate developments—that of relativity theory and atomic physics—shattered all the principal concepts of the Newtonian world view: the notion of absolute space and time, the elementary solid particles, the strictly causal nature of physical phenomena, and the ideal of an objective description of nature."[13] These new developments all appear to lean towards a world view that bears surprising parallels to the ideas of Taoism and other religious philosophies of East Asia. They have been examined in detail by Fritjof Capra in his brilliant book *The Tao of Physics*.

My discussion of Tao and Physics will be very brief. I shall only deal with one aspect of the problem, the nature of matter and the nature of electromagnetic waves. The atomic theory was well established when the twentieth century began. Atoms are the smallest divisible part of matter. They are the ultimate "solid, massy, hard, impenetrable, movable particles" envisaged by Newton. But when Earnest Rutherford bombarded atoms with alpha particles from radioactive elements, he obtained totally unexpected and astonishing results. It turned out that atoms consist of vast regions of empty space in which minute charged particles, electrons, revolve around a nucleus, which is made up of tiny neutrons and protons. Electrons, neutrons, and protons, however minuscule, thus appeared to be the real "elementary" particles of the atomic theory. But, as we all know, that was not the end of the story. The chasing of the real elementary particles has been the major preoccupation of nuclear physics for the last half century. More than two hundred "elementary" particles are now known, but they have not brought us any closer to the structure of the atom. The words of Arthur Eddington, written in 1928, still ring true today: "We have chased the solid substance from the continuous liquid to the atom, from the atom to the electron, and there we have lost it."[14]

Moreover, the particles of the subatomic world do not behave at all like the solid particles of classical physics. Depending on how they are examined, they can appear sometimes as particles and sometimes as waves. To add to the confusion, electromagnetic waves can also sometimes appear as particles. Indeed, light can sometimes behave as if it is a stream of particles called photons. This paradox is solved by quantum mechanics, which tells us that at the subatomic level matter or events do not exist or occur with certainty at definite times and places, but rather show a probability to exist or occur. These probabilities in quantum theory are expressed mathematically as wave functions. Thus, matter dissolves into waves, and waves into probabilities, probabilities not of things but rather of interconnections, a conclusion so esoteric that it goes against the grain of our everyday experience. But it is not at all inconsistent with what we have seen as the basic aspects of the Tao.

Let us now compare the world view of modern physics with what the *Tao Te Ching* tells us about the Tao:

1 Like the Taoists' vision of the Ultimate Reality, i.e., Tao, the reality of matter, as revealed by modern physics, is a mystery. It cannot be defined or explained in words. It can only be expressed as wavelike patterns of probabilities. We do not even know whether, in the final analysis, it is composed of particles or waves. Indeed, the physicists' vision of matter is just as difficult to attain as the Taoist mystics' vision of the Tao.

2 Like the Taoists' vision of Nature, polar opposites in the world of modern physics, for example, wave and particle, electron and positron, matter and antimatter, are aspects of a fundamental reality. The universe is a unified entity. In the atomic world an object can only be discerned in terms of the interaction between the object and the observer. All things are interconnected.

There is, therefore, a remarkable parallel between the worldview obtained by theoretical and experimental research in modern physics and that achieved by meditation and intuition by the ancient followers of the Tao.

Since Tao is seen as the mother of all things, it has to be regarded as the source of all living as well as non-living things. It is, thus, appropriate for us to carry this exploration further to see if

Tao has anything to say about modern discoveries in biology, the study of living things.

· · · · · · · · · ·

Tao and Biology

The eminent role of nature in the Taoist worldview is reflected in the fact that through the centuries Taoist temples have been known exclusively as *kuan*, whereas Confucian and Buddhist temples are always called *ssu* or *miao*. The character *kuan* (Figure 2, page 172) is composed of two radicals. The one on the right means "to look or see." The one on the left is derived from an ancient graph that depicts a bird. Thus, *kuan*, could be taken to mean a place where one observes nature, both the nature around us and the nature within us.

We have already pointed out the importance of opposite polarities in Taoist thought. Beauty is defined by ugliness, goodness by evil. Both polar opposites exist within us. They are the defining qualities of our being. The ultimate polarities in the universe are *Yin* and *Yang*, two Chinese words that have become almost as familiar in the west as they are in the east. Originally, the two terms meant "shady" and "sunny," respectively. For example, the northern side of a mountain is *yin* and the southern side is *yang*. Then they came to mean "female" and "male." Finally, they became general terms for the fundamental yet opposite forces or principles of nature.

Indeed *Yin* and *Yang* are inherent attributes of nature. Chapter 42 of the *Tao Te Ching* tells us:

Tao gives birth to One,
One gives birth to Two,
Two gives birth to Three,
Three gives birth to all things.
All things have their backs to the *yin*
And stand facing the *yang*.
When the two principles combine,
All things achieve harmony.
—*(Mitchell, mod.)*

The dynamic character of *yin* and *yang* is illustrated in the ancient Chinese symbol called the *t'ai chi t'u* (Diagram of the Supreme Poles), shown in Figure 3 (page 174). The bright *yang* half and the dark *yin* half are shown to be in continuous rotation. The *yang*

FIGURE 2. *The Two Parts of the Character* Kuan.

returns cyclically to the beginning from maximum to minimum. It is then displaced by *yin*, which then returns cyclically to the beginning. The process continues without end. The two dots in the diagram convey the idea that when each one of the two forces reaches its maximum, it already contains within itself the seed of its opposite. This continuous reversion of the opposing attributes is the fundamental motion of Tao, as indicated in *Tao Te Ching*, Chapter 40, The Principle of Reversion:

> Reversion is the action of Tao,
> Gentleness is the function of Tao.
> The things of the world come from Being,
> Being comes from non-being.
> —*(Lin)*

Since Life is a form of Being, Life must arise from Non-being, that is, inanimate or lifeless matter. We are, of course, more accustomed to thinking that the opposite of Life is Death. In Taoist philosophy life and death are the opposing aspects (*yang* and *yin*) of a unified whole. This concept is beautifully expressed by Chuang-tzu, in his discourse on Life and Death:[15]

> Life is the companion of death, and death is the beginning of life. Who can appreciate the connection between the two? When a man is born it is but the embodiment of a spirit. When the spirit is embodied there is life, and when the spirit disperses, there is death. But if life and death are companions to each other, why should I be concerned? Therefore, all things are one. What we love is the mystery of life. What we hate is corruption in death. But the corruptible in its turn becomes mysterious life, and this mysterious life once more becomes corruptible.

Although Chuang-tzu is talking here about human life, there is no reason to think why the passage should not apply to all forms of life on earth. Thus, life itself does not remain static and it becomes possible to conceive of one form of life changing into another. This idea is implied in another passage from the Chuang-tzu:[16]

> All species contain certain germs. These germs, when in water, become *chüeh*. In a place bordering upon water and land, they become lichens or algae, like what we call the 'clothes of frogs

FIGURE 3. *Diagram of the Supreme Poles.*

and oysters'. On the bank they become *ling-hsi*. Reaching fertile soil the *ling-hsi* become *wu-tsu*. The roots of this give rise to *ch'i-ts'ao*, the leaves become *hu-tieh*, or *hsü*. The *hu-tieh* later changes into an insect, born in the chimney corner, which has the appearance of newly formed skin. Its name is *ch'ü-to*. After a thousand days the *ch'ü-to* becomes a bird called *han-yu-ku*, the saliva of which becomes the *ssu-mi*. The *ssu-mi* becomes a winefly, and from this in turn comes the *i-lu*. . . . Mosquitoes are produced from the rotting *huan* . . . [which] produce the horse, which ultimately produces man. Man again goes back into the germs. All (living) things come from the germs and return to the germs.

It is an extremely difficult passage for the translator, as the identity of many of the living forms referred to is long lost. It is probably inspired by what the ancient Chinese knew of the metamorphosis of insects. Some of the transformations are based on highly dubious observations. Nevertheless, the passage remains noteworthy in its recognition that existing forms of life are not immutable and that one form of life can evolve into another. Other passages in Chuang-tzu (as pointed out by Needham, *SCC* II, p. 79) denote an awareness of the struggle for existence among animals and the notion of the survival of the fittest.[17]

Although the *yin-yang* symbol gives equal play to both feminine and masculine elements of life, it should be noted that in the very term *yin-yang*, the feminine *yin* precedes the masculine *yang*. Indeed, the *Tao Te Ching*, wherever appropriate, tends to emphasize the role of the feminine aspect of Tao in the universe and those qualities which characterize the female—childbearing, forbearance instead of dominance, kindness instead of hostility, and gentleness instead of harshness. For example, Chapter 6 of the *Tao Te Ching* (The Spirit of the Valley) says:

> The Spirit of the Valley never dies.
> It is called the Mysterious Feminine.
> The Door of the Mysterious Feminine
> Is the Root of Heaven and Earth.
> It is like a veil barely seen.
> Use it and it will never fail.
>
> —*(Lin, Feng-English, mod.)*

We see the theme repeated in Chapter 28, Keeping to the Female:

> He who is aware of the Male
> But keeps to the Female

Becomes the Valley of the World.
To be the Valley of the World is
To move constantly in the path of Virtue
Without swerving from it
And to return again to (the innocence of) Infancy.
    —*(Lin, mod.)*

It is repeated in Chapter 61, Big and Small Countries:

A great country is like the lowland towards which all
    streams flow.
It is the reservoir of all under heaven, the Feminine of the
    world.
The Feminine always conquers the Masculine by her
    quietness,
by lowering herself through her quietness.
    —*(Wu)*

It is, thus, not surprising that in the *Tao Te Ching* Tao is usually
perceived as the Mother—but never the Father—of the myriad
creatures ("ten thousand things") in the universe. The stress on
the feminine complements another metaphor that is used to
denote the character of the Tao—water, which like the Tao flows
into the lowest level that is available for occupation, as stated in
Chapter 8, Water:

The highest goodness is like water.
It benefits all the ten thousand creatures
But does not compete with them.
It dwells in the lowly places that all disdain,
Wherein it comes near to the Tao.
    —*(Wu, Lin, mod.)*

In spite of the leaning towards the feminine qualities of
tolerance, compassion, and mercy, a key concept of Taoism is that
Tao is entirely impersonal and impartial in its manifestations. This
is stated in Chapter 5, Nature:

Heaven-and-earth is not sentimental,
It treats all things as straw-dogs.[18]
The Sage is not sentimental
He treats all his people as straw-dogs.
    —*(Wu)*

This passage tells us that Tao does not look at living things and what happens to them through human eyes. What is considered predatory to a human, may be natural to another creature. Chuang-tzu has expounded this idea in a story:[19]

> Prime Minister Tang of Shang asked Chuang-tzu about love.
> "Tigers and wolves are loving animals," said Chuang-tzu.
> "What do you mean?"
> "The tiger loves his cub. Why isn't he a loving animal?"
> "What about perfect kindness?" asked the prime minister.
> "Perfect kindness has no regard for particular relations."

Let us summarize what we have considered as Taoist concepts that I think are relevant to modern discoveries in Biology.

1 Being arises from non-being. Life must have evolved from lifeless matter when *yin* and *yang* are harmonized in a particular configuration.
2 *Yin* and *yang* follow each other in continuous rotation. Life and non-life (death) must also follow each other continuously. Within the rotations, changes in life forms can occur. Life and death are the polar opposites of a unified whole—all of existence.
3 In natural processes *yin* (the female) plays a greater role than *yang* (male).
4 Nature is impartial and unsentimental. It is not influenced by human values in its evolutionary manifestations.

Now let us see what modern science can tell us about the nature and behavior of living things, how they arose, and why there is such a bewildering variety of them. The key to our understanding of these issues was discovered more than a hundred years ago, in 1859, when Darwin published his epoch-making book, *On the Origin of Species by Means of Natural Selection, or the Preservation of Favoured Races in the Struggle for Life*, now known simply as *The Origin of Species*. In a nutshell, new species of life evolve from existing species through natural selection. A great deal has been learnt about the mechanics of evolution through progress in the life sciences since Darwin first propounded his theory, particularly through discoveries in genetics and molecular biology. Today, we can briefly sketch the natural history of living things on our planet as follows:[20]

1 *Chemical Evolution.* Life began with the rise of self-replicating molecules (replicators) from the primordial soup on the earth's surface. The most successful species (RNA or DNA) presumably crowded out other replicating molecules that might have also been formed. (But error can sometimes occur during replication. Not all copies were faithful to the original—thus we have mutations.) These "naked" replicators presumably kept on replicating until the raw materials available (i.e., food) began to run out.

2 *Evolution of Cells.* Replicators found it useful to be enveloped in a sort of membrane, thus giving rise to organelles. The membrane protected the replicator and helped it to retain food that had diffused into the organelle. The organelles evolved into unicellular organisms, and the replicators became what we know as genes. In the prokaryotes the genes are distributed within the cell; in eukaryotes they are assembled into a nucleus. The genes can now only replicate when cells divide and multiply. Multicellular organisms then evolved from the single-cell organisms.

3 *Evolution of Higher Animals and Plants.* Some organisms then developed the capability to reproduce by sexual fusion, during which the genes from two individuals were mixed and the rearranged genes handed down to the offspring. The process greatly enhanced the chance of evolving new variants in a species. In most higher animals only the female can bear the young, and thus the female of the species takes on a larger role in the propagation of the species. The enormous variety of plants and animals that exist on planet earth is a vivid indication of the power and wonder of the evolutionary process. This phase culminates in the evolution of *Homo sapiens.*

4 *Exogenetic Evolution.* With the advent of *Homo sapiens,* evolution has entered a new phase, one that is based on our capacity to think and feel. This new phase no longer deals exclusively with genes, but rather with products of the human mind and emotion, *viz,* intuition, knowledge, know-how, and products thereof, such as books, laws, customs, religious practices, and technological inventions. They have enabled mankind to develop the great civilizations of the world, marked by magnificent accomplishments in religion, art, literature, science, and technology.

The driving force behind the first three processes, that is, the evolution of inanimate chemicals into replicators, replicators into cells, and cells into whole animals and plants, is the imperative of replicators to keep on replicating. The ones most stable (or in Darwinian terminology, the fittest) in the environment will survive and endure. The replicator has only one purpose in its existence, that is, to make as many copies of itself and its progenies (and their progenies) as possible. This singlemindedness of purpose is carried over when replicators become genes enveloped in cells and when cells evolve into organisms. All the types of behavior of animals and plants can be explained in this way. As Richard Dawkins pointed out in his book *The Selfish Gene*, the unit of natural selection is not the species, not the individual, but rather the gene. In Dawkins's view the organism is merely the vehicle, the so-called "survival machine," which protects the genes and through which genes can exert their influence. Individual organisms live and die, but the gene can almost live on forever, provided their survival machines reproduce before they die. In anthropocentric terms, the gene is selfish. Thus, by nature an individual living thing, plant, animal, or human being, is basically selfish. It will only look out for itself or its own kind.

It goes without saying that a human society based solely on the gene's selfish ruthlessness, would be a vicious society in which to live. But fortunately, as we ascend into the evolution of humans, another factor begins to come into play, that is, evolution of the products of the human mind, which Medawar has called exogenetic heredity.[21] These are human ideas and artifacts which are transmitted (or replicated) from one generation to another. Thus, human values such as love, kindness, generosity, etc., can evolve, be selected, and taught even though such qualities go against the grain of the selfish gene. Dawkins has called these exogenetic factors "memes." They are replicated by being copied from one human mind to another.

We can now consider how these discoveries compare with the teachings of the *Tao Te Ching*:

1   Tao is in consonance with the evolution of replicators, cells, and organisms from inanimate matter that we have outlined.
2   Mutations occur constantly; hence, new forms of life are being evolved all the time. Thus, the theory of evolution does not conflict with Taoist thought.
3   In sexual reproduction, as in the manifestations of Tao, the female usually plays a more prominent role than the male.

4 Human ideas and values are part of the Tao; they have their own *yin* and *yang* aspects. Thus, when there is selfishness, its polar opposite, love, cannot be far behind.

All in all, Taoist philosophy is remarkably receptive to modern currents of biological science.

· · · · · · · · · ·

Taoism and Christianity

By now it should be clear to all readers who are Christians that there is an important difference between Taoism and Christianity. Tao is entirely impersonal and impartial, but in the Christian view God is intensely personal and partisan. And yet, in many respects, Christian and Taoist ideas show a remarkable consonance. First of all, there is an unmistakable affinity between the Christian idea of God and the Taoist idea of Tao. Take, for example, the opening passage of the Gospel according to Saint John:[22]

In the beginning was the Word, and the Word was with God, and the Word was God. He was in the beginning with God; all things were made through him, and without him was not anything made that was made.

This mystical passage has a distinct Taoist flavour. Indeed, one could replace "Word" with "Tao," and it would read like a chapter from the *Tao Te Ching*.

Tao has been translated into English most often as *Way*. Is it a coincidence that the early Christians were known as the people of the *Way* or those who followed the *Way* of God? It was Jesus himself who first started to use the word *Way*.[23]

"And when I go and prepare a place for you, I will come again and will take you to myself, that where I am, you may be also; and where I am going you know, and the *Way* you know." But Thomas replied, "Lord, we do not know where you are going. How can we know the *Way?*" Jesus said to him, "I am the *Way*, and the Truth and the Life, and no man can come to the Father but by me."

Way was already used to identify Christians before the conversion of St. Paul:[24]

But Saul, still breathing threats and murder against the disciples of the Lord, went to the high priest and asked for letters to the synagogues at Damascus, so that if he found any belonging to the *Way*, men or women, he might bring them bound to Jerusalem.

Later, Paul himself was proud to say that he followed the Way.[25] But even for those who profess to know the Way, the nature of God remained a mystery and has remained throughout the history of Christianity. Let us hear what Saint John Chrysostom, one of the early fathers of the Church, had to say about God in the fourth century:[26]

God's judgments are inscrutable, his ways inaccessible. His peace passes all understanding. The gifts which he has prepared for them that love Him are more than human hearts can imagine. His grace has no bounds, his intelligence is unimaginable. If all these things are incomprehensible, how could He Himself be comprehensible?

This theme was echoed by Saint Thomas Aquinas almost a thousand years later in the thirteenth century:[27]

Wherefore man reaches the highest point of his knowledge about God when he knows that he knows him not, inasmuch as he knows that that which is God transcends whatever he conceives of him.

Thus, in the tradition of the early and medieval Christian Church, God is the Word and the Way. He is incomprehensible and transcends human understanding. As we have seen, Tao is the Word and the Way, and Tao is beyond comprehension.

Secondly, there is a similarity in the way Christians and Taoists perceive the relationship between the high and mighty and the lowly and meek. One of the most moving passages from the New Testament is the Magnificat from the Gospel according to Saint Luke, in which the expectant Mary, in praise of God, sang:[28]

He hath showed strength with his arm, he hath scattered
 the proud in the imagination of their hearts.
He hath put down the mighty from their seats, and hath
 exalted the humble and meek.

He hath filled the hungry with good things and the rich he hath sent empty away.

This theme, that God is on the side of the poor and the downtrodden, was repeated often by Jesus during his ministry. Here are a few samples from the Gospel according to Saint Matthew:

Blessed are the poor in spirit: for theirs is the kingdom of heaven.
Blessed are the meek: for they shall inherit the earth. (5:3)
But many that are first will be last, and the last first. (19:30)
Whosoever shall exalt himself shall be abased; and he that shall humble himself shall be exalted. (23:12)

Similar sentiments are also prominent in the *Tao Te Ching:*

Therefore, the Sage puts himself last,
And finds himself in the foremost place.
Regards his body as accidental,
And his body is thereby preserved. (Chapter 7)   —*(Lin)*
To be proud with wealth and honor
Is to sow the seeds of ones own downfall. (Chapter 9)   —*(Lin)*
Truly, one may gain by losing
And one may lose by gaining. (Chapter 42)   —*(Wu)*

Lastly, perhaps the most astonishing coincidence is the presence of a doctrine of the Holy Trinity in both Christian and Taoist theology. This doctrine was a matter of intense debate in the early Christian Church; it was finally adopted at the Council of Nicea in AD 325. We have no idea how the Taoist concept of Trinity came about. It may have had its origin in Chapter 42 of the *Tao Te Ching* (quoted earlier, page 171), which says that "Tao gives birth to One, One to Two, and Two to Three; and Three gives birth to all things." In any case, the belief in a trinity of three supreme beings was already a part of Chinese popular religion in the second century BC, while Taoism as an institutional religion did not come into existence until the second century AD.[29] There is no evidence that the Taoist Trinity was in any way influenced by Christian theology or *vice versa.* After the idea was fully adopted by the Taoist religion, the three deities became known as the "Three Pure Ones" (*San-ch'ing*). We can still see their images enshrined in the major Taoist temples in China today.

This fascination with Trinity is carried further both in the New Testament and in the *Tao Te Ching*. In I Corinthians 13:13, Saint Paul said:

So Faith, Hope, Love abide, these three; but the greatest of these is Love.

Let us compare this statement with the triad of virtues cited in Chapter 67 of the *Tao Te Ching*:

I have three treasures; guard them and keep them safe.
The first is Love,
The second is Frugality,
The third is Humility.
Having Love, I can be courageous;
Being Frugal I can afford to be generous;
Being Humble, I can learn the wisdom of the world.
—*(Wu, Lau, Lin, mod.)*

Love is central to both religions, but I cannot help noticing that besides Love the other virtues Saint Paul stresses, Faith and Hope, are *yang* values, whereas those stressed by the *Tao Te Ching*, Frugality and Humility, are *yin* values. Clearly humanity needs both sets of values. These differences in emphasis do not nullify the fact that there are strong sympathetic echoes between Taoist philosophy and Christianity.

From this exploration of the connections between Taoism, modern science, and Christianity, it seems to me that several strains of Taoist thought deserve our attention when we consider the survival of the human race.

First, Nature is impartial. Evolution is impartial. It will be folly to think that in the on-going process of biological evolution the survival of the human race would be automatically favored.

Second, *yin* and *yang* characters are part of our nature. Both good and evil are within us. Hence, our worst enemy is ourselves. To counteract the destructive manifestations of our "selfish genes" we need to cultivate and strengthen the unselfish tendencies we hold in our exogenetic, cultural heritage.

Third, we are a part of Nature, not above it or beyond it. We must respect and follow the Order of Nature, and balance the *yin* and *yang* forces on our planet so that human society and Nature can coexist in a stable, unified, and harmonious whole.

With this note, I would like to close this paper with one more quotation from the *Tao Te Ching*, Chapter 56:

He who knows does not speak,
He who speaks does not know.

· · · · · · · · · ·

Notes

1. When I arrived at Chicago for the World's Parliament of Religions on 27 August 1993, I was greeted by a headline on the front page of the *Chicago Sun-Times*, "Religious Leaders Flock to Chicago." On the second page, there was a list of the twenty major religions of the world. Confucianism was one of them, but Taoism was not. I hope, in a small way, this article will help to make Taoism better known to the religious communities and the public in the Western world.
2. Lin Yutang, *The Wisdom of Laotse* (New York: Modern Library, 1948), p. 4.
3. *Ibid.*
4. Quoted by Joseph Needham, *Science and Civilisation in China*, Vol. 2 (Cambridge: Cambridge University Press, 1956), p. 33.
5. Biography of Lao-tzu in the *Shi Chi* (*Records of the Historian*) by Ssu-ma Ch'ien, 90 BC. The passage is quoted in D.C. Lau's translation of the *Tao Te Ching*, (Harmondsworth: Penguin Books, 1963), p. 8.
6. *Ibid.*, p. 7.
7. Robert G. Henricks, *Lao-tzu: Te Tao Ching: A New Translation Based on the Recently Discovered Ma-wang-tui Texts* (New York, Ballantine Books, 1989).
8. H. G. Creel, *What is Taoism? and Other Studies in Chinese Cultural History* (Chicago: University of Chicago Press, 1970), p. 55.
9. In this and subsequent passages from the *Tao Te Ching*, the names of translators whose versions are utilized are given at the end of the quotation. The modifications, if any, are mine.
10. Wang-tsit Chan, *The Way of Lao Tzu* (Indianapolis: Bobbs-Merrill, 1963). This translation is not listed in Table 1.
11. Alan Watts, *Tao: The Watercourse Way* (New York: Pantheon Books, 1975), p. 41.
12. Quoted in Fritjof Capra, *The Tao of Physics* (Boston: Shambhala, 1975), p. 56.
13. *Ibid.*, pp. 61–62.
14. Arthur Eddington, *The Nature of the Physical World* (Cambridge: Cambridge University Press, 1928), p. 318.
15. *Chuang-tzu*, Chapter 22, section 1. Cf. Lin Yutang, *ibid.*, p. 234 (50: 1).
16. *Chuang-tzu*, Chapter 18, section 6; trans. by Hu Shih, *The Development of the Logical Method in Ancient China* (Shanghai: Oriental Book Co., 1922), p. 135; quoted in Joseph Needham, *Science and Civilisation in China*, Vol. 2, pp. 78–79.
17. Joseph Needham, *Science and Civilisation in China*, Vol. 2, p. 79.

18. According to section 3, Chapter 14 (*T'ien yün*) of *Chuang-tzu*, "straw dogs were treated with the greatest deference before they were used as an offering, only to be discarded and trampled upon as soon as they had served their purpose." Cf. D. C. Lau, *ibid.*, p. 61.
19. *Chuang-tzu*, Chapter 13, section 2, trans. Lin Yutang, *ibid.*, p. 67.
20. Richard Dawkins, *The Selfish Gene* (Oxford: Oxford University Press, 1976; 2nd ed., 1989). The ideas expressed in this summary are based largely on Dawkins's explanation of the process of evolution.
21. P. B. Medawar and J. S. Medawar, *Aristotle to Zoos* (Cambridge, MA: Harvard University Press, 1983), pp. 94–97.
22. John 1: 1–4 (all New Testament translations are from the Revised Standard Version)
23. John 14: 4–6.
24. Acts of the Apostles 9: 2.
25. Acts of the Apostles 24: 14, 22.
26. St. John Chrysostom, *On the Incomprehensibility of God* (*Peri Akataleptou Theou*), trans. R. Flacelière, with Introduction by F. Cavallera and J. Daniélou (Paris: Cerf, 1951), p. 706c.
27. *De Potentia*, q. 7, art. 5. English translation, *On the Power of God* (London: Burns, Oates & Washbourne, 1932–34), Vol. 3, p. 33.
28. Luke 1: 46–56.
29. Julia Ching, *Chinese Religions* (Maryknoll, NY: Orbis Books, 1993), pp. 103–4, and 113–14. See also John Blofeld, *Taoism: the Road to Immortality* (Boston: Shambhala, 1978).

. . . .

The Ultimate Origin of the Universe Is Unknowable

1 What are your views on cosmic beginnings, particularly with reference to the origin of the universe, of life, and of *Homo sapiens*?

The Big Bang theory provides a satisfactory explanation of how the present universe came into being, but we still have no idea of what was there before the Big Bang. Thus, the ultimate origin of the universe is unknowable.

The wonder and diversity of life on Earth can be explained by the theory of evolution, by the progression from inanimate matter to self-replicating molecules (genes), to plants and animals, and finally to *Homo sapiens*. But something is gained in each stage in the progression that cannot be deduced from the laws of physics and chemistry. Aristotle (fourth century BC) introduced the concept of *psyche* or 'spirit' to denote this something extra in terms of levels of being.

Matter: Inanimate
Plants: Vegetative spirit
Animals: Vegetative spirit + sensitive spirit
Human: Vegetative spirit + sensitive spirit + rational spirit

We can interpret Aristotle's 'rational spirit' as those attributes which make *Homo sapiens* human, that is, the capacity to love, to think, to appreciate beauty and experience a sense of the numinous. How did such entities as 'sensitive spirit' and 'rational spirit' evolve, and where do they come from? Perhaps the "spirits" are inherent properties of all matter which only become manifest when the appropriate level of organization is achieved. How such spirits emerge from matter remains obscure. Thus, a large element of mystery remains in our understanding of the origin of life and *Homo sapiens*.

2 What are your views on human ends, especially as this relates to the framework of cosmic beginnings?

Human ends will depend on the future course of biological evolution. Popper claims that biological organisms possess *a priori* knowledge which can influence the course of evolution. If he is right evolution can be active as well as passive which implies that *Homo sapiens* has the ability to influence what happens to his own future. But at the same time evolution is subject to cosmological forces that are totally outside the control of humans on earth. Evolution, like Tao, is impartial and unsentimental. Above all, it is unpredictable.

I suspect *Homo sapiens* will last a long time on earth if he does not pursue policies that will destroy himself or the environment in which he lives. But there is no guarantee.

3 What do you think should be the relationship between religion and science?

Religion and science are two vital aspects of human experience. The relationship between the two should be one of mutual respect. "Render under Caesar the things that are Caesar's, and unto God the things that are God's." It will be tragic for human existence if religion dominates science or *vice versa*.

11

Gaia: Cosmic Beginnings, Nonhuman Ends

Lynn Margulis and Michael Dolan

Lynn Margulis, a Distinguished University Professor in the Department of Biology at the University of Massachusetts, Amherst, is best known for her research and writings championing the Gaia hypothesis (with James Lovelock) and the symbiotic theory of cell evolution, two of the most influential departures from mainstream biology today. A current member of the National Academy of Sciences, she chaired from 1977 to 1980 their Space Science Board Committee on Planetary Biology and Chemical Evolution. She is a co-director of NASA's Planetary Biology Internship (PBI) and is active in the development of science teaching materials at levels from elementary and middle schools to graduate schools.

Michael Dolan is a graduate student in the Organismic and Evolutionary Biology program with Lynn Margulis at the University of Massachusetts, Amherst, having collaborated with her and Karlene Schwartz on the writing of *The Illustrated Five Kingdoms: A Guide to the Diversity of Life on Earth.*

Abstract

By focusing on the totality of life on Earth (as a component with the atmosphere and lithosphere of a single self-regulating system), the Gaia perspective deals with planetary phenomena rather than human biology. The nonhuman ends implicit in the hypothesis have implications for how we view nature, how we address environmental problems, and how we organize science itself. Rather than facing an inert environment, the biota produces and is produced by its environment in a continually changing global ecosystem. The gaian perspective on environmental problems such as the rising CO_2 level reveals the fundamental, long-term Earth processes that conventional environmental science ignores. Rather than fragmenting science into exclusive disciplines, the Gaia hypothesis calls for an integration of biology with geology and climatology. With an organic orientation the Gaia hypothesis exposes the limits of mechanistic, reductionist science.

The Gaia hypothesis holds that "the atmosphere, the oceans, the climate and the crust of the Earth are regulated at a state comfortable for life because of the behavior of living organisms.

Specifically, the Gaia hypothesis said that the temperature, oxidation state, acidity, and certain aspects of the rocks and waters are at any time kept constant, and that this homeostasis is maintained by active feedback processes operated automatically and unconsciously by the biota" (Lovelock 1988). The basic tenet of Lovelock's Gaia hypothesis (in contrast to either the prevalent strictly physicochemical concept of Earth or Vladimir Vernadsky's view [1945] of life as a special kind of moving matter) is that life acts physiologically to regulate the global environment (Margulis and West 1993). The regulation results from the consequences of growth and metabolic activities of those organisms prevailing at the moment. What is usually considered to be the "physical environment," the atmosphere, oceans, and land, is part of the gaian system connected through space (by atmospheric and hydrospheric interaction) and through time (by life's evolution). The gaian view rejects the claim that the background for life is an inert physical environment. The environment is inseparable from the living. The rocks, the air, the biota, and the water are parts of a continually changing global ecosystem at Earth's surface. As we regard Earth's surface, life enmeshed in its surroundings, as a single set of ecosystems, our attitude toward the planet dramatically changes. The extensive modifications of the global environment by human population expansion, deforestation, and urbanization are ominous not for gaian regulation, which reflects the activities of all organisms on the planet, but for gaian regulations around values of temperatures and atmospheric composition best for humans. Indeed, the new gaian regulatory values are likely to be best not for humans but for those organisms that thrive on human waste.

The Gaia hypothesis was developed beginning in the late sixties as J. E. Lovelock was requested by committees of NASA to help seek life on Mars. He contrasted the atmosphere of Earth with that of Mars, noting how Earth's exists in a state of chemical disequilibrium: relatively large amounts of oxygen (O_2) are present simultaneously with gases highly reactive with oxygen such as nitrogen (N_2), methane (CH_4), and even hydrogen (H_2). Whereas Earth's atmosphere contains only a small relative quantity of carbon dioxide (0.03% CO_2), the atmospheres of its neighbors Mars and Venus are composed mostly of carbon dioxide (> 90%) as shown in Figure 1 (facing page).

In recent years the Gaia hypothesis has been used to predict the biological production of compounds such as dimethyl sulfide

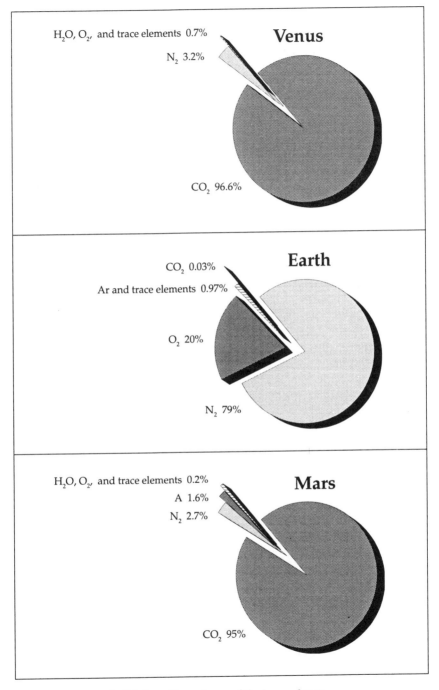

FIGURE 1.   *Atmospheres of the inner planets.*

and methyl iodide, required to transfer essential elements from the oceans to the land surfaces. Climate regulation via cloud formation is suggested to be linked to algal sulfur gas emissions. Lovelock has further developed the hypothesis by augmenting it with mathematical models (Lovelock 1988). He has introduced or re-introduced concepts such as planetary medicine and geophysiology to help describe its regulatory properties (Lovelock 1991).

While Gaia has presented exciting new ways of viewing Earth, the evolution of its environment, and its natural chemical processes, it has also profoundly influenced debate over humanity's place in nature. The Gaia idea generates philosophical query into nature and into the organization of scientists and their sciences. Gaia concepts require that we replace our priority on human ends with concern for nonhuman life. Microbial organisms (e.g., microbes, bacteria, protists, fungi; see Figure 2, facing page) have a place in Gaia far more crucial than as "disease agents" in humans. Environmental problems of people are perceived as part of Gaia's long-term future, with or without humanity. Gaian analyses seriously challenge the structure of scattered, mutually-exclusive scientific disciplines and the conventional responses of scientists and other rationalizers to environmental problems. Perhaps most importantly, the mechanistic philosophy of conventional science itself is called into question.

· · · · · · · · ·

Nonhuman Ends

The growing number of environmental concerns associated with industrialization and urbanization include air pollution, the greenhouse effect, the ozone hole, soil erosion, cancer, radioactive and chemical waste, and deforestation (Figures 3A, 3B, 3C, pages 194, 196, and 198, respectively). In recent years reaction to fears of increases in these effects has sparked a widespread concern for environmental protection; the rally cry expresses itself as a desire to "Save the Earth!" Naturally enough the focus has primarily centered on people: how we're being made sick, poisoned, or denied our needed resources. By hypothesizing a planetary entity that regulates itself by changing the chemical composition of the atmosphere and the surface sediments, Gaia adds a radical twist to our understanding of Earth and our place here. Not humans but microbes, in the interactions with plants and other animals, have become the most important organisms on the planet. Only

Prokaryotic microbes

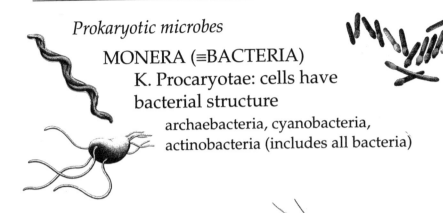

MONERA (≡BACTERIA)

K. Procaryotae: cells have bacterial structure

archaebacteria, cyanobacteria,
actinobacteria (includes all bacteria)

Eukaryotic microbes

PROTOCTISTS

K. Protoctista: eukaryotic microbes and their larger descendants

diatoms and other algae,
slime nets, water
molds, amebas,
ciliates, slime molds, etc.

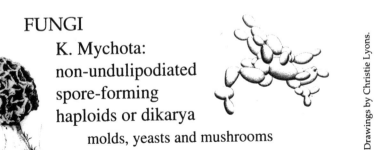

FUNGI

K. Mychota: non-undulipodiated spore-forming haploids or dikarya

molds, yeasts and mushrooms

Drawings by Christie Lyons.

FIGURE 2. *Microorganisms of the Five Kingdoms (microorganism = microbe, a living being visualized with a microscope).*

microbes produce food from nitrogen in the atmosphere (N_2 fixation), generate methane under oxygen-poor conditions (thus returning carbon to the air), and produce dimethyl sulfide, necessary to bring sulfur from the ocean (where it is plentiful, to the land, where it is in short supply and needed to make protein). Only bacteria, inside or outside plant cells, fix CO_2 into usable organic compounds for food and energy. Microbes and plants influence the albedo (reflectivity of light) through cloud formation far more than do animals. On land especially the action of microbes is augmented by environmental maintenance by plants. Trees and herbs make food and air. Fungi and bacteria clean and maintain moisture. In short, Gaia calls for a reorientation toward plant ends, fungal ends, coccolithophorid and other protoctisto-logical ends, cyanobacterial ends, and methanogenic bacterial ends (Table 1). What these organisms do is far more important, from a planetary perspective, than what humans do. The largely unseen planetary processes, the so-called "ecosystem services", i.e., the oxygen, carbon, and nitrogen cycles, the transfer of sulfur and iodine from the sea to the land, the genesis of cloud cover, all are directly regulated by microbes, not by people.

TABLE 1. Microbial Contributions to Gaia

Group of microbes	Examples	Uses/Metabolic modes
Prokaryotes	cyanobacteria	conversion of sunlight into usable energy; sugar and oxygen producers
	sulfur bacteria	removal of hydrogen sulfide; producer of elemental sulfur and sulfate; conversion of sunlight into usable energy
	methane bacteria	production and removal of methane; influences oxygen concentrations
	nitrogen fixers	provision of usable nitrogen from air to food
Protoctists	coccolithophorids	food, oxygen, sulfur gases, cloud cover
	diatoms	food for marine life; secrete silica (opal)
	foraminifera	help to find petroleum reserves
	green, brown, and red algae	food for marine life; energy and food from sunlight and carbon dioxide
Fungi	mushrooms	supply nitrogen and phosphorus to plant roots
	molds	recycle dead animal bodies

In elaborating on the Gaia hypothesis in his first book (1979), Lovelock explicitly indicated the preeminent role of microbes:

> The parts of the Earth responsible for planetary control may still be those which carry the vast hordes of microorganisms. The algae of the sea and of the soil surface use sunlight to perform the prime task of living chemistry, photosynthesis. They still turn over half of the Earth's supply of carbon, in co-operation with the aerobic decomposers of the soil and the sea-bed, together with the anaerobic microflora in the great mud zones of the continental shelves, sea bottom, marshes, and wetlands. The large animals, plants, and seaweeds may have important specialist functions, but the greater part of Gaia's self-regulating activity could still be conducted by micro-organisms.

We concur with his advice against too drastically disturbing those regions where planetary control is likely to be strongest: swamps, marshes, and other wetlands, and especially the regions of the continental shelves. Tropical lakes, rivers, and forests need protection from our rapacious intent that so often results in denuding the land and irreparably drying it out.

It follows, then, that many of the environmental concerns that preoccupy us are no great problem to gaian environmental maintenance, while matters vital to Gaia are ignored by us. As Lovelock bluntly put it,

> Gaia theory forces a planetary perspective. It is the health of the planet that matters, not that of some individual species of organisms. This is where Gaia and the environmental movements part company. The health of the Earth is most threatened by changes in natural ecosystems. Agriculture, forestry, and to a lesser extent, fishing are seen as the most serious sources of this kind of damage with the inexorable increase of the greenhouse gases, carbon dioxide, methane, and several others coming next (Lovelock 1988).

From this perspective the sensitive areas such as the tropical moist forests should be preserved as carbon sinks and climate regulators; they ought not be removed. This gaian pronouncement obviously has different implications for human economy than conventional environmental analysis offers. (How much do we reward Brazilians for preserving their forests as "air conditioners of Earth"?) But Gaia is not necessarily anti-human in its orienta-

FIGURE 3A. *Rhondonia, Brazil: burning the forest (NASA Landsat photos courtesy C. J. Tucker).*

tion, it's simply nonhuman. To paraphrase Lovelock, we should not delude ourselves that we are managing the Earth; we should appreciate that it manages us.

This disparity between gaian versus human views of humanity's place in nature has long-term implications as well. In short, the gaian environmental regulatory system does not need us. Humans play no vital role in gaian planetary maintenance and, particularly regarding the greenhouse gases, are instead seriously insulting it. If the current trend continues, carbon dioxide concentration may double in the next century, with a concomitant increase in global mean temperature. The anthropogenic CO_2 increase, including that resulting from deforestation in the tropics, could induce a gaian shift to a new atmospheric steady state with higher temperatures and CO_2 levels. Such a change would favor greater plant and microbial growth but not necessarily the kind of plants and microbes we prefer. As Lovelock suggests, "[T]he single-minded quest to save humankind conflicts with the greater need to sustain the Earth as a fit and comfortable place to live. If we lose our habitat, the system of life and its environment on Earth, Gaia will go on. But humankind will no longer be part of it" (Lovelock 1991).

. . . .

Gaian Science

The Gaia hypothesis holds that Earth's surface system is greater than the sum of its parts. Similarly, the hypothesis itself is greater than an explanation of maintenance of life on Earth. The Gaia hypothesis, in part due to Lovelock's unique career, challenges conventional science organization. Because it deals with the whole Earth, its atmospheric chemistry, geology, microbiology and evolutionary biology, and so forth, Gaia can not fit into any single fragmented discipline of science. No science department by itself can properly teach it. As with the research of Vladimir I. Vernadsky (1863–1945, Russia), G. Evelyn Hutchinson (1903–1991, UK and USA), Heinz A. Lowenstam (1912–1993, Germany and USA), and others, gaian research requires scientists to develop a familiarity with many disciplines and to integrate or synthesize the results of these fields, literally, into a single, organic worldview. Lovelock reintroduced the Gaia concept as "geophysiology." Its public vocation is planetary medicine.

The Gaia idea is less of an hypothesis than it is a radical change of scientific orientation, as Joseph (1990) described in his

FIGURE 3B.   *Rhondonia, Brazil: ground view of deforestation.*

history of the notion. Just the word "Gaia" generates a visceral negative response in certain scientists. The taking seriously of the gaian idea does threaten these investigators with exposure of their limitations and prejudices. Insight into the malaise of the specialist provoked in the philosophical discussion of "Gaia theory" at the American Geophysical Union, the first and only debate on Gaia in "polite scientific society", is described by Sagan (1988). One difficulty in "proving" the Gaia hypothesis is that its tests transcend any single traditional field of scientific inquiry (Margulis and Karlin 1994). Gaia hypothesis testing mandates interaction among scientists with different training. The hypothesis continues to be modified as communication between its proponents and critics accelerate. Geologists and climatologists recognize that many of the phenomena they measure have at least some microbiological and protoctistological aspects to them. Geologists begin to understand that sedimentation, stratigraphy, paleontology, and even geochemistry require some knowledge of microbes, including protoctists (like foraminiferans and coccolithophorids) and fungi that form and breakdown minerals. The study of biology experienced a similar revolution three decades ago as physical scientists made it clear that knowledge of chemistry was crucial to understanding biology. After early resistance, biologists embraced chemistry. Geologists and other environmental scientists do not yet study biology because they fail to see its relevance, but the Gaia hypothesis exposes the necessity of the study of microbiology, geology, and atmospheric science in understanding Earth. Evolutionary theory in the absence of knowledge of meteorology, chemistry, and geology is inadequate. This gaian viewpoint is not popular with scientists and instructors who prefer to continue their business as usual. Before gaian thinking is integrated into the rest of science, more academic disputation is expected.

The Gaia hypothesis represents a paradigm shift in that many a worldview involving interlocking assumptions are affected. Lovelock notes that the original Gaia hypothesis (Margulis and Lovelock 1974) was not so much controversial as it was just ignored. Although gaian ideas have generated both technical and popular science literature for twenty-five years (see Margulis and West 1993 for an extensive bibliographic list), only recently has it become part of mainstream scientific discussion. gaian research per se still has not been funded by government or other official agencies.

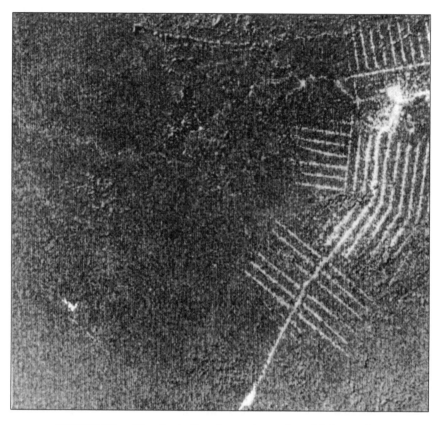

FIGURE 3C. *Rhondonia, Brazil: remote sensing of deforestation.*

Like dissected tissue samples in the search for the whole animal, the conventional disciplines can reveal only pieces of Gaia. Scientists, in general, have not faced up to the challenge of gaian environmental problems. As Lovelock again provocatively puts it,

> I am not saying that we do not need organized science; only that we need to recognize its frailty as a human institution, that it is slow, and its record in handling immediate environmental problems is far from good. It tends to do only those things that scientists find easy to do and want to do anyway. It concentrates almost obsessively on minor matters that happen to worry the public, such as carcinogens in the environment, or on phenomena in the stratosphere that are intensely interesting to scientists, but that are easily managed environmental problems requiring only common sense for their solution. I find it deplorable that so much scientific effort has gone to research the depletion of the ozone layer when the large issues, such as forest clearance and the atmospheric greenhouse, have been, relatively speaking, ignored (Lovelock 1991).

The microbial and plant contribution to acid precipitation, the insect-borne production of methane, an important greenhouse gas (Hackstein and Stumm 1994), and the human acceleration of desertification are other areas of gaian science that need research. But as "planetary physicians" (Lovelock 1991), with more of an organic than a mechanistic view of the Earth's processes, we realize that we cannot postpone decisions until results from all the research are in: chlorofluorocarbons contribute to greenhouse warming, so they must be seriously regulated and properly discarded, *today*; deforestation accelerates desertification and therefore should cease, *today*.

Even we still speak of "gaian mechanisms" as if Gaia were a machine. We admit that through this "bottom-up" conventional science, some of Gaia's details have been and will continue to be discovered. Yet this restricted, reductionist view cannot see Gaia as a whole and therefore must be supplemented. Neither ordinary atmospheric chemistry nor animal ecology could predict dimethyl sulfide production as the sulfur transfer medium for animals, for example. Gaia has, in short, exposed the limits of mechanistic science. In this way the gaian worldview opens new opportunities in science, beyond the fragmentation. "The Gaia hypothesis may well signal the emergence of just such a mature science—a

FIGURE 4. *James E. and Sandra Lovelock. The second international scientific meeting on Gaia organized by Sandy Lovelock took place at Oxford, England, in April 1994.*

FIGURE 5. *V. I. Vernadsky in 1911.*

science that seeks not to *control* the world but to *participate with* the world, not to operate on nature, but to co-operate with nature" (Abram 1988).

Such an organic view of the natural world was implicit in Vernadsky's work itself. "Actually no living organisms exist on Earth in a state of freedom. All organisms are connected indissolubly and uninterruptedly first of all, through nutrition and respiration, and secondly, with the circumambience material and its energetic medium" (Vernadsky 1945). Hutchinson (1957, 1967, 1975 and Hutchinson and Edmondson 1993) and Lowenstam (Lowenstam and Weiner 1989) were nearly the only western scientists to share Vernadsky's organic perspective. Although independently of Vernadsky, Lovelock's imaginative perspective from space of the living Earth greatly developed Vernadsky's views by showing the regulatory or physiological capacity of life to create and modify, control and moderate its own environment. (The two scientists are shown in Figures 4 and 5, facing page.)

The acceptance of the gaian viewpoint has many consequences. It is expected to alter our behavior toward each other and lead us to recognize that no science is "objective," for none can be seen from the outside. This shift in orientation will lead us, we hope, to see life as a planetary phenomenon—one far more complex, robust, and long-lived than the human portion. The preservation of many kinds of life transcends the aesthetic need for biodiversity because diversity is essential to gaian function, that is, to survival. Without the little-known and even less appreciated nitrogen, carbon, sulfur, and other metabolic modes of our bacterial, protoctist, and fungal planetmates (Table 1, page 192), we would die of thirst, asphyxiation, starvation, and constipation, to say nothing of boredom!

. . . .

References

D. Abram, "The Mechanical and the Organic: Epistemological Consequences of the Gaia Hypothesis," in *Gaia: the Thesis, the Mechanisms and the Implications*, P. Bunyard and E. Goldsmith, eds. (Cornwall: Wadebridge Ecological Centre, 1988).

J. H. P. Hackstein and C. K. Stumm, "Methane Production in Terrestrial Arthropods," Proc. Nat Acad. Sci., 1994, 91:5441–45.

G. E. Hutchinson, *A Treatise on Limnology*, 3 volumes (New York: John Wiley and Sons, 1957, 1967, 1975).

G. E. Hutchinson, and Y. H. Edmondson, *A Treatise on Limnology*, Volume IV (New York: John Wiley and Sons, 1993).

L. Joseph, *Gaia: Birth of an Idea* (New York: St. Martin's Press, 1990).

J. E. Lovelock, *Gaia: A New Look at Life on Earth* (New York: Oxford University Press, 1979).

————, *The Ages of Gaia: A Biography of Our Living Planet* (New York: W. W. Norton, 1988).

————, *Healing Gaia* (New York: Harmony Books, 1991).

H. A. Lowenstam and S. Weiner, *On Biomineralization* (New York: Oxford University Press, 1989).

L. Margulis, and E. F. Karlin, "Gaia, a New Look at the Earth's System," in *Technology and Global Environmental Issues*, W. J. Makofske and E. F. Karlin eds. (New York: HarperCollins, 1994).

L. Margulis and J. E. Lovelock, "Biological Modulation of the Earth's Atmosphere," *Icarus* 21 (1974), 471–489.

L. Margulis and O. West, "Gaia and the Colonization of Mars," *GSA Today* 3 (1993), 277–280, 291.

D. Sagan, "What Narcissus Saw: The Oceanic "I"/Eye," in *The Reality Club* 1, J. Brockman, ed. (New York: Prentice Hall, 1988).

————, *Biospheres: Metamorphosis of Planet Earth* (New York: McGraw-Hill, 1990).

V. Vernadsky, "The Biosphere and the Noosphere," *The American Scientist* 33 (1945), 1–12.

• • • • • • • • • •
A Part of the Whole Gaian System

1 What are your views on cosmic beginnings, particularly with reference to the origin of the universe, of life, and of *Homo sapiens*?

Scientists conclude, based on strong cosmological inference, that the universe originated between 10 and 20 billion years ago in the Big Bang. Our best guess now is that life originated on Earth through a type of spontaneous generation from carbon and nitrogen chemicals over 3.5 billion years ago. The details of this primordial spontaneous generation are hotly debated. First life was bacterial. Larger life evolved from symbiotic mergers of bacteria that formed nucleated cells. *Homo sapiens*, as well as all other animals, plants, fungi, and protoctists, are composed of nucleated cells, which means they evolved by "symbiogenesis." Thus all organisms larger than bacteria originated not only by accumulation of random mutation but also through a series of microbial fusions. Therefore, we humans are in fact composite beings. So are our food, our pets, and all other familiar forms of life. If we feel as if we are falling apart . . . it is because we are.

2 What are your views on human ends, especially as this relates to the framework of cosmic beginnings?

From a scientific perspective human history and civilization, which are very recent, played no significant role in the origin and evolution of the biosphere, which is very ancient. While we can seriously harm ourselves and perhaps even drive ourselves to extinction, people, even if we consciously strive to do so, cannot destroy all life on Earth. We call "Gaia" the concept that living beings make, regulate, and change their immediate aqueous, atmospheric, and terrestrial environments when they metabolize and grow. If we see ourselves as part of the whole gaian system, that is, a part of all interacting "life on Earth," we conclude there is a limit to our perversion. We *Homo sapiens* are only one of some 30,000,000 extant species of life. Rather than giving us a license to pollute as we please or to convert forest and prairie to stadium and shopping mall, this gaian view of Earth should lead us to humility and to recognize our place in the rest of the shockingly complex and unknown biosphere. Respect for our planetmates, the nonhuman life forms of Gaia, leads us to plant trees and limit our population growth. We might work to safeguard our planetwide support systems and learn to enjoy the microbes' munificence and the prodigality of plants.

3 What do you think should be the relationship between religion and science?

The gaian view is consistent with those religions, such as Buddhism, that deny the finality of purely human ends. The traditional Judeo-Christian and Moslem religions dismiss, oppose, or ignore science-faith contradictions. Scientific scenarios delegitimize religious myths. Most people have a vast tolerance for contradiction: peace lovers work on weaponry, conservationists purchase Brazilian hardwood sculpture, and cancer researchers smoke cigarettes. Scientists work at the lab bench one day, querying nature and leaving her to her own devices, and beseech special favors from an all-powerful God at church, temple, or mosque the next. Since western religion is irrational, it bears much less requirement to make sense or to be internally consistent than does science. Although many scientists may see science as "a controlling influence for the good in their lives," few would identify it as a "higher power" (the religious criterion). The relationship between western religions and modern science, then, is one of suspicion and antagonism. Science, basking in its arrogant conviction of its proximity to the truth, may free us from the religious superstition of the Inquisition while religion may protect us from giving free reign to the Nazi doctors and other fascist purveyors of the technological fix. That any influence, religious, scientific, or cultural, will reduce our propensity for coupling, procreating, and expanding the *Homo sapiens'* sphere of influence we judge doubtful. Thus it is all too easy to anticipate continued clashes of tribalism and self-righteous screeches of petty nationalism punctuated by rape and murder as part of the forthcoming human species' demise on a finite Earth.

12

The Smallest Cells Have Important Lessons to Teach

James A. Shapiro

James Shapiro is Professor of Microbiology in the Department of Biochemistry and Molecular Biology at the University of Chicago. His unusually broad academic experience includes undergraduate years at Harvard (B.A. in English Literature) and graduate studies in Cambridge (Ph.D. in genetics) followed by post-doctoral work in Paris and extended visits to Cuba, Israel, and Scotland, where in 1993 he was a Darwin Prize Visiting Professor in Edinburgh. The author of numerous scientific papers and an organizer of several international meetings, he is known worldwide for his fundamental research on the multicellular reactions of bacteria.

Abstract

The conventional wisdom about bacteria is that they are primitive, single-celled organisms. Actually, bacteria (the smallest living cells) are essential and sophisticated actors on the stage of life, often outwitting larger organisms for their own (the bacteria's) benefit. Bacteria have an intricate social life that provides them with many adaptive advantages. This means that multicellularity is not an invention of so-called "higher" organisms. Like all cells, bacteria are outstanding genetic engineers, and they have used this capacity to withstand antibiotic chemotherapy. Bacterial antibiotic resistance is one of the best-documented examples of evolution by natural genetic engineering. The discovery that genetic change results from regulated, biological processes instead of random errors and physico-chemical damage to DNA has profound implications for theories of life and evolution.

Changes in the Way We Think about Nature

This setting offers the working scientist the challenge to communicate intelligibily with a diverse audience of non-specialists and the opportunity to deal with some of the broader and more fundamental implications of one's research, which must normally focus on very detailed and highly technical questions. As a microbiologist who studies often underappreciated cells, I find it interesting that the title of the symposium, "From Cosmic Beginnings to Human Ends," covers vast realms of nature but yet is far from comprehensive. I hope that we can focus some of our attention on the majority of the living world which is not human, because it is imperative to see humanity in the context of nature as a whole. Our perspectives on the human place in the natural order have undergone dramatic changes over time, and they continue to develop. If we simply compare the ways we look at mankind today with the way our predecessors did one hundred years ago we can all agree that there have been some very dramatic changes in thinking.

Major conceptual changes have occured in science over the past century. Our view of how nature is organized has shifted dramatically, away from Cartesian reductionism and Cartesian dualism towards a more connectionist or integral view of nature. While this movement actually began in the physical sciences, it is most dramatically accelerating in the life sciences. More and more, my colleagues and I now think about the interdependency of all life. We emphasize ecology and symbiosis and the interactions between different organisms. Scientifically, we must see humanity as part of the natural order and not as its master. Further, the great advances in microelectronics, computers, and information systems (which may be thought of as a kind of silicon-based life) have made it easier for us to recognize the central roles that communication, information processing, and control play in vital systems at all levels of biological organization. This trend truly represents a reintegration of soma and psyche.

· · · · · · · · · ·

Bacteria as Victims of Prejudice and Sustainers of the Biosphere

The conceptual movements away from reductionism and dualism have been particularly helpful in making sense of many new discoveries about the organisms I study: bacteria, the smallest living cells which have long been the victims of prejudice. It has periodically been fashionable in biology to disregard bacteria as atypical because they lack the same kind of nuclear apparatus as the cells of so-called "higher" organisms. The truth is that this difference in cellular structure is minor compared to the fundamental biochemical similarities between bacteria and all other living organisms: DNA, RNA, proteins, lipids, and so on. As the title of this presentation indicates, bacteria are generally very small, but there are exceptions. Very recently, large symbiotic bacteria living in the intestines of surgeonfish have been discovered, and bacterial cells visible to the naked eye were displayed on the cover of *Nature* magazine in March 1993 (Angert et al. 1993). The size of these cells indicates that, contrary to what many people had believed, bacteria are not just featureless bags of enzymes but instead must have very elaborate internal structural organization to facilitate the movement of intracellular components. Sophisticated bacterial physiologists had already reached this conclusion based on clear thinking about the problems of carrying out the myriad tasks basic to all living cells, bacteria not excepted (Matthews 1993).

I am convinced that bacteria have suffered from a kind of "bum rap" among the general public, who think of them only as germs or merely so-called "primitive" life forms. This latter idea almost certainly incorporates certain assumptions about the direction of evolution but also reflects the idea that only large organisms, like ourselves, can be truly complex and intelligent. The truth is quite the contrary. Bacteria are quite sophisticated actors on the stage of life, and they are in fact extremely beneficial. Indeed, bacteria can live without us, but we can't live without them. They are essential for the maintenance of the biosphere. To begin with, bacteria are the most talented chemists on the planet, and they are the earth's principle biogeochemists. All of the fundamental mineral cycles depend on bacteria which carry out the bulk of the decomposition of organic wastes. The nitrogen, sulfur, carbon, phosphorus, and other cycles are mediated by bacteria. It is useful to think of bacteria as the main interface in the biosphere between the organic and the inorganic aspects of nature. For example, nitrogen fixation (the cycling of nitrogen from the atmosphere into organic chemicals where it can be used for biosynthesis and growth) is essential for life. One of the main sites of nitrogen fixation is in the root nodules of leguminous plants; these nodules are stuffed full of *Rhizobium* bacteria which contain the enzyme nitrogenase that actually converts atmospheric nitrogen to fixed nitrogen.

Bacteria permit life to develop in some of the most exceptional regions of the planet, such as the deep sea vents at the bottom of the ocean where there is no sunlight (Gaill 1993). These vents are in contact with the hot inner core of the earth. Surprisingly, there is abundant life surrounding them, including vast fields of tube worms and giant clams. These unusual organisms can grow because they contain symbiotic bacteria which use the chemical energy coming out of the molten rocks under the sea floor to fix carbon. The tube worms have no digestive system but instead have an elaborate system of gills where the bacteria grow and produce sufficient biomass to support the proliferation of their hosts. These bacteria are capable of what is called chemolithotropic metabolism, that is, growth using chemical energy from minerals. This is how they support life where the sun never shines.

In his book on the *Gaia* hypothesis, James Lovelock is explicit about the importance of bacteria (Lovelock 1979). He views them as the fundamental homeostatic organisms within the biosphere, controlling the level of oxygen in the atmosphere as well as the chemical composition and pH of the planet's soils and waters. Thus, in contrast to one aspect of the conventional "wisdom" about bacteria—that they are just harmful germs—the truth is that they are absolutely essential to our survival, which should incline us to take a friendlier view of them. Another aspect of the conventional wisdom about bacteria is that they are stupid and totally lacking in social graces. The typical view of bacteria in a colony containing many millions of cells is that they are just piled willy-nilly on top of each other. The scientific way of expressing this concept is to say that bacteria lack the genetic capacity for multicellular interactions and, in groups, are totally disorganized and randomly associated so that they are unable to do anything for each other—indeed, that they interfere with each other. We shall see later how far off the mark such ideas are.

· · · · · · · · · ·

Changing Ideas of the Physical Basis of Complexity

The notion that bacteria are primitive, unsophisticated organisms stems from what I would call size chauvinism. Bacteria have traditionally been considered simple because they are small and consequently difficult to see into. They are at the size limit of structures that can be resolved by the light microscope, and until recently even electron microscopy did not reveal much of the structure and organization in bacteria that we have come to associate with plant and animal cells. Now, though, these technological limits are being superseded, and I'll give an example of this shortly. In addition to possessing more powerful technology, we have also changed our whole attitude towards size, in response to the major shifts in scientific thinking accompanying the microelectronics revolution. As silicon-based systems become increasingly complex and lifelike, small is no longer viewed as stupid or simple. Silicon chips show us how microscopic dimensions and complexity can go hand-in-hand. Thus, nowadays, small actually means sophisticated and powerful rather than unsophisticated and primitive. So it is appropriate to consider examples of bacterial sophistication and of what we might even call bacterial cleverness.

Bacteria display their sophistication in the first instance by their extraordinary metabolic and chemical versatility. But they also exhibit stunning behavioral versatility. In the last twenty-five years, one of the most active current fields of bacterial research, on a property called "chemotaxis," has been resuscitated by Julius Adler of the University of Wisconsin (Adler 1975). Chemotaxis is the ability of bacteria to detect chemical differences in their environments and to move appropriately for their benefit— towards those chemicals which are useful to them, such as food sources, and away from those chemicals which are harmful, such as damaging substances like acid and phenol. As molecular biologists have studied chemotaxis, they have come to realize that a very complex apparatus within the bacterial cells is involved in detecting specific chemicals, in transferring information about the presence of those chemicals and their levels in the environment, and in controlling the cellular motility apparatus accordingly. To use the current terminology, there is a signal transduction network within the bacterial cell which allows it to control the rotation of motors which power the organelles of swimming motion, called flagella, in response to chemical changes. This control allows the cells to migrate in the proper directions for optimum growth and survival. Using modern techniques that combine electron microscopy and immunology, a young postdoctoral fellow at Stanford University has discovered that all of the chemical receptor proteins and signal transduction molecules are clustered at one end of the bacterial cell in what has been dubbed the "nose spot" (Maddock and Shapiro 1993; Parkinson and Blair 1993). So we are beginning to learn about the internal organization of these tiny cells. As we do so, we realize more and more that this organization is just one aspect of a sophisticated cellular architecture which allows bacteria to control their behavior so that they can interact in a very sensitive and purposeful way with their chemical environment.

· · · · · · · · ·

Bacteria as Symbionts and Pathogens: Outsmarting Bigger Organisms

Even more dramatic examples of bacterial sophistication are apparent as we study how bacteria interact with other organisms. One beneficial interaction is the nitrogen-fixing symbiosis I've already mentioned. Analysis of this symbiosis is one of the hottest areas in contemporary microbiology, particularly deciphering the very elaborate chemical dialogues which go on between the bacteria and the plants as they form root nodules in a highly orchestrated fashion (Fisher and Long 1992). This amazing interspecific ballet involves migration of the bacteria to the plant roots, morphological changes in the roots in response to bacterial signals, bacterial attachment to the roots, the induction of "infection tubes" in the roots, and bacterial travel through these structures to penetrate plant cells and establish the nitrogen-fixing populations within those root cells that, obligingly, undergo hypertrophy to form the nodule structure.

Other interactions involve symbiosis that has gone awry and produced disease. Most of us have heard about the enteropathogenic *E. coli* strains which have recently been hitting fast food restaurants and causing intestinal disease in people who eat undercooked hamburgers. We now know a great deal about how these pathogenic bacteria attach themselves to the lining of the intestine and elaborate virulence proteins which induce specific changes in the basic structure of the intestinal cells so that they actively transport the bacteria inside themselves (Rosenshine and Finlay 1993). These bacteria proliferate by consuming the nutrients they find in the interiors of these cells, and the cell membrane also protects them from the immune system. So we can legitimately say that these disease bacteria have "outsmarted" the intestinal cells and tricked them into taking them up where they then act to their own advantage at the expense of their hosts.

While the cellular interactions in pathogenesis are already very sophisticated, bacteria can do even better, taking over the development of whole organisms. We can see this in another important plant-bacteria interaction involving a group of organisms called *Agrobacterium*. These bacteria are used as one of the main vectors for plant genetic engineering, and we shall shortly see why. When *Agrobacterium tumefaciens* infect wounded plants, they induce the formation of massive tumors called crown galls.

Normal plant development has ceased and aberrant neoplastic growth takes over. The species name *tumefaciens* actually means "tumor-making," and the way this process occurs is quite remarkable (Duban et al. 1993). The *Agrobacterium* cells can sense that a plant has been wounded because the damaged tissues emit certain compounds that act as chemoattractants. After the *Agrobacterium* cells move into the wound, they transfer a specific segment of DNA, called "T DNA" (for tumor DNA), into the surrounding plant cells, and the T DNA then becomes incorporated into the plant chromosomes (Zambryski 1989). The T DNA then directs the synthesis of plant hormones which redirect the growth process to produce a crown gall tumor. Why do they do this? They do it because the crown gall tumor produces one or more compounds called "opines" which only the bacteria can metabolize. So these particular bacteria are capable of taking control of the genome of a higher plant and subverting the plant to produce substances only the bacteria can feed on. That seems pretty clever, and contemporary genetic engineers in the biotechnology industry are taking advantage of this system by inserting their own preferred genetic structures into T DNA so that it can subsequently be introduced into plant chromosomes (Chilton 1983).

. . . .

Bacteria as Multicellular Organisms—Unexpected Social Capabilities

Another important lesson about the need to discard notions of bacterial simplicity and primitiveness and adopt a deeper appreciation of their sophistication comes from observations about their vocation for living in organized multicellular groups (Shapiro 1988). Such structured communal living is actually quite common for bacteria in nature. My colleague John Breznak at Michigan State University has studied the symbiosis between intestinal bacteria and the termite. This symbiosis is essential to the termites because they cannot digest cellulose without their bacterial flora. When John and one of his students examined the lining of the termite intestine, they found several different kinds of bacteria in highly ordered multicellular populations, not in disorganized jumbles of disconnected cells as predicted by conventional ideas (Breznak and Pankratz 1977). Similar findings were made by John Sieburth of the University of Rhode Island when he examined the microbial flora adhering to the surfaces of marine plants and animals (Sieburth 1975). Back in the 1920s, one of the founders of

FIGURE 1.
Four E. coli colonies stained for enzyme activity (ß-galactosidase). The colonies all display form and biochemical differentiation. Distinct populations can be seen growing in sectors descended from individual cells. Sometimes these sectors have quite different growth properties and, in cases like lower left and upper right, form neoplastic "tumors" growing out of the main colony.

soil microbiology, Sergei Winogradsky, who worked at the Institut Pasteur in Paris, actually used what he called "la methode directe" and examined soil particles with a microscope to see where the bacteria were located (Winogradsky 1949). He found that they were not isolated free cells that could be washed away but were almost invariably stuck to soil particles in what he called "families"; that is, small biofilms or microcolonies. While isolated bacterial cells do exist in nature, they are generally dispersal forms, much like the spores of fungi and lower plants, and probably do not represent the bulk of the bacteria in the biosphere.

In the laboratory, we also see this vocation for organized group living in the form of regular, highly organized colonies on standard bacteriological media. Many bacteria produce pigments, and their colonies reveal a great deal of internal order and differentiation through color changes. The species *Serratia marcescens*, for example, produces a brilliant red dye called "prodigiosin." (This species might particularly interest readers because pigmented *Serratia* colonies were once thought to represent miraculous appearances of drops of the blood of Christ.) When we look at *Serratia* colonies, we see right away that these populations are not just lumps of cells but are actually structured, highly reproducible multicellular entities which must have undergone a regular process of development and morphogenesis.

When we look at colonies produced by *E. coli*, the laboratory workhorse of the bacterial world which is widely considered the prototype species for all bacteria, we likewise see structure, organization, and pattern. At the macroscopic level, *E. coli* colonies have form and a certain aesthetic appeal, as illustrated in Figure 1, facing page (even though a fondness for bacterial colonies is certainly a very specialized taste). At the microscopic level, observing *E. coli* cells growing on a layer of agar on a glass slide under a coverslip, we likewise observe a high degree of order (Shapiro and Hsu 1989). Of course, we always wonder whether the beautiful patterning we find on a slide might not be an artefact of the special physical conditions created by the coverslip, and so we also look at the bacteria directly on the petri dish, where they are less physically constrained. Here too we see order, and we also observe many of the interactions that occur between developing microcolony populations. It is quite interesting to note from watching *E. coli* develop on agar plates that the tendency of the bacteria is to maximize cell-to-cell contact and to join together

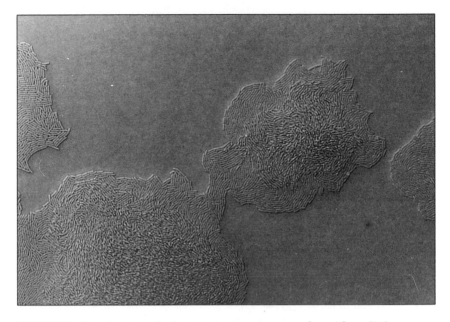

FIGURE 2. E. coli *microcolonies growing on an agar surface. After a little more than six hours incubation, these microcolonies displayed a great deal of order among their constituent cells. Note the highly aligned cells connecting two microcolonies which are in the process of merging. 600× magnification.*

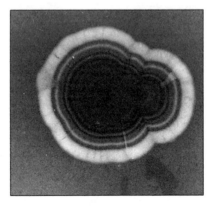

FIGURE 3. *Two* E. coli *colonies coordinating their biochemical activities. The larger colony on the left was inoculated about thirty hours before the smaller colony on the right. Both colonies displayed concentric ring patterns of differential enzyme activity which have come into register where the colonies merged.*

into increasingly larger colonial populations. Sometimes we see ordered phalanxes of bacteria connecting two microcolonies which are about to merge (Figure 2, facing page), and these striking patterns raise many questions about how these bacteria line up this way and what systems are controlling this kind of multicellular growth process.

At this point, we might ask some basic questions. Why do bacteria grow in organized multicellular populations? What good does it do for them? There are actually many ways that bacteria benefit from a multicellular life-style, and I would just like to mention two. Certain bacteria are photosynthetic and are called *Cyanobacteria* because of their blue-green color. They are very important photosynthetic organisms and play a major role in maintaining oxygen levels in the atmosphere. Many cyanobacterial species, such as those in the genus *Anabena*, live in long multicellular chains called "trichomes." What is particularly interesting about these *Anabena* is that they not only carry out photosynthesis but, if starved for nitrogen, also carry out nitrogen fixation. Both processes are critical in the geochemical cycles I've already mentioned. There's a biochemical problem, however: photosynthesis generates oxygen, and oxygen poisons nitrogenase, the enzyme that catalyzes nitrogen fixation (Fay 1992). So the same cells cannot simultaneously carry out both photosynthesis and nitrogen fixation. *Anabena* uses its vocation of multicellularity to solve this problem. It makes specialized cells called "heterocysts" in which the photosynthetic apparatus degenerates and a rather elaborate process establishes the nitrogen fixation apparatus within an anoxic environment. Thus, after nitrogen starvation, the *Anabena* filament undergoes a cellular division of labor so that most cells are photosynthetic but a few heterocysts are present to fix nitrogen. For such a division of labor to be effective, of course, all of the cells in the filament are connected to each by small pores; through these, the photosynthetic cells pump energy-rich compounds to the heterocysts to fuel nitrogen fixation, and the heterocysts in turn can pump out compounds rich in fixed nitrogen.

Another advantage of multicellularity is seen in the group of organisms known as *Myxobacteria*, which are so named because they make elaborate fruiting bodies and have long been known to have a very elaborate social life (Shimkets 1990). The myxobacteria are micropredators, preying on other microorganisms by synthesizing and liberating into the immediate environment a large number of enzymes and antibiotics which cause other bacteria and fungi to disintegrate. The envelopes of these prey microorganisms fall apart, and they lyse, so that the myxobacteria (who are resistant to their own enzymes) can come in and sop up the liberated nutrients. This turns out to be an efficient form of predation. Some species, such as *Myxococcus xanthus*, actually graze upon cyanobacteria in ponds. But wait— there's a problem. If the predators are in water and liberate enzymes to lyse their prey, the enzymes will be diluted and lose their effectiveness. Moreover, if the prey organisms lyse in water, the liberated nutrients will also be diluted and largely inaccessible to the predatory *Myxoccoccus* cells. How do they solve this problem? Jeffrey Burnham and his colleagues discovered the solution: the *Myxococcus* cells construct large spherical colonies filled with pockets where they trap the cyanobacterial filaments (Burnham et al. 1981). In this way, both excretion of lytic factors and lysis of prey cyanobacteria are localized and contained within an elaborate multicellular structure. So the ability to form an organized, multicellular structure gives these bacteria access to a food resource which would otherwise be very difficult for them to exploit.

If bacteria can form ordered multicellular populations for their own benefit, the natural impulse of a scientist is to try to explain how they do it. What natural principles are involved? One fundamental aspect of multicellular organization that we know about is communication between the cells. In some cases we can see the communication at work, as in the case of *E. coli*. Videotapes of early microcolony development show how separate cells and their descendants seek each other out and grow together, as we saw above in the merging microcolonies (Figure 2, page 214). Contrary to conventional expectations that each bacterium would maximize its access to substrate, the tendency of *E. coli* cells growing on an agar surface is, instead, to maximize cell-to-cell contact (Shapiro and Hsu 1989). In other words, these "prototypical" bacteria have evolved to grow cooperatively, and if we measure their rate of cell division in intimate microcolony populations, we find that it is just as rapid as when the cells are kept separate by putting in a great deal of work to agitate them in liquid medium (Shapiro 1992a). As people study bacterial growth and DNA transmission, we have uncovered a large array of different signalling molecules, which range all the way from individual amino acids and their derivatives through oligopeptide and polypeptide pheromones to large structures, such as bacterial sex pili. Recently, in fact, I spoke to the National Institutes of Health official who manages a review panel on microbial physiology, and he said that most of his grant proposals deal with cell-to-cell communication in bacteria, a topic which would have been greeted with ridicule only a few years ago.

· · · · · · · · · ·

Bacterial Sensitivity and Responsiveness

Sometimes communication is not limited to cells but involves whole colonies. I was privileged to observe this a couple of years ago when I noticed that the ring patterns in my colonies lined up when two colonies happened to grow together. These ring patterns indicated concentric zones of cellular differentiation within the colonies. Wondering whether these alignments were just coincidences because two independent colonies happened to develop synchronously or whether there was some type of active coordination between the colonies, I followed the suggestion of a student, Marc Lavenant, and inoculated colonies next to each other but at different times. Since the colonies were no longer synchronous, alignment would indicate some form of ongoing coordination between enzyme synthesis in the two populations. The result was always the same: the ring patterns lined up, and the alignment even included the surface terracing contours of the two colonies (Figure 3, page 214; Shapiro 1992a). Thus, colonies can communicate, and several lines of evidence suggest that they do it by creating chemical fields in the agar growth medium. While there is considerable controversy among my colleagues as to how appropriate it is to apply the term "communication" to coordination by these chemical fields (which are largely products of bacterial metabolism), it is definitely the case that, as the colonies grow, they modify their environments, sense the environmental changes, and adjust their cellular activities accordingly. Thus, we can consider them to be sentient organisms.

Not only do the bacteria display sensitivity and responsiveness to regular changes in their environment as they proliferate in populations, but they can also adjust to unexpected and unpredictable situations. Let me give two examples. The first is an experiment I performed to test for developmental regulation in young *E. coli* microcolonies. I irradiated the edge of a population with the fluorescence beam from my microscope. The irradiation damaged the cells in a small area near the edge so that development began unevenly, with a notch in the microcolony perimeter.

However, after about an hour, the deformity was corrected, and the perimeter had a normal profile. This is just one of several kinds of experimental interventions that can be done to show that the integrity and form of the whole colony is something which the bacteria actively maintain. An even more spectacular example was published ten years ago by Martin Dworkin of the University of Minnesota (Dworkin 1983). This experiment investigated predatory behavior by *Myxococcus xanthus*, which search for prey bacteria in mobile groups of several dozens of cells called "flares." The flares migrate as coherent units and can detect clumps of prey bacteria, move towards them and then stay to feed on them. Dworkin was interested in finding out how the *Myxococcus* detected their prey. He tested the theory that they were using chemoreceptors by placing chemically inert glass or polystyrene latex beads on the agar and observing whether the *Myxobacteria* responded to them. They did respond, and two aspects of the response were remarkable. The flares did not respond to all the beads on the agar surface, but once one flare detected a bead (over a distance of many cell lengths), the entire group made a turn towards the bead. These turns were not completely accurate however, and once a flare came closer to the bead, it would make a mid-course correction and home in on the target. This ability to detect the presence of these beads and control group movement towards them is not yet understood, but it is quite an extraordinary display of sensory perception and coordinated control of the activities of many cells. However, what is perhaps even more remarkable was the behavior of the *Myxococcus* flares after they had contacted the target beads. Rather than linger and feed, as they would have done if the object had been a mass of prey bacteria, the flares quickly left the beads, which had no food value, and continued their search. In other words, the *Myxococcus* were able to evaluate the nature of their target object and make an appropriate behavioral decision.

· · · · · · · · · ·
Bacteria as Genetic Engineers

Bacteria are not unique in their ability to act as genetic engineers. One of the major discoveries in molecular genetics has been that all cells have this capacity. But bacteria provide excellent examples of natural genetic engineering and its relationship to fundamental questions of evolution and biological diversity. We have already seen how *Agrobacterium* cells genetically engineer plants for their own benefit by injecting a specific piece of DNA that leads to formation of crown gall tumors. This is one example of bacteria engineering the genome of another organism, something other pathogens do as well. (One could say, for example, that HIV genetically engineers the lymphocytes of infected people.)

Bacteria are, in fact, continually engineering their own genomes. The origins of bacterial genetics in the 1940s was based on the discovery of sexual exchange between different strains of *E. coli*. It was my Ph.D. advisor, William Hayes, who figured out that this exchange was based on the presence of a plasmid which he called F (for fertility factor), which allows one *E. coli* cell to transfer its DNA to another (Jacob and Wollman 1961). Today plasmids comprise one class of basic tool that we use in recombinant DNA-based genetic engineering (Cohen 1975). As we worked out the structure of the F plasmid, we learned that it has a very elaborate organization with many sophisticated components. It is a kind of genetic engineering machine whose function is to move DNA between cells.

The realization that such genetic engineering machines existed in bacteria quickly assumed real-world significance. The postwar decade when bacterial genetics was developing as a science was also the era of the first massive use of antibiotics for chemotherapy to combat infectious diseases. As different antibiotics, first penicillins and sulfa drugs and then tetracycline, chloramphenicol, streptomycin, and so forth began to be applied, bacteria evolved strains that were resistant to these agents. In fact, antibiotic resistance has become a worldwide crisis of major proportions. We underestimated the bacteria, and now we find that antibiotic chemotherapy is less and less effective in dealing with growing pandemics of diseases such as cholera and tuberculosis. The way bacteria evolved antibiotic resistance is quite important both practically and scientifically. Interestingly, the emergence of bacterial drug resistance is our best studied case of contemporary evolutionary change. There is a conventional theory of evolution which suggested that resistance emerged through a series of small genetic changes. These changes were assumed gradually to alter the cellular targets of antibiotic action so that the bacteria would no longer be sensitive. Indeed, such small changes could in fact be demonstrated in the laboratory. However, that is not what happened in nature. It was a tremendous surprise in the late 1950s when Tsutomu Watanabe and his colleagues in Japan figured out that antibiotic-resistant bacteria had picked up plasmids which contained specific DNA segments that encoded mechanisms for resistance to penicillins, chloramphenicol, sulfa drugs, tetracycline, streptomycin, and so forth (Watanabe 1967). In other words, the evolution of bacterial drug resistance had not occured by the accumulation of small genetic changes but rather by the incorporation of DNA encoding whole new biochemical systems. These systems are themselves remarkable. For example, the mechanism for resistance to tetracycline consists of a set of proteins that form a pump to remove tetracycline from the cell and prevent it from inhibiting bacterial growth. Moreover, we have also learned that DNA segments encoding these resistance systems are capable of "transposing" or moving from one place in a cell's genome to another, thus facilitating both their spread and their maintenance in bacterial populations (Cohen and Shapiro 1980). The dramatic emergence of bacterial antibiotic resistance is but one of many examples of evolution by natural genetic engineering. The idea that living cells can reorganize their own DNA and are not subject to the vagaries of physico-chemical accidents to acquire new characteristics is extremely important to our understanding of life and the origins of biological diversity. But that is the subject of a whole different lecture (Shapiro 1992b).

· · · · · · · · · ·

Bacteria as Material for studying Self-Organization and Pattern Formation

As mentioned in the introduction, major changes are going on in science today. One of these is the shift in emphasis from reductionism to complexity and interconnectedness. A second change is the breakdown in traditional disciplinary boundaries. Both of these changes are reflected in the growing interest of many physicists in biological problems and the complementary eagerness of biologists to find useful mathematical forms of analysis in the physical and information sciences. The ability of bacteria to organize themselves is beginning to serve as a paradigm for the experimental study of self-organization and pattern formation in complex systems. Let me cite two recent examples.

When chemotactic *E. coli* cells are cultured in viscous media, they form patterns. Sometimes these patterns are quite spectacular, as shown by the work of Elena Budrene at Harvard. She has incubated these bacteria under highly oxidative conditions, and such treatment results in the bacteria forming a series of regularly spaced spots that are visible to the naked eye (Budrene and Berg

1991). These spots contain millions of bacterial cells that have aggregated together. In order to aggregate, the bacteria responded to oxidative stress by excreting the amino acid aspartate, which is a powerful chemoattractant and serves as an autoaggregation signal. Since the bacteria are better able to protect themselves against damage from oxidizing agents at high cell densities (enzymes such as catalase work more effectively under such conditions), the autoaggregation response is part of a defense mechanism (Ma and Eaton 1992). Depending upon the exact starting conditions, the distribution of aggregation centers can assume a variety of very striking geometries, some of which were recently published in the *New York Times* (October 13, 1992). Significantly, it is information processing (that is, detection of the oxidative stress and activation of the aspartate excretion system) that underlies this example of bacterial pattern formation.

Another system of bacterial pattern formation has been studied by physicists in both Israel and Japan. My colleagues Eshel Ben-Jacob in Tel Aviv and Mitsugu Matsushita in Tokyo have long been interested in patterns that develop in non-living systems, such as snowflakes or metals electrodeposited on glass surfaces. Independently, they began looking at patterns produced by bacteria growing under conditions of nutrient deprivation on the surfaces of laboratory media. What they found was that the bacterial colonies assumed different geometries depending upon the exact composition of the medium (Ben-Jacob et al. 1992; Ohgiwara et al. 1992). More nutrient and less agar (the hardening agent for solid media) meant more symmetrical, circular colonies. As nutrients were diminished and the agar concentration increased, the colonies assumed ever more branching forms. Many of these forms were geometrically similar to patterns observed in physical systems, some of which are well-understood, such as fractal geometries generated by diffusion-limited aggregation (DLA) models. DLA morphologies are formed under the most stringent conditions, when growth is dependent upon the arrival of limiting nutrients. Under other conditions, less well understood geometries are formed, such as the so-called dense-branching morphology (DBM). There is no theoretical explanation for DBM shapes. It is altogether possible that the origins of DBM (and other) forms will first be solved with the bacterial colony systems. One great experimental advantage that bacteria have is genetics: by DNA manipulations, we can modify the indescribably complex entities that are bacterial cells one molecule at a time without destroying the integrity of the whole system. Thus, these very small cells have the potential for making major contributions to this growing interdisciplinary field of complex self-organizing systems.

• • • • • • • • •

Summing Up

What lessons have bacteria, these tiny but highly sophisticated cells, taught us? First of all, I think they teach us a great deal about the interconnectedness and complexity of nature. Part of the ongoing scientific revolution away from Cartesian reductionism focuses on the connections, hierarchies, and redundancies of natural systems. We see all these features exemplified within bacterial cells and in their interactions with each other and with other organisms. A second lesson of bacteria is the importance of communication and information processing as fundamental to life at all levels, including the supposedly most primitive cells we know. Information processing is not a monopoly of man or of higher organisms. We have seen examples of signalling between bacteria eliciting appropriate responses, both in metabolism and morphogenesis. We have seen examples of signalling between bacteria and plants, in symbioses such as nitrogen-fixing root nodules as well as in crown gall tumor formation, and examples of bacteria signalling intestinal cells in animals to take them over during pathogenesis. The final lesson that we can glean from these amazing creatures, and this is a fundamental lesson of modern genetics, is that the evolutionary process is not just a matter of random changes in DNA due to chemical or physical events. Evolution is not anarchic. Rather, it is, at least in part, a process involving natural genetic engineering under biological control that has produced the diversity of exquisitely adapted organisms we find in the biosphere.

In brief, bacteria teach us about complexity, communication, and interconnectedness in life and about the cell biology of evolution. They also hold out promise as prime experimental material for studying fundamental issues of self-organization and morphogenesis in complex biological and physical systems. Not bad for such tiny cells!

• • • • • • • • •

Acknowledgements

My research has been generously supported for nearly twenty years by grants from the National Science Foundation. I deeply appreciate both the helpful comments of Deborah Epstein on the manuscript and the suggestion by Lynn Margulis that I pinch-hit for her and speak at the Parliament.

· · · · · · · · · ·

References

J. Adler, "Chemotaxis in bacteria," *Ann. Rev. Biochem.* 44 (1975): 341–56.

E. R. Angert, K. D. Clements, and N. R. Pace, "The largest bacterium," *Nature* 362 (1993): 239–41.

E. Ben-Jacob, H. Shmueli, O. Schochet, and A. Tenenbaum, "Adaptive Self-organization during Growth of Bacterial Colonies," *Physica A* 187 (1992): 378–424.

J. A. Breznak and H. S. Pankratz, "In situ Morphology of the Gut Microbiota of Wood-eating Termites *(Reticulitermes flavipes* [Kollar] and *Coptotermes formosanus* [Shiraki])," *Appl. Environ. Microbiol.* 33 (1977): 406–26.

E. O. Budrene and H. C. Berg, "Complex Patterns Formed by Motile Cells of *Escherichia coli,*" *Nature* 349 (1991): 630–33.

J. C. Burnham, S. A. Collart, and B. W. Highison, "Entrapment and Lysis of the Cyanobacterium *Phormidium luridum* by Aqueous Colonies of *Myxococcus xanthus* PCO2," *Arch. Microbiol.* 129 (1981): 285–94.

M. D. Chilton, "A Vector for Introducing New Genes into Plants," *Sci. Amer.* 248 (1983): 51–59.

S. N. Cohen, "The Manipulation of Genes," *Sci. Amer.* 233 (1975): 25–33.

S. N. Cohen, and J. A. Shapiro, "Transposable Genetic Elements," *Sci. Amer.* 242 (1980): 40–49.

M. E. Duban, K. Lee, and D. G. Lynn, "Strategies in Pathogenesis: Mechanistic Specificity in the Detection of Generic Signals," *Molecular Microbiology* 7 (1993): 637–45.

M. Dworkin, "Tactic Behavior of *Myxococcus xanthus,*" *J. Bacteriol.* 154 (1983): 452–59.

P. Fay, "Oxygen Relations of Nitrogen Fixation in Cyanobacteria," *Microbiological Reviews* 56 (1992): 340–73.

R. F. Fisher and S. R. Long, "*Rhizobium*-plant Signal Exchange," *Nature* 357 (1992): 655–60.

F. Gaill, "Aspects of Life Development at Deep Sea Hydrothermal Vents," *Faseb Journal* 7 (1993): 558–65.

F. Jacob and E. Wollman, "Viruses and Genes," *Sci. Amer.* 204, 6 (1961): 93–107.

J. E. Lovelock, *Gaia: A New Look at Life on Earth,*" (London: Oxford University Press, 1979).

M. Ma and J. W. Eaton, "Multicellular Oxidant Defense in Unicellular Organisms," *Proc. Nat. Acad. Sci. USA* 89 (1992): 7924–28.

J. R. Maddock and L. Shapiro, "Polar Localization of the Chemoreceptor Complex in the *Escherichia coli* Cell," *Science* 259 (1993): 1717–23.

C. K. Matthews, "The Cell—Bag of Enzymes or Network of Channels?" *J. Bacteriol.* 175 (1993): 6377–81.

M. Ohgiwari, M. Matsushita, and T. Matsuyama, "Morphological Changes in Growth Phenomena of Bacterial Colony Patterns," *J. Phys. Soc. Japan* 61 (1992): 816–22.

J. S. Parkinson and D. F. Blair, "Does *E. coli* Have a Nose?" *Science* 259 (1993): 1701–02.

I. Rosenshine and B. Finlay, "Exploitation of Host Signal Transduction Pathways and Cytoskeletal Functions by Invasive Bacteria," *Bioessays* 15 (1993): 17–24.

J. A. Shapiro, "Bacteria as Multicellular Organisms," *Scientific American* 256, 6 (1988): 82–89.

———, "Concentric Rings in *Escherichia coli* Colonies," in *Oscillations and Morphogenesis*, L. Rensing, ed. (New York: Marcell Dekker, 1992), 297–310.

———, "Natural Genetic Engineering in Evolution," *Genetica* 86 (1992): 99–111.

J. A. Shapiro, and C. Hsu. "*E. coli* K-12 Cell-Cell Interactions Seen by time-lapse Video," *J. Bacteriol* 171 (1989): 5963–74.

L. J. Shimkets, "Social and Developmental Biology of the Myxobacteria," *Microbiol. Rev.* 54 (1990): 473–501.

J. M. Sieburth, *Microbial Seascapes* (Baltimore: University Park Press 1975).

T. Watanabe, "Infectious Drug Resistance," *Sci. Amer.* 217, 6 (1967): 19–27.

S. Winogradsky, *Microbiologie du Sol: Problemes et Methodes* (Paris: Masson, 1949).

P. Zambryski, "*Agrobacterium*-plant Cell DNA Transfer," in D. Berg and M. M. Howe, eds. *Mobile DNA* (Washington, D. C.: American Society for Microbiology, 1989).

· · · · · · · · ·

A Relationship of Mutual Respect

1 What are your views on cosmic beginnings, particularly with reference to the origin of the universe, of life, and of *Homo sapiens*?

2 What are your views on human ends, especially as this relates to the framework of cosmic beginnings?

I think that questions of cosmic beginnings and human ends are outside the realm of scientific investigation until we solve the problem of time travel.

3 What do you think should be the relationship between religion and science?

I think that the proper relationship of science and religion should be one of mutual respect for the distinct role that each plays in helping human beings to understand their place in the scheme of things. Historically, we have run into great trouble when we tried to substitute religion for science or science for religion.

13

Crucial Conversations:
Theology, Feminism and Science

. . . .

Mary E. Hunt

Mary E. Hunt is a feminist theologian who is co-founder and co-director (with Diann Neu) of the Women's Alliance for Theology, Ethics and Ritual (WATER) in Silver Spring, Maryland. A Roman Catholic particularly concerned with liberation issues, she spent several years teaching and working on women's issues and human rights in Argentina after completing her theological studies at Marquette University, Harvard Divinity School, and the Graduate Theological Union in Berkeley, California. Among her many publications as writer and editor is *Fierce Tenderness: A Feminist Theology of Friendship*, which was awarded the Crossroad/Continuum Women's Studies Prize for 1990.

. . . .

Abstract

Feminism is having a profound impact on theology, but that impact is all but absent in the religion and science discussions which are currently in fashion. This essay addresses the problem, with particular attention to the contributions of Rosemary Radford Ruether, Carol Adams, Shamara Shantu Riley, and Sallie McFague, each of whom offers a hint toward its solution. Unless the "feministization" of religion is taken seriously, it is hard to imagine an adequate dialogue since scientists will continue to be in conversation with an outmoded version of religion.

. . . .

Introduction

My topic is a modest one, commensurate with the humble attitude which it strikes me we might all well adopt in the face of such far-reaching themes and our finite abilities to reflect on them. I want to invite what for me are "crucial conversations" about the relationships between science and religion from a feminist theological perspective. I am indebted to May Sarton for her novel of the same title and hope that my approach will be as engaging as her book.

I come to the topic of religion and science as a feminist theologian from the Roman Catholic and women-church traditions with an interest in science, not as a scientist with an interest in religion. I am grateful to colleagues who have done such a fine job of laying out the scientific contours of the problems; I intend to do something similar from the theological side, albeit with a far reduced scope.

My concern is at once theoretical and pragmatic. Given the intense interest in religion and science by western Christian theology to which I will confine my remarks (although, happily, the conversation is far more varied than that), and given the quantum leaps in the "feministization" of religious consciousness, I am concerned that religion and science dialogues reflect that consciousness in programmatic as well as theoretical/theological ways; otherwise, we run the risk of reinventing the theological wheel and discovering once again that it is square and limiting our religious imaginations unnecessarily, hence truncating an important dimension of theology's contribution to the conversation.

My concerns take shape in three parts:

1 a reflection on the dialogue which thus far seems, at least from the western Christian theological side, to have recycled many of the problems of patriarchal religion;

2 a summary of the major issues, especially methodological ones, which feminist and womanist work in religion contribute to the discussion; and

3 a modest conclusion aimed at making best use of the emerging resources.

· · · · · · · · · ·

A Reflection on the Dialogue Thus Far

Theological interest in science has ebbed and flowed for centuries, with scientific paradigms challenging theological claims, and vice versa. The current focus invites yet another generation of theologians and scientists to grope with unanswered, and in many instances unanswerable, questions as if we all had something mutually intelligible to say.

I share that presupposition, but I wonder if in fact what we have to say is as important as how we say it to one another. Put another way, if we are bringing our best thinking to bear on issues for which there is finally a range of meaningful approaches, then the quality of our conversation is at least as important as the conclusions we draw. Perspectives, starting points, and diversity of data all point toward new ways of doing theology both within the western Christian tradition on which I concentrate, as well as among the various world religions where the dialogue is thriving. I await the reflections of members of those groups who, I believe, will echo some of my central concerns and surely add valuable ones of their own.

The late twentieth century focus on the interface of religion and science emerges at a time when theology has undergone significant changes. Liberal and neo-orthodox schools of theology in the first half of the century, which had their innings with science as well as with one another, gave way to the death-of-God movement in the late 1960s. It was, arguably, the turning point when the combined forces of psychology, economics, and political science converged to call a halt to the use of what had become for many people an empty language about the divine for dealing with questions of meaning and value. It was not that the divine had rolled over and played dead, rather that the mechanistic talk about God no longer made sense even in a technological world.

The political and liberation approaches to theology which followed in the second half of the century, and of which the feminist work I do plays a part, signaled a very different approach to the discipline. They involved changes both in how theology is done, namely, from the bottom up, not from the top down, and most important, in who does theology. Unfortunately, little if any of that difference—specifically, the inclusion of women, people of color, young people, and others who have been marginal to the process—is reflected in the contemporary religion and science conversation. I suggest that its absence must be remedied for the sake of the quality of the conversation itself as well as for the impact of its results.

What I am most concerned about is not intellectual affirmative action, nor President Clinton's dreaded bean counting, though I think both are more positive than those pejoratives would indicate. Rather, it seems that the central conversation of religion and science as carried out in the pages of journals, in conferences, in classes, or at the annual meetings of societies and sections which take on these issues as professional responsibilities seems to go on without apparently being (or having been) influenced by the "feministization" of religion.

By the "feministization" of religion I mean the extent to which the heretofore missing voices, perspectives, values, and priorities of women are reshaping the face of religion. This is going on in virtually every major religious tradition, on every continent, and without benefit of centralization. It does not mean that men's experiences are left aside, rather that they are joined with women's for a fuller, richer starting point for theological reflection. An overview of the basic issues is beyond the scope of this essay, indeed it is presumed in my analysis, just as elementary physics, biology, and cosmology are presumed in the work of other scholars in this collection.

The problem is that the religion-science discussion seems devoid of feminist concerns and analyses which have transformed religion in the direction of wider participation and greater diversity of perspective. It seems untouched by efforts to demystify language and to provide informal opportunities for exchange. By this I do not mean a certain "dumbing down" of theology or science for the masses, but a deeper commitment to accessible, clear discussion with focused attention on social consequences. Both disciplines have been challenged from within and without by women practitioners and by those who are most deeply affected by the implications of the discussion, claiming not simply a seat at the table but that the table be round and open, and that the agenda be shaped by those who have been absent yet whose lives and livelihoods are at stake. This is not simply a political concern, but one which is now deeply embedded in the fabric of feminist theological work.

As the liberation theologies (in this country especially feminist [with Euro-American roots], womanist [with African-American roots], and mujerista [with Hispanic-American roots], as well as the work of African-American and Latin American liberationist men) have taken hold, the shape and face of theological education and the religious academy have changed.[1] These changes have been difficult and, frankly, contentious. Issues of class, race, gender, sexual preference, and national origin have become essential, not accidental, parts of the theological mix, with resulting shifts in the canon of things theological. My point is simply that any dialogue between religion and science which does not reflect these advances is the equivalent of scientists coming to the table with a pre-Einsteinian worldview and trying to carry on a conversation with process theologians. It simply will not happen, or if it does it will be like ships passing in the night.

These theological changes take a range of forms. Language is one of the most obvious examples, with words and concepts to talk about the divine, human beings, and the world now far more plentiful, if also more problematic, than ten years ago when a seemingly monolithic vocabulary (e.g., lord, God, ruler, King) held sway. Changes in liturgy and ritual, the gender, class, and racial makeup of clergy, and styles of decision-making and ministry are undergoing similar shifts. These are not to accommodate, but are because of, the increasingly normative value placed on rethinking and reconfiguring the theological enterprise which has heretofore been a predominantly white, male one. Again, a dialogue between science and religion which does not also reflect these changes risks becoming outdated before it begins. That some scientists are unaware of it is further proof of the hegemony of one kind of starting point that is not feminist.

The diversity dynamic is replicated in virtually every denomination to varying degrees, including Roman Catholicism, which is the religion I observe with greatest attention. Gallup and news service polls taken around the time of Pope John Paul II's 1993 visit to the United States revealed that upwards of two-thirds of Catholics hold a different view from that of the institutional church on such contentious, though admittedly not doctrinally central, issues as ordination of women, homosexuality, celibacy for clergy, use of birth control, and abortion.

What this means is that even within individual denominations, much less within the western Christian experience taken as a whole, there is enormous variety as well as elasticity to accommodate the many perspectives which now, as never before, are being taken seriously on their own terms. There no longer exists such a thing as "the Catholic position," for example, on an issue without more nuance as to which kind of Catholic position: institutional church, base community, women-church, and so on. Granted the Vatican Observatory has research resources that outstrip the potential of local groups, I am merely suggesting that we not overgeneralize anymore as to who represents what.

I am not suggesting that just because a church, in this case Roman Catholicism, outlaws birth control that it ought to be banned from the larger scientific conversation. But at the same time I do not think such positions can be ignored as if they were inconsequential with regard to science without serious intellectual losses. I am simply proposing that such deep changes have taken place in the world of religion that it is not helpful to pass over them in the name of ecumenical politeness or scientific objectivity.

The rise of the religious right has eclipsed the efforts of middle and progressive sectors to "claim the center" of the political, therefore theo-political, debates. But the larger point is that with particularities now obvious, it is clear that religious issues are more theo-political than simply theological. We know that we are dealing not with Truth but with power in the final instance, power to communicate one's view of truth. In such a context, authoritarian models contradict relativity and have been rendered irrelevant by many religious people. This accounts for the many and varied changes in how religious people act who belong to faith traditions, like my own, which used to function effectively in the way of a spiritual and ethical monarchy. Now that we think for ourselves and still claim identity with our traditions, those traditions are, de facto, changing. Such is clearly the case with Roman Catholicism, and because of it, other changes can be expected.

What does this mean for the science and religion discussion? Much of that emerging discussion in the past ten years has gone on at the same time that the debates and power struggles in religion have been in ferment. There have been hints in religion that the new enthusiasm for religion and science has paralleled diminishing enthusiasm for the political and liberation struggles, providing a way for splintered constituencies to regroup around "big questions" with few women and/or members of racial/ethnic minority groups providing any significant leadership.

By dealing with very different, and, of course, "very important" questions of cosmic consequences and human results, there is the temptation, or perhaps for some, the strategic effort, to bring about the appearance at least of a common agenda. I prefer not to think that for religionists to delve into science has been to create a "safe space" for people who do not want to contend with the messy, sometimes distasteful, and always painful problems of diversity within one's own intellectual field and spiritual home. But often the topics chosen for discussion have been so far removed from the urgencies and exigencies of racism, class divisions, and sexism that there is at least the appearance of "fiddling while Rome burns," or worse.

I think that the religion-science discussion has indeed fallen into these traps, however unconsciously. It has become in too many instances, and this from the side of religion, a topic and a field which is in vogue on its own rather than as a tool for sharpening the analysis and strategizing needed to deal across the board with the very issues about which the newly enfranchised voices in the theological conversation speak. For example, the very dimension of the question about cosmic beginnings is beyond the scope of most people who struggle for tonight's dinner. Granted that the intention of asking the cosmic question is meant to make dinner more widely available, the explicit link is not always readily apparent.

While I appreciate the difference between the two questions, as well as the impact that refinements of the "Big Bang" can have for social consciousness and the construction of a just society, the way in which the questions are usually framed and the often abstract and esoteric ways in which they are debated make it at least an open question whether such connections are foremost in the minds of the askers. More specifically, I wonder if those who have found some of their interests decentered in the rough and tumble of theological diversity have not moved into a realm where both their questions and their ways of asking and answering them are normative once again.

It is my suspicion that this is the case. It is my conviction that it is simply not in the best interests of anyone to limit the conversation so narrowly nor to structure it so ideologically as to form, however unintended, a kind of backlash against the strides made in the past several decades. In short, we cannot let the science and religion conversation take place alongside of, but without being influenced by, the theo-political agenda of which it is a part. Scientists who enter it as if that were the case are simply missing some of the richest theological insights of our time.

I offer these reflections with the requisite tentativity. I advocate a socially focused use of the rich resources of both fields. But when religionists and scientists speak and act without specific reference to or participation by those who are most deeply affected by the results, in our time mainly women and dependent children, especially those who are economically exploited, then I have serious doubts about the results. Happily, it must not be this way given the many contributions of feminists and womanists, among other liberationists, to theology. A glance at some of these provides suggestive material for informing future debates.

A Summary of the Major Issues

While the bad news may be that the larger conversation is not yet affected by this work, the good news is that feminist theology is in the process of transforming itself into ecofeminist work, with ecowomanist work developing as well.

I offer four central works which persuade me that feminist theology has a major contribution to make in this regard. I have selected these issues on the basis of their applicability to the wider conversation, as well as their complementarity in forming a foundation for future work.

Rosemary Radford Ruether

In her recent book *Gaia and God: An Ecofeminist Theology of Earth Healing,* one of her dozens of scholarly works, Dr. Rosemary Radford Ruether conducts a sweep of intellectual history with reference to the concrete implications of creation stories and religious images as they have shaped contemporary consciousness.[2] She juxtaposes the strengths and weaknesses of various options, modelling that one can at the same time ask questions of historical value as well as ethical value, of scientific as well as moral adequacy. Ruether concludes:

> Rebuilding human society for a sustainable earth will require far more than a plethora of technological "fixes" within the present paradigm of relations of dominance. It will demand a fundamental restructuring of all these relations from systems of domination/exploitation to ones of biophilic mutuality. New technologies may well have their place, although there may also be a need to rediscover old techniques of agriculture, architecture, artisanry, and community-building as well.[3]

Dr. Ruether's holistic approach, fundamentally religious in vision but scientific in application, provides the science-religion conversation with a feminist truism, namely, that dualistic models must go, and hierarchically dualistic models must go first. Newer is not necessarily better, and common, mutual work is preferred over glitz. While this seems trite in the telling, it is, I think, sage in the doing.

Carol Adams

Carol Adams, writer and vegetarian activist, in the introduction to her edited anthology *Ecofeminism and the Sacred* insists on a related point, namely that ecofeminism has discerned the false dualisms in various "patriarchal theological tenets" which she lists as "transcendence and dominance of the natural world, fear of the body, projection of evil upon women, (and) world-destroying spiritual views," with the second part of the dualism always "in service to the first."[4] This means that elements of a renewed theological agenda are available from the religion side of the religion-science debate. They are widely accessible in books, courses, even tapes and artistic expressions, so that their absence from the debate is curious, if not intended. She rejects, as I do, the notion of feminism as a unitary voice of all women. Rather, she lifts up the need for solidarity across differences in this "diversity amidst relationship" way of understanding the many and the one.[5]

Adams goes on to insist that the diversity called for in a broad-ranging ecofeminist conversation is meant to provide increasing opportunities to critique racism, class difference, and other particularities from a range of perspectives. It is a programmatic concern, not simply a methodological one. For Carol Adams, and for many of the contributors to her excellent collection, this translates into a wonderfully ecumenical conversation which goes beyond Christian and Jewish dialogue to include other world religions, as well as Goddess Spirituality. Carol Adams builds on Rosemary Ruether's rejection of hierarchical dualism and insists that its absence creates the space for solidarity in diversity. This is especially critical given the life-threatening situations which are so common, ironically, in the midst of technological plenty.

Shamara Shantu Riley

Shamara Shantu Riley is a graduate student in political science at the University of Illinois, Champagne/Urbana, just beginning what I predict will be a major contribution to the discussion. She is developing an Afrocentric "ecowomanist" perspective which she defines as "the interconnectedness of the degradation of people of color, women, and the environment . . ." and includes efforts "to eradicate this degradation."[6] This is what Carol Adams has in mind, and Ms. Riley's work adds an important piece to the foundation for an inclusive, strategically adequate conversation about religion and science.

Riley understands why Alice Walker (among earlier African-American womanists) was so discouraged by the overwhelming burden of racist patriarchy that she could write "Let the earth marinate in poisons. Let the bombs cover the ground like rain. For nothing short of total destruction will ever teach them anything."[7] Increased recognition of the ways in which environmental destruction has its most devastating impact on communities of people of color, as well as the ways in which population policies disfavor women from oppressed racial and ethnic groups, in short, the ways in which survival is threatened, make it imperative that African-American women, as well as African-American men, make ecological concerns a priority.

She goes on to suggest that the both/and approach of precolonial African societies and certain African words and concepts for power, energy, and the like can be very useful for responding to these problems in non-dualistic ways. Ms. Riley's contribution, pointing out the urgency of the ecofeminist/ ecowomanist task because of the threats to individual and social survival, is an essential dimension to weave into the conversation.

Sallie McFague

Sallie McFague, a Christian theologian in the reformed tradition, in her recent publication *The Body of God: An Ecological Theology* adds an explicitly theological dimension to this feminist/ womanist foundation.[8] Dr. McFague, after the fashion of Harvard theologian Gordon Kaufman, understands theology as imaginative and constructive work for which models and metaphors are essential tools.[9] She proposes "the body" as a metaphor for dealing with the divine in a society which systematically forgets bodilyness.

She suggests that we consider what it means to say that God is or has a body just as we do. She argues that all of creation is best understood as a body so that God, or Goddess if one prefers, is not simply a theological abstraction but something literally "corporeal" to which we can relate as analogous to ourselves. At the same time "the body of God" is analogous to all of creation which is "bodily" in its form—the body of a rock, or of a river, or of a tree, to borrow Maya Angelou's images.

What is so suggestive in this imagery is that embodied experiences, indeed our bodies which experience the results of every scientific and technological event, are the common ground of creation. It is this body which has its cosmic beginning and its human end.

· · · · · · · · · ·

A Modest Conclusion

These four useful insights point the way toward a renewed religion-science discussion. Rosemary Radford Ruether's claim that dualistic models must go and hierarchically dualistic models must go first can begin to close the gap between the two fields. Carol Adams's commitment to solidarity in diversity invites broader participation in the discussion. Shamara Shantu Riley's insight into the urgency of the ecofeminist/ecowomanist task because of the threats to individual and social survival alerts participants to just how important this conversation is. And Sallie McFague's proposal that embodied experiences, indeed our bodies which experience the results of every scientific and technological event, are the common ground of creation suggests a common starting point.

When taken together, they offer a powerful antidote to the compartmentalized, segmented kind of conversation which is so often passed off as the heart of the religion and science dialogue. It is my contention that these elements are the seeds for far richer, more productive conversations, and that without them the dialogue can degenerate into an even more idealized form of theology than that which it replaces. It remains for feminist scientists to provide their input as well, since one could reasonably suspect that similar contributions are being ignored on the science side.

I do not expect, nor am I proposing, that all participants in the science-religion conversation will make ecofeminist/ecowomanist work a priority. But insofar as it has had and is having a broad impact on religion as such, spirituality in particular, and increasingly on the theo-political scene as a whole, I suggest that we begin the crucial conversations within our fields and within our religious communities to understand and apply these insights.

A concrete way to move in this direction is to use the four insights I have outlined as evaluative criteria for discussions and debates in religion and science. Another way is to develop a similar framework from the work of feminist/womanist scientists which, when taken together with the theological work, would, I submit, radically alter the conversation.

Yet another step in the right direction is to incorporate these insights into the worship and education programs of religious groups that are concerned about the cosmos. What could be more counterproductive than imagery, hymns, and even prayers that reflect outdated cosmologies and theologies? Likewise, imagine how quickly children will incorporate these concerns into their religious consciousness so that as they deepen in scientific sophistication they will not experience the radical discontinuity between religion and science. This is where my hope lies: that our crucial conversations, those now in progress and those which we will engage in in the future, will indeed make a cosmic difference.

· · · · · · · · · ·

Notes

1. Note that *womanist* is a term used by African-American women to distinguish their positions from those of Euro-American feminists and African-American men. Alice Walker, who popularized the term, claims that "Womanist is to feminist as purple to lavender." Cf. Alice Walker, *In Search of Our Mothers' Gardens* (New York: Harcourt Brace Jovanovich, 1983), xii. Likewise, *mujerista* takes its roots from Hispanic women's experiences which, like womanist work, falls between Euro-American feminist and Latin American male liberation theologies. Cf. Ada Maria Isasi-Diaz, "Mujeristas: Who We Are and What We Are About," *Journal of Feminist Studies in Religion*, 8, 1, 105–9.
2. Rosemary Radford Ruether, *Gaia and God: An Ecofeminist Theology of Earth Healing* (San Francisco: Harper San Francisco, 1992).
3. Ruether, 258–59.
4. Carol J. Adams, ed., *Ecofeminism and the Sacred* (New York: Crossroad, 1993), 2.
5. Adams, 4.
6. Shamara Shantu Riley, "Ecology Is a Sistah's Issue, Too," in Adams, 191–204, especially 204, n. 5.
7. Shamara Shantu Riley quotes this from Alice Walker's "Only Justice Can Stop a Curse," in Walker, 341.
8. Sallie McFague, *The Body of God: An Ecological Theology* (Minneapolis, MN: Fortress Press, 1993).
9. For an excellent systematic treatment of this approach to theology, cf. Gordon D. Kaufman, *In Face of Mystery: A Constructive Theology* (Cambridge, MA: Harvard University Press, 1993).

· · · · · · · · · ·

The More Pressing Question Is Why It All Began

1 What are your views on cosmic beginnings, particularly with reference to the origin of the universe, of life, and of *Homo sapiens*?

I look to scientists to make sense of the heat and light that seems to have brought all of what we know into being. For me, the more pressing though unanswerable question is *why* it all began. I simply acknowledge that I do not know but that I am grateful that it did.

2 What are your views on human ends, especially as this relates to the framework of cosmic beginnings?

The ends seem as interrelated to me as the beginnings. I have no notion of individual immortality; rather, I see us as part of a cosmic whole into which we are enfolded before birth and after death. Efforts to separate any one from All seem doomed from the outset.

3 What do you think should be the relationship between religion and science?

I view the two fields as delightfully intertwined. Both rest on faith-filled assumptions which make sense to those who share their world views, but seem utterly odd to those who do not. Likewise, the cosmos seems to go its merry way despite all of our best intentions to understand and shape it. For theologians and scientists to acknowledge this relieves us of a heavy burden and signals our respect for all that is.

14

Is Participatory Science Possible?

Alice J. Dan

Alice Dan is a Professor in the College of Nursing and the School of Public Health at the University of Illinois at Chicago and is also the Director of the Center for Research on Women and Gender. Her many activities in these fields, including the publishing of numerous books and articles, are directed towards the well-being of women in our society. Recently she founded WISENET/Midwest, a collaborative network to promote access to careers in science and engineering for women.

Abstract

Despite the deeply egalitarian spirit of science, its practitioners are largely limited to middle- and upper-class males and, in the United States, to whites. Discriminatory attitudes are not consciously practiced, yet the effect is to exclude minorities and women from becoming scientists. Feminist analysis offers some explanation of the forces within science which cause these limitations and explores the transformative potential of a truly multicultural science.

Mary Hunt has outlined for us some of the ways in which theology has become more broadly participatory in recent years. Her book *Fierce Tenderness: A Feminist Theology of Friendship*[1] takes even further the development of a model for inclusive, non-hierarchical relationships. The question I want to address in some brief comments is whether science can be organized according to such a model or whether the barriers to inclusivity within science are too great.

Within science there is a tension between the established structures of research, with their reputation for elitism, and the inner impetus of the scientific process (what I think of as its *chi* energy, from my experience with Tai Chi Chuan), which is profoundly populist. By this I mean that shared knowledge, shared observation, is the key to building science. Science depends on consensus and provides a means to achieve consensus, even among those with greatly varying world views.

In what way is science dependent on consensus? Certainly not in the sense that a vote is taken on results or conclusions of experiments, but rather that definitions of concepts and variables are socially constructed and reflect particular realms of discourse.[2] *What* things are called influences *how* they are studied, and the naming process is key to the progress of science. Most of science involves naming a phenomenon and measuring it in a way that can be replicated. Only when that phenomenon can be reliably measured by other researchers do we really grant validity status to a named phenomenon.[3]

Despite the necessity of common understandings for the building of science, despite science's participatory energy, entry to science is limited by many factors. We are all familiar with the "pipeline" analogy in which the large majority of students initially interested in science drop out at many points along the way, leaving a more homogeneous group (mostly white, mostly male) to become practicing scientists.[4] Available data show that white males make up about 47% of the total US workforce but over 80% of the scientific and engineering workforce; white women make up about 42% of the total US workforce but only about 15% of the total number of scientists and engineers; African Americans make up about 12% of the entire US population but only about 2% of the scientific and engineering workforce. Except for Asian Americans, other minority groups are even less well represented in science and technology.[5] If this disparity continues as the US population becomes increasingly diverse, science will become less and less representative of this diversity.

Sheila Toblas has made a powerful argument for the value of diversity in science in *They're not Dumb, They're Different.*[6] She documents how science is taught so as to exclude those who are different from the teachers, those who are *capable* of science but are turned off by the limited approach. Her research on approaches to university-level science teaching in the US indicates a lack of interest on the part of instructors in students with learning styles different from their own. They do not consciously discriminate by race or gender; but the competitive, individualistic model of work and personality characteristics like their own appear necessary to them in science. Recent data on gender and science from other countries[7] show how cultural differences in training environment, expectations of students, and social roles of women in different societies affect their entry into science.

Another recent report, from the National Research Council,[8] presents findings on women scientists and engineers in industry. Comprising about 12% of the scientific workforce specifically in industry, women show an attrition rate twice that of men. They cite a hostile, male-oriented work culture that discourages them from advancement. These criticisms are not novel, but they have had little impact on changing the scientific culture for women and minorities in the US. Recent feminist and post-modernist theorists have helped to clarify the obstacles to diversity in science.

Perhaps the harshest criticism has been leveled at the notion of scientific objectivity.[9] The biases that characterize our everyday lives, the political commitments, the perspectives from particular social locations, are all part of the scientific work that we do. There is no universal, unbiased, "objective" place from which to judge truth. As Catharine MacKinnon puts it, "Objectivity, as the epistemological stance of which objectification is the social process, creates the reality it apprehends by defining as knowledge the reality it creates through its way of apprehending it. . . . Its point of view is the standard for point-of-viewlessness, its particularity the meaning of universality."[10]

Another important lesson from post-modernist theory has been consideration of the relationship of power to definitions of reality. Hierarchical systems, such as doctor-patient or doctor-nurse relationships, define reality from the standpoint of the dominant group. This means, for example, that "health" for the subordinate is defined as what looks good to the dominant. For an example of a definition based on a dominant group norm, here is the NIH definition of women's health concerns: "Diseases or conditions unique to women or some subgroups of women, . . . more prevalent . . . or more serious among women, . . . for which risk factors are different for women, or for which interventions are different for women."[11] Although the word "man" doesn't appear, it lurks in every phrase! It is a definition in which only the ways women differ from men are important. It does not express women's perspectives on their own health. It doesn't even suggest that women's perspectives might have something to offer to men's views of health. It makes it easy to see women as some sort of special interest group, rather than as the majority of the population. (How would a definition value women's perspective? An example of a definition that provides access to women's experiences: "Women's health addresses the health concerns of women, as consumers and providers of health care."[12])

As Mary Hunt has noted, the inclusion of previously excluded groups not only extends the possibilities for knowledge but also transforms the shape of knowledge in ways we cannot predict.

"That theory which is the product of the most inclusive scientific community is better, other things being equal, than that which is the product of the most exclusive. It is better not as measured against some independently accessible reality but better as measured against the cognitive needs of a genuinely democratic community. This suggests that the problem of developing a new science is the problem of creating a new social and political reality."[13] The transformative potential of a truly multicultural science can only be realized when we start from changing relationships among the people who want to do science.

• • • • • • • • • •

Notes

1. Mary E. Hunt, *Fierce Tenderness: A Feminist Theology of Friendship* (Silver Spring, MD: Waterworks Press, 1990).
2. H. E. Longino, *Science as Social Knowledge: Values and Objectivity in Scientific Inquiry* (Princeton, NJ: Princeton University Press, 1990).
3. This is one reason why god and religion are problematic for science: spiritual phenomena are difficult to access for scientific evaluation.
4. S. Widnall, "AAAS Presidential Address," *Science* 241 (1988), 1740–45.
5. A. Fausto-Sterling, "Race, Gender and Science," *Transformations* 2 (2, 1992), 4–12.
6. Sheila Tobias, *They're Not Dumb, They're Different: Stalking the Second Tier* (Tucson, AZ: Research Corporation, 1990).
7. M. Barinaga, "Overview: Surprises across the Cultural Divide," *Science* 263 (1994), 1468–72.
8. National Research Council, *Women Scientists and Engineers Employed in Industry: Why So Few?* (Washington, DC: National Academy Press, 1994).
9. S. Harding and J. F. O'Barr, eds., *Sex and Scientific Inquiry* (Chicago, IL: University of Chicago Press, 1987); D. J. Haraway, *Simians, Cyborgs, and Women: The Reinvention of Nature* (New York: Routledge, 1991). S. Harding, *Whose Science? Whose Knowledge? Thinking from Women's Lives* (Ithaca, NY: Cornell University Press, 1991).
10. C. A. MacKinnon, "Feminism, Marxism, Method, and the State," *Violence Against Women: the Bloody Footprints*, edited by P. B. Bart and E. G. Moran (Newbury Park, CA: Sage Publications, 1993).
11. United States Department of Health and Human Services, *Action Plan for Women's Health* (DHHS publication no. [PHS] 91-50214) (Washington, DC: U. S. Government Printing Office, 1991), 149.
12. A. J. Dan, ed., *Reframing Women's Health* (Newbury Park, CA: Sage Publications, 1994).
13. H. E. Longino, *Science as Social Knowledge: Values and Objectivity in Scientific Inquiry* (Princeton, NJ: Princeton University Press, 1990), 214.

. . . .
Science and Religion Are Different Ways of Knowing

1 What are your views on cosmic beginnings, particularly with reference to the origin of the universe, of life, and of *Homo sapiens*?

> Probably because my own research has focused on the menstrual cycle, I tend to think of the forces in the universe as rhythms and cycles, rather than as driving events. I particularly like Winfree's description of the universe as a "clockshop," with many mechanisms operating more or less in synchrony, coming into phase with each other, decoupling and entraining again. I don't think any "master clock" is necessary, simply this characteristic of the cosmos to ebb and flow.

2 What are your views on human ends, especially as this relates to the framework of cosmic beginnings?

> Human "ends" of course has a double meaning: the end of human life and/or the goals of humanity. These are not unrelated. I believe that some goals of patriarchal religion (e.g., "be fruitful and multiply") need revision, in order to avoid contributing to the end of human life. While there may have been a time in human history when hierarchical relationships gave advantage to societies, at this time it is critical to develop complex social structures that fully utilize information from all segments and individuals in society.

3 What do you think should be the relationship between religion and science?

> Science and religion are different ways of knowing. Religion is personal knowledge, it does not require explanation to anyone; it is individualized and can be different for every person. This is why religious freedom is so important: because spiritual truth is deeply individual. Science, on the other hand, is accountable for its assertions. It is the cooperative effort to build knowledge through systematic observation and requires that we agree to certain premises in order to participate. I think of these as very separate processes, although they coexist in society and in individuals. I think of their relationship at best as one of mutual support. However, because religion takes responsibility for defining values while science avoids this responsibility, there are religious values embedded in science.

15

The Ethics of Scientific Knowledge and Technological Power

· · · · · · · · · ·

Kenneth Vaux

Kenneth Vaux is Professor of Theological Ethics at Garrett-Evangelical Theological Seminary, Northwestern University, with a particular interest in ethical questions in the life sciences, the human sciences, medicine, and technology. Since obtaining degrees in theology from Princeton Theological Seminary (1963) and the University of Hamburg (1968), he has been a widely respected teacher at Texas Medical Center, Houston; Baylor University College of Medicine, Houston; and at the University of Illinois Medical Center, Chicago. A prolific author of journal articles, reviews, and reports, he has edited, co-authored or written books on topics of deep concern to our society, including most recently *Death Ethics: Religious and Cultural Values in Prolonging and Ending Life* and *Birth Ethics: Religious and Cultural Values in the Genesis of Life*, as well as *Ethics and the Gulf War: Religion, Rhetoric and Righteousness*.

· · · · · · · · · ·

Abstract

The coalescence of religious and humanistic wisdom in the Nuremberg Canons morally guides modern medicine. This ethical wisdom resonates with the science and technology derivative of Greek and Hebrew-Christian culture. It provides a secular/sacred perspective to deal with the ethical crises emergent in the tradition, such as sexuality and terminality.

The landmark centennial celebration of the Parliament of World Religions and its symposium on "Cosmic Beginnings and Human Ends" provides us opportunity to reflect on the theme of religious values and the ethics of scientific knowledge and technological power.

The fact that both Parliaments convened in Chicago enables us to mark another event, in this case the fiftieth anniversary (1996) of the Nuremberg Code of medical research ethics. In the second Nuremberg trial Andrew Ivy, the Chicago scientist-physician, was chosen to represent American medicine and its ethical standards of research and care. As sixteen eminent Third

Reich physician-scientists were tried for medical crimes and violation of the "laws of humanity," it was Ivy who set forth the perfectionist-Wesleyan ideals, that extreme version of our Hebraic-Hellenic tradition that became the substance of the Nuremberg Code. Though his own career would be marred by inordinate ambition and the Krebiozin scandal, the puritan and perfectionist ideals he espoused at Nuremberg do capture the essence of that inherent and intensive ethic that alone can constrain, guide, and animate biomedicine in these extraordinary decades at the close of this millennium.

In this essay I will first draw on the insights of that same tradition that Ivy invoked to show how its moral constraints and imperatives have indeed shaped modern medicine. I will secondly delineate the elements of an ethic of knowledge and technology rooted in this same tradition constituted by Graeco-Roman and Judeo-Christian beliefs and values. Finally, I will apply this humanistic and theocentric ethic to two zones of modern health science and care—zones at once mundane and mysterious and therein requiring a profound ethic. We will consider the question of human sexual function and the AIDS crisis and the question of euthanasia in the presence of terminal and incurable disease.

In the unfolding story of modern medicine, knowledge on the one hand and technical action on the other have now collapsed into one human enterprise. The intellectual and technical act of biomedicine itself is actually shaped by value constraints and possibilities; and epistemology itself has changed in the recent history of science—our concept of what it is to be a knower has changed since the sixteenth and seventeenth centuries. Knowledge now involves doing.

The distance between thought and act though once great is now minute. Today knowledge and power have become instantaneous and coincidental. Centuries had to pass between Da Vinci's perfect theory of human flight and the Wright Brothers' first craft. Decades transpired from the conception of electromagnetic theory to the invention of the radio. Within a few years the theoretical physics of Einstein, Oppenheimer, and the collective genius that gathered in Göttingen became technically manifest in the Manhattan Project. Only months separated genetic theory from praxis. Today the act of knowing is often identical with the act of doing; think, for example, of patenting life and Dr. Chakrabarty's DNA work. Knowing has become doing.

The scientific tradition itself is also a reflection of the underlying beliefs and values of the embodying culture. These values both animate and constrain scientific activity.

In this day when thought and act are so apt to be one, we see that the enterprise of science and biomedicine is shaped by the political and economic ethos. First, we remember that human medicine and experimentation is now in some sense manipulation. Our therapies, all of which are in some sense investigative, seek, through a personalized design or a collective trial, to make someone something. Recall Dr. DeVries's words to an early artificial heart patient, Mr. Schroder: "Bill, we'll make you better than you are." Experiments are framed today so that theoretical constructs control the knower. We are no longer so naive as to think we can perceive the *Ding an sich*—the thing in itself. Self-conscious constructions of our minds determine what we shall seek and what we shall find to be real. So we inevitably shape what we will know and what we shall do by what we believe and what we value.

We need also be cognizant of a fact that is painfully obvious in this day of DRGs, cost containment, Health Care Reform, and sponsored research, both by industry and government: vested interests, expectations, and demands indeed determine what will be known and what will be done. This is especially true today as free, disinterested, university-based inquiry diminishes, and industry, the defense department, and the entrepreneureal factor define and determine what shall be known and done.

If this is the case, and if biomedicine is ideologically and culturally driven, I would then argue that we must become explicit about the moral vision and values that we will seek to realize by means of science and technology. I will also argue that we need to recover the moral genius of our informing ethical tradition so that we remember what our quest is about and consider what we need to know, identify what we want to do and then get on with it, with greater clarity and conviction. With Leon Kass, I am calling for a more natural science, one responsive to the deep Hellenic and Hebraic spirit in our scientific consciousness and conscientiousness.

In this second part of the essay let me sketch the contours of a moral perspective on knowledge and power as that perspective is found in the biblical and humanistic tradition.

The primal image about what the human quest for knowledge

and technology mean is found in the paradise and Prometheus myths. These stories say two things: on the one hand they witness to the fact that humans are possessed with irresistible and insatiable inquisitiveness. The world is the divine playground or experiment—humans are the divine instruments to creatively play in this arena. Science and technology, if you will, constitute human happiness, delight, and creativity. The capacity to know, to learn, to create is fashioned in us by virtue of our created nature, *Imago Dei*. We are by nature and intention creatures who ask Why? and How? and What can be done? We are also uncomfortable with boundaries and limitations. We are by nature assaulting creatures—Prometheus unbound. We don't want to be told what we can know and can't know, or what we can do and cannot do. This autonomy verging on arrogance objects even to the idea that our knowledge and power should only be used for human fulfillment in justice. Here is found the glory and the tragedy of human experience. A moral impulse both compelling and constraining lies at the heart of the Western ethical tradition.

Paradise and Prometheus are our constitutive mythic stories, that is, they have become in tradition deeply true depictions of who we are meant to be and how we are intended to act. They are, if you will, our moral charters.

Initially, it is interesting and important to note that both pictures, though ultimately about the seizure of knowledge and power from the gods, are *literally* about life and death in the body. The literal and symbolic features of these stories are equally important. At one level the biblical paradise narratives, like all old Oriental creation sagas, cast the question of the moral burden of knowledge into stories not only about obedience and defiance, but also about sexual awareness, childbirth, and death.

First hear the *Genesis* texts: God created man in his own image and said to them, "Be fruitful and multiply, replenish the earth and subdue it: have dominion over every living thing that moves upon the earth. I have given you all that is necessary for life. Eat freely; but of the tree of knowledge of good and evil you shall not eat—lest you die." But the serpent said, "You shall not die, for God knows that your eyes shall be opened and you shall be like God, knowing good and evil." But the tree was good for food and it was to be desired to make one wise, so they ate and their eyes were opened. And the LORD God said, "Behold, the man is become as one of us to know good and evil—now lest he put forth his hand and take of the tree of life and eat and live forever—" therefore the LORD God sent him forth from the garden of Eden.

In Judaism, the Fall becomes the rise, the expulsion becomes the beginning of the quest. The God of Israel is the God of the Exodus—the God of liberation, leading forth into the unknown. Prometheus, the Greek counterpart of Adam, becomes explicit in the old tragic tradition at about the same period as the Hebraic insight. Prometheus seizes not divine wisdom, but power—not only for its intrigue and delight but for the good of humankind; for which he is cast down to Tartarus, chained by the divine agencies of might and force, and subjected to cruel and perpetual torture, ongoing hepatic degeneration and regeneration— gnawing-away and regeneration of the liver, reducing him to that sullen but splendidly unrepentant existence.

Into the Hellenic *oikumene,* amid the seeming apocalyptic ruins of Hebraism, is born another *episteme* and ethics, another *scientia* and *conscientia*—a science with a moral accompaniment. Christianity sustains the twofold moral contours that Jerusalem and Athens brought to knowledge and power. There is compulsion and constraint: "Do it—but carefully." To the Hebraic drive for free delight in and exploitation of the world and the Hellenic *logos* provoking inquiry, is now added the Gospel theme of gracious invitation into cooperative knowledge in the divine spirit. Then apocalypse is transformed into eschatology and then secularized eschatology. This spirit adds a redemptive hope for renewal of the cosmos.

In the tradition the theme of constraint is also amplified. To Hebrew idolatry and injustice is added the Greek *hybris* and *hamartia* (pride and violation [sin]). These elements are then transformed into the Christian *conscientia*—the moral analogue of scientific knowledge.

What are the positive ethical imperatives from the tradition that bear on knowledge and power? What are the warnings? There is first, I believe, a moral distinction drawn between knowledge and power when enacted as discovery, as invention. Discovery is the licit, indeed mandated work of the human race. In the tradition we are encouraged, in Newtonian language, to "think God's thoughts after him." To discern the secrets of nature, to discern patterns and causal connections, to uncover what is there, is noble and encouraged activity. Indeed, knowing and building the world, in this sense of discovery and imitation, is seen in most

Western theology and philosophy as the essence of human destiny. We were placed in this world or we find ourselves in the world for that explicit purpose. Utilizing the principles of physics to construct a viaduct system or build a house is benign. Of course, principles of gravity, propulsion, ignition, heat, pressure, and so forth can also be used to harm and destroy. As a rule, though, knowing and fashioning according to natural patterns is a salutary activity. Inventing or innovating is another story. Breaking out or moving beyond natural teleology is particularly cautioned in the Hellenic spirit. To contravene natural process is also condemned from Homer to Aristotle to Aquinas. Whether it be artificial contraception, making tetraparental chimeras in the lab, or making *in vitro* fertilized babies for a single woman, the pejorative "unnatural" is invoked.

The tradition does, however, extol the art of knowing and the act of making. The normative features bearing on *episteme* and *techne* contend that this activity should be (1) *evocative*, (2) *ameliorative*, (3) *distributive* and (4) *tentative*.

There is also an underside to each possibility. In each of these qualities we find an element of imperative and injunction. Reflecting the normative character of our moral tradition with its double message of no and yes, it says "Don't become this as you seek for yourself," "Don't do this as you do the good."

. . . .

Evocative / Provocative

In the first place knowledge and power should be evocative and not provocative. Knowledge cries out to be known from the cosmos: "Thy word has gone out into all the earth." The Puritans, among whom science flourished, took their cue from the apocalyptic Book of Daniel:
"In that day knowledge shall increase" (Dan. 12:4). Think of Ray and Sydenham, Locke and Boyle. Listen to these Puritan passages from Milton and Petty (quoted in Charles Webster, *The Great Instauration*, chapter III [New York: Holmes & Meier, 1975]):

> So at length, when universal learning has once completed its cycle, the spirit of man, no longer confined within this dark prison-house, will reach out far and wide, till it fills the whole world and the space far beyond with the expansion of its divine greatness. Then at last most of the changes and changes of the world will be so quickly perceived that to him who holds this stronghold of wisdom hardly anything can happen in his life

which is unforeseen or fortuitous. He will indeed seem to be one whose rule and dominion the stars obey, to whose command earth and sea hearken, and whom winds and tempest serve; to whom, lastly, Mother Nature herself has surrendered, as if indeed some god had abdicated the throne of the world and entrusted its rights, laws, and administration to him as governor.

From the moment of creation God hath plac'd Metals and Minerals in the Mountains, Valleys and Veins of the Earth, and causeth them to grow there.

Knowledge is evocative—it opens itself to our perception. Kepler in his great system of physics wrote of *Betrachten*, that meditative expectant openness to the disclosure of knowledge, that disposition necessary in any insightful scientist. But knowledge is also seen in the tradition as provocative, not only alluring and inviting, but potent, awesome, terrifying. Marlowe and Goethe rightly capture that paradoxical lure and snare in their renderings of the Faust legend. Faust is the modern Adam or Prometheus who with Paracelsian ambition grasps for secret inner meanings of reality, even at the risk of losing his soul. Knowledge, and certainly power, implemented knowledge, is provocative. Naïveté in nuclear knowledge disappears forever at Alamagordo, then at Hiroshima and Nagasaki. Oppenhemier reflects from the Vedas, the Torah, the Greeks, and from the grand tradition when he cries, "We physicists have known sin!"

In advancing biomedicine, the frontier that best exhibits this evocative/provocative tension is human genetics. In *gnosis*—diagnosis and prognosis—and in intervention we feel this two-edged sword. How is responsibility different when one knows before it is born that a child is afflicted with Tay-Sachs disease or with Down's Syndrome? Now that innocence and naïveté have yielded to foreknowledge and prediction, what is the force of culpability?

A good example is found in one of the first examples of genetic therapy. Today some scientists feel that the drug 5-azacytidine has the effect of awakening the dormant gene that was able to produce fetal hemoglobins. In persons with beta thalassemia and sickle cell anemia, the adult hemoglobin gene is faulty. It is thought that using this drug to activate the dormant fetal gene might compensate for this flaw and improve the patient's blood picture. The problem is this. The mechanism of the drug, a process called hytomethalization, has also been associated with activating malignancy. So often in our scientific and technological interventions into nature's process, we discover that it is impossible to do just one thing.

Eugenic manipulations may often have such two-sided effects. Here again we find knowing involving doing, doing good involving the probability of doing harm, the known verging into the unknown—these are the moral features of knowledge and power.

· · · · · · · · · ·

Ameliorative/Punitive

A second feature of our normative ethic for knowledge and technology is the ameliorative/punitive axis. We are to seek to lessen the pain of life all the while taking care not to add to that pain.

The Hebrew God of the Exodus and the Greek god of reason now lead to the Christian God of Resurrection. The age of knowledge is the age of salvation, of healing. In the messianic age the blind see and the lame walk. Here is born the genius of opthamalogic neurology; here is the reason for Herb Vaugh's research to stimulate images in the optic centers of the brain and imitate sight in the blind. Here also is moral grounding for the search for neural pathways and for functional computerized stimulation restoring gait to a parapalegic.

But today we have fashioned a vast picture of pains in life from which we seek release. The ameliorative imperative is strongest where functions are lost, where babies fail to survive and thrive, where life is cut short in its prime and chronic disability saps life's delight: premature renal and hepatic failure, prematurity in birth, heart and vessel disease secondary to hypolipoprotein disorders, malignant tumors—these are affronts to the human spirit and challenges to thought and technique.

Equally intense are the agonies of the mind: the wretched convolutions of Alzheimer's disease, end-stage brain disease in AIDS patients, intractable schizophrenia; the personality disorders—neuroses—all the way to mild dissatisfactions, even sadness and boredom. How far shall the demand for amelioration be allowed to go? How much pharmacologic and psychotherapeutic care will be offered?

Our societal quest for knowledge and the incentives that spur on that search—teaching in the schools, university priorities, government funding, private philanthropy, the choice of careers —all should be shaped by some moral index of suffering. We need to know more about the genetic bases of intellegence and creativity. We need to do more to maximize the inherent potential of persons.

At this point you will sense that I am objecting to a prevalent moral view about knowledge and skill which says in effect, "If the mountain is there, climb it" or "If it can be done, do it." This view of intellectual freedom and technological necessity has much to commend it, especially if the underlying providence of nature and history that I've espoused is true. If the knowledge and technology that need be is given us in due season, we should then claim with that knowledge that we have become ready to know and to do what now can be done. We should never lie back and hesitate. There is certainly power in the advocacy of completely free and disinterested inquiry—to know just because it can be known. But the view of technical necessity is more problematic. Oppenheimer decried the fact that what was technically sweet always became irresistible. With Oppenheimer and against the point of free science, I would argue that the quest for knowledge and power should be subject to our finest values. If our normative tradition from Sinai and Athens to Nuremberg teaches us anything, it is that knowledge is given to people in order to heal. The Nuremberg Code at its heart asks: why do you want to know? what are you going to do with it? is this investigation necessary? do benefits clearly outweigh risks? has fully informed consent been obtained? can the subject back out if he or she chooses? We are offended, perhaps, that Barney Clark had a suicide key so he could shut down the experiment if he wished. Dr. DeVries was merely being faithful to point nine of the Nuremberg Code. It may be the case that medical treatments and trials, which we have argued are manipulations of knowledge and technique, constrictions of what we wish to know and do, may ultimately require some kind of thanatologic manipulation as seems to already be the case in the Netherlands' death practice, which we will shortly consider.

Knowledge and derivative technique can easily be turned from the ameliorative to punitive purposes. Whenever we seek to know in order to harm, we violate the ethos of our heritage. Actually the line between the ameliorative and the punitive is very thin. Often seeking to do good, we do harm. The Third Reich medical researchers invented the science of ktenology—the medical art of killing.

. . . .
Distributive / Exploitative

A third moral antinomy that we find in the knowledge/power dialectic is the distributive/exploitative tension. The Hebrews, Greeks, primitive Christians, European Catholics, and Puritans were first and foremost *communities*. Our tradition, in short, is one that accents solidarity, not solitariness. What is known is meant to benefit the community. What is done is to serve, to protect, and to enhance life in the whole community. In addition this tradition tends away from the provincial and toward the universal. In Abraham's covenant his people were to be "as sand on the seashore." The Hellenic vision was toward the *oikumene,* the whole inhabited world. The Puritan commonwealth, a social experiment that very much shaped the emergence of Western scientific culture, believed that the millennium had dawned and the whole human community was being drawn into a single fellowship that could and should be enriched by the benefits of science and technology.

Francis Bacon recites this exuberance:

> This is a thing which I cannot tell whether I may so plainly speak as truly conceive, that as all knowledge appeareth to be a plant of God's own planting, so it may seem the spreading and flourishing or at least the bearing and fructifying of this plant, by a providence of God, nay not only by a general providence but by a special prophecy, was appointed to this autumn of the world: Daniel spoke of the latter times it is said, Many shall pass to and fro, and science shall be increased; as if the opening of the world by navigation and commerce and the further discovery of knowledge should meet in one time or age.
>
> (*Bacon Works,* pp. 220–21)

To press towards universal dissemination is a feature of the scientific age. It is in the very nature of science. Studies must be verified and corroborated. That which is claimed to be true in physics or psychology must be true in India, Iceland, and Illinois. Trying to hide knowledge, to develop it under political and military auspices so that the Russians wouldn't get it, was inimical to the intellectual endeavor itself. The new supercollider and even Star Wars proposals, their intrinsic merit aside, were interesting for the fact that some proposed that they be shared step by step with the Soviet Union.

The antithesis of dissemination is privatization which finally leads to exploitation. The gnostic heresy which claims that only the chosen, the specialist, or the worthy should know (or in terms of power, that only the privileged, the deserving, or our kind should receive) usually implies insulation from the many and ultimately constitutes assault on the many.

The most difficult question at this point comes when there is a probability that some knowledge and technical application will be misused, for instance, the ability to build a nuclear bomb or genetically recombine some lethal virus. Is there knowledge that must forever be quarantined? Is there a forbidden experiment? Despite the legitimate fears we have in this terrorist age, it seems clear that concealment and attempted exclusivist control are not the answer. Eventually, everything we know and can do gets out. Whether it be the bomb—a Princeton undergrad recently had it all together, theoretically at least—or a biological technique, nothing is as intriguing as something that is classified.

At this point, we ponder what may be the most alarming question possible. Fact: throughout history, everything that can be known becomes known, and yes, everything that can be done is eventually done. Now, with new destructive capacities, if that precedent continues, we are finished. For the time being we have not used chemical weapons nor have we released biological weapons as the main instruments of war. Will we for the first time in history refuse to do what could be done? My view on this point is that knowledge should be extended (published, in the literal meaning of that word) and facility shared. But this commitment to an open system must be accompanied with a structure of moral guidance and control which conveys our beliefs and values. Fetal research should only be done under careful guidelines. The same is true for genetics, in vitro fertilization, indeed all biomedical research and innovation. Dr. Lejune should not just cry out in anger when NIH makes his insight into trisomy 21 into a societal search-and-destroy policy of prenatal diagnosis and abortion. He and we should bring that knowledge and technique to the community *only* within a carefully drawn moral framework.

· · · · · · · · · ·

Tentative/Utopian

A final quality that should envelop the activity of knowledge and power is the recognition of fallibility and tentativeness. What we know, and ever will know, about anything is only a fragment of the truth. The more profound our knowledge, the more we acknowledge this point. President Bok once told a graduating class at Harvard: "one half of what we have taught you is not true, and we do not know which half." Most theories are refined across history, often completely displaced. This recognition saves us from the dangers of utopianism, where we erroneously believe we possess consummate knowledge. Today this humility is desperately needed. The theories and praxes of the biological, human, behavioral, and social sciences are at best faint approximations of the realities they study.

In conclusion, let me now relate this analysis to two critical areas of health care activity: human sexual function and health policy vis-à-vis AIDS and the question of medical euthanasia in the face of incurable and immanently terminal illness. These topics, of course, open vast horizons, but I do believe some tentative responses can be suggested from the moral ideology of knowledge and power I have sketched.

· · · · · · · · · ·

Human Sexual Function and AIDS

Knowledge of human sexual being and function seems to be moving today in two directions. On the one hand we are coming to understand the basic ethological, endocrinal, biochemical, and phylogenetic determinants of our sexual being. Edwin Wilson's award-winning book *On Human Nature* moves in this direction, showing the basic biological givenness of homosexuality, ethics, even religion. On the other hand, popularists such as Leo Buscaglia and scientists like Erich Fromm and Karl Menninger have shown the transcending qualities of love and fidelity. Our knowledge is disclosing the mundane and mysterious dimensions of human sexual function.

This polar development of knowledge is leading us to see human sexuality more in functional and technical terms, all the while we yearn for care and meaning. How might this help us respond to the AIDS crisis? Surely we need to abandon our secretive and essentially amoral posture. We can't continue to bury our heads in the sand, hope the crisis will go away, or seek a technological fix, a magic bullet. We need to confront squarely the public health crisis and deal with that in mercy and nondiscriminating care. At the same time we need to recover the prophylactic ethic that alone can safeguard our personal and public health in this domain. The insipid injunction of "do your own thing" sexual ethics with simmering glee and contempt for victims cannot survive. This process is as reprehensible as our baby ethic, which Dr. Bill Bartholome outlined in a lecture at the University of Illinois, where we parrot a "right-to-life," save-the-kids ethic out of one side of our mouths then abandon them with contempt in our social policy of continuing care. Amelioration means to prevent and heal. Hippocrates said predict the future, heal the sick, do no harm; only a morally guided knowledge and technology will do this.

· · · · · · · · · ·

Euthanasia

The crisis of care at end of life may be the most profound issue before the human community in the remaining years of this century. Here too the knowledge base is objective and empirical and also transcendent. First there are the empirical questions: how do the body and brain die? what do EEG tracings tell us? what do ventricle flow studies show us? what constitutes brain death?

But then questions move beyond the empirical and rational into the metaphysical: when does a person die? what is a person? is the soul or personality coterminous with the biological organism? Both concrete and spiritual knowledge are needed to inform our moral responses. Today the Netherlands has a euthanasia practice where one in every six deaths is a medical euthanasia— persons with terminal illness are put to sleep under medical care. Oncologists and anesthesiologists do the work. Again, in America we are reluctant to practice open euthanasia; people hoard pills ready for when the moment comes. We speak of ceasing treatment, deciding to forego life-sustaining treatment. As we enter this twilight zone, we will need the profoundest spiritual wisdom, technical skill, and moral concern.

In knowledge, we therefore confront the deep. What is at stake is the meaning of our being and the prospect of our non-being. Only memory and hope can then serve us. The morality of knowledge should be informed by memory and undertaken on faith. It needs to be chastened by remembrance and inspired by hope. The moral drama of knowledge and power is the drama of ignorance and insight, of darkness and light, of night and day. This drama is captured by the words of T. S. Eliot as set to music by Andrew Lloyd Webber and sung by Grizella in *CATS:*

Memory, turn your face to the moonlight;
let your memory lead you.
Open up, enter in;
If you find there the meaning of what happiness is,
then a new life will begin.
Daylight, I must wait for the sunrise;
I must think of a new life,
and I musn't give in.
When the dawn comes, tonight will be a memory, too,
and a new day will begin.

· · · · · · · · · ·
Integral and Synergetic Endeavors

1 What are your views on cosmic beginnings, particularly with reference to the origin of the universe, of life, and of *Homo sapiens?*

In *The City of God,* Augustine referred to human beings as *terra animata*—living earth. The origins of cosmos, life, and human existence are an intertwining reality as the person reflects into the substratum of vitality and physicality that explains but fails to exhaust his being. There would not be the question of cosmic, animistic, or ontic reality without the human person as an imaginative (scientific) being. The cosmos, the phenomenon of life, and the human epiphenomenon therefore can properly be called the Body of God.

2 What are your views on human ends, especially as this relates to the framework of cosmic beginnings?

The ends or purposes of the cosmos, bios, and anthropos are intrinsic and extrinsic. Internal codings and laws shape the history of nature in these three dimensions. They also are all animated by transcending force and purpose—no dimension is fully explained in and of itself. The end of the cosmic entity, including the living world and humanity, is light or glory. This enlightenment grows in creation as darkness (entropy) descends.

3 What do you think should be the relationship between religion and science?

Religion and science are therefore integral and synergetic endeavors. Religion provides the metaphors—cosmic, vitalistic, and anthropic—to explain *raison d'être;* science describes details of the·process.

16
The Equations of *Maya*
· · · · · · · · · ·
John L. Dobson

John Dobson, founder of the Sidewalk Astonomers in 1968, is a man with a mission. He travels widely in the United States and abroad, usually with telescopes, lecturing on astronomy in the cities and in state and national parks and helping people make their own telescopes (a much-used design known to all amateur astronomers as Dobsonians). He was born in China, the grandson of the founder of Peking University. Having received his degree in chemistry from the University of California at Berkeley, he went to work at the Lawrence Radiation Lab, which he left in 1944 to join the San Francisco monastery of the Vedanta Society of Northern California. He left the monastery in 1967 to help people see and understand the universe.

· · · · · · · · · ·

Abstract

Modern cosmologists usually take non-existence for granted and hope to get the universe out of nothing. But must we assume that in the absence of the universe and in the absence of space and time there would be nothing? Or can we, without so rash an assumption, find clues to what might remain if instead we take existence for granted but leave out space and time? Could what remains, through apparition or *maya*, appear as this universe? Can we, from what remains, get a universe of gravity, electricity and inertia?

· · · · · · · · ·

Introduction

This is the one-hundredth anniversary of the 1893 Parliament of Religions at which Swami Vivekananda[1] so eloquently proclaimed that all religions are true and that the proof of one is the proof of all. He said,

> If the Parliament of Religions has shown anything to the world it is this: it has proved to the world that holiness, purity, and charity are not the exclusive possessions of any church in the world, and that every system has produced men and women of the most exalted character. In the face of this evidence, if anybody dreams of the exclusive survival of his own religion and the destruction of the others, I pity him from the bottom of my heart and point

259

out to him that upon the banner of every religion will soon be written, in spite of resistance: 'Help and not fight; Assimilation and not Destruction; Harmony and Peace and not Dissension'.[2]

It was my hope in attending this present Parliament of the World's Religions, a hundred years after the swami's ringing words were spoken, that the conflict between the various religions had been largely put behind us and that we could now address the conflict between science and religion. It was my hope that the conflict between science and the church which reigned in terror through the Spanish Inquisition might finally be put to rest. And I came here to say that if anyone dreams of the exclusive survival of religion and the destruction of science, I pity him from the bottom of my heart. And likewise, if anyone dreams of the exclusive survival of science and the destruction of religion, I pity him from the bottom of my heart. In my mind, the proof of one is the proof of both.

Can we, by now, square science with religion? In particular, can we square relativity and quantum mechanics with Swami Vivekananda's Advaita Vedanta?[3] Since there cannot be two worlds—one for the scientists and one for the mystics—it must be that their descriptions are of the same world but from different points of view. Can we, from the vantage point of the swami's Advaita (non-dualism), see both points of view? Swami Vivekananda said that science and religion would meet and shake hands. Can we see things from his vantage point?

Since the notion of *maya* or apparition as the first cause of our physics is central to the swami's Advaita, I have chosen as my subject "The Equations of Maya." Can we find them in our physics? According to the philosophy of the Advaita Vedantins, as the swami himself has said, there cannot be two existences, only one. And *maya* is, as it were, a veil or screen through which that oneness (the Absolute) is seen as this Universe of plurality and change.

First, we have to know what equations are. Second, we have to know what the Vedantins mean by *maya*. And finally, we have to take a hard look at our physics to see if any of our equations can be taken as descriptive of *maya*.

· · · · · · · · ·
What Are Equations?

So, what are equations? They are a kind of mathematical short-hand. They are just brief statements, usually in symbolic form like $2 + 2 = 4$. If you put that into English, it reads, "two plus two equals four." There's nothing scary about it. But essentially, there are two kinds of equations: mathematical equations, like the one just mentioned, and the equations of our physics. But mathematics is not about anything. "Two oranges plus two oranges equals four oranges" is about oranges, but $2 + 2 = 4$ is not about anything. Now physics is about something; it is about how matter behaves. So the equations of physics are about the behavior of matter, and that's what concerns us here. Newton's famous equation $f = ma$, put into words, means that the force required to accelerate an object is proportional to the product of the mass of that object and the rate of change of its velocity. That means that when you're pushing a car to speed it up, how hard you have to push depends on how heavy the car is and how fast you have to speed it up. All that is contained in that little statement, $f = ma$. It's just a kind of shorthand, and it's not scary.

· · · · · · · · ·
What is **Maya?**

We've talked a little about equations; now we have to talk about *maya*. What do the Vedantins mean by *maya*? First, we know from the Upanishads[4] that it is made of three *gunas: tamas, rajas,* and *sattva. Tamas* has its veiling power, *avarana shakti* in Sanskrit. *Rajas* has its projecting power, *vikshepa shakti* in Sanskrit, and *sattva* has its revealing power, *prakasha shakti* in Sanskrit. Now this language, "veiling" and "revealing," is the language of perception, not the language of manufacture. You can't make anything out of a *guna* as the Sankhyans[5] wanted to do. These three *gunas*, of which *maya* is said to be made, are just three aspects of a misperception. They are not substances, like wood, stone, or gold, out of which objects could be made. They are simply three aspects of an apparition. In order to mistake a rope for a snake, you must fail to see the rope rightly; that's the veiling power of *tamas*. Then you must jump to the wrong conclusion; that's the projecting power of *rajas*. You yourself project the snake. But the length and diameter of the rope are seen as the length and diameter of the snake; that's the revealing power of *sattva*. If you hadn't seen the rope, you might have jumped to some other wrong conclusion.

But many of the Vedantins, when they write about the veiling and projecting powers of *maya*, leave the revealing power out. You look in the books—you'll find they leave it out. But you cannot leave it out, or the theory would be lame and the universe wouldn't run.

So we see from the Upanishads that *maya* is made of three *gunas*, that it is a misperception, a kind of magic, and that the universe is therefore apparitional, like the snake for which a rope has been mistaken. But why does the apparition take the form of this universe? Why do we see the physics that we see? Partly it is the *gunas* and partly it is space and time.

Swami Vivekananda said in one of his lectures[6] that the universe is the Absolute seen through the screen of time, space, and causation (*kala, desha, nimitta*). He said that time, space, and causation are like the glass through which the Absolute is seen, and when It is seen on the lower side, It appears as the universe. So not only is the universe apparitional, it's the Absolute seen through time and space, and that allows us to understand why the physics of the universe takes the form that we see. (Swami Vivekananda said that he could write a whole book on a single statement of Sri Ramakrishna, and I could write a whole book on this single statement of the swami.)

Now Swami Vivekananda's statement that the universe is the Absolute seen through the screen of time, space, and causation allows us to get some interesting information, albeit in negative terms, about what he calls the Absolute. Since it is not in time, it cannot be changing; change takes place only in time. And since it is not in space, it must be undivided, because dividedness and separation occur only in space. And since it is therefore one and undivided, it must also be infinite, since there is no "other" to limit it. Now "changeless," "infinite," and "undivided" are negative statements, but they will suffice. We can trace the physics of our universe from these three negative statements. If we don't see the Absolute as what it is, we'll see it as something else. If we don't see it as changeless, infinite, and undivided, we'll see it as changing, finite, and divided, since in this case there is no other else. There is no other way to mistake the changeless except as changing. So we see a universe which is changing all the time, made of minuscule particles, and divided into atoms.

But because of the revealing power, the changelessness, the infinitude, and the undividedness show through. The changeless shows through in us as our yearning for peace and security, and it shows in what we see as matter as its mass or inertia. The infinite shows in us as our yearning for freedom, and it shows in what we see as matter as the electrical charge on the minuscule particles. And the undivided shows in us as love, and it shows in what we see as matter as gravity and the attraction between opposites like positive and negative electrical charges. The universe is "wound up" against gravity only because the undividedness shows through. And it is "wound up" against electricity only because the infinitude shows through. Gravity, electricity, and inertia are simply the nature of the underlying existence showing through, just as the length and diameter of the rope show through in the snake for which it has been mistaken. What we see as energy is simply the underlying existence showing through. Everything that happens, happens because of that.

Causation

So we have seen from the Upanishads that *maya* is made of three *gunas*. The Sankhyans call it *prakriti*, the first cause, and we have seen that the first cause must be apparitional. As Swami Vivekananda said, the universe is the Absolute seen through the screen of time, space, and causation. Here I need to say a few words about causation, because what we ordinarily see as causation is not apparitional. It is transformational. Chevys do not arise by apparition; they come from Detroit. Although, as we have seen, the first cause of our physics is apparitional, it leaves us with a universe wound up with energy, and the transformations run on of their own accord. Gravity arises by apparition, but falling is transformational. The gravitational energy is transformed to kinetic energy without any change in the amount.

As you may know, philosophical systems in India are catalogued according to their understanding of causation. The Sankhyans were Parinamavadins. They believed in *parinama*, transformational causation, like making milk into buttermilk—the milk is transformed into buttermilk. The Advaita Vedantins are Vivartavadins. They believe that the first cause is *vivarta*, apparition, like mistaking a rope for a snake. Now these are very different things. When milk is transformed into buttermilk, it's a change that takes place in time. It's a happening, and there's a shelf life on your buttermilk, there's a date on it. But mistaking a rope for a snake is not a happening in that sense. It is not that you mistook the rope for a snake yesterday and now there's a snake in your kitchen and you don't dare open the door; it's a mistake you are making now, it's something you're doing now.

Transformational Causation

Now the rules that govern transformational causation are very well understood at the universities. The energy that goes into an operation at the beginning comes out at the end. Although the form of the energy may change, you never get any new energy that way. It's like pouring gold: you melt it and pour it into a set of forms, then you remelt it and pour it into another set of forms. You never get rich that way. No matter how many times you remelt it, you never get any new gold. Transformational causation is like that. What you put in at the beginning comes out at the end. It is governed by the conservation laws. Whether it's matter, energy, momentum, or electrical charge—whatever you put in at the beginning comes out at the end. And since the universe is made out of energy, the changes of which are governed by these conservation laws, the universe cannot have arisen through transformational causation, it cannot have come out of nothing.

Apparitional Causation

But what I have referred to as apparitional causation is a very different thing. When you mistake a rope for a snake, the rope is not transformed into a snake. It's just a mistake, and it's something you're doing now. So the question is not "How did the Absolute become the universe?"—that can't be answered: the Absolute has not become the universe. The question is "Why do we see it that way? (that is, Why do we feel that we are bound? Why do we continue to make this mistake? Why are we unable to see through the apparition?"). And that can be answered.

On December 14, 1882, Vijaykrishna Goswami asked Sri Ramakrishna this question: "Sir, why are we bound like this? Why don't we see God?" And Sri Ramakrishna answered:

> Maya is nothing but the egotism of the embodied soul. This egotism has covered everything like a veil. 'All troubles come to an end when the ego dies.' If, by the grace of God, a man but once realizes that he is not the doer, then he at once becomes a jivanmukta. Though living in the body, he is liberated; he has nothing else to fear.[7]

What is Egotism?

So *maya*, the first cause, is made of three *gunas* and consists of seeing the Absolute through the screen of time, space, and causation—and we continue to see it thus because of egotism. What is this egotism?

Those of you who have read Erwin Schrödinger's little book, *What Is Life?*,[8] may already see that egotism is a genetic invention to keep a living organism alive. The defining characteristic of a living organism is that it must be able to direct a stream of negative entropy upon itself. It must find and use a source of energy less scrambled at the start. Entropy is a measure of the scrambledness of the energy. Every living organism scrambles the energy in its environment. Negative entropy is a measure of the usability (the unscrambledness) of the energy. We get our negative entropy by eating and breathing. The plants get their negative entropy from the Sun. In most transformational processes, the scrambledness of the energy goes up. The entropy goes up. It never goes down. At least locally, entropy is going up; the universe is running down. *Every living organism must direct a stream of negative entropy upon itself to stay alive;* so life is impossible except in a situation that is going from bad to worse. If you want to enjoy the "good old days," do it now! All living organisms live in this cascade of increasing entropy by directing streams of the increase through their forms. And egotism is a genetic invention required by this necessity.

Prime Directives

The prime directives of the genetic programming are to direct a stream of negative entropy upon the organism and to pass on the genetic line. And the egotism required for the fulfillment of these prime directives is what Sri Ramakrishna referred to as the "unripe ego." The discrimination is made between the organism and its environment for the sake of fulfilling these directives. Sri Ramakrishna, when speaking to men, referred to these prime directives as "woman and gold"—"gold" for directing a stream of negative entropy upon the organism and "woman" for passing on the genetic line. When speaking to women, he said "men and gold." He often said, when speaking to men, *"Maya* is nothing but woman and gold."

Genetic Programming

It should be noted that this language—"genetic programming"—was not current in Sri Ramakrishna's day. So far as I know, some of the first things that were published on the subject of genetics were Mendel's experiments, and I don't think they hit the press until 1900. But if we translate Sri Ramakrishna's remarks into that language, they say very clearly that *maya* is nothing but our genetic programming.

You remember that the question was not how the Absolute has become the universe but rather why we continue to see it that way. And the answer is that it is because of egotism, and that egotism turns out to be nothing but our genetic programming. It is this genetic expectation that keeps the wool pulled over our eyes. It is the expectation that by following the dictates of the genes we'll reach the peace and security of the changeless, the freedom of the infinite, and the bliss of the undivided. But that is just a genetic mirage.

We are programmed to eat, breathe, and mate. But not so fast! It goes in steps, and the male programming for passing on the genetic line goes like this: in the absence of females, seek females; in the presence of females, select; in the presence of a selected female, start a conversation: ask her where she's from, ask her where she's going, ask her out to dinner; and the rest you know. We are all descended from ancestors who were programmed this way and who passed on the genetic line. So much for that problem. But how about our negative entropy?

Negative Entropy

We get our negative entropy by eating and breathing, and we get it from the plants. The plants get their negative entropy from the Sun. They make reducing agents for their own use and dump oxygen out as waste. We munch down the reducing agents and huff and puff on the oxygen and run around on the canned sunlight. And we feel that we are the doers. It's just a genetic mirage. We are not the doers. It is just recycled sunlight.

Sometimes when you read in *The Gospel of Sri Ramakrishna* that he says that we are not the doers, you might think that he is asking us to *pretend* that we are not the doers—but no, he never makes that kind of mistake. He is not asking us to make-believe anything. He is asking us to discriminate between the real and the make-believe and to let the make-believe go.

I once wrote to Swami Yogeshananda that this earth can't bloom a flower. Without the Sun, no plants would bloom. Without the falling hydrogen, no suns would shine. And without the entire universe, no hydrogen would fall. I said that this whole universe blooms the flower. By this whole universe, the robin sings. But by what blooms this Universe? It is the nature of the Absolute showing through in space and time that blooms this universe. It is the revealing power of *maya*. The dream is in the dreamer, and the dream is alive.

So, it's the genetic programming that keeps the wool pulled over our eyes. But our genetic programming comes in batches, and that gives us a loophole—a genetic loophole. No other animal on the face of this planet has a childhood like yours.

Childhood

We have a whole batch of programming for being children and another whole batch for being adults and a third whole batch for being parents. But no one has a childhood like yours. And we owe our childhood to our parents. Directing a stream of negative entropy upon ourselves and on our children falls mostly to the parent batch. Passing on the genetic line falls mostly to the adult batch. But the children are free. Children do not direct streams of negative entropy upon themselves—"Mommy does it." And children don't pass on the genetic line—"Mommy does it." Children don't follow the prime directives. If you ask a child what he's going to do, he says, "I'm going to play. That's what kids do." As Sri Ramakrishna said, "The ego of a child is nothing like the ego of a grown-up man." You see, they both make sand castles at the beach; then the kids run through them with their feet, but the grown-ups take pictures.

The Beach

We owe our childhood to our sojourn on the beaches of northeast Africa, where we were probably marooned on an island a few million years ago, and where, in the absence of the jungle, we were forced to eat at the beach. It was there, when our body language failed in the surf, that we learned to talk. And it was there, to accommodate the change, that we prolonged our childhood.[9] That is why our parenting batch is so different from that of other animals. And that is why the curiosity and the wonder of our childhood never comes to an end. We are the children of children who never grow up. And there is an escape route through this genetic loophole. Don't forget it! *Children don't follow the prime directives of the genetic programming.* And neither did Sri Ramakrishna. Although he practiced all sorts of spiritual practices, his native way to go was to think of himself as a child and of God as Mother.

· · · · · · · · · ·

The Equations of Maya

We have talked a little bit about equations and a great deal about *maya*. Now we have to take a hard look at our physics to see if any of our equations can be taken as descriptive of *maya*.

First of all, let me remind you that the physics of the last century—the physics of Swami Vivekananda's day—was nothing like the physics of this century. In those days it was taken for granted that the mix of the chemical elements in the universe had been given at the time of creation—if there was a creation—or had been around forever—if there was a forever—and that if you just kept shuffling the mix long enough, it would come out in the present configuration again. The swami sometimes referred to that view. Don't take it as "gospel truth"; he was just quoting the scientific view of his day. In those days it was taken for granted that the universe consists of real particles with real mass and real energy moving through real space in real time. It was taken for granted that mass and energy were different things, that space and time were independent of each other, and that if we knew the present position and momentum of the particles, we could predict the entire past and future of the universe. No one thinks like that now. There have been some major revolutions in our understanding of physics since then, and they began just after Swami Vivekananda passed away.

Relativity

In the winter of 1895–96, Swami Vivekananda met Nikola Tesla and asked him if he could show that what we call matter is just potential energy. The swami said, "I am to go and see him next week to get this new mathematical demonstration,"[10] which apparently never came. It is probably unfortunate that Tesla didn't get it shown, because if relativity theory had arisen out of a suggestion by Swami Vivekananda, the history of modern physics might have looked very different. The notion that what we see as matter is just potential energy was published as an appendix to

Einstein's relativity paper ten years later, in 1905.

In 1905, Einstein changed our geometry from 3-D to 4-D. He put time into our geometry where it belongs. Time and space come into the geometry as a pair of opposites, so that if the space separation and the time separation between two events, say here-now and there-then, are equal, the total separation between those two events is zero.

Euclid had assumed that space separations are objective, but Euclid's geometry is a theoretical geometry about a theoretical space that does not, in fact, exist. Space separations and separations in time are not objective. Observers moving with respect to each other measure different distances between there and here and different times between then and now. What is objective is the *total* separation, the space-time separation, between there-then and here-now.

Einstein's equation looks very much like Pythagoras' equation for the hypotenuse of a right triangle. In Pythagoras' equation you square the two sides of the triangle, *add* the squares, and take the square root of that *sum*. But in Einstein's equation, to get the space-time separation between two events, you square the time separation and *subtract* it from the square of the space separation, and take the square root of that *difference*.[11] So that if the space and time separations between those two events are equal, the total separation between them is zero. And that puts the separation between the perceiver and the perceived at zero, because always we see events away from us in space by the trick of seeing them back in time in just such a way that the total separation is zero. That separation equation, as I see it, is one of the equations of *maya*. If this universe is apparitional, like a dream, then the separation between the dreamer and the dream must be zero.

It was this change in the geometry that allowed Einstein to realize that what we see as mass (matter) is just potential energy: $E = m$. That is the equation that Swami Vivekananda hoped to get from Tesla. So now we see that matter (mass), as well as energy, is just the underlying existence showing through in the apparition. So that equation, too, is an equation of *maya*.[12]

There are many things which are easier to see now than they were in Einstein's day, before the discovery of neutron stars and before the suspicion of black holes went public. It is easy to see now that the gravitational energy transformed to kinetic energy in the fall of an object to the surface of a neutron star would be a tenth of its rest mass, so that the energy released in the splash of a ten-gram marshmallow on a neutron star would be enough to vaporize a town. It is easy to see now that, falling to the event horizon of a small black hole, one-third of the energy would be released, and that all of it would be released if the black hole contained all the rest of the matter in the observable universe. It is easy to see now that, as Einstein said in 1917, "There can be no inertia relative to 'space', but only an inertia of masses relative to one another." And it is easy to see now that that inertia is related to their separation in the gravitational field, and not to their proximity to each other, as Einstein seems to have thought.[13]

It is easy to see now that the universe is wound up against gravity because the undivided shows through in the separation. And it is easy to see now that the universe is wound up against the electrical charges of the minuscule particles because the infinite shows through in the smallness.[14] And we owe a great deal of these considerations to Einstein. But there is another revolution that has taken place in our physics which is considered even more basic than Einstein's change in our geometry. That is quantum mechanics.

Quantum Mechanics

Matter does not behave according to our genetic expectations. Our genetic expectations are Newtonian. They assume Euclidean geometry, and they assume Newtonian physics. They take for granted that space separations are real and that causation is transformational. That is why so many people have so much trouble "understanding" relativity and quantum mechanics. Our genetic expectations are offended. We cannot easily accept the fact that it is impossible to know everything about a physical system, just as it is impossible to identify the snake for which a rope has been mistaken. But there is this deep uncertainty lying at the bottom of our physics.

In the late 1920s, Werner Heisenberg pointed out that the product of our necessary uncertainty in where a particle is and our necessary uncertainty in its momentum can never be smaller than Planck's constant over two pi; he also pointed out that the product of our necessary uncertainty in when something happens and our necessary uncertainty in the energy of the happening can never be less than that same amount. This is Heisenberg's uncertainty principle, which I take to be another of the equations of *maya*.

What it says is that if we see what we see through the screen of time and space, we cannot quite tell what it is that we see.

Richard Feynman has said that every statement in quantum mechanics is a restatement of Heisenberg's uncertainty principle. This quantum behavior is what keeps the electron from sitting down on the proton in a hydrogen atom, in spite of the enormous electrical attraction between them. If we knew that much about its position, our necessary uncertainty in its momentum would be so large that the momentum associated with that uncertainty would be enough to drive it off. That is why we don't fall through the floor. If the electrons are pushed too close to the nuclei, they simply buzz harder and keep us up. That's why the planets don't collapse. It's the uncertainty necessitated by the fact that the first cause of our physics is apparitional.

Summary

These three equations, as I see it, are some of the equations of *maya*. Einstein's separation equation sets the separation between the perceiver and the perceived at zero. *The dream is in the dreamer.* We see the bright star Sirius eight-and-a-half light years away from us by the trick of seeing it eight-and-a-half years ago. And the distance away comes in squared with a plus sign, but the time ago comes in squared with a minus sign, so that if the two are equal, the total separation goes to zero. Einstein's more famous equation, $E = mc^2$, ". . . In which energy is set equal to mass," is the equation which Swami Vivekananda had hoped to get from Tesla, because, as he said, "There cannot be two existences, only one." And Heisenberg's uncertainty principle includes the notion that the observer is always mixed up in what he sees. There is no longer any talk of a universe independent of the observer any more than there is talk of an apparitional snake independent of the person who is seeing the apparition.

Whence and Whither?

For a long time I have felt that the physicists were just on the verge of noticing that the first cause of our physics is apparitional, that our physics is the physics of an apparitional universe. I mentioned it to Johnny Carson when I was on his show a couple of years ago. I said that when you mistake a rope for a snake, what you do is look at it very carefully, and you notice that it has these diagonal markings on its back. And you think, "It looks like a rope. Have we had ropes long enough for the snakes to imitate them?" And you call it a rope-snake. Then you look carefully at the end where the rattles should have been and you see hemp fibers. "Aha! Rope-snake hempii." There was so much laughter that I couldn't finish. We were cut off by the music. But what I wanted to say was that when you find that the head end is also hemp fibers, you realize that it really is a rope. I wanted to say that only this last step has not yet been taken by the physicists. Relativity and quantum mechanics are not about an actual universe. We already have the physics of an apparition.

There are some interesting differences between the physicists and the mystics. The mystics take existence for granted and want to get from here to there; they want to see beyond the apparition. And the physicists are likely to take non-existence for granted and want to get from there to here. The Big Bang cosmologists want to get the universe out of nothing. It's like asking us to believe that nothing made everything out of nothing. But that's not what shows in our physics. If behind what we see there were only a zero, then where would gravity come from, and electricity, and inertia? I have to side with the mystics. On observational grounds I have to take existence for granted.

Another interesting difference is that the physicists are Parinamavadins. They believe that causation is transformational and that the universe is actual, whereas the mystics are Vivartavadins. Regardless of what they write in their books or what they say from the pulpit, all the mystics and religious aspirants agree that *faith is at the root of spiritual experience; and that would not be possible unless the universe were apparitional.* If the milk has been made into buttermilk, faith that it's milk will be of no avail; whereas, if you have mistaken your friend for a ghost, faith that it's your friend ends the problem.

Here let me remind you that physics and philosophy are our maps. They can be judged as true or false according to whether they correspond or do not correspond to fact. But mysticism (or religion) is a journey, and about a journey one does not ask whether it is true or false, but only where it goes. Will it take me to the goal?

Our problem is to reach the goal, to see beyond the screen. You remember that Swami Vivekananda said that the universe is the Absolute seen through the screen of time, space, and causation. It's no use asking how the Absolute became the universe.

The Absolute has not become the universe any more than the rope has become a snake. Our problem is to see it straight. And you remember that Sri Ramakrishna said that *maya* is nothing but the egotism of the embodied soul. And that is genetic. The prime directives of the genetic programming are to direct a stream of negative entropy upon ourselves and to pass on the genetic line. That is why we feel ourselves to be the doers of action and the enjoyers of its fruits. It is just a genetic mirage. The genes have us persuaded that by following their dictates we'll reach the peace of the changeless, the freedom of the infinite, and the bliss of the undivided. They don't have it to give. We don't get the undivided; we get a family. You must have noticed.

Our problem is to reach the goal and not be hoodwinked by the genes. But this is not a journey from one place to another in an actual world: It is a journey from one point of view to another. That is why it is often referred to as an "inner journey." It is a journey from an erroneous point of view, dictated by the genes, to a point of view from which we can see through the genetic mirage.

Countercheating the Genes

It is important to remember that our problem is genetic. As James Burke says, "If you don't know how you got somewhere, you don't know where you are." And as I say, "If you don't know where you are, how will you know where to go?" In order to "countercheat" the genes, we need to know how they have cheated us.

In an apparitional universe, seen in time and space, there are only three drives to catch hold of—the drive for the changeless which we see in matter as inertia and in ourselves as our yearning for peace and security; the drive for the infinite which we see in matter as electricity and in ourselves as our yearning for freedom; and the drive for the undivided which we see in matter as gravity and in ourselves as our yearning for love and bliss. There are no other drives for the genes to catch hold of; so they have caught hold of these three and persuade us to run after them in ways that get their genetic necessities fulfilled, in ways that fulfill their prime directives. But the fulfillment of a genetic necessity does not confer on the organism the fulfillment of the yearning that drives it. The yearnings have been borrowed by the genes. But the genes have left some loopholes which we built in at the beach long ago.

All our spirituality began at that beach—our breath control, our speech, our music and our hymns, our worship, our mantras and our prayers. And there at the beach we built in parenting and childhood and the ability to pass on what we know. And now we are smart enough to countercheat the genes, to use the genes themselves to help us see behind the screen. Every human emotion can be redirected from the fulfillment of a genetic necessity to the fulfillment of our spiritual quest. And remember, our childhood batch is unique; children don't go along with the prime directives of the genetic programming. "The ego of a child is nothing like the ego of a grown-up man."

And let me remind you that space is not that which separates the many, but that which seems to separate the one. And in that space that oneness shines, therefore falls whatever falls. And space is not that in which we see the small, but that in which the infinite appears as small. And in that space that vastness shines, therefore bursts whatever bursts, therefore shines whatever shines. And finally, time is not that in which we see the changing, but that in which the changeless seems to change. And in that time that changeless shines, therefore rests whatever rests, therefore coasts whatever coasts.

Swami Vivekananda said that science and religion would meet and shake hands. I think that time has come.

· · · · · · · · ·

Notes

1. Swami Vivekananda was a Hindu monk whose friends sent him to the Parliament to represent Hinduism. He was a disciple of Sri Ramakrishna, who lived in a temple garden near Calcutta and who realized that all religions lead to the same goal. Sri Ramakrishna was born in 1836 and passed away in 1886. Swami Vivekananda was born in 1863 and passed away on the Fourth of July, 1902.
2. *The World's Congress of Religions: The Addresses and Papers Delivered Before the Parliament* (New York: John Williams, 1894).
3. Advaita Vedanta is a philosophy based on the notion that there can be only one existence behind the plurality which we see. The word *advaita* means 'non-dual.' The word *vedanta* means 'the culmination of knowledge.' It refers also to some ancient Sanskrit scriptures (the Upanishads) where this philosophy is discussed.
4. The Upanishads are the philosophical sections of the ancient Sanskrit scriptures called the Vedas.
5. Sankhya is one of the six systems of Indian philosophy. Sankhyans held that nature, *prakriti*, is one and that souls are many. They believed that *prakriti* is active and the souls are passive, but *prakriti*

dances for the souls. The ultimate aim of Sankhya is *kaivalya*, 'isolation' (of the soul from *prakriti*).

6. Swami Vivekananda, *The Complete Works of Swami Vivekananda*, volume 2, "The Absolute and Manifestation" (Mayavati: Advaita Ashrama, 1948).

7. Swami Nikhilananda tr., *The Gospel of Sri Ramakrishna* (New York: Ramakrishna-Vivekananda Center, 1942).

8. Erwin Schrödinger, *What Is Life?* (Cambridge, Mass.: Cambridge University Press, 1967).

9. Elaine Morgan, *The Aquatic Ape* (New York: Stein and Day, 1982).

10. Vivekananda, volume 5.

11. $S^2 = x^2 - t^2$, where x and t are the space and time separations between the two events and S is the total space-time separation.

12. This equation is often written $E = mc^2$, where c is the speed of light, 3×10^{10}cm/sec. In Einstein's day the unit for energy was the erg, and the unit for mass was the gram, and when we found out that mass and energy were the same thing, we had to know how many ergs make a gram. Now one gram is the energy of an atomic bomb, and one erg is the kinetic energy of a two-gram beetle walking one centimeter per second. So $E = mc^2$ says that, carefully handled, the kinetic energy of 9×10^{20} two-gram beetles walking one centimeter per second would vaporize Berkeley.

13. Martin Gardner, *The Relativity Explosion* (New York: Vintage Books, 1976), 123.

14. Just as the gravitational energy of the universe would go to zero if and only if the dividedness went to zero, just so, the electrical energy of an electrical particle would go to zero if and only if the size of that particle went to infinity.

· · · · · · · · ·

The Universe May Be Apparitional Rather than Actual

1 What are your views on cosmic beginnings, particularly with reference to the origin of the universe, of life, and of *Homo sapiens?*

For one who feels that the Big Bang cosmology is not well supported by the observational evidence, and for one who suspects that the universe may not have had a beginning at all, any discussion of "cosmic beginnings" with respect to the "origin" of the universe must take on a rather odd look. If the universe could be "actual," that is, if it could have arisen through some process of physics, then its beginning could be considered to be a "happening in time," and a discussion of "origins" would be in order. But if, as I have suggested, the universe might be apparitional, rather than actual, then the discussion of origins must take the form of an investigation into the nature of the apparition. *We must know what might be behind the apparition, what are the consequences of such an apparition, and whether they correspond to what we see.* Also, we should see whether or not the notion that the universe is apparitional might help to explain some of the things which heretofore we have had to take for granted.

For instance, Newton's laws of motion take inertia for granted. Special relativity takes space and time for granted. General relativity takes gravity for granted. Quantum electrodynamics takes electricity, as well as Heisenberg's uncertainty principle and Pauli's Verbot (Pauli's exclusion principle), for granted. But must we take all this for granted? Or can we, with the Advaita Vedantins, put an apparitional first cause under our physics?

Although in the Big Bang models everything we see must be traced back to the original fireball, in a Steady State model everything must be traced back to the primordial hydrogen, made of electricity and inertia, and falling together by gravity to galaxies and stars. And the question is: can we understand that this primordial hydrogen with its gravity, electricity, and inertia could arise apparitionally from what underlies the apparition? And can we, in the light of this apparitional model, understand why the electron doesn't sit down on the proton in a hydrogen atom (in spite of the enormous electrical attraction between them), and why the spin-one-half particles obey Fermi-Dirac statistics (that is, why they obey Pauli's Verbot)?

To ask what might exist behind such an apparition is to ask what might exist in the absence of matter, energy, space, and time, and it is easy to get an answer to that question in terms of negation. In the absence of time we are left with the changeless, since change can take place only in time. And since smallness and dividedness can exist only in space, in the absence of space we are left with the infinite, the undivided.

So what I am suggesting is that by seeing what we see as if in space and time, we might have mistaken the changeless, the infinite, the undivided for something else. And the question is whether that something else could be expected to take the form of the universe as we see it. I am suggesting that the nature of the apparition is seeing what we see as if in space and time, and that what's behind the apparition is the changeless, the infinite, the undivided. So our remaining question is: what would be the consequences of such an apparition, and do these consequences correspond to what we see?

Now this apparitional causation, as I call it, was analyzed a long time ago in India by the Advaita Vedantins and the Buddhists, and they came to some very interesting conclusions. They pointed out that in order to mistake a rope for a snake you must fail to see the rope rightly (as in the twilight). This they called the veiling power of *tamas*. Then you must jump to the wrong conclusion (that it's a snake); this they called the projecting power of *rajas*. But also they pointed out that you must have seen the rope to start with (in the partial light of twilight) or the mistake might have taken some more arbitrary form; this they called the revealing power of *sattva*. The length and diameter of the rope are simply misinterpreted as the length and diameter of a snake.

This apparitional causation was referred to by the Vedantins as *vivarta*, and it was contrasted with *parinama*, transformational causation, (as when milk is transformed into buttermilk, or as when gravitational energy is transformed into kinetic energy in the downward swing of a pendulum). What we ordinarily think of nowadays as causation is what the Vedantins called *parinama*. It involves the transformation of energy from one form to another without any change in the amount. And it is governed by the conservation laws. The energy that goes into a process at the beginning comes out at the end. The form may change but not the amount. Now, since the universe is made out of energy, it cannot have arisen by transformation, except from energy. It cannot arise from nothing. You can get a universe out of a universe by transformational causation, but you can't get it out of nothing. However, it can arise from the underlying existence by apparition.

So if the "origin" of the universe is apparitional, and if the nature of the apparition is seeing what we see as if in space and time, and if what's behind the apparition is the changeless, the infinite, the undivided, then the consequences of such an apparition would be that we would see the changeless as if changing, the infinite as if finite, and the undivided as if divided. But, because of the revealing power, we must have seen the changeless in the changing, and that is what I see as inertia; we must have seen the infinite in the finite, and that is what I see as the electrical charge of the minuscule particles; and we must have seen the undivided in the divided, and that is what I see as gravity. And thus far these consequences *do* correspond to what we see. And they also provide a possible explanation for gravity, electricity, and inertia, which heretofore we have had to take for granted.

As I see it, the only reason the universe is energetically wound up is because it is apparitional. (In an apparition the underlying existence *must* show through.) Otherwise the dispersed particles could stay dispersed. What would be the need for gravity if the undivided didn't have to show through in the apparition? And the minuscule particles could remain uncharged. What would be the need for the electrical charge if the infinite didn't have to show through in the apparition? And why should matter show inertia? Why should it fight every change in its state of motion except for the fact that the changeless has to show in the changes of the apparition? As I see it, gravity, electricity, and inertia are simply the nature of the underlying existence showing through in the apparition through what the Vedantins call the revealing power.

We see (as a pair of opposites) a gravitational "plurality" against an electrical "duality." That is, the gravitational rest energy of the proton is related to its separation in the gravitational field from all the rest of the matter in the observable universe, whereas its electrical rest energy is related only to its smallness in the electrical field and to its separation from a single electron. But if the universe is apparitional, something must prevent the demise of the electrical duality in the presence of the gravitational plurality. As I see it, that is why matter obeys Heisenberg's uncertainty principle. And likewise, something must prevent the demise of the gravitational plurality in the presence of the duality. And that, as I see it, is why spin-one-half particles obey Fermi-Dirac statistics, or Pauli's Verbot. (The demise of the electrical duality is not prevented for an electron and a positron or for a proton and an anti-proton. But in the presence of the gravitational dissimilarity of the electron and the proton in the primordial hydrogen, it is prevented by Heisenberg's uncertainty principle.) Similarly, two spin-one-half particles (i.e., protons, electrons, and neutrons) in the presence of that spin-duality cannot occupy the same energy state. (That is, they obey Fermi-Dirac statistics, or Pauli's Verbot.) That's what prevents the gravitational collapse of a neutron star.

As I see it, the reason we had to take space and time, gravity, electricity, and inertia, as well as Heisenberg's uncertainty principle and Pauli's exclusion principle for granted is simply because they all arise by apparition and not by any transformation. So in the absence of an understanding of the "first cause," we had no model on the basis of which we could understand them.

If there is anything to this suggestion that the universe might have arisen by apparition—that the first cause might be apparitional (and it's certainly counter-intuitive)—then it would seem to me that in order to avoid representing any change in the change-less, it must have arisen as pairs of opposites so that the total linear momentum, the total angular momentum, and the total electrical charge of the observable universe should be zero. If it could be shown that there is an overall residual momentum or electrical charge, I should deem this suggestion to have failed. And if, as this suggestion seems to imply, hydrogen is the primordial apparition, then it would seem that neither the proton nor the electron should decay. If they arise by apparition, how could they decay by transformation within that apparition? If it can be shown that the proton does indeed decay, then I should suspect that this sugges-tion may have failed. (It will be of no use to suggest that this is metaphysics and need not be taken seriously. Anything which influences the existence or behavior of what we see as matter is within the domain of physics.)

Since this apparitional cosmology rather favors a Steady State model over the Big Bang models, perhaps I should say something about what drives the cosmic expansion. Perhaps, also, I should discuss the source of the microwave background radiation and the "new hydrogen" needed to keep up the cosmic density. Then, too, I should say something about the helium abundance and about what has come to be called the "dark matter."

Observationally, what we see is that all the distant galaxies seem to be running away from us. And the simplest and most straightforward explanation is that long ago there was this Big Bang explosion and that that is what drives the cosmic expansion. (In the Big Bang models, this explosion stands without explana-tion.) In the Steady State model, on the other hand, the energy which drives the cosmic expansion is simply the energy of the radiation which is lost in the expansion. As the galaxies and stars condense, their gravitational energy is transformed to radiation and radiated away into the expanding spaces of the universe. If the energy of the radiation is lost in the expansion, then it must drive the expansion.

In this Steady State model, it is the conditions at the border of the observable universe imposed by the expansion that are the source of both the background radiation and the "new hydrogen." As seen by us, the radiation from matter seen to be approaching the border is redshifted approaching zero energy. But if the radiation energy approaches zero, so does the particle energy and the particle mass. Then, since radiation going through a field of low-mass particles would be thermalized to 3K, it would appear to us as the background radiation. The amount of 3K radiation predicted by this model matches what we measure. The amount predicted by the Big Bang model is at least one order of magnitude too high.

Also, near the border, where the mass approaches zero, the momentum of the particles must also approach zero, and with it, our uncertainty in that momentum. (You can't have a big uncertainty about a very small momentum.) Then, by Heisenberg's uncertainty principle, if our uncertainty in the momentum approaches zero, our uncertainty in where the particles are must approach infinity. The hydrogen simply "tunnels" back in.

For the Big Bang models, the observed helium abundance is far too low unless most of the matter of the universe involved in the fireball explosion was of such a nature that it could not be made into helium. It has therefore been suggested by some proponents of the Big Bang model that some 90% to 99% of the matter in the universe is of such a nature that it responds only to gravity and not to any of the other forces such as electricity and magnetism which might allow us to detect it. This "dark matter," as it is called, is thought to surround the visible galaxies but not to reside within them. And the problem is, if it responds only to gravity, why doesn't it all fall in?

For a Steady State model, though, there is no problem about the dark matter being ordinary matter, because the visible galaxies could be expected to be surrounded by what I call "hovering layers" of ordinary matter blown out by the stellar winds. When a cluster of stars condenses from a cloud of gas, some 90% to 99% of the material in the cloud could be expected to be blown away by the stellar winds of the cluster. Since the diameters of these hovering layers may be five to ten times the diameters of the associated galaxies, their densities might be well below one percent of the densities of the associated galaxies. The detection of this material might be rendered problematical simply by its low density.

For a Big Bang cosmology, in which the early universe was extremely hot, a discussion of the origin of life is of course appropriate, since life could not have been with us from the beginning. But for a Steady State model, in which the universe is without beginning, perhaps life itself could be without beginning. However, the question then arises: how could it spread from solar system to solar system or from galaxy to galaxy? Somehow it seems that life must have had a start, that somehow life must have arisen spontaneously from non-living matter. Yet thus far there is no evidence for this.

Pasteur thought that he had shown that life does not arise from non-living matter but only from previous life. Darwin seems to have taken the other view, namely, that it might have arisen from "some warm pool." The evidence, of course, is simply that life does exist on this planet, which presumably had a beginning; so if life didn't come from elsewhere, it must have arisen here. But how? What could pull non-living matter across the border into life?

Natural selection as Darwin sketched it is a very good mechanism for selecting between two or more genetic programmings, but it makes no suggestion as to the origin of the programs. And as yet this is an unsolved problem. But how about the origin of sentiency and intelligence? Could they have arisen from inert matter?

For any cosmological model in which the universe is considered to be "actual," the problem of the origin of sentiency and intelligence is insoluble. But if the universe is apparitional, sentiency is in it from the word "go." Even the atoms are "sentient." We have senses for the perception of gravity, kinetic energy, radiation, electricity, and magnetism, because the individual protoplasmic cells can respond to these same five kinds of energy. And the cells can respond to them because the atoms respond to them. The atoms themselves respond to gravity, kinetic energy, radiation, electricity, and magnetism. The plumb bob "knows" where the Earth is, and the electron "knows" where the proton is. Sentiency is in this from the word "go" because the underlying existence is "involved" in what we see and must show through.

It is hopeless to expect that something like sentiency or intelligence, or anything, for that matter, could arise by "evolution" (as a rose evolves from a bud), unless it was first put in by "involution." The reason the oak tree can "evolve" from the acorn is because it was first put in the acorn through "involution" by the parent trees. But in the case of the tree and the acorn, the involution is by transformational causation, *parinama*. Whereas, in the case of the underlying existence and the universe, the involution is by apparitional causation, or *vivarta*. What underlies the universe is involved by apparition in us and what we see. And since what underlies all this is infinite, there is no knowing what may evolve; in this connection I cite Teilhard de Chardin: "In the world, nothing could ever burst forth as final across the different thresholds successively traversed by evolution (however critical they be) which has not already existed in an obscure and primordial way . . ." (*Phenomenon of Man*, Book One, Chapter Three, Section 1B [New York: Harper and Row, 1955]).

The expectation that sentiency and intelligence might arise from "inert matter" is contrary to all the experience of our race. But matter is not inert; it is "ert" (it moves by itself), because what underlies the apparition shows through. And the notion that what is more might evolve from what is less is beyond the domain of reason.

So sentiency arises by apparition and is with us from the word "go." But how about intelligence? Intelligence, as we know it, is associated with the egos of poly-celled organisms, like ourselves, who have brains. And brains come down through a long transformational past. Even our individual brains have a transformational past from a single cell, to where we are now. Each of our bodies is made up of a very great number of cells, and we have no awareness of the egos of the individual cells. Yet each of us, at the time of conception, was a one-celled organism without a brain. However, that single cell had a complete human form transformationally involved in its gene code through the grace of our parents.

So, although sentiency might arise apparitionally, it looks as though intelligence arises transformationally. It looks as though intelligence arises from sentiency as a genetic invention of the ego. It looks as though intelligence, like egotism, is a genetic invention which favors survival. And it looks as though what we proudly think of as our advanced state of intelligence was forced upon us by the use of tools and language.

So the underlying existence shows through in what we see. What difference does it make whether you think of it as The Formless, or call it Mother, or Father? The questions that remain are these: does the pull of the underlying existence (the changeless, the undivided, the infinite) pull matter across the border from the non-living to the living? Does it pull sentiency to intelligence? And does it pull the saints to final beatitude?

Through the discrimination between plus and minus in the electrical duality, that oneness holds the electrons near the protons in the hydrogen. Through the discrimination between up and down in the gravitational plurality, that oneness falls the hydrogen together into clouds. And through the discrimination between spin-up and spin-down, it pulls the particles together in pairs to make molecules and the entire atomic table. Does that oneness, through molecular discrimination, pull what we see as matter into life? Does it, through the discriminations of the ego, pull sentiency to intelligence? And does it, through the discrimination between the real and the make-believe, pull the emotions of the saints to the goal?

We are like Xerox machines looking for Xerox machines to copy. And because the underlying existence shows through in us, we are pulled toward peace and love and freedom, and we look for them in others. If we see a special manifestation of peace and serenity, or of love and happiness, or of strength and freedom, or of compassion, our hearts open and we are drawn to it. All animals, when they mate, pick out species characteristics, and so do we. It is probably our tendency to breed in this direction that has separated us so far from other animals. And in this tendency, I see the hope for our future.

About the origin of *Homo sapiens sapiens,* it should be said that although formerly it was considered a great mystery, and there was a great deal of talk about the missing link (that is, what happened between the chimps and ourselves), by now this mystery has been largely cleared up. And what happened between the chimps and us has been fairly well investigated by Sir Alister Hardy, Desmond Morris, Elaine Morgan, Leon P. La Lumiere, Jr., and others (see, for example, Elaine Morgan, *The Aquatic Ape* [New York: Stein and Day, 1982]). It now seems more than likely that a few of our chimp-like ancestors, dwelling in a mountainous area of northeast Africa some ten or fifteen million years ago, were cut off from the mainland by a rise in sea level which reduced our homeland to an island. Gradually, as our local jungles dwindled, we were forced more and more to forage at the beach. And what I should like to say here is that it is what happened at that beach that led up to our meeting at the Parliament of Religions; it is what happened at that beach that separated us from the chimpanzees and led to our propensity for science and religion.

Often in my youth it was suggested by the anthropologists that first we somehow (miraculously?) developed this big brain and then invented language and the use of tools. But no one thinks like that now. Nowadays it is more or less taken for granted that we were forced by our situation to the use of tools and language and that that is what imposed on us the need for a bigger brain.

Anyone who has foraged at the beach knows that the easily available protein supply comes mostly packaged in calcium carbonate shells which require to be broken open with a stone. Any chimp could see that. Louis Leaky found that the early stone tools of our ancestors in Olduvai Gorge were made of "stream-rounded boulders." Why? Because we came from the beach, where all the stones were rounded and where we used them for procuring food.

And surely it was there at that beach, where our body language failed in the surf, that we were forced to use speech. Elaine Morgan, in *The Aquatic Ape*, rightly points out that speech cannot arise until breath control arises, and breath control arises in the water. We already had our body language, which, as Desmond Morris points out in *The Naked Ape*, is easily understood by the chimps, the gorillas, the orangs, and ourselves. But what good is dancing in the sea? We needed another means of communication more suitable in the water. All the other animals on this planet who talk (namely the dolphins and the whales) do it in the sea.

Although the temperature of the water at our beach was nearly 90°F, the shift from the jungle to the beach must have imposed on us a severe pressure to change. We needed feet instead of hands on our lower extremities for paddling sand and water. We needed a cushion on our buttocks for sitting on the sand. We needed fat under the skin for buoyancy and streamlining in the water, and we didn't need our fur. We grew hair on our heads for the sake of children in the water and learned to fight with our fists to protect them from the sharks. It is fortunate for us that the dolphins beat us back to the sea and reprogrammed the sharks against blunt punches. No land animal will yield to your fists.

Now one of the genetic mechanisms which we used in our forced adjustment to the beach is what is called *neoteny*, the retaining into later life of juvenile characteristics. We delayed the invasion of our childhood by our more adult point of view. House cats, like most animals, reach the adult stage in about a year, and the insatiable curiosity of the kitten dies away. But not for us. Our brain continues to grow, and our insatiable curiosity lingers on. Out of that lingering curiosity arose science and religion. It is our lingering curiosity that has led us up to this Parliament.

We are the children of children who never grow up. And it is the lingering wonder of childhood which gave rise to Newton's *Principia*, to relativity, to quantum mechanics, and to all the religions of the world. It was there at that beach that we learned the breath control of the yogis. It was there at that beach that we learned to talk and to sing. Our hymns and our prayers and our yearning to know arose at that beach and follow us still. And the beauty and freedom of childhood follow us still. But in order that our childhood could be free, the responsibility for our upkeep has been thrown on our parents. The prolonging of our youth has imposed on us the prolonging of our parenting. Our youth and our parenting are not like those of other animals. Like them, we have genetic programming to see us through our adult phase and to persuade us to pass on the genetic line. But unlike them we have genetic programming to see us through a prolonged childhood and a prolonged period of parenting which is required to support it. Children don't fulfill the prime directives of the genetic programming, namely, to keep ourselves alive and well and to pass on the genetic code. Our parents do it for us. Out of this beauty and freedom of our childhood, monasticism arose: ". . . Turned from home and toil and kindred, leaving all for His dear sake." The monks and nuns neither earn their keep, nor pass on the genetic line, but continue instead in the wonder of childhood: "What or Who is beyond what I see?"

2 What are your views on human ends, especially as this relates to the framework of cosmic beginnings?

The aim of science is to make a better map, and what is needed is a better understanding of the first cause. The aim of religion is to help the pilgrims on their way, to help them see beyond the screen, and what is needed is a better map by which to chart the journey. Both science and religion are investigations into the nature of the world and our place in it. How did we get here, and where do we go? What is also needed is the simple recognition that we are all pilgrims on whatever paths, headed for the same goal. Our problem now is to get beyond the thralldom of the genes, to discriminate between the underlying existence and the apparition, between the real and the make-believe, and to let the make-believe go. Individually, we can do it even now. Can we do it as a race? Will our genetic programming ever reach a point where this is easier?

3 What do you think should be the relationship between religion and science?

I feel that religion and science should meet and shake hands. But it won't happen until the first cause is put under our physics. If some important, well-known physicist, say John Archibald Wheeler or Stephen Hawking, were to notice that relativity and quantum mechanics are evidence that the universe is apparitional rather than actual, then the news would spread worldwide in a week. I used to hope that Richard Feynman would notice it, but he is gone.

The mystics already see that the world is apparitional. Regardless of what they say from the pulpit or what they write in their books, they all see the universe as apparitional because they all agree that faith is at the root of spiritual practice. And if the world were actual, faith would have no part in it. When milk has been made into buttermilk, faith that it's milk will get you nowhere. But if you have mistaken a rope for a snake, faith that it's a rope ends the problem.

Fritjof Capra wrote a very interesting book called *The Tao of Physics* in which he points out similarities in the language of the mystics and the physicists. Now as I see it, the reason for these similarities is that they are both describing an apparitional world. In an actual transformation, like milk into buttermilk, there is no confusion of language. First there is milk, then there is a process, and finally there is buttermilk. But if one has mistaken a rope for a snake and I ask "Is there a snake?" and you answer "Yes," then I say "Show me!" If you answer "No," I say "Kick it!" This sort of confusion runs all through the writings of the mystics and the scientists simply because the world is apparitional. If the mystics and the scientists could agree that the first cause behind what we see is apparitional, we could all sit down together and have a talk—we could meet and shake hands.

The mystics take existence for granted and want to get from "here to there" (to see behind the apparition), and that is possible. But for the most part the scientists take non-existence for granted and want to get from "there to here," and that is not possible. Nothing does not become something. And even if you accept Swami Vivekananda's point of view that the universe is the Absolute seen through the screen of time, space, and causation, still you cannot ask how that became this. The Absolute does not become the universe. It is only an appearance, a misinterpretation. "When will they ever learn?"

The question is not "How did that become this?" but "Why do I continue to see it this way?" And that comes down through a long line of ancestry as a genetic predilection. The undividedness which shows in matter as gravity shows in us as love, but the genes have us chase it in ways that give rise to offspring. This doesn't require an explanation. The infinite which shows in matter as electrical charge shows in us as our yearning for freedom, but the genes have us chase it by eating and breathing and keeping the body strong and well. And the changeless which shows in matter as inertia shows in us as our yearning for peace and security for the body. These are prime directives of our genetic programming which have come down to us from a distant past through a long line of ancestors who followed the dictates of the genes. But because of our long sojourn at the beach in Africa a few million years ago, our children don't follow the prime directives of the genetic programming. They neither procure their own food nor pass on the genetic code, and neither do monks and nuns.

Science is a map to tell us where we are and how we got here. Religion is a journey. But there needn't be a conflict between the cartographer and the pilgrim.

17

Scientific and Christian Thought: Phenomenological Reflection*

Raimon Panikkar

Raimon Panikkar is Professor Emeritus of Religious Studies at the University of California, Santa Barbara, where he has taught since 1972, having also been a professor at Harvard and at the Universities of Madrid and Rome. Born in 1918 in Barcelona and now residing close by in the village of Tavertet, he has lived and studied in Spain, Germany, Italy, India, the United States, and Latin America. Ordained a Catholic priest in 1946, he has taken an active part in the cultural and philosophical life of Europe, India, and the Americas, where he is highly regarded for the pluralistic vision arising from his Indian and European, Hindu and Christian background and his wide interest in science and the humanities. The founder of several journals on philosophy and culture, he is the prolific author of many books and articles, including most recently *A Dwelling Place for Wisdom* and *The Silence of God: The Answer of the Buddha*, as well as *The Cosmotheandric Experience: Emerging Religious Consciousness*. Soon to be published are his Gifford Lectures of 1989 entitled *The Rhythm of Being*.

Abstract

Two particular and restricted forms of thought, one due to modern science and the other to christianity, are compared here in the form of six theses in such a way as to clarify discussion of the so-called conflict between science and religion.

The oft-debated question of the last century between science and faith, even though it has been a poorly formulated problem, continues to worry many spirits.[1]

Before saying anything else it would be useful to situate this problem from a philosophically descriptive point of view.[2] I imagine that the reader will get my intentioned speech, composed of theological jargon when speaking of science and of words of scientific use when speaking of religion. No one has a monopoly over words.

For heuristic reasons I present these reflections in the form of theses.

. . . .

Modern Science Is a Novum Not Yet 400 Years Old

The roots of modern science are submerged in the night of time. Predecessors were the nominalists, the platonists, the civilizations of India and Egypt, to name a few. However, there is a novum at around 1600, to mention a date, and around Galileo, to mention a name.

There is next a difference between traditional and modern science. The former understands itself as a *scientia, gnôsis, jñâna* that is to say, as a wisdom which gives fullness, joy, salvation . . . , because in fact knowledge is supposed to be an assimilation of reality, since it is believed that Man is *homo sapiens*.[3] The latter is fundamentally a calculus which does not pretend to lure the whole of Man nor in any way to offer a salvific knowledge, since it is believed that Man is *animal rationale*.

This modern science is characterized by the following traits:

1   *An intellectual construction*

i   based on a very particular form of observation, i.e., the quantifiable;

ii   that is generally about experimentation, i.e., a more or less artificial modification of observable facts that allow the projection of their behavior on spatial-temporal coordinates;

iii   that applies mathematical rationality, i.e., a coherent system of deductions starting from previously postulated axioms— originating in pragmatic or a-prioristic reasons.

2   *A social fabric* which is practically the most important in the modern world. This church stands on three pillars that mutually reinforce themselves: the *magisterium* (the teaching body), the *priests* (the scientists), and the *administration* (the technicians). States and nations, universities, multinational businesses, and other modern institutions respect, accept, and count on this impressive fabric which is considered so solid that it does not seem imaginable that the doors of Hell can ever prevail against it. "It will endure for centuries on end." Or, saying it with a simile that already reveals an equal mentality, "one cannot go back." Modern science is an indisputable element, a strong and forceful institution which has extended over the whole world. It believes itself modifiable (*scientia semper est reformanda*) but not mortal.

3   *A cultural world* which dominates the way of thinking about and seeing the world for a great part of humanity, even though these people may not be directly connected with technoscience. Modern science is not just a collection of "known facts" and a socio-political institution, it is also a *forma mentis*, a way to see reality and to interpret facts and events that appear to human consciousness. There is a scientific ideology, just as there is a scientific myth that dominates modern culture. That which is "scientific" has the guarantee of seriousness, quality, and even of truth.

Science has influenced in a nearly totalitarian way, generally working on the unconscious, the ways of thinking of modern Man. Such a balanced thinker, for example, as David Jou, when formulating the three fundamental cosmological questions, does not ask about the nature or the essence of the universe, life, and intelligence, but rather he asks, as if they were neutral questions, about "the *origin* of the universe, the *origin* of life, and the *origin* of intelligence." It is the scientific evolutionary way of thinking that makes us believe that to explain the genesis of a phenomenon is to know it.

Let us not forget that culture does not primarily give us answers but rather it offers us the horizon from which the questions are formulated. The question of the origin of things, which replaces that which asks about its being or its essence, conditions the entire scientific culture. The question takes for granted a dynamic conception within a linear vision of time. The same question is already presupposing evolution—which in the same assumption leads us to classify peoples as developed and as not developed, or as in the process of development, to say it more euphemistically.

• • • • • • • • •

Scientific Thought Is a Very Particular and Restricted Form of Thought

I understand thought as that human activity by which Man arrives at the intelligibility of a thing or event. The form of scientific thought is conditioned by its method. This method is characterized by:

1 *An active abstraction.* Scientific thought in fact abstracts from reality a part of it, only that which is susceptible to being measured. Those aspects of reality that show things as bad or good, menacing or satisfying, beautiful or ugly, invisible to the senses or carriers of non-rational messages, do not fall directly under the purview of scientific thought. Modern science is content with extracting the quantifiable parameters of the (observable) phenomena, with the more or less explicit presumption that this algebra (with its deductive operations of rational logic) reveals to us the (pragmatic) behavior of the phenomena thus described. In this way, it can predict, control, calculate, and formulate laws about the behavior (but not about the nature) of the phenomena thus observed.

2 *A passive abstraction*—that is to say, by dismissing that which does not fall under its parameters: in other words, by excluding any other element which is not intrinsically objectifiable, as could be the intentions of the thinker, the ethical aspect of thought, or any other extrapolation foreign to the scientific enterprise. This does not mean that scientists (who are people and usually the most intelligent, sociologically speaking) do not have many other intentions and worthwhile preoccupations, such as to do good and extend the benefits of science around the world. Just like the missionaries of years past who wanted to save souls and have everyone go to heaven, today's missionaries want to save the bodies and spread well-being and peace around the world.

3 *The refusal to say anything about other aspects of reality*—limiting itself to the possibility of establishing scientific laws warranted by the underlying mathematics and by the possibility of falsification by other data and theories. For this reason, unique events (phenomena) fall outside of the range of scientific thought. Just like in the olden time a very clear distinction was made between the supernatural and the natural, the religious and the political (the church, for example, did not want to involve herself in temporal doings), now there is a similar distinction between the scientific and the non-scientific fields. It is the same myth that continues in another form. (Myths are very resistant to death indeed.)

· · · · · · · · · ·

Scientific Kosmology Is Monocultural, Monorational, and Self-sufficient

I understand by kosmology (*sic*) the set of organized experiences of reality which is proper to each culture. Each kosmology arises from a horizon where, more or less instinctively, all human perceptions are situated, so that in such a way they have a certain meaning or are in some way intelligible. Kosmology is the description of how the world appears to human consciousness. I distinguish it from cosmology, that is the vision that modern science has of the cosmos, where the word "cosmos" already has the particular meaning of the scientific object just as modern science understands it. The world of astrology and the world of alchemy, for example, do not form part of the scientific cosmology. This cosmology is just one of the many kosmologies.

This kosmology is:

1 *Monocultural.* It is not by chance that modern science was born in christian Europe just half a millenium ago and that it follows in the footsteps of platonic tradition in trying to install the concept of objective reality—even though platonic conceptual objectivity is wider than conceptual scientific objectivity. (Platonic concepts represent the ideas of the platonic world; scientific concepts are algorithms.) This means that modern science finds itself at home in this culture of western origin. To understand the difference, let us think for example of the vedico-upanishadic culture in which the fundamental categories of thought are not concepts but rather states of consciousness or fields of meaning. And these are states or fields that "objectivize" themselves, we could add, to underscore the solidity and validity of these categories—always using western metaphors, since we are speaking a western language. To ask what things *are*, speaking within the hellenic framework, amounts (homeomorphically) in the vedico-upanishadic culture to asking oneself what things feel and how we feel them. And it would be a methodological error to qualify this as anthropomorphism. Let us remember that there are ways of thought in other cultures where what counts is the uniqueness and not the repeatability, the resistence to comprehension and not the noetic (epistemic) transparence.

I have to add that I don't criticize monoculturalism: I am only saying that we need to be aware of it. Lest we defend a totalitarian view of the evolution of culture in which each new "progress" subsumes all the previous steps, with scientific Man representing the highest degree in the evolution of human perfection, we have to recognize that the other kosmologies can have a validity as relative as the scientific cosmology—which therefore we should also relativize.

2 *Monorational.* The modern scientific worldview strives to be rational; and this putative last word is interpreted as a mathematical rationality (this would certainly include Heisenberg, Gödel, and non-euclidian geometries and probabilities). All that which does not fall under the type of rationality thus defined either is not included in such cosmology or is regarded as false.

Angels, for example, cannot be part of a scientific cosmology because they are scientifically uncontrollable. Love will have to be explained as movements of attraction moved by some feelings that are the fruit of a major or minor psycho-physiological affinity. When all of this becomes scientifically calculable and therefore controllable, it will permit a possible scientific interpretation. Science knows how to wait, and it is convinced that it has not yet deciphered all the enigmas of the universe. Science deals with enigmas to be deciphered (decoded) and not with mysteries to be experienced (observed). The world is written in mathematical characters, Galileo said. Modern science is this reading.

This monorationality does not need to be absolutist, however. It is an open monorationality that can very well admit that phenomena which now do not (yet) fall within the scientific field could in the future be a part of it, as has happened more than once. Science can admit without difficulty that people believe in angels and in maddening love (as Ramon Llull would say), even though these things do not have citizenship in the scientific world. They might have such citizenship in the future, if we wait patiently without abandoning the enterprise. Scientific hope is of the future; religious hope is of the invisible.

3 *Self-sufficient.* (One could as well say self-regulating [self-contained].) It is self-sufficient in the way that a corporation is self-perpetuating by choosing new executives from among its members. Science is not stubborn with its contents; it is open, enough even to change the paradigm if the need is proven, of course, within the recognized parameters. Science does not have dogmas of content but only of method and of assumptions; it is open to dialogue but in a language that it has to understand, and this is called rational language.

The great lesson of modern science is the methodological precision and rigor of its observations, together with its liberty in terms of preconceived ideas. In the last instance, the great value of science as a heuristic method is its humility: it knows itself limited, fallible, and provisional. It is therefore always ready to change hypotheses when it is proved to be needed. Science as a scientific activity (but not as a techno-scientific institution) does not have created interests. It is not afraid of scaring or disorienting all of those who have placed their hopes on obsolete hypotheses.

Another way of saying the same thing, but in a less scientific manner, is to say that modern science does not have any need of God. It does not need this hypothesis. God can be very welcome to the scientist who needs certainty, but deity is superfluous to science. Modern science does not thirst for foundations: it can function and exist in provisionality. It is not absolute, it has a protean nature. And because of this, paradoxically, it can believe that *extra scientiam nulla salus* ("there is no salvation outside science"). It is very open and tolerant—within its own limits.

· · · · · · · · · ·

Christianity Is a Novum Not Yet Two Millennia Old

The roots of christian faith are submerged in the night of time. Predecessors were the prophets of Israel, Zoroaster, Egypt, and so forth. But there is a novum around 753 years after the foundation of Rome, to give a date, and of Jesus of Nazareth, to give a name; and there is a profound difference between the traditional religions and christianity.

The first ones are understood, very generically speaking, as religions of salvation and paths of cosmic awareness, since in them Man is believed to be part of the cosmos. The second one is understood as a unique incarnation of the divine in a historic man and, indirectly, in history itself, because it is believed that Man is the king of creation.

This christianity is characterized by:

1 *An intellectual construction*

i based on a spiritual experience originated by the impact provoked by Jesus of Nazareth and continued by Christ, which is the name that is usually given to the risen Jesus. I am referring to the personal experience of the christian, without which one cannot speak of christian faith;

ii justified by the cordial interpretation of not only historical facts but experiences that have been growing throughout the centuries. I am referring to the interpretation done with the whole being, not only by the particular individual but rather by the entire tradition, that has led the christian faith to crystallize in a set of more or less integrated beliefs;

iii the fruit of a self-understanding within the semitic-hellenic cultural matrix with gothic and later elements. One should not forget that christianity is an intellectual and fundamentally mediterranean spiritual construction. The whole Bible is of a semitic mentality. Bread and wine are mediterranean symbols, just to give an example.

2 *A social fabric* that for many centuries was the most important in the european world and its colonies, that has been fused with the political and cultural powers for more than a thousand years. The states, nations, universities, social entities, and public laws accepted the church's principles in the life of the peoples. This ecclesiastical institution stands on three pillars: a body of doctrine, a practical application, and a subtle administration. The church is a strong and powerful institution that has extended itself throughout the world. It strives to become "inculturated" in any existing culture.

3 *A cultural world.* Even though the institution of the church has lost power almost everywhere in the world, the way of thinking in modern societies, be they christian or not, is overwhelmingly shaped by what could be called christian culture, be it orthodox or secularized. Not only the ideas but the *forma mentis* of the contemporary world that has suffered the impact of the West are predominantly of christian origin: the sense of history, the conviction of a spiritual-material duality, the notion of linear temporality, and the consciousness of individuality could be some examples. Christians may remember that in the time of Advent the biblical readings of the liturgy speak of a peace when all the peoples will be subjected to Jahweh and walk in the light of the Lord. The secularized translation of all this is the belief that the future peace will come when all the peoples of the earth will have a world government, a global democracy, a single market and therefore a world bank, and so forth. Many of the so-called alternative movements share the same ideals.

· · · · · · · · · ·

Christian Thought Is a Particular and Restricted Form of Thought

I understand by christian thought a thought which thematically endeavors to see reality in the light of a personal christian experience and its cumulative interpretation by christian tradition. Christian thought could be characterized, among other things, by the following traits:

1 *Exegetic.* Even though many like myself would like to understand christianity (or at least christianness) as the religion of the Word, one cannot deny that christian history shows that it has been more a religion of the Book than of the Word, as practically all of the abrahamic religions are. Indeed, an important role has been given to tradition especially in the orthodox and catholic interpretations but one always subordinated to Scripture, which, evidently, requires interpretation, that is to say, exegesis.

Even though today this conception is in crisis, due to contemporary hermeneutic awareness, christian self-understanding interprets itself as an intellectual elaboration starting from that which used to be called "revealed facts." It is all a question of interpreting them well.

A great part of the past polemics between "science and faith" were seen in terms of conflict or harmony between the facts of revelation and the data of science—believers saying that between the two there could be no contradiction because they had in God the same origin. The fact that a minority is today against this opinion and that we would like to reevaluate experience as a more genuine origin of christian thought, according to a more mystic trend, cannot allow us to forget that the prevalent form of christian identity is based on the interpretation of Scripture.

2 *Exclusive.* Because of the fact that christianity believes itself to be on a path, even though asymptotic, towards truth, christian thought believes that faithfulness to this truth requires exclusion of anything that contradicts its own fundamental intuitions, since they were considered as revelation of an omniscient God. One can and should be tolerant, but thought cannot betray itself and condone error. *Extra ecclesiam nulla salus,* in spite of its many possible interpretations, could be a formulation of this attitude. This has made christian thought very sensitive to unity. Who gets saved is not one undiscriminated being among a series of many individuals but rather a unique being, and therefore incomparable. For centuries christian thought has not found it to be repugnant that only a few were saved. This implies a very different anthropology from that which is currently dominant. In contrast to scientific objectivism we find here an extreme subjectivism. It is the subject that counts.

3 *Existential.* Christian thought has always claimed to be a science of salvation. Without faith there is no salvation, but the act of faith is a free and intellectual act. The method, that is to say, the path, is an existential path—it wants to lead to liberation, to the

fulfillment of Man, be it called heaven, blessed vision, diviniza-
tion, happiness, or whatever. No matter the ideological baroquism
of a good part of christian thought, christianity has declined to
give a total explanation of reality and has concentrated instead on
finding a meaning to the pilgrimage of *homo viator* towards his
goal. The Bible, theologians will underscore, is not a science or
history book, but it simply narrates what is necessary for Man's
salvation. Christian thought wants to be about Man's salvation.

· · · · · · · · · ·

Christian Kosmology Is (Mono)Theistic, Homocentric and Acritical

1 *Monotheist.* I eliminate the parenthesis here in order to maintain the parallelism with scientific kosmology and because, in fact,
the greatest bulk of the christian tradition during the last two
millennia has not (yet) overcome the monotheistic scheme of the
deity which was inherited from its most important matrix, the
hebrew bible: christian kosmology believes in one God, creator of
heaven and earth, be it because this is the interpretation of the
bible narrative or be it because it is a confirmation of a more
original insight according to which the world has neither made
itself nor has in itself a reason of its existence.

In the course of the christian dialogue with the world around
us, this God has been variously interpreted as the soul of the
universe that gives life to the world, which would be then its
organism (panentheism); as the architect of the universe, which
then would be the result of the divine plan (platonism); as the
divine watchmaker that would keep the world order (Newton,
Leibniz); as the omnipotent engineer that would make it work
(many current scientists); or as a creator God that would give
existence (being) to all things. But in one way or another the
christian God is cause (creator) and the world his effect (creature).

This could be the moment to mention that the great challenge
of christian thought for the incoming third millennium consists in
overcoming theism, deepening the experience of the Trinity in the
direction of a cosmotheandric intuition.[4]

2 *Homocentric.* Man is the center of the universe; maybe not
spatially, but the christian vision of reality is fundamentally
interested in Man and his salvation. The Incarnation is for the sake
of Man, even though Saint Paul tells us that all creation takes
advantage of it. God becomes not a star, one could say echoing
Saint Augustine, but Man. Christianity is not interested in the way

the heavens go but in the way one goes to heaven, we could add, echoing Galileo. Christian kosmology is seen in Man's function. What the medieval christian thinkers called *curiositas*, and considered a sin, was the desire to want to find out what is irrelevant for the fulfillment of human life. God has become Man so that Man may become God; the cosmos merited only relative and secondary interest.

That earth was the center of the universe did not mean that our planet was in the middle of the spatial scientific coordinates; it did not have a cosmological meaning but a kosmological one. That modern Man continued believing the center of reality to be within a marginal galaxy within the astronomic universe remains an incongruence. This is an example of the kosmological imbalance of the current christian vision. And this leads us to our third point.

3 *Acritical.* Christian kosmology is not the fruit of a thematic reflection, as scientific cosmology is. Christian thought has made progress in the world and has been accepting, often grudgingly and with delay, of the worldview that surrounded it. In a certain sense there is no specific christian kosmology. Christian thought has only declared non-christian those visions of the world that were thought incompatible with the christian vision of things. But despite all, it has been adapting to the kosmology of each era, due mainly to the influence of science. We may think not only of Ptolemy, Copernicus, but also of Miquel Servet, Pasteur, and now of the Eucharistic and Resurrection problems.

I have defended elsewhere that the *Divine Comedy* represents the last kosmology of the West, and in fact, Dante's work consists of a christian vision of the world where each event has a place and acquires a meaning. From Pythagoras to Dante, the West has had a homogeneous kosmology. From that point on, western civilization has not had any other global vision of reality, despite the effort (genial, but failed) of the *Faustus* of Goethe. The latest kosmology has proceeded to dismantle piece after piece of the preceding one because it did not consider it convincing (because it did not explain the phenomena); but it has not been entirely supplanted by any other. Christian thought has been accommodating itself more or less adequately to the cosmological reforms that were being brought about, but without possessing its own kosmology. Almost all of the so-called christian "theology" is not such (logos over God) but kosmology (and anthropology)—a vision about the World and Man compatible with what was believed to be God.

This phenomenological description, even though I have loaded it with irony, can help us to obtain a certain clarity in the conflict wrongly called "science and religion" that still worries many people. This I reserve for another occasion.

• • • • • • • • • •

Notes

*Translated from Catalan by Paula Sprague and Natalia Francis, Department of Romance Languages, University of Wisconsin, Madison.

1. During the fall of 1992 the Fundació Joan Maragall of Barcelona organized an international symposium about *Scientific Thought and Christian Faith*. The author of this work took part in the roundtable discussion of the symposium, orally presenting the more explicitly elaborate ideas. The work is still unpublished, given that the Foundation will not publish the summary or the article. The *Revista de Catalunya* will publish it in two independent articles, of which this is the first.

2. For over a dozen years I have been preparing a study on *The Conflict of Kosmologies* (*sic*) that I hope to publish soon.

3. I write Man for *homo* (with capital M), not giving males the monopoly on *anthôpos*, nor splitting Man into "man" and "wo-man," nor making of Man just a number of the set "humans." Every person is unique.

4. Cf. the explanation of this word in *La nova innocència I* (Barcelona: Llar del llibre, 1991), 57–65 and more extensively in my book *The Cosmotheandric Experience* (Maryknoll, N.Y.: Orbis Books, 1993).

• • • • • • • • • •

"Cosmic Beginnings" Is a Meta-Cosmic Notion

Before plunging into the sea of the possible or plausible answers to the three questions, it may be advisable to pause, not because we are afraid of the sea, but because we want to know the height and be aware of the firmness of our springboard. As Buddha's wisdom warned us, not every question is proper: not because we cannot fathom the answer, but because we do not understand the question. We simply do not know, sometimes, what we are asking about.

The three questions, in point of fact, are contemporary questions: they belong to our contemporary world, the springboard is our present-day sensibility. And the height comes from our scientific worldview. They are related not only to our *time;* they are also linked to our *spatial* world, that is, to our prevalent culture. Other times and other cultures may give different answers because they are already putting different questions—although sometimes under similar wordings. Language is a *human invariant,* but no particular language is a *cultural universal.*

I shall distinguish a threefold level on each of the three questions. Needless to say, I offer these reflections to an enlightened scientific community for dialogue and critique. The field of modern cosmology is too young and needs to be extremely prudent, and even fearful, when indulging in such momentous and yet unavoidable problems. I am very grateful to have been asked to voice my comments which to some may seem as coming from another world—another world, however, which is also human and real.

1 What are your views on cosmic beginnings, particularly with reference to the origin of the universe, of life, and of *Homo sapiens?*

2 What are your views on human ends, especially as this relates to the framework of cosmic beginnings?

3 What do you think should be the relationship between religion and science?

These are the three levels of the question: the first, most important and mainly neglected level, is the crosscultural problematic. Western (or westernized) Man is not alone in this world, nor is that culture a universal and unique culture.

The second level is the often despised and mainly misunderstood metaphysical field. Modernity has a very peculiar notion of the non-measurable and tends to cast it altogether into the pit of the non-verifiable (or falsifiable) so that it can be easily dispensed with.

The third level belongs to the strictly scientific field. The contemporary citizen tends on the one hand to revere Modern Science as Bible, and to ignore it when it becomes impractical or complicated on the other. (It is the same reaction as the old citizens with the actual Bible, by the way.)

I shall make a few comments on each level.

The Crosscultural Question

"Beginning" in English stands for an almost exclusively temporal concept, although it is used to translate words which often do not connote just the modern idea of temporality. When the *Hiranyagarbha* hymn of the Rig Veda (X, 121, 1), the Prologue of John's Gospel (I, 1), or other cosmogonies say *agre, en arché,* or use similar expressions, they do not mean fundamentally a temporal beginning and much less the beginning of a linear time. They do not indulge in an idle discussion on what was 'before,' since the very concept of "before time" is a contradiction in terms—"before" being already a temporal notion. *Cosmic beginnings* in this context is, strictly speaking, a meta-cosmic notion; it has nothing to do with a time zero.

The Christian scholastics already discussed whether the cosmos can be *ab aeterno*, and many of them found no contradiction in it. The philosophical idea of creation could very well be a *creatio ab aeterno* since there is no time in which God was not Creator.

Even more, a common idea of scholasticism was that God is constantly and continuously creating the world. It is called *creatio continua*. The image of an architect, or worse an engineer, working for a while and keeping afterwards an indefinite sabbath was considered a rather childish and unconvincing interpretation of the Bible. The Lifegiver or Father of many traditions was not the divine clockmaker of a mechanical construct. The world is the Body of God, says more than one human tradition.

Cosmic beginnings means here the Foundation, the Ground, the ultimate Stuff, the Support (*skambha*), the Self of the universe (cf. *Atharvaveda* [AV] X, 7). A prevalent insight was that this universe needs such a Ground—even if sometimes called *Ungrund*. This is the idea of contingency, that is, that the cosmos is tangent to that Base, that it touches in one 'point' (*cum-tangere*) something which is 'more,' 'firmer,' more real, truer . . . than itself. The problems are complex. And our ancestors were not so stupid after all.

I will say here only this much. Victims of monoculturalism, we tend to evaluate ancient kosmologies (*sic*) with the parameters of our modern scientific cosmology. Fair enough, since we do not have other available parameters. But we tend to forget that our own parameters are as relative as those of the ancient cosmogonies. We tend to forget, to put an example closer to us than the ancient kosmology of, say, the jainas, that even the categories of the ptolemaic universe were not those of Copernicus. Gods, spirits, a material heaven, a qualitative space, an earthbound human nature, and the like were essential ingredients of the ptolemaic universe which were practically dismissed in the copernican system. We tend to read those systems as if they were two different texts, forgetting that the comparison of contexts requires a different hermeneutic than that of texts. This is the field of what I have called *diatopical* hermeneutics.

In a word, the relativization of any ancient vision of the world, which we so easily acknowledge, should also include the relativization of our own worldview.

I may be allowed to put it facetiously like this. How did that handful of fellows of the twentieth century figure out the nature of the universe after they put their foot on the moon and invaded the planet with electronic gadgets? They dismissed a God Atlas sustaining the world because they naively imagined that to sustain is what they did with their own hands (or shoulders). They dismissed a creator Jahweh because they again naively imagined that once the Demiurge might have done 'his' job the universe was left to its own laws, which the scientific mind was capable of formulating. Nevertheless they were asking "what It is this all about?" Now, they equated this question with "how did it all begin?" And they understood the verb "begin" as a ride backward in the linear temporal succession of phenomena. The It was reduced to an irrelevant question, being substituted by the How it 'evolved.' The It is as mysterious today as it was millennia ago, but by displacing the curiosity to the How of the past we seem to allay kosmological and metaphysical qualms. To be sure, the contemporaries of the "New World Order" are consoled by the belief that the kosmological and metaphysical problems are unanswerable and concentrate on the scientific question. But a small group among them seem to fathom that there may be more to 'it.' And here we are.

Condensing this very complex issue, I would say that the problem of the cosmic beginning asks for a *tempiternal* foundation of the cosmos. My answer is the cosmotheandric intuition, an intertwining of the cosmic, the human, and the divine.[1] But I imagine that the questionnaire was not meant to put such a question.[2] So I turn to the second level.

The Metaphysical Problem

Beginning is certainly also a temporal concept. It refers to time. Now, time is related to change. We could parallel Newton's first law (leaving aside whether Galilei had already formulated or at least applied it[3]), saying that if there were no change, time would be totally meaningless.

We may say that time is the measure of change using the word *metron* in the original meaning of the first of the Seven Sages of Greece. *Metron ariston*, said Kleobuos of Lindos (Fragment 1, Diels-Kranz I, 63). All things occur 'in' time because time is that 'thing' which 'allows' things to occur. The universe has almost always been considered alive, and time is the respiration (*prana, brahman, Atem*) of it. The ancient greeks already described life (ζωή) as the time of being (χρόνος τοῦ εἶμαι, Hesychios); and the Veda speaks of time as the God supreme upon whom all the worlds repose (*AV* XIX, 54).

The inquisitive human spirit wants to travel 'in time' and asks about cosmic beginnings. We are haunted by the "origins of the universe" (as we are asked about). We see things and events succeeding each other. We want go back, to climb up, or come down, to the origins of everything. It is easier to look for the origins along a temporal road than to descend deep down an ontological well. Furthermore, the human mind seems to hesitate whether the origins are at the beginning or at the end, whether things move because they are pushed or because they are pulled. Modern culture is prevalently archeological. Other cultures, not excluding that of which Aristotle is a paradigm, seem to think that the originating energy is rather eschatological, that is, that it lies at the end and not at the beginning. God moves as final cause, they would say, or as Aristotle beatifully puts it, ὡς ἐρώμενον, as loved, as desired—as an erotic magnet. And, in fact, sometimes we know better a thing knowing what it will become than ascertaining what it has been. Many a marriage and friendship would be spared shipwreck if we were to take this wisdom into account. The mirage of the future may change the swamp of the present.

We are thereby making the distinction between "origin" and "beginning." Perhaps to know the origin, the source from where an event comes, we should wait a little, learn patience, and direct our attention to the *telos*, the end, to eschatology.

But we are asked about cosmic beginnings, we are questioned as to how we see the start of the universe coming from its past. It is common knowledge that most human civilizations do not have a linear and much less a straight-line idea of the temporal processes.

Here is where the plural of the question becomes very meaningful: there may be many beginnings. Things may have many beginnings, and even the same thing may have a plural beginning, even many sources.

We have no evidence whatever whether time is a straight line, a curb, a sinusoid, a spiral, a broken surface, or whatever.

Cosmic beginnings in this sense amounts to asking where the present world comes from, whence comes the dynamism governing the changes we see in this our cosmos, whereby the very question of what this cosmos is remains open. The traditional cosmos was centered on the solar system surrounded by other mindblowing lights (stars), which undoubtedly was meant to indicate that we are not alone in the universe. The medievals distinguished very carefully between what happens in the ordinary *sublunar* world from the events *sub sole* and the meanings *sub specie aeternitatis.*

How did this cosmos begin? The question underlying this query and confering importance to it, is this: how does this answer help us to understand this present cosmos and our existence in it?

And here we need to introduce another momentous remark: the evolutionistic thinking.

One thing is the evolution of the species à la Darwin (and subsequent refinements); social darwinism is another thing; and a third problem is the theory of evolution as a *forma mentis* which I have just called evolutionistic thinking. The three are related, but they should be distinguished. It is this latter one I am refering to and which also confers plausibility to the other two. I would sum it all up in one single sentence: evolutionistic thinking is prompted by the belief that genesis amounts to evolution and that knowing the evolution of a process amounts to understanding the process. In other words, the conviction that detecting the *how* of a phenomenon (how it appears, evolves, unfolds, . . .) amounts to the knowing of the *what* (the phenomenon is).

Indeed, the *natura* or *physis* of a phenomenon is intrinsically related to its birth, genesis, becoming. We should not get stuck in immutable esences, but we should not get drowned either in the swamp of sheer bottomless and marshy lands. *Ousia* and *physis*, substance and nature, the static and the dynamic, identity and difference belong together. To know the beginning of a phenomenon is of paramount value, but this knowledge alone is not enough.

Evolutionistic thinking tends to let us be satisfied with the mere explanation of how a thing has come to be. We know for certain that we come from our parents, as is the case with any other animal. We know how crystals have come to be and probably also how the earth's surface has evolved throughout past ages. It is all precious knowledge. It gives us clues for the future and allows us to advance patterns of behavior and even to formulate certain laws. But all this mass of knowledge does not disclose to us the nature of ourselves, of an animal, a crystal, or the earth. If we concentrate ourselves exclusively in knowing how the past has reached the present, we may easily overlook what I have called the tempiternal present. In one word, the cosmic beginnings do not provide the clue to understand the cosmos; the temporal unfolding of the universe still maintains the secret of what this universe is. Nature has a history and its unfolding shows patterns, gives hints, and allows us to draw some laws, but the narrative is ever new. To deduce from the present situation of the world how it was millennia ago is not the same as to know from the political situation of contemporary Spain the life of the spaniards during the muslim period. Nature is less whimsical than Man, but to assume that it is just dead 'matter' which follows deterministic mechanical laws is a big and unwarranted assumption.

Perhaps we do not even need to know the "cosmic beginnings" in order to have a sufficient knowledge of what this cosmos is. Perhaps a knowledge of a sufficiently large span of its life may enable us to live conciously and efficiently in it. I am saying that knowing sufficiently well the plains, rivers, and mountains of my country may suffice to know this aspect of the world and that a satellite picture of the planet may not increase the quality and depth of my knowledge.

I am saying even more. I am raising the question of whether driving down the neatly constructed highway of (linear) time may be the only or even the best method to come to know the nature of the universe.

I may exemplify this "with reference to the origins of . . . *homo sapiens.*"

If we want to understand what *homo sapiens* is, we shall first of all try to find one, and if possible more than one such specimen. We have plenty of them around us. We shall very soon discover common traits and individual differences. We elaborate then a complex scientific anthropology. But at a certain moment we shall come across what for us is a very special specimen of *homo sapiens:* ourselves. I will discover myself and try to apply all our known anthropology to me. I will then realize one thing: that all our anthropological knowledge leaves aside what interests me most: me. I will then make the discovery that each of us is unique and as such not an object of scientific knowledge nor susceptible of classification. All can be classified except the classifier (and the criterion of classification). The knowledge of a certain beginning of myself and of others will undoubtedly help me to understand *homo sapiens* better. I know that it has evolved and that some thousands of years ago was somewhat different and somewhat the same. The differences will help me in sifting what is more and what is less important (and even essential) in *homo sapiens*. But the knowledge of *homo sapiens* will not be the same as my understanding of myself (and my Self). Even more, to understand the present-day mystery of Man, our pain and pleasures, anguishes and certainties, our dreams and desires, our self-knowledge and our âtman, our assumptions and our myths, our loves and our hatreds, our oceanic feelings and our freedom, our thinking and its foundations, . . . to understand that reality that I am and my neighbors are we may need many other means, parameters, introspections, and reflections than to ponder the evolution of *homo sapiens*, its ancestors, or the way a DNA molecule influences our linear protein chain—interesting as this latter problem is for molecular biology. The "know thyself" of the temple at Delphi is not covered by the knowledge of *homo sapiens*. Our uniqueness is not explained by our cosmic beginnings. And if we deny being unique, we destroy our freedom, dignity, and joy.

The patient reader will have the impression that I am beating around the bush and skipping the 'real' scientific question. I do not think so, but I turn now to the third level.

The Scientific Query

Cosmic Beginnings in the context of the entire set of questions has most probably an entirely different connotation: the connotation of *modern science*. By 'modern science' I do not understand the modernized *scientia, gnôsis, jñâna* of ancient cultures, but the scientific paradigm of the "nuova scienza" since roughly five hundreds years ago: Galilei, Newton, Einstein, to quote just three names, that we could multiply up to contemporary scientists, in spite of the paradigm shifting that is taking place more recently.

We all know the admirable restraint of most of the propounders of the Big Bang hypothesis and the scientific criticism it has received; we all know also that modern science refuses to offer us a model of the universe. It limits itself to finding out mathematical parameters which tally with the observations of some experiments and may therefore serve at foreseeing physical behaviors, controlling some phenomena, and in our case at suggesting that we may reckon within fifteen billion years the 'age' of our known universe. The appeal and fascination of the Big Bang hypothesis is that, in spite of all its healthy provisos, it offers us a picture of a possible factual evolution of our material, mainly energetical universe. And in fact the query about cosmic beginnings is not an interrogation about mathematics or even modern science but the legitimate question of the present-day cosmology: what is the origin of our universe?

There may be many other *kalpas*, many other universes, and our cosmic beginnings may not be an absolute beginning, but the question arises, however, whether we can say something by the dint of modern science to the human question of the first and second levels. Our human destiny seems linked with the fate of the universe, and this universe seems to have revealed to modern physics how old she is.

If the first level asks about the tempiternal and the second the temporal character of the universe, this third level puts the question about the sequential series of material events which may disclose to us the age of our universe, the hourly beginning of our cosmos. For how many seconds has our cosmos existed? When did it all begin? (Beginning here means time zero, and time the relationship between space and velocity: $(dt = ds/dv.)$ If the universe expands (because we observe distances to increase or rather density to decrease) and we can calculate velocity, going in the inverse direction we may be able to reach that point which has haunted so many spirits, when "there will be no time" (Apoc. X, 6).

This apparently so-simple scheme is full of practical and theoretical difficulties, well known to mathematicians and physicists. I shall skip them. What interests us here is not the actual procedure but the meaning, the cosmological meaning, of the intent. And it is here, and only here, where I shall insert my criticism.

To begin with we are not dealing with time as all other human cultures understand this word. We are dealing with *chronons*, the physico-mathematical unity of time considered constant. This unity may be the second, as a practical way of dividing the solar movement or the infra-atomic movement. In a popular way we may say that if we cross the minimum of distance (because otherwise the attraction forces prevail) at the highest speed, using an anthropomorphic or rather materiomorphic model, we may assume that we have a time unit, which could be called the *chronos*.[4] What is important to us here is the cosmological model, if the expression "cosmic beginnings" has to refer to a real cosmos, to our universe.

I have personally some scientific difficulties concerning the

Big Bang hypothesis, but our point here is cosmological. Assuming its correctness, what can it possibly mean for our real world and for the religious quest of humanity? This is our exclusive concern here.

I shall limit my remarks to three, paralleling the three levels of my commentary.

1   The universe here under question is the accepted astronomical universe disclosed to us by modern science based on a very thin assumption of the speed of light and the shifting of the colours in the spectrum. Although we have some meagre information about the extra-solar world and even thinner about the extra-milkyway we assure the sameness of those physical laws throughout the universe, and the constancy of the same laws in an extrapolation which far surpasses the limits of verifiability.

I am by no means saying that it is not fascinating and important. I am only avering that the jump, even within the physico-mathematical field is so enormous as to caution us of hurried conclusions and cosmological applications.

Even assuming that we have found the unification of the four physical forces (electromagnetic, gravitational, weak and strong nuclear) in the so-called Grand Unified Theory (which so far has not been found) we are dealing here with exclusively physical 'energies.' Unless we reduce the cosmos to a bundle of forces, we have to confess that other dimensions of reality are left outside. We would then have only the approximation to the point of singularity of a time zero which is, as such, beyond any scientific approach.

2   Our second remark is more important. It all depends on words, but this is what we have. My contention is this. Physico-mathematical time is not kosmological time; it is not real time, as practically all human cultures have understood this word. The time of modern science is a physico-mathematical parameter, it is a quantifiable magnitude, the measure of an objectifiable relation between space and speed. A very real and important magnitude indeed, but not that 'reality,' entity, or whatever which other cultures have called by this name. We have here a vicious circle, for speed is already intrinsically related to time so that to measure time we already need time.

Having relativized, when not having ridiculed, all other kosmologies, we should not absolutize the modern scientific cosmology as the only one superseding all the others and offering us the only real model of the universe. As I have tried to elaborate elsewhere, I distinguish between our modern cosmology (as a global scientific theory of the cosmos) from all the other traditional kosmologies (as the vision they have of the universe in which they live).

We may agree that my age is an expression of my time, but the age of a stone needs another measure than the *metron* of my personal time, and so the age of the universe. Time, after all, is one of those words which defy objectification (time without a subject perceiving change is no time) and subjectification (things have to really change and thus require also an unchanging canvas). Time is not an objective entity, nor is it a subjective entity. Time is very real, but it is neither "over there," so that there is the same 'time' for everybody, nor "over here," so as to be a private aspect of every one of us. Time is a very real relation. The time of the universe cannot be measured with human time or vice-versa.

Cosmic beginnings is probably an anthropomorphism. We have had a beginning, because we define the ego as that which began with our birth (or conception). The earth has had a beginning, because we define the earth as that particularly shaped piece of matter which we call this planet; but this does not mean an absolute beginning of that 'matter' which 'later' becomes the planet. But the beginning of the cosmos seems to point towards an absolute beginning, and this is a rather ambiguous concept. A beginning is a beginning in relation to something from which it is the beginning. Such a 'something' 'prior' to the beginning cannot exist—otherwise it would not be an absolute beginning. In other words, we may conceive 'something' beginningless (without a beginning) but not an absolute beginning, because something is only beginning in relation to something else, therefore it is not absolute. The very notion of beginning is a relative notion. To play with Non-being as if it *were* a being is not a fair play.

3   Would this mean that God or religion cannot receive any support from scientific thought or that scientific thought needs to be, as such, intrinsically a-theist and a-religious? Not necessarily; but it means that our human reflections on cosmic beginnings cannot invoke an already-shaped concept of God or religion in favor of or against the existence of such beginning.

Religion and science are two specific human activities of Man. In general terms when Man aspires to know, he cultivates knowledge; when Man aspires to be saved (realized, liberated, . . .), he cultivates religion. In traditional cultures true knowledge had a saving effect and true religion had a knowing ingredient. Many problems nowadays arise from the cultural schizophrenia of having converted necessary distinctions into lethal dichotomies.

And with these considerations I have implicitly reacted to the other two questions.

· · · · · · · · · ·

Notes

1. Cf. R. Panikkar, *The Cosmotheandric Experience* (Maryknoll, N.Y.: Orbis, 1993).
2. There are scores of modern accounts of old cosmogonies. Still useful is the collective volume of "Sources Orientales I," *La naissance du monde* (Paris: Seuil, 1959).
3. A. Zimmermann, "Galileis Überlegungen und ihre Nachwirkungen," in the Festschrift for Elisabeth Gössmann, *Theologie zwischen Zeiten und Kontinenten*, T. Schneider and H. Schlügel-Straumann, eds. (Freiburg: Herder, 1993), 173–184.
4. Cf. my old calculations of 1949, republished in my book *Ontonomía de la ciencia* (Madrid: Gredos, 1961), 309–354. The value of 10^{-24} seconds has been today superseded by double, and the Big Bang reckoning would consider an infinitesimal approach to zero–which is a mathematical but not a physical hypothesis.

18

A Search for Beliefs to Live by Consistent with Science*
• • • • • • • • • •
Roger W. Sperry

Roger Sperry, a principal shaper of modern views of how the brain works, received a Nobel Prize in Physiology or Medicine in 1981 "for his discoveries concerning the functional specialization of the cerebral hemispheres." By then he had already turned away from the experimental science that in his hands had been so brilliantly successful and had begun concentrating on the relationship between mind and consciousness and ethical values, as described in his 1983 book *Science and Moral Priority: Merging Mind, Brain and Human Values*, and more recent publications arising from his continuing intellectual activity at the California Institute of Technology, carried out in spite of a disease that has robbed him of mobility for many years (see the postscript to the Preface on page ix).

• • • • • • • • • •

Abstract

Instead of separating religion and science into "mutually incompatible realms," the new macromental paradigm of behavioral science permits integration of the two within a single consistent worldview. A new form of causal determinism combines conventional "bottom-up" with emergent "top-down" causation. Traditional materialist tenets are overturned, along with the science-values dichotomy, clearing the way for a science-based value/belief system. Intrinsic ethicomoral directives emerge in which a revised sense of the sacred would help protect the evolving quality of the biosphere and the rights and welfare of future generations. Subsequent versions of today's changing worldview raise questions of which interpretation to believe. An analysis of "New Age" thinking is called for, and a brief attempt at such analysis is included.

With a scientist's faith in empirically verified truth and a long commitment to research in the brain, behavioral, and life sciences, I spent most of my working years accepting the scientific accounts of the nature and origins of life and the universe. If science said that human life is lacking in any ultimate purpose, value, or higher meaning—that we and our world are driven merely by mindless, indifferent physical forces—I was prepared to face this. Like many scientists, I preferred to seek out and confront the truth, however harsh, than to live by false premises and illusory values. The more I learn about the workings of the brain and how it processes information, the stronger becomes my allegiance to the type of truth that receives consistent empirical validation in the outside real world.

Nevertheless, without abandoning or compromising scientific principles, I have come around almost full circle today to reject the type of truth science traditionally has stood for, along with its dominant central tenet that everything in our universe, including the human psyche, can be accounted for in terms entirely physical—that science has absolutely no need for recourse to conscious mental or spiritual forces. As a brain scientist, I have come to believe in the reality and power of conscious mental/ cognitive entities of the mind or spirit and the indispensability of their causal control for both brain function and its evolution—and that science has been wrong all along in its categorical denial of this. In particular, I take the subjective value-belief system of the brain to be a powerful intrinsic force that, above any other, shapes human culture and the course of affairs in the civilized world.

This turnabout in my system of belief began with some changed ideas about consciousness and the fundamental relation of mind to the physical brain. It soon became apparent that if these revised mind-brain concepts were to hold up, they would transform our scientific views of both human and nonhuman nature and of the kinds of forces that control them, with wide-ranging humanistic as well as scientific consequences. Among the many ideologic and value-belief consequences, I could foresee the foundations for a naturalistic "global ethic" for all nations and cultures, based in the neutral universality and credibility of science: an ethic promoting values that would tend to preserve and enhance, instead of destroy, our world. The bottom-line message that emerged said we should be looking to science to save the world, not through more or better technology (which would only stave off and thereby magnify our impending downfall) but, instead, by providing reformed value-belief guidelines to live and govern by.

As these and other ramifications began to unfold, I found myself drawn more and more away from the world of the laboratory and split-brain research and toward these more compelling and timely issues. Our experiments to determine whether different mental states are more left or right hemisphere, though still intriguing and productive (Trevarthen 1990), began to seem less crucial in the light of our worsening global predicament and imperiled future, especially when compared with the new issues being raised by the idea that mental states have an interactive causal role. By the 1970s, this causal view of mind had become the center of a paradigm battle in behavioral science, with a possibility of further spread into all science. Meantime, as more implications continued to unravel, and with the left-right research already well under way, I decided it would be better to shift my top priority in order to concentrate on the issues of consciousness and mental causation.

Many people fail to see how a "save the world" strategy derives from a concept of consciousness in relation to brain physiology. The answer, put very simply, goes as follows: the fate of the biosphere will depend on human value priorities, which will depend upon assumptions about human life and its meaning —which the new theory modifies in critical ways. The new view of consciousness radically revises the kinds of beliefs upheld in science about ourselves and the world, with conceptual impacts that reach deeply into religion, science, philosophy, and social priorities in general.

Consciousness pervades nearly all aspects of the human enterprise. Everything ever known or felt, seen, heard, believed, imagined, or experienced in any form has to be processed through this universal medium, the conscious mind. Conveyor of all our values, our sense of purpose and meaning, of right and wrong, of beauty, joy, and so on, consciousness is central to all that matters most in life. Any basic revision in its conception, therefore, or in its role, or how it relates to the physical brain or to outside reality is bound to produce sweeping reverberations. An implied answer, for example, to just the one question "Is consciousness mortal or immortal?" would have repercussions in all dimensions or levels of the social structure.

The shift from a noncausal to a causal view of consciousness, asserting that subjective awareness counts and makes a real difference in the physical world, has enormous and far-reaching implications. It abolishes the traditional science-values dichotomy and leads to a new resolution of the old free will-determinism paradox (Deci 1980; Grenander 1983). The very nature and causal influence of belief itself is changed.

Subjective belief, in our new theory, is no longer a mere impotent epiphenomenon of brain activity. It becomes a powerful impelling force in its own right. From the standpoint of the brain's functional organization and cognitive processing, one can hardly overrate the commanding, central-control influence of the human belief system as a shaper of both individual and social behavior. What we believe determines what we value, what we choose, how we act, and what we decide in social policymaking. It is no surprise that our current global crises, viewed historically, can be ascribed in no small part to the kinds of religious beliefs that have long prevailed (White 1967). I think human destiny and the fate of our whole biosphere hang critically on the kinds of beliefs and values the next few generations (let us hope, to come) elect to live and be governed by.

The beliefs that count most are not those about ordinary, day-to-day concerns and basic subsistence, but the higher religious, philosophical, and ideological beliefs: the kind people live and die for—beliefs that concern life's purpose and meaning, beliefs about God, and the human psyche, and its role in the cosmic scheme. Such beliefs determine a society's judgment of how things ought to be in the world, the cultural sense of value, of moral right and wrong, and of social justice. Any belief about the ultimate value and meaning of life tends to condition all subsidiary values throughout one's value hierarchy. The force of an overriding worldview belief system in thousands of millions of minds, determining how people think, what they value, and what they decide, shapes the course of history. It is important that we try to perceive the role of such belief systems in creating the current precarious state of the human condition.

· · · · · · · · ·

Two Great Credos in Conflict

Trouble comes, as daily headlines and history affirm, when such powerful movers and shapers of the human endeavor come into conflict, either with each other or with reality. Despite great advances in our knowledge about the cosmos and the ways of human and non-human nature, belief systems around the world remain so diverse, and even incompatible, that if we accept as true the cherished beliefs of one people, it follows that truths upheld as sacred by other peoples must be false or misleading. While there appear to be advantages in a healthy religious diversity, belief differences, carried to the extent of mutual incredibility and civil intolerance, become a major cause of world conflict—not to mention serious doubts about which of the various versions of belief represents real truth.

Probably the widest, deepest rift in contemporary culture, and the source of its most profound conflict and mutual misunderstanding, is the incompatibility that separates the two great credos of our time: science and mainline religion. Two fundamentally opposed views of existence are upheld, in two totally different reference frames for "truth." Science asks us to accept a purely impersonal, materialistic, mass-energy account of the cosmos. Religion, on the other hand, demands faith in the opposite: in a universe infused and dominated by spiritual intellect, caring, and intentionality. As emphasized by Andrew Greeley (1986), Francis Schaeffer (1981), and many, many others (see Jones 1965; Provine 1988), it comes down to a choice, in the last analysis, between these two great antithetical conceptions of ultimate reality: a universe with a supreme plan, spiritual values, purpose, and higher meaning, or a spiritually void, value-empty cosmos, governed throughout by quantum physics.

For me personally, as a scientist, the salient aspect of this conflict has been that science, so demonstrably successful and in touch with reality in most respects—and which otherwise I regard as the proven best, most credible approach to truth we have—teaches that we and our world are but the product of a passing fluke of physics, utterly lacking in any ultimate purpose or meaning (Provine 1988). Science insists that there is no real freedom of will or choice, nor any actual moral right and wrong—that ours is a deterministic universe in which the flow of events is causal and inexorable. Science tells us, further, that the entire conscious content of the life experience is merely an accessory artifact, a superfluous by-product of brain activity, with no effect whatever on the sequence of events, either in the brain or in the real world—an impotent epiphenomenon that initially arises out of, and in the end sinks into, oblivion.

In any case, it is painfully evident that present-day civilization is obliged to operate from two very different and irreconcilable frameworks of ultimate belief. One lacks credibility in the light of modern science; the other is repellent in humanistic appeal and flies in the face of everyday experience and common sense. In coping with this dilemma, I followed for many years the usual practice of accepting each scheme within its realm but keeping the two alternatives strictly separate. When matters of moral, religious, or related humanistic concerns were involved, my scientific convictions had to be set aside. Conversely, in matters of the laboratory, any mental or spiritual explanations were emphatically excluded.

This double standard has pervasive political and legal manifestations. It is involved in the separation of church and state and is widely endorsed throughout Western society. The U.S. National Academy of Sciences introduced its 1984 booklet, *Science and Creationism* (Press 1984), with a formal pronouncement that "religion and science are separate and mutually exclusive realms of human thought whose presentation in the same context leads to misunderstanding of both scientific theory and religious belief."

As a brain-behavior scientist concerned with the brain's modes and methods of cognitive processing, I find this kind of double thinking leaves much to be desired. If two systems of belief concerning such vital things as the nature, origins, and destiny of all life and the universe, and the kinds of forces in control, are perceived to stand in direct contradiction to each other, and indeed to be "mutually exclusive," then certainly something must be seriously wrong!

A Better Way to Go

During the past twenty-five years I have become increasingly convinced that there is another, better alternative. I can see another kind of answer to this dilemma, a third choice, based in a different conception of ourselves and the natural world that emerged from my revised view of consciousness and how it relates to the workings of the physical brain. A different scientific mode of thinking is involved, specifically, a different conception of causal explanation. It brings a different, "compromise" view of the kinds of powers that govern the universe and created humankind.

Incompatible objective-versus-subjective frameworks of the past are reconciled in a unifying, intermediate position that departs from previously accepted philosophical dichotomies. Standard philosophic terms must be given new meaning, or new terms must be invented (Ripley 1984). Features from both sides of the old dichotomy—the mental and the physical, fact and value, subjective and objective, freedom and determinism—are blended, without contradiction, within a single, consistent, worldview synthesis (Natsoulas 1987; Sperry 1988, 1990).

In practice, the outcome means that I have no longer been

obliged to vacillate between two mutually antithetical schemes for ultimate reality. Instead, I can rely only on this single third choice, which preserves and integrates what seem to me the most credible aspects from each of the earlier views. On one hand, it relinquishes dualistic supernatural beliefs, such as unembodied minds or spirits. On the other, it denies that the traditional (reductive physicalist) accounts of science have been giving the true story.

After more than a quarter century, I find that this "third choice" continues to measure up to its initial impression as a valid reconciliation of earlier polar disparities in a consistent, long-sought unifying view of man in nature (Sperry 1965)—a credible and functional worldview of a kind I can live and work with. Since using this new reference frame, with its intrinsic, almost self-evident global ethic (outlined later), I have much less trouble perceiving moral solutions, for example, to issues between fundamentalists and secular humanists, prochoice versus prolife factions on abortion, environmentalist interests versus those of human subsistence, animal rights issues, and so on. Further, I no longer need to keep my religion and my science separate.

This new outlook on existence did not come out of any quest on my part for new beliefs but arose as the unforeseen, secondary result of a long search for a better answer to the age-old mind-brain problem. Wrestling with questions of conscious unity back in the 1960s, in the surgically separated hemispheres of split-brain animal and human subjects, we were forced to view the relation of brain to conscious awareness in new, more direct ways. In the course of applying and comparing the merits of the available mind-brain theories, I discovered that our long-trusted, supposedly irrefutable and airtight logic for banning consciousness from explanations of brain function rested, in fact, on an unrecognized logical oversight or shortcoming. On further analysis, the whole case for excluding consciousness proved to be outweighed, in my own mind at least, by a newly perceived reasoning about causation.

This new reasoning does not change older assumptions regarding the chain of causation at neurocellular levels in the brain. In cognitive processing, however, these neurocellular events are seen to be enveloped within, and thus controlled by, higher-level types of causal phenomena. In a train of thought, for example, the causal progression is determined at each step by the holistic network properties of mental images, percepts, insights, cognitive associations, and the like, thereby obliging the constituent neurocellular components to fire in patterns determined largely at conscious mental levels. It is an unproven, but widely accepted, assumption of this hypothesis that the conscious qualities are irreducible emergent properties of a special class of brain processes which are. conceived to have their own special dynamics.

In brief, the new answer hypothesizes that conscious experience appears in the causal chain of brain activity at upper (that is, cognitive) levels of brain processing in the form of irreducible emergent properties. These emergent mental entities are conceived to interact on a holistic, "functionalist" basis at their own cognitive level in brain integration and also to exert a concomitant supervenient form of downward control over their constituent neurocellular activities. In contradiction to prior behaviorist doctrine and that of neuro-science, the subjective qualities of inner experience become ineliminable causal contructs for explaining conscious behavior. In effect, the mind is put back into the brain of objective science (see Sperry 1965, 1990). A different model of causal determinism is invoked that combines traditional bottom-up with emergent top-down causation in a "reciprocal" or "doubly determinate" form of hierarchic control.

Though contradicting the reigning presuppositions of the 1960s about causality in brain science, this revised view of brain function gave more satisfying answers to split-brain issues concerning unity of the mind and the conscious self (Bogen 1986; Trevarthen 1990). Instead of concluding, for example, that the normal intact brain must have two separate, left and right minds (harboring, in effect, two separate conscious selves), I could think of conscious experience in the intact brain as an overriding unified entity that normally is "different from and more than" the sum of the conscious experience of the two separate hemispheres. It followed, further, that the unified subjective intent must causally program the patterns of neuronal firing within each hemisphere without interfering with the physical or chemical laws of the neuronal processing at physiological levels.

Most importantly, this revised view provided a breakthrough in our reasoning about causation, a way out of the logic in which science had been locked for more than two centuries and which had forced us into the reductive materialist-behaviorist worldview. The new holistic, emergent downward-control reasoning provided a legitimate, rationally sound way to circumvent the logic of the conventional microchain of causation without violating the empirical principles of science. Though the day-to-day practice and methodology of science are little affected, the kind of life-view science stands for is vastly changed. What previously had been a rigorously objective, atomistic, value-free, and purpose-devoid cosmos is now infused with a new subjectivity and intentionality.

My turnabout on consciousness was thus not so much a product of particular research findings as a coming together in a new light of previously separate threads of thought. For example, I had been teaching evolution in terms of downward causation for years but had not applied it to the riddle of consciousness until I was forced to think in new ways by our split-brain studies, in which surgical midline division of the brain was found to correspondingly divide the mind.

The shift of mental qualities from a noncausal to a causal status demanded basic revisions in our prior materialist/ behaviorist convictions. Brain function could no longer be thought to be fully explainable in terms of its chemistry or molecular biology. The higher organizational network properties must also be included as irreducible control factors. Instead of excluding mind and spirit, this view retains all the rich subjective qualities as integral and ineliminable functional agents—not, of course, in any disembodied, free-floating, or ethereal form but as holistic properties in upper-level brain processing. The long-banned subjective states and qualities are now put up front—in the driver's seat as it were—as a crowning achievement of evolution (Sperry 1965) and are given primacy in determining what a person is and does.

Not only within the brain but throughout the natural world the same basic principle of emergent causal control applies. The more highly evolved "macro" or holistic properties at all levels gain added status and legitimacy in science as irreducible and ineliminable causal entities in their own right, exerting downward control over their lower, less-evolved components. The "mental" is just a special instance of this universal macrocausation, but sufficiently special to merit separate mention. Bottom-up micro-controls are retained throughout but are no longer exclusive.

· · · · · · · · · ·

Trial Tests

My first attempt to act on these newfound beliefs was to test them in the marketplace of professional opinion through lectures and articles (Sperry 1964, 1965). Definitive proof was not the object, any more than proof had been obtained for the preceding behaviorist or materialist paradigms. Even so, I believe that someday we will obtain convincing demonstrations, at least for the general principle of emergent causation, by closing in on the issues, using simple mechanical models such as a rolling wheel (Klee 1984; Smart 1981). The best I could do at the time, however, was to put the ideas in print, where the new reasoning could be pondered, weighed, and analyzed from different specialist angles by thousands of critical minds.

The majority feedback over an initial four-year trial period encouraged more formal presentations within neurology, philosophy, and psychology, and to our National Academy of Sciences (Grene 1969; Sperry 1969, 1970). The abrupt swing in American psychology shortly thereafter, away from the long-dominant behaviorist doctrine denunciating mentalism to acceptance of subjective mental phenomena as legitimate causal constructs for scientific explanation (Dember 1974; Matson 1971; Palermo 1971; Pylyshyn 1973; Reese and Overton 1972; Segal and Lachman 1972), was most reassuring.

This conceptual turnabout of mainstream psychology in the early 1970s (the so-called cognitive, consciousness, mentalist, or humanist revolution) meant that the causal view of consciousness had been lifted out of the realm of mere philosophic conjecture into that of the history of science. Whether the test of time proves it right or wrong, the new paradigm already has replaced behaviorism and has reigned for nearly two decades as the dominant working conceptual framework for the whole scientific discipline that specializes in mind and behavior (Baars 1986; Gardner 1985; Sperry 1987).

Meanwhile the more basic sciences, such as physics, chemistry, and molecular biology, have continued to adhere (predominantly) to the traditional bottom-up microdeterminism. The result is that we now have, within science and philosophy, two competing, fundamentally opposed paradigms for causal determinism. One opposes, while the other affirms, emergent causation: the irreducible, holistic interaction and downward control by the higher, more-evolved forces of nature over their lower, less-evolved constituents.

In simple terms, the dispute comes down to whether a newly evolved whole (entity or system) interacts entirely through the properties of its component parts or whether its interactions are also governed by novel emergent properties of its own as a whole which, at the same time, carry along and thereby control all the parts. In the brain, it is a question of higher mental over lower neuronal properties, but the issue is universal. Ultimately, it's a question of the types of forces that are in control in our world and within ourselves—the forces that made and move the universe and created humankind.

. . . .

Competing Paradigms in Science

On one side, in accord with traditional microdeterminist views in science, we and all our thoughts, behavior, and decisions, as well as everything around us, are controlled from below by strictly physico-chemical forces that reduce ultimately to quantum physics. Everything in the brain and elsewhere is subject to the laws of physics and chemistry. There is no freedom, no choice, no values, no intention, no moral priority. All such are merely subjective epiphenomena of mind which may parallel, but in no way causally influence, the course of physical events in the brain or in the natural world. "Mind does not move matter" is the familiar bottom line for this classic position, or "No physical action waits on anything but another physical action."

On the other hand, if our new mentalist thinking is correct, the physical and chemical forces in the brain, though still present and operating as before, are enveloped or embedded within, and thereby controlled and programmed ("pushed and hauled around" [Sperry 1965]), by the higher laws and dynamics of conscious and subconscious mental processes. The more highly evolved, "macro," or holistic mental properties of brain action determine when, where, and how the component molecular events will occur, but without interfering with the physicochemical laws at the molecular level—much as TV or computer programs shape patterns on the viewing screen without interfering with the physics of the system.

Brain cell excitation, in this view, no longer waits solely on biophysical forces but also obeys a higher command, involving subjective feelings, wants, choice, intentions, moral values, and all other "things of the mind." The subjective events of mind and consciousness have their own dynamics and laws of causal progression. These transcend and control the events of brain physiology in an enveloping supervenient sense—at the same time that they are determined by them. This reciprocal, two-way control in opposing directions is not in conflict because different forms of causation are operating in the upward and downward directions.

Following adoption of the mentalist paradigm in psychology, with its new approach to causal explanation, the central idea was soon incorporated into systems theory (Laszlo 1972) and has since been gaining ground in science and philosophy. Even physics, the long time bastion of opposing materialist doctrine, has in the past decade started a swing in the same direction (via "chaos" and computer science). The macromental paradigm has thus come to pose a major challenge to traditional micromaterialist principles of explanation and knowing. Review of the chronology reveals an ironic twist in that psychology, long put down by the more physical sciences, should now be the first to adopt what promises to be a more valid basic paradigm for all science.

As things stand, I no longer need to believe, as a scientist, that I and my world are governed solely from below upward through the "fundamental forces of physics" in a totally mindless and purposeless cosmos, indifferent to human concerns. In our new downward-control paradigm we are moved and surrounded in the modern world by higher, more-evolved vital, mental, cultural, and other social forces. The forces embodied in politics, religion, education, business, and so on are full of purpose, caring, value, and meaning and are interpreted to be just as real and causal as the properties of molecules and atoms. In our new reasoning these higher, more-evolved forces of nature and all reality are given their due as well as physics and chemistry.

The resultant new emphasis for science is not on the ultimate subatomic building blocks of creation but on the supersedent properties of the new forms, patterns, and shapes into which the building blocks are successively assembled. I can still believe, for example—despite quantum physics—that the proverbial solid table is just as solid and hard as ever and, regardless of having similar subatomic makeup, is very unlike soft pudding. All in all, the result is a vastly transformed scientific view of both human and nonhuman nature. A kind of cosmos and vision of reality are upheld that, to me, seem much more credible and satisfying than either of the earlier, more polar views.

· · · · · · · · · ·
Science-based Moral Code: a Global Ethic

This intermediate outlook, moreover, though based in the worldview and truths of science, no longer clashes with common experience nor with traditional views in the humanities, nor is it incompatible with liberal nondualistic religious belief and values. Subjectivity and the qualitative aspects of reality are no longer shut out. A sense of higher meaning is provided in the cosmic scheme of things, with rich value and moral directives.

In these and other ways, the consciousness revolution has turned around the traditional science-values dichotomy and is thus, in effect, also a *values* revolution. Further, the scientific about-face on consciousness is one of the few scientific revolutions that also qualifies as a combined *ideological* revolution, in the sense described by Karl Popper (Popper 1975). The overall outcome is that, for the first time, our most advanced scientific theories need no longer be kept separate from religious values in "mutually exclusive realms" of human thought (Byers 1987; Pugh 1977; Rottschaefer 1987, 1988; Sperry 1988).

The most precious and sacred things in life are no longer reduced to subatomic physics or set apart in another, dualistic existence. Transcendent guidelines for judging moral right and wrong are established in terms consistent with mainstream science. Humanity's creator becomes the vast interwoven fabric of all evolving nature. The creative forces and creation itself are inextricably interfused. What is done to one is done to the other, making it immoral, even sacrilegious, to degrade earthly existence or to treat it as only a way station.

The implicit "supreme plan for existence" by which morality is judged (Fletcher 1987) becomes the grand design of the evolving cosmos itself, with special focus on our own evolution (Sperry 1972, 1983). Evolution, no longer seen to be governed merely from below by chance gene mutations, becomes a gradual emergence of increased direction, purpose, and meaning among the forces that move and govern living things. The highest good is an ever-evolving quality of existence, and an open-end future becomes a *sine qua non* for higher meaning. Extinction of humanity in the absence of other-worldly preservation would mean the entire human enterprise and all the eons of creation that went into it sink into meaninglessness (Provine 1988). A strong moral basis emerges, on these and related grounds, for environmentalism, population control, conservation, and other mainstays of sustainability and quality survival.

Combining such considerations with the inherent system of values already inbuilt in human nature by evolution and forming a basic common denominator from which all human value systems are built (Pugh 1977), I arrive at a system of beliefs and associated values that by its very nature carries intrinsic ethicomoral directives. My ultimate criteria for meaning and value, and for how things ought to be in the world—for what is ethically right and wrong and what is most sacred—are accordingly based on this single integral reference frame, consistent with empirically verifiable reality and the worldview of science in its reformed macromental description. In a sense, the theologist's "divine will" translates into that which is in harmony with and contributes to the creative pattern of evolving nature, and thus works with the forces that made and move the universe and created humankind. Evolving nature is assumed to include human nature, not only the biological but also its cultural aspects, extending into the highest aesthetic and spiritual dimensions of the human psyche.

In simple terms and for practical purposes, the measure of the good and morally right becomes the extent to which the quality of this-world existence is preserved or improved in an enduring, transcendent perspective. The reference here is not to my own existence, or to yours, or to this or that nation's, or even to this or the next generation's—though it may be, and usually is, all of these. When conflict arises between the "rights" of this or that individual, nation, or species, however, a higher standard for resolving right and wrong is needed and becomes the quality of existence in a broad, long-term, transcendental (eternal, evolutionary, or "godlike") perspective.

Most people readily agree that this criterion (enhancing the evolving quality of life) accords with common intuition, that it is almost obvious. It is not, however, a simplistic measuring stick. Diversity, contrast, competition, and even conflict and death play vital roles in the evolutionary advancement of the quality and meaning of life. Goodness and morality would lose meaning if everyone were good and moral all the time—just as humanity is bound to undergo a profound loss in meaning if our world is turned into one vast human habitat, designed throughout to sustain a maximized, homogenized human population.

As with any ethical system, only broad principles are stated, leaving the need for debate and judgment in settling specific issues. Assessment of moral priority, however, becomes much more subject to constructive discussion once agreement is reached regarding the ultimate criteria and highest good. In the present scheme, moral values are not absolute or immutably prefixed, or preconceived by either natural or divine law. Instead, like other values, they are evolutionary, interrelated, and conditional on the context in which they evolve and are applied.

Such a moral code, based in the credibility and universality of scientific truth, would seem to be something a sufficient majority of nations and peoples might be willing to compromise on as a common-core foundation for world law and justice and international policymaking, for control of nuclear devices, of pollution of oceans and atmosphere, and other steps to maintain world order and an evolving quality of life—perhaps through world federation. The kind of global ethic that is visioned—much more than with otherworldly guidelines or more anthropocentric humanistic, hedonistic, or relativistic ethics—could help to combat the looming crises in our worsening world conditions. As a prescription for the plight of the planet and the human predicament (Sperry 1972, 1988), it provides a single (noncatastrophic, even humane) remedy directed at the root cause.

· · · · · · · · · ·

Emerging New World Outlook: Alternative Views

It remains to mention some other recent proposals along similar lines. Once the rationale for refuting the traditional materialist ideology was evident and established in behavioral science, it was not long before other variations for a new worldview began to appear (for example, Augros and Stanciu 1984; Berry 1988; Bohm 1982; Capra 1975, 1983; Birch and Cobb 1982; Harman 1988; Kaufman 1985; Lazlo 1972; Peacocke 1979; Popper 1972; Popper and Eccles 1977; Prigogine and Stengers 1984; Starr 1984).

Nearly all of these proposals appear to depend, either explicitly or implicitly, on the overthrow of traditional materialist doctrine in favor of a more holistic paradigm. The proponents, however, instead of ascribing the changeover to the turnabout on consciousness and emergent causation, as done here, advance other grounds for their outlook. Quantum physics is cited frequently, for example, as are ecology, systems theory, panpsychism, process philosophy, nuclear annihilation, economic theory, and so on. Most of these proposed new outlooks are also said to have important, even vital implications for social reform and the acquisition of more sustainable values. Accordingly, it is a matter of some concern to appraise the differences in these alternatives, along with their futurist implications. Although this is not the place to undertake a full assessment of their many pros and cons, these proposals have so much in common that a point-by-point comparison of any one will serve to illustrate many of the main issues and the general type of arguments. One proposal that seems in overall outlook to come close to the view presented here, and which has had wide popular influence and acclaim, is that of Thomas Berry (1988). Moreover, its outlook is quite broad, enabling fairly extensive comparisons.

The answer to our worsening global predicament is seen by Berry, like the others, to lie in reformed values and beliefs (with resultant changes in behavior, aims, social priorities, and so forth) based in a revised conception of nature and all reality, arrived at through reinterpretation of the scientific evidence. When I tried, over twenty years ago, to suggest that we could look to science for more realistic and sustainable values (Sperry 1965, 1972), my proposal was strongly rejected on principle, by both ethicists and scientists. Mainstream science in 1970 still prided itself on being materialistic and value free, while ethicists still honored the fact-value dichotomy. By the late 1970s, however, and especially in the 1980s, we were in a new era with respect to values (Edel 1980; Rottschaefer 1988). Specifically, the idea that ethicomoral values can be derived from the worldview of science had become not only acceptable but almost an unquestioned starting assumption for many of these new proposals.

In general, again like the view presented here, Berry also gives ultimate respect to the natural forces of creation, referring to his "new story" as "creation-oriented," in contrast with dualistic, otherworldly oriented theology (Berry 1988). As a Christian monk and gifted historian of culture, Father Berry is able to express this position more persuasively than most of us in science, adding rich insights into the historical and cultural background. Before probing the basic differences in our views, I list some of the many points of agreement to be kept in mind as we focus on points of contention:

1   A changed sense of the sacred is centered in the natural world, as opposed to dualistic schemes, and is held to be consistent with a reconceived cosmology of science.

2   Traditional materialistic thinking is replaced by an emergent, holistic approach in which the worldview of science
is infused with a new subjectivity and with rich
macroqualities.

3   The growing chasm between the "two cultures" of the
humanities and the sciences is bridged in an integrated
new worldview that restores due emphasis on the humanities.

4   Some basic incompatibilities between the reference frames
of religion and science are reconciled in a unifying
worldview.

5   Today's global crisis is attributed in large part to inadequate mind-sets of the past, both in religion and in science.

6   A new outlook on existence is called for—a new *Zeitgeist*
with a new ethic and a changed sense of ultimate value.
Adoption would lead to fundamental social change and
improved prospects for quality survival.

7   Anthropocentric values are replaced by more biospheric
priorities in a shift from human-centered norms to nature-
centered norms.

8   The proposed value-belief system is of a natural, neutral,
non-exclusive type, with potential for acceptance by different ethnic, cultural, and national communities.

9   A new or changed concept of evolution, driven more holis-
tically (Sperry 1964) or more numinously (Berry 1988), is
more directed and less subject to chance and accidents of
genetic mutation.

10 The careless exploitation and despoiling of earth becomes
immoral, as does demeaning and trivializing other species,
to say nothing of forcing their extinction.

(Other lesser points and shades of similarity are apparent on
examination.)

Differences between our two views lie principally in the
means by which the foregoing similar features are arrived at and
justified. Instead of relying on the consciousness revolution and
resultant new mentalist paradigm, Berry uses what he calls the
principle of subjectivity, known otherwise as *panpsychism*, a teaching that everything in the universe has a psychic/spiritual, as well
as material, component. Berry refers to "the interior subjective
numinous aspect of the entire cosmic order," to "the universe as a

psychic-spiritual as well as a material-physical reality from the beginning" (Berry 1988, 81), and to "the numinous and consciousness dimensions of the emergent universe from its primordial moment" (Berry 1988, 120).

This idea of an interior psychic aspect even in inorganic nature is ancient, and its modern adherents include Lloyd Morgan, Alfred Whitehead, Teilhard de Chardin, and the followers of process philosophy. No definitive proof or disproof is available. Panpsychism, however, has not succeeded in the past in overthrowing the doctrine of scientific materialism because it does not alter its purely physical laws and equations. The psychic element is present, supposedly, in parallel and is not causally interactive. Berry's and any other view that purports to replace the "old story" of science with a new one needs to have a strong, logically effective basis, such as the consciousness revolution, for refuting the firmly entrenched, highly successful, and time-tested paradigm of scientific materialism.

Although our new mentalist paradigm in behavioral science infuses a new subjectivity into the scientific worldview, this does not extend to entities without brains. An "ecophilosophy," based on panpsychism, obviously yields rather different ethical principles from the view I describe, which is based on emergent macromental causation, including its use in comparative animal behavior (Griffin 1981). It is worth noting that those who work in neuroscience, and in related areas of brain and behavior (Doty 1975), have not been encouraged by the collective evidence encountered there (by far the most extensive and directly pertinent evidence available on consciousness and its variables) to adopt the idea of panpsychism.

Another difference concerns the concept of evolution. Berry sees the governing, directive forces of creation as present from the start, rather than self-built in graduated stages. He writes favorably of the anthropic principle (Berry 1988, 16), refers to "the primordial intention of the universe," and states that "the governing principles of the universe have controlled the entire evolutionary process from the moment of its explosive origin" (Berry 1988, 44). In the view I present, the principles governing evolution are, instead, developed in graduated stages as evolution proceeds. In accord with standard biological thinking, they are self-generated and self-organizing, not preplanned or preconceived in a "primordial intention" or "anthropic design."

Though deploring the driving values of the technological-industrial age and its shattering "assault on the earth," along with its dream of creating a wonderworld through endless material progress and growth, Berry does not implicate overpopulation. In contrast, my approach since 1965 has centered on what even then was viewed as the planet's "human surplus," which sees the environmental crisis and desecration of life as a crisis primarily of overpopulation. Our advancing technology, if separated from the population factor, I take to be part of the advance in the evolving quality of existence, something that gives added meaning and higher dimensions to the human venture—and also, let us hope, will provide space travel in time to escape our dying planet and, perhaps, control over the aging process, along with other yet-unimagined wonders of an ever-evolving open-end future (Sperry 1988). Our two views largely agree on the profit-driven Industrial Age mindset, bent on endless material growth regardless of the effect on nature. In my view, however, Utopia is tomorrow's technology, combined with and adapted to the population levels of centuries past.

A further difference in the two positions is Berry's stress on an extreme "interconnectedness" or "communion" between all entities of the universe, described as part of his "ecological age" perception of reality. Everything is inferred to be in intimate touch with everything else. This suddenly popular concept, in many of the new proposals and in "ecophilosophy" and "New Age" thinking, apparently derives from developments in physics relating to Bell's Theorem and the Einstein-Podolsky-Rosen (EPR) thought experiment. The interpretations are still contested, even in physics. In my case, this universal "interconnectedness," and the type of "wholeness" and/or "holism" inferred from it, are treated simply as another misinterpretation of quantum physics (Clifton and Regehr 1990). The majority of physicists still think in the old microdeterministic, exclusively bottom-up mode. They discover something they think applies to subatomic reality, then tell us the whole world works this way, forgetting that in most of nature the subatomic properties are trapped within and downwardly controlled by layer upon layer of higher systems, for which Newtonian laws work nicely but not quantum physics. Common-sense views of interconnectedness would seem adequate for the actual interdependence of different individuals, species, and habitats as stressed by ecological theory for more than fifty years. In today's context, ecology gains new appreciation and strengthened significance but is considered (for the most part) a nonissue, with respect to a shift of worldview, in that it has not been in conflict with the preceding, materialist paradigm.

A main question one keeps coming back to in trying to analyze the alleged emerging new world outlook is, namely, What developments precisely caused the downfall of the old paradigm? That is, What new evidence, concepts, or theory served to overthrow reductive materialism in favor of the new, emergent holism? The answer holds the key to the new paradigm and to understanding its implied changes for new social beliefs and values.

Having reexamined the history (Sperry 1987, 1988), I remain convinced that what caused the current outlook was primarily the turnabout on consciousness and emergent causation rather than quantum physics or relativity theory, ecology, or panpsychism— or systems theory, dualist interactionism, counterculture activism, dissipative structures, or any of the many other developments that have been implicated. Many of these other developments contribute important features to the new world picture, but they seem to me, in themselves, either not powerful enough to have dislodged the earlier paradigm or, as with quantum physics, to lack an adequate basis for the turnabout in the scientific treatment of consciousness and values (Sperry 1987)—as well as being some fifty years off in the timing.

The related, so-called New Age Movement of the past two decades, which has increasingly challenged Judeo-Christian and other traditions of Western culture, I believe also has its foundation in the consciousness revolution. I see the spreading impacts of the new mentalist paradigm as constituting a sound core of the movement, largely obscured by a confusing welter of associated spurious (antiscientific, even occult) features. It is this sound foundational core, however, which, in my view, has kept the movement alive and growing, despite continuous and well-taken criticisms. The timing of the appearance and rise of the New Age Movement closely parallels the rise of the new mentalism in science: both were launched in the 1960s, were in full swing by the mid-1970s, and were visibly established by the mid-1980s.

Viewed in this light, the many confusing, even conflicting, facets among New Age trends fall into place and become subject to a consistent understanding. A standard is provided by which to separate those features that genuinely belong and are sound from those that are spurious or unrelated. For example, reincarnation (or "channeling"), mental telepathy, all occultisms, "Gaia" self-awareness, "Omega point," and anything else not accepted in mainstream science are ruled out. On the other hand, a transformed perception of ourselves and of physical reality, as well as a moral basis for environmentalism, population control, and sustainable economics, with rejection of the older materialist and endless-growth values—are among the features confirmed, given our new macromental model. If, as some contend, there is nothing genuine or substantial among the New Age claims—no new mode of thinking, no global mind change, no new culture emerging with new mindsets to drive humankind toward more sustainable value priorities—then our entire species, and many others, appear to be in grave danger.

At the same time, it needs to be stressed repeatedly that our new acceptance in science of consciousness and subjectivity, the mental, cognitive, or spiritual, does *not*—as is frequently inferred—open the doors of science to the supernatural, the mystical, the paranormal, the occult, the otherworldly—or, in short, to any form of unembodied mind or spirit. The strength and promise of the new macromental outlook is in just the opposite—that is, in taking our ultimate guideline beliefs and resultant social values out of the realm of the supernatural and otherworldly uncertainties and grounding them in a more realistic realm of knowledge and truth, consistent with science and empiric verification.

• • • • • • • • • •
Note

* *Author's note.* This article responds to a request to write a nonspecialist, personalized account of the beliefs I live by as a scientist and how I arrived at them. Planned for a popular volume, the original version (Sperry 1986) is here expanded and updated for readers more professionally concerned with relating religion and science. I thank Robert Doty, Charles Hamilton, and Colwyn Trevarthen for helpful comments on the manuscript, and Patricia Anderson for assistance in compiling the references.

• • • • • • • • • •
References

R. M. Augros and G. N. Stanciu, *The New Story of Science* (New York: Bantam, 1984).

R. J. Baars, *The Cognitive Revolution in Psychology* (New York: Guilford, 1986).

T. Berry, *The Dream of the Earth* (San Francisco: Sierra Club Nature and Natural Philosophy Library, 1988).

C. Birch and J. B. Cobb, *Liberation of Life: From the Cell to the Community* (New York: Cambridge University Press, 1982).

J. E. Bogen, "One Brain, Two Brains, or Both?" in *Two Hemispheres—One Brain*, ed. F. Lepore, M. Ptito, and H. H. Jasper (New York: Alan R. Liss, 1986).

D. J. Bohm, *Wholeness and the Implicate Order* (London: Routledge and Kegan Paul, 1980).

D. M. Byers, ed. *Religion, Science, and the Search for Wisdom* (Washington, D.C.: United States Catholic Conferences, 1987).

F. Capra, *The Tao of Physics* (East Lansing, Mich.: Shambhala, 1977).

———, *The Turning Point* (New York: Bantam New Age Books, 1982).

R. K. Clifton and M. G. Regehr, "Toward a Sound Perspective on Modern Physics: Capra's Popularization of Mysticism and Theological Approaches Reexamined," *Zygon: Journal of Religion and Science* 25 (March 1990): 73–104.

E. L. Deci, *The Psychology of Self-determination* (Lexington, Mass.: D. C. Heath, 1980).

W. N. Dember, "Motivation and the Cognitive Revolution," *American Psychologist* 29 (1974): 161–68.

R. W. Doty, "Consciousness from Neurons," *Acta Neurobiologiae Experimentalis* 35 (1975): 791–804.

A. Edel, *Exploring Fact and Value*, Vol. 2 (New Brunswick, N.J.: Transaction Books, 1980).

J. Fletcher, "Humanism and Theism in Biomedical Ethics," *Perspectives in Biology & Medicine* 31 (1987): 106–16.

H. Gardner, *The Mind's New Science: A History of the Cognitive Revolution* (New York: Basic Books, 1985).

A. Greeley, *Courage of Conviction*, P. L. Berman and T. G. Schlitz, eds. (New York: Dodd, Mead, 1986), 113–19.

M. E. Grenander, "The Mind Is Its Own Place," *Methodology and Science* 16(3, 1983): 181–92.

M. Grene, "Workshop on 'Concepts of Mind'," in *The Understanding of Nature* (Dordrecht: Reidel, 1974), xiv–xv.

D. R. Griffin, *The Question of Animal Awareness* (New York: Rockefeller University Press, 1981).

W. W. Harman, *Global Mind Change* (Indianapolis: Knowledge Systems, 1988).

W. T. Jones, *The Sciences and the Humanities* (Berkeley: University of California Press, 1965).

G. D. Kaufman, *Theology for a Nuclear Age* (Philadelphia: Westminster, 1985).

R. L. Klee, "Micro-determinism and Concepts of Emergence," *Philosophy of Science* 51 (1984): 44–63.

E. Laszlo, *The Systems View of the World: The Natural Philosophy of the New Developments in the Sciences* (New York: Braziller, 1972).

F. W. Matson, "Humanist Theory: The Third Revolution in Psychology," *The Humanist* 31(2, 1971): 7–11.

T. Natsoulas, "Roger Sperry's Monist Interactionism," *Journal of Mind and Behavior* 8(1987): 1–21.

D. S. Palermo, "Is a Scientific Revolution Taking Place in Psychology?" *Science Studies* 1(1971): 135–55.

A. R. Peacocke, *Creation and the World of Science* (Oxford: Clarendon Press, 1979).

K. R. Popper, "Of Clouds and Clocks," in *Objective Knowledge*, K. Popper, ed. (Oxford: Clarendon Press, 1972), 206–55. Second Arthur Holly Compton Memorial Lecture, presented April 1965.

———, "The Rationality of Scientific Revolution," in *Problems of Scientific Revolution*, R. Harre, ed. (Oxford: Clarendon Press, 1975), 72–101.

K. R. Popper and J. C. Eccles, *The Self and Its Brain* (New York: Springer International, 1977).

F. Press, *Science and Creationism: A View by the Committee of the National Academy of Sciences* (Washington, D.C.: National Academy Press, 1984).

I. Prigogine and I. Stengers, *Order Out of Chaos: Man's New Dialogue with Nature* (New York: Bantam, 1984).

W. Provine, "Evolution and the Foundation of Ethics," *MBL Science* 3(1988): 5–29.

G. E. Pugh, *The Biological Origin of Human Values* (New York: Basic Books, 1977).

Z. W. Pylyshyn, "What the Mind's Eye Tells the Mind's Brain: A Critique of Mental Imagery," *Psychological Bulletin* 80(1973): 1–24.

H. W. Reese and W. F. Overton, "On Paradigm Shifts," *American Psychologist* 27(1972): 1197–99.

C. Ripley, "Sperry's Concept of Consciousness," *Inquiry* 27(1984): 399–423.

W. A. Rottschaefer, "Roger Sperry's Science of Values," *Journal of Mind and Behavior* 8(1987): 23–35.

———, "The New Interactionism between Science and Religion," *Religious Studies Review* 14(1988): 218–24.

F. A. Schaeffer, *A Christian Manifesto* (Westchester, Ill.: Crossway Books, 1981).

E. M. Segal and R. Lachman, "Complex Behavior or Higher Mental Process? Is There a Paradigm Shift?" *American Psychologist* 27(1972): 46–55.

J. J. Smart, "Physicalism and Emergence," *Neuroscience* 6(1981): 109–13.

R. W. Sperry, "Problems Outstanding in the Evolution of Brain Function," James Arthur Lecture Series of the American Museum of Natural History (New York: American Museum of Natural History, 1964).

———, "Mind, Brain and Humanistic Values," in *New Views of the Nature of Man*, J. R. Platt, ed. (Chicago: University of Chicago Press, 1965), 71–92. Reprinted (1966) in *Bulletin of the Atomic Scientists* 22(7): 2–6.

———, "Toward a Theory of Mind" (Abstract), *Proceedings of the National*

Academy of Sciences 63(1969): 230–31. (Presented in full in "A Modified Concept of Consciousness," *Psychological Review* 76: 532–36.)

————, "An Objective Approach to Subjective Experience: Further Explanation of a Hypothesis," *Psychological Review* 77(1970): 585–90.

————, "Science and the Problem of Values," *Perspectives in Biology and Medicine* 16(1972): 115–30. (Reprinted in *Zygon: Journal of Religion and Science* 9 [March 1974]: 7–21.)

————, "Changed Concepts of Brain and Consciousness: Some Value Implications," *Perkins Journal* 36, 4(1983): 21–32. (Reprinted in *Zygon: Journal of Religion and Science* 20 [March 1985]: 41–57.)

————, "The New Mentalist Paradigm and Ultimate Concern," *Perspectives in Biology and Medicine* 29, 3(1986): 413–22.

————, "Structure and Significance of the Consciousness Revolution," *Journal of Mind and Behavior* 8, 1(1987): 37–65.

————, "Psychology's Mentalist Paradigm and the Religion/Science Tension," *American Psychologist* 43, 8(1988): 607–13.

————, "Turnabout on Consciousness: A Mentalist View," *Proceedings of the First International Conference on the Study of Consciousness within Science* (University of California at San Francisco, 1990).

D. Starr, "The Crying Need for a Believable Theology," *The Humanist* 44(1984): 13–16.

C. B. Trevarthen, *Brain Circuits and Functions of the Mind* (New York: Cambridge University Press, 1990).

L. White, Jr., "The Historical Roots of Our Ecological Crisis," *Science* 155(1967): 1203–7.

19

Creation Stories, Religious and Atheistic

John Leslie

John Leslie is Professor of Philosophy at the University of Guelph, Ontario. His interests include metaphysics, ethics, philosophy of religion, and philosophy of cosmology. He has served as secretary of the Canadian Philosophical Association and is one of the leading contemporary authorities on the Anthropic Principle. His book *Value and Existence* (1979) defends a neoplatonist picture of God, while *Universes* (1989) and his edited volume *Physical Cosmology and Philosophy* (1990) investigate the claim that our universe is "fine tuned" in life-permitting ways.

Abstract

A possible religious story describes an eternal magician, existing reasonlessly and creating by mere will-power. A contemporary atheistic tale describes an eternally inflating field that gives birth to bubble universes with randomized properties which are sometimes life-permitting. However, even an eternal magician or field calls for explanation. Neoplatonism explains things in terms of an ethical requirement that the good should exist. The requirement needs no help from anything further: it itself acts creatively. Philosophically defensible, this is compatible with scientific findings and with a spinozistic God, or with a divine person whose existence can be explained.

I

Attempting to account for our complex universe, and especially for the existence of life and consciousness, people have generated two main types of narrative: the religious and the atheistic. Which of these two is the better? Are they in serious conflict? Might science prove that atheistic creation stories are wrong and religious ones right, or *vice versa*?

Consider a typical religious story. God is an invisible person, eternally existing, infinitely knowledgeable and powerful. Benevolently motivated, he created our universe by a mere act of will, from nothing. That is to say, there was no pre-existing clay from which he formed it. He simply wished it into existence. Yet perhaps the time of his creative act of will was the very first moment of time so that there were no previous hours in which he had been idle, unbenevolent, surrounded by emptiness. Instead he created time and the world together. Still, his benevolence involved no great hurry to create beings who would benefit from it. He was content that their appearance should be delayed for several billion years. He even entrusted the manufacture of these beings (or at least of their material bodies, for they may also have immaterial souls which he created when the bodies became available) to the particles of the material world. To these particles he gave powers to interact in various ways: powers which might, indeed, amount simply to the fact that he always willed them to pirouette in these or those fashions around one another, but which might alternatively have been powers truly delegated to them so that protons, electrons, and so forth, were directly responsible for one another's movements. In either case, he used immense ingenuity to ensure that the mathematical equations describing those movements were such as would lead to the appearance, eventually, of very intricate living things. Although the picture of God as specifically creating eyes, hands, the human appendix, plague germs, and so forth, is still occasionally defended, it has been very widely abandoned. A creator whose specific acts of will produced deadly bacteria, or something as useless and dangerous as the human appendix, or beetles with wings permanently sealed over so that they cannot fly, or even something as imperfect as the human eye, impresses many people as neither very clever nor very benevolent. If the human optic nerve has to tunnel through the retina, producing a blind spot, then would this not best be explained as an unfortunate by-product of a Darwinian process? God, it is said, could not have made the laws of physics so supremely elegant—he could not have used anything like laws of physics but would instead need to have resorted to mere magic—if he had wanted to guarantee that there would be no plague germs, or that eyes would never start evolving with their nerves on the wrong side.

Here we have, as it were, the divine magician and his card tricks. The magician is no ordinary conjuror. He created his packs of cards by simply wishing them into existence. Yet he decided to produce his theatrical effects by using ingenious laws of card-manipulation plus, perhaps, a clever initial arrangement of the cards. True, the results may not demonstrate his power as convincingly as if he were constantly creating new cards, but he had reasons for not demonstrating it in that way, which would have led to a performance rather tedious in the long run. The interest of the patterns generated by his cards depends on their not being simply magical. The details of those patterns may occasionally be ugly, but that cannot be avoided when one acts by laws and not by mere magic. Now, if God had employed mere magic then he would have been altogether too dominant. Any living beings created by him would have been little better than puppets. They would have possessed too little free will.

Next consider a story such as might be told by an atheistic modern cosmologist. It is the story of the perpetually inflating cosmos, the bubble universes, the randomization of universe properties and the "anthropic" observational selection effect.

Physics describes two main types of energy, namely, the energy tied up in particles and the energy of fields: gravitational fields, electromagnetic fields, scalar fields, and so on. According to the story now to be examined, there exists a rapidly inflating field. It always has existed, so we must not ask what first brought it into being. The field is so strong that particles are constantly fluctuating in and out of existence inside it. Quantum theory describes events of this kind as happening even in empty space. In the case of a space filled with a very strong field, the ferment of particle creations and annihilations becomes extremely violent. Now, a curious feature of the ever-inflating field is that its intensity remains the same despite its expansion. Just as electric charge can be negative instead of positive, so can energy. The binding energy, for instance, which holds the atomic nucleus together, enters the physicist's equations as a negative quantity. Again, it has long been maintained that the total energy of our universe is zero when its gravitational component is taken into account: gravitational binding energy exactly cancels out all the energy present in atoms, light rays, neutrinos, and so on. The same principle applies to the ever-inflating field and the particles fluctuating in and out of existence inside it: the total energy of this rapidly expanding system is zero, so that it can continue to inflate endlessly with no loss of field strength and at no energy cost.

Although the field inflates eternally, it is for ever producing "bubbles" in which the rapid inflation ceases, giving way to much slower expansion such as characterizes the cosmic region visible to us. These bubbles can be much larger than the volume probed by our telescopes. Among modern cosmologists, at least the larger bubbles would typically be referred to as "universes" in recognition of how events deep within them formed their own worlds, unaffected by events in other bubbles or in the inflating ferment between the bubbles. No limit can be set to the number of such universes. What is more, their individual characteristics would be, according to a widespread opinion which we can make central to our story, *immensely varied.* Each bubble-universe would cool as it expanded. At very high temperatures, Nature's main forces— gravity, electromagnetism, and the nuclear strong and weak forces—are unified into a single force. With cooling they split apart, and the manner of their splitting could differ from one universe to another because of scalar fields whose intensities varied randomly from universe to universe. Interacting with such fields, particles which would otherwise be massless (as is the photon) would become massive to various degrees, depending on what the particles were and on how intense the scalar fields were. This would in turn have an effect on force strengths: on the strength of electromagnetism, for example. Obviously a force is effectively weaker when the particles on which it acts are more massive, and also, although less obviously, a force is stronger when the "messenger particles" which carry it are less massive. The bubble-universes could thus differ in such respects as the extent (if any) to which electromagnetism was stronger than gravity, or the mass difference between the electron and the proton. And they might differ as well in their expansion rates, their degrees of turbulence, the total number of particles in each, the relative numbers of matter particles and photons, and much else.

Many cosmologists have been impressed by how the force strengths and particle masses which we observe, and the rate at which the visible universe expands and its (extremely low) degree of turbulence, and many other matters, all seem "fine tuned for producing life" in the following technical sense: tiny changes in these matters would have prevented the evolution of living beings of any plausible kind. For instance, a change by one part in many billions in the early expansion rate would seemingly have led to a scheme of things which either recollapsed almost immediately or else flew to pieces so fast that it would soon have been entirely composed of very dilute, very cold gases. Again, an equally small change in the relative strengths of electromagnetism and gravity could have prevented the existence of stable stars like the sun. Or again, if the neutron-proton mass difference had not been twice the mass of the electron, more or less exactly, then there would have been no chemical interactions. And so on, down a long list: upwards of thirty factors would appear to have needed tuning, often with very considerable accuracy. Religious thinkers might wish to treat the observed fine tuning as evidence of God's power and ingenuity. Atheists will prefer to appeal to the anthropic principle. As enunciated by Brandon Carter roughly twenty years ago, this states "that what we can expect to observe must be restricted by the conditions necessary for our presence as observers."[1] Carter's anthropic principle is in no way religious. It does not state that our universe was compelled to contain observers, for instance because God wished this. It has, furthermore, no special concern with humankind. Instead it concerns observership. It can remind us that if there were vastly many universes (or gigantic cosmic regions, if the word "universes" is disliked) and if they differed in their properties, then observers would be able to detect only those universes, perhaps very rare ones, which had life-permitting properties.

Let us tell another story. Monkeys are tapping at typewriters randomly. There are so vastly many monkeys that, almost certainly, several will generate sonnets. Beside each monkey is a sleeping man who will be wakened if a sonnet is typed: otherwise he will remain asleep. In view of all this, no such man has a right to be totally astonished at being wakened and finding that his own monkey has typed a sonnet.

The case would be similar, it is suggested, if there were vastly many universes with randomized properties. Somewhere or other, at least a few would have life-permitting properties. The living beings who evolved to observe them would have little reason to be astonished by those properties. Their fine-tuned surroundings would not be remarkable evidence of God's hand.

· · · · · · · · · ·

II

The religious and the atheistic stories both merit serious consideration. Let us support this by considering further tales which suggest that our universe's fine-tuned character truly is a sign either of God's hand or of the existence of multiple universes with randomized properties. The tales all illustrate the importance of analogies. Arguments from analogy are scorned by many philosophers, yet they do not deserve scorn. They can remind us of simple principles of reasoning which we are liable to forget.

First, there is what could be called the Merchant's Thumb

principle. The world's events do not come to us neatly labelled as those, on the one hand, which specially call for explanation and those others (such as happening to see a friend in town) which presumably do also have explanations but explanations only of highly complex, untidy varieties, so that we call them "matters of mere chance." How, then, are we to know that something specially needs to be explained? A fairly reliable sign is that a tidy explanation springs to mind. When does a dealt hand of cards call for explanation by something other than chance? It quite probably calls for it when cheating is easy, when this particular hand is certain to bring great profit to the dealer, when the dealer is in sore need of great profit, and so on. A poker hand which at first looks worthless, not specially calling for explanation, can come to be thought very special indeed when one realizes that a million dollars are at stake, that poker has many variants, and that in the variant actually being played this apparently valueless set of cards that the dealer has dealt to himself is a powerful hand. Again, what is so specially in need of explanation in the positioning of a merchant's thumb as he exhibits a silk robe? Every thumb must be somewhere or other. However, the merchant hopes to make a sale, and his thumb is covering a hole in the silk. We see a tidy explanation and so, we are inclined to think, the thumb's position is not a chance affair.

Just how can the Merchant's Thumb principle be applied to our cosmological situation? The answer is that when people are introduced to the fine tuning—when they learn that the force strengths, the particle masses, and so forth, are just right for producing life—then their reaction is often that this proves nothing. Every force strength, they point out, has to be something or other, leading to some effects or other. What is so special, they ask, in the fact that the actual force strengths permit life to exist? However, we can reply to them as follows. Our universe's life-permitting character can be thought in special need of explanation because there are two tidy ways in which it might be explained. It might be explained by reference to God, or it might be explained (rendered unmysterious) by reference to greatly many, greatly varied universes and to an observational selection effect. Only a life-containing universe could be seen by anyone, as the anthropic principle reminds us.

Consider a Fishing Story. Hungry, you catch a fish measuring 23.2576 inches. What is so special there? Every fish must have some length or other, you reflect. But what if you then find that the only fish which your fishing apparatus could catch and present to your contented eyes would be fish of exactly this length? Two seemingly tidy explanations suggest themselves. Perhaps there are vastly many differently-lengthed fish in the lake, or perhaps a beneficent fish-creator has created a fish "fine-tuned" to your needs. Suppose that these explanations really were tidy: they appealed to supposed facts which were not themselves implausible and which, if they really were facts, would readily account for the catching of the fish. You ought then to be reluctant to believe that there had been just the one fish in the lake, its length just chancing to be exactly the right one.

Ought it to be objected, though, that if our universe had failed to be a life-permitting universe, the type of universe which contented eyes could detect or which divine beneficence would create, then there would be nobody discussing it and that therefore its fine-tuned, life-permitting character is nothing remarkable? A Firing Squad story suggests that this line of objection fails. If fifty sharpshooters all miss you, then you should think twice before shrugging your shoulders and commenting that, had they not missed, then you would not be considering the affair. It might well be better to believe in a benevolent set of sharpshooters, or perhaps in firing-squad situations in numbers huge enough to have made it quite likely that at least one of the intended victims would survive.

Ought it now to be objected that huge numbers would be irrelevant? Suppose I am in a forest and a randomly fired bullet hits me. Would my sad case be any the less surprising if the forest were filled with hugely many people? How could others in the forest have helped me personally to be hit? A good reply could be that a well-populated forest would not make me any the less a victim of bad luck, but it could have made it quite to be expected that somebody or other would have bad luck. Now, every somebody must be "me" to that person. A vast number of universes with randomized characteristics could make it unsurprising, not a mere matter of luck, that some universe or other was "my universe" to a living being. If a thousand coins are tossed, it can be misleading to talk of "mere luck" when at least one of them falls Heads.

· · · · · · · · · ·

III

Suppose that we agree that our fine-tuned universe does specially call for explanation. Let us now ask whether an atheistic or a religious account of it can explain it satisfactorily.

The religious and atheistic stories considered above could both be found dissatisfying. It could be objected that they offered no ultimate explanations.

The first story might seem to introduce an inexplicably existing, inexplicably powerful wizard. The order of the created world reflects the order of his infinitely knowledgeable mind, yet how did he come to have any mind, let alone an orderly one? And how could he have replicated his mind's orderliness by merely willing things to exist? And why, if benevolent, did he allow so many years to pass before conscious beings appeared?

The second, atheistic story might sound equally inadequate. It tells of a cosmos which has always existed. It states that the laws of this cosmos are such that it continues to generate more and more universes as bubbles inside itself, bubbles with widely varying properties. But why does it obey those laws instead of others? Why, even, does it have any orderliness of a type which makes the word "laws" appropriate? And why has there always been a cosmos, rather than nothing?

It is sometimes suggested that a cosmos which had always existed would need no further explanation: its existence at any one instant would be explicable by its having existed at the previous instant, and so on *ad infinitum*. Leibniz told a story against this, however: a story of a geometry book with pages exactly copied from a previous book, which was itself a copy of a still earlier book, and so on backwards for ever. As he commented, this would seem not to explain why the book was a book about geometry.

Cosmologists now often try to avoid believing in infinite past time. In particular, many of them admire the Hartle-Hawking theory that time becomes more and more spacelike at ever earlier moments: the result is that, despite not stretching backwards for infinitely many years, the cosmos has no instant at which it began. Asking what existed before it began, to cause it, is like asking what Earth is like to the north of the North Pole. The cosmos has no cause; it just *is*.[2] Yet even this can sound very unsatisfactory. Cannot we ask why there is this system with its laws which fuse space with time in this particular manner? Cannot we ask such a question even if those laws leave no room for the system to be caused by something at a previous time? Philosophers often work with a concept of cause, or at least of responsibility, which is non-temporal. Augustine's God was creatively responsible for the universe although he had not existed before it: he created time and the world together. Believing that God was self-explaining, Descartes was correspondingly willing to speak of God as "self-causing," although he agreed that this would be nonsense if causation necessarily involved temporal priority.

Still, what would be the point of continuing to ask "Why?" when no answer could be had? Now, it might be thought obvious that existence as a whole could not possibly be explained. To explain it by reference to something else could seem an admission that it was not really existence as a whole. And how could it be explained by saying that it, or part of it which created all the rest, was "self-causing"? Would not this be entirely absurd? So are we not forced to accept that something or other, perhaps God or perhaps the cosmos, exists for no reason whatever?

· · · · · · · · · ·

IV

Science relies on principles—in particular the inductive principle that the past will be a reliable guide to the future—which seemingly cannot themselves be justified by appeal to anything further. (Will the past always be a guide to the future? It is, as Hume noticed, question-begging to appeal to the fact that earlier events have in the past always been a guide to later ones.) It perhaps ought not to worry us, therefore, if we could not prove that existence as a whole needed an explanation. We could still think an explanation needed. It would be one of our basic principles that nothing existed reasonlessly. But of course we should have to abandon this principle if the concept of an explanation of all existence could be proved to be logically absurd.

If there were to be an ultimate reason for all existence, then it would have to be an eternal or timeless reason. There never would have been an empty situation, a situation in which there was nothing in existence (although, as Augustine saw, it would not at once follow that time stretched backwards infinitely). Similarly, there never would be an empty situation in the future. It could none the less be useful to tell oneself a story in which the cosmos was removed and any divine person was also removed, so that there were no existents whatever. What could there be, in this imaginary situation, to bring about the existence of anything, thereby ensuring that the situation was only imaginary?

The sole viable answer may be the one offered by a neoplatonic position whose basics are as follows. (1) Even if there were absolutely no existents, there would still be facts, truths, things-which-were-so: for instance, the contingent fact that there were no existents, and the eternal, unconditionally necessary fact that, were there to exist three groups of five frogs, then there would exist more than twelve frogs. Again, there would be the fact that misery, were it to exist, would be worse than happiness would be. (2) There would be the fact, too, that the absence of a world whose people were all of them in torment was something really excellent, something ethically required. And there would be the fact that the absence of certain other things, perhaps of a good divine person or perhaps of a good world of life and consciousness, would be really unfortunate. That is to say, the presence of such other things would likewise be ethically required. It would be good that they should come to exist. (3) Consistent sets of ethical requirements *can themselves bear creative responsibility* for the existence of a good thing or things: possibly of a divine mind, possibly of an entire cosmos. Logic allows this; experience does not refute it.

Perhaps those three neoplatonic points are correct. Perhaps ethical requirements are directly responsible for the existence of something. Logic does not tell us that ethical requirements are at times creatively powerful, but nor does it say they never are. A creatively effective ethical requirement is not like a wifeless husband. There is clearly a sense of "as such" in which no ethical requirement *as such* could create anything, yet this is just the sense in which no cow as such is brown: contrast how, as a matter of definition and in this way "as such", cows as such are female. It might be that, as a matter not of analyticity, of definitions, but of *synthetic necessity*, necessity of a kind which is absolute without being analytic, some ethical requirements were creatively effective. (Although himself believing that our universe exists inexplicably, J. L. Mackie writes that it would be "a gross error" to argue "that merely because ethical requirement and creative requirement are conceptually or logically distinct, there cannot be a real, and perhaps necessary, connection between them"; it is right, he says, to resist "the prejudice that it can be known *a priori* to be impossible" that a thing's value "can itself tend to bring that thing into existence".[3]) Furthermore, none of this is in clear conflict with actual experience. What experience seems to show is that greatly many ethical requirements lack creative power. Yet a widely accepted explanation of why a good divine person would allow evils, that is, matters whose absence was ethically required, is that it is impossible to satisfy all ethical requirements simultaneously. This is crucial to the standard Free Will Defence against the Problem of Evil. When, therefore, an ethical requirement failed to be creatively effective, this might be because it had been overruled by a stronger ethical requirement. It might be ethically required, for example, that there be no murders, but even more strongly ethically required that the world be one in which people find it physically and mentally possible to murder instead of being mere puppets who cannot do wrong.

Such a neoplatonic way of thinking raises many very difficult issues, far too many for us to consider here.[4] Let us instead ask how this way of thinking relates to the religious and atheistic stories with which we began.

· · · · · · · · · ·

V

The neoplatonism of Plotinus and Dionysius, and of such modern writers as Tillich, is, some would say, an atheistic doctrine. Others would call it theistic. Who is right on this matter may in the end depend merely on how one chooses to define the word "theism." What is clear is that the doctrine, although it involves talk of God, does not conceive God as *a person* like the God of our first story. God could instead best be described as the principle that the cosmos owes its existence to its ethical requiredness and to nothing else. No divine creative volitions enter the picture.

Once, however, one has accepted that ethical requirements can themselves be creatively responsible for this or that, then one can quickly find oneself believing that God is a divine mind which owes its existence to its ethical requiredness: one can thus accept the Cartesian notion that God is self-causing or self-explaining.[5] One might further join Descartes in viewing the divine mind as the creative ground of a cosmos which existed beyond it. Yet alternatively this mind might be thought to be all that exists, as is suggested by Spinoza's *Ethics*. Spinoza's world-picture is not in conflict with actual experience, for Spinoza imagines God as eternally knowing absolutely everything. It follows that he knows what things would be like in a world like ours, and even precisely what it would feel like to be you, with all your experiences: for instance, experiences of being ignorant of vastly much. How then could your experiences prove that Spinoza was wrong? Certainly, you are not vividly aware of being part of God's all-knowing mind. Yet if God were to know precisely what it felt like to be you, then there would have to be parts or aspects (or "modes," in technical parlance) of God's eternal, all-knowing mind which were not vividly aware of being parts of an eternal, all-knowing mind, but were instead characterized by considerable ignorance. These parts would, for example, have vivid awareness of time's successive moments without having vivid awareness that these moments were, as would be required by God's eternal knowledge, all of them real together. And there could seem to be nothing too very odd in such a situation. Einstein pictured a very similar situation when he described temporal progress as a matter of "a four-dimensional existence instead of the evolution of a three-dimensional existence."

This last point might be found baffling. Perhaps another story could throw light on it. Take the case of your own mind as you perhaps picture it: a succession of mental states such that, when any one of them is present, the earlier ones are all annihilated absolutely instead of being in some sense "there." Suppose for argument's sake that the mental states are brain states, which are physical states. (The words "a physical state" function in such a way that something can be a physical state even when it is a mere aspect of another physical state. Mental states could thus be physical states even if they were not filled with neurophysiological details, let alone details of quark and electron positions.) Imagine that a demon records all the details of the physical world's successive states, including those of your brain. He then reproduces the patterns of these states side by side along a fourth dimension. Granted that the succession of your brain states involves experiences of change, of temporal progress, just why should it be true that the succession of states along the fourth dimension of the demon-created world would fail to involve experiences of change, of temporal progress? Why should the fact that the states were all in existence *together* make any difference? Perhaps it would make a difference, yet this is surely hard to establish. The B-theory of Time, which makes *being now* as relative as *being here*, is popular among philosophers, largely owing to the influence of Grünbaum.[6] It does not deny temporal progress. Instead it pictures it in Einstein's way. It does not assert that you are at present aware of the past experiences which you have forgotten, but it maintains that those past experiences are in an important sense "there" and not annihilated. Your mental life contains really existing parts, temporal sections, of which you are not now conscious, because the section of your mental life which is *now* exists *elsewhere* in time than those parts do. As Spinoza saw, a mental life can readily include parts which are not each of them vividly aware of all the rest.

. . . .

VI

It would be easy to gain the impression that this short article is much in favour of religious stories. Rejecting such things as the eternally inflating cosmos, bubble-universes, randomization of properties, and an anthropic observational selection effect, it must regard God as very evidently the explanation of our world's fine tuning. However, this is not in fact so, for three main reasons.

First: It seems impossible to prove that there must be an ultimate reason for all existence. Perhaps, therefore, the cosmos exists for no reason whatever.

Second: Although God—God as a person creating a world beyond himself, or Spinoza's God, or the God of Plotinus, Dionysius, and Tillich—might explain the fine tuning plausibly, an equally plausible explanation might be provided by multiple universes, variation between universes, and anthropic observational selection. A. D. Linde, whose eternal inflation with bubble-universes supplied the subject-matter for our atheistic story, is by no means the only cosmologist whose universes come in great numbers and great variety. Universes could take the form of successive oscillations of J. A. Wheeler's oscillating cosmos, or of gigantic regions in the infinitely extending cosmos of G. F. R. Ellis. They could exist as huge quantum fluctuations in the superspace of E. P. Tryon, or as the "worlds" of H. Everett's many-worlds quantum mechanics, or as the "child-universes" of K. Sato's cosmos, pinched off from the bodies of their parents, et cetera.[7]

Third: There is little need for believers in God to reject the existence of greatly many, greatly varied universes. If God were a benevolent person, for instance, then why should he exhaust his benevolence on a single universe, leaving others uncreated? Or if he created many universes, why should he ensure that all had identical properties? Might there not be goodness in variety? True enough, a believer in God could be reluctant to accept totally lifeless universes, yet even these might be acceptable if their existence, perhaps as bubbles inside an ever-inflating whole, would give completeness to what God had created. (After all, belief in God can be thought compatible with belief in lifeless deserts and in flowers born to bloom unseen. Descartes's story of an evil demon expresses the view that completeness is desirable even when it transcends consciousness: the demon is imagined as wickedly filling souls with experiences which exactly counterfeit those of beings in a world that is complete, a world in which there is more than mere consciousness.)

This does not mean, however, that whether one believes in God should have no influence on one's cosmology and one's physics. Its influence could very reasonably be rather great. If accepting a religious creation story then we shall, for example, tend to find nothing preposterous in the currently rather unpopular idea that the Big Bang started as an infinitely hot, infinitely dense "singularity." We shall feel no pressing need to prefer such alternatives as the Hartle-Hawking picture which spatializes and smears out the singularity, thereby getting rid of any point definitely identifiable as time's very first moment. God could explain even an infinite density and a first moment, we may well think.

Again, we shall presumably think that God could account very adequately for any fine tuning. God as a benevolent person, or neoplatonism's more abstract God, could select life-permitting force strengths, particle masses, and so on. Believers in God need not feel forced to accept a physics which plays dice with these affairs, and multiple universes, and anthropic observational selection of the rare universes where the dice have fallen life-permittingly. Those who find God incredible, in contrast, are nowadays under much pressure to believe in all of those things.

Derek Parfit discusses this general area somewhat similarly in his "Why Does the Universe Exist?"[8] Like his article, this one has been deliberately non-technical. The field's difficulties may be so great that only something non-technical can have much chance of being right.

• • • • • • • • •

Notes

1. "Large Number Coincidences and the Anthropic Principle in Cosmology," in *Confrontation of Cosmological Theories with Observational Data*, M. S. Longair, ed. (Dordrecht: Reidel, 1974), 291–98. See also J. D. Barrow and F. J. Tipler, *The Anthropic Cosmological Principle* (Oxford: Clarendon Press, 1986).
2. See S. W. Hawking, "Quantum Cosmology," in *Three Hundred Years of*

Gravitation, S. W. Hawking and W. Israel, eds. (Cambridge: Cambridge University Press, 1987), 631–51.

3. *The Miracle of Theism* (Oxford: Clarendon Press, 1982). The quotations are from chapter thirteen, which is devoted to a discussion of neoplatonism. See also J. Leslie, "Mackie on Neoplatonism's 'Replacement for God'," *Religious Studies* 22 (1986): 325–42.

4. They form the main subject-matter of my *Value and Existence* (Oxford: Blackwell, 1979), which further includes discussion of neoplatonist philosophy from antiquity to modern times. See also J. Leslie, "The World's Necessary Existence," *International Journal for Philosophy of Religion* 11 (1980): 207–23.

5. This may be the most intriguing theme in A. C. Ewing's *Value and Reality* (London: Allen and Unwin, 1973); see chapter 7 in particular.

6. *Philosophical Problems of Space and Time* (Dordrecht: Reidel, 1973, 2nd edition).

7. Details are given in my *Universes* (London and New York: Routledge, 1989), which also summarizes the evidence of fine tuning, and in the contributions of Linde, Wheeler, Tryon, and others to my edited volume *Physical Cosmology and Philosophy* (New York: Macmillan, 1990). G. Gale surveyed the field for pages 189–206 of the volume, under the title "Cosmological Fecundity: Theories of Multiple Universes." The volume further includes essays on the fine tuning by B. J. Carr, R. Swinburne, and others.

8. *Times Literary Supplement* (3 July 1992): 3–5. Another non-technical comparison of neoplatonist, multiple-universe, and other theories of creation fills chapter seven of J. J. C. Smart's *Our Place in the Universe* (Oxford: Blackwell, 1989).

Nothing Could Exist Groundlessly

1 What are your views on cosmic beginnings, particularly with reference to the origin of the universe, of life, and of *Homo sapiens*?

Nothing could exist groundlessly. There must be some reason why there is a cosmos, not an absence of all existing things. Mere logic, however, cannot prove this, because the reason couldn't be just a logical reason—a mere need to avoid contradiction.

On the other hand, it's contradictory to imagine an absence of all *truths*. If nothing had existed, it would have been true that no good cosmos existed and that this was unfortunate.

Perhaps the reason why the cosmos exists is that it ought to exist. Its existence is required ethically, with creative effect. The God of neoplatonism just is *the creative ethical requiredness of the cosmos*.

Our universe began in a Big Bang about fifteen billion years ago, yet this is little additional reason for belief in God. Even a universe which had a beginning could, many folk think, just happen to exist. And remember, mere logic cannot refute those folk.

Much evidence indicates that life evolved only because the strengths of our universe's main forces (gravity, and so on) and the masses of its particles (the proton, and so forth) fell inside very narrow, life-permitting ranges. This could be evidence that it was a God-created universe. Or it might indicate that there existed hugely many universes, force strengths and particle masses varying randomly from universe to universe—perhaps because of random "symmetry breaking" at early instants.

Talk of *many universes* makes sense because the cosmos may extend much further than our universe—the universe which came out of what we call "the" Big Bang. Maybe there have been infinitely many such Bangs.

2 What are your views on human ends, especially as this relates to the framework of cosmic beginnings?

By "human ends" I mean what humans ought to aim at. At first glance, no theory of cosmic beginnings should affect this. What if the cosmos were God-created? There would still be no obvious need for the monkish virtues of celibacy, fasting, penance, mortification, self-denial.

On second thoughts, belief in a God-created cosmos might reasonably strengthen one's conviction that some things really are better than others, in an absolute way. That's important to human strivings.

Again, cosmological theorizing might tell us how long the human race—or any races descended from it—could possibly survive. If the early cosmic expansion speed was below a certain figure, then the universe is doomed to recollapse in a Big Crunch. This of course couldn't imply that all human strivings were pointless. But it would set interesting limits to them.

I mentioned the idea that force strengths and particle masses fall inside life-permitting ranges which are very narrow. A currently popular theory is that the strengths and masses which we observe are fixed by scalar fields which have different intensities in different cosmic regions. Experiments in high-energy physics might conceivably upset our local scalar fields, creating a bubble which expanded at nearly the speed of light and destroyed us all. Humans should strive to avoid that danger—which has been seriously discussed by leading physicists and cosmologists.

God would be no clear guarantee against doom, either in a Big Crunch or through a bubble expanding at tremendous speed. It's wrong to think that all God's eggs, so to speak, would have to be in the one basket—our own little universe.

3 What do you think should be the relationship between religion and science?

Religious people often decry a God "who fills gaps in our scientific understanding." What if we could be certain, for example, that force strengths and particle masses were "fine tuned" in life-permitting ways? This, they say, might reasonably fortify religious faith but should never help topple anyone into such faith.

Their approach strikes me as schizoid. Yes, a universe-creating divine person might have reasons (perhaps connected with a wish to preserve human freedom) for not making his presence too obvious. But for him to hide all traces of his creative activities might seem more than a little deceitful, mightn't it? And how absurd to think that religious faith could reasonably be "fortified" by various scientific discoveries, yet that the discoveries provided no reason whatever for developing such faith!

Whether God "fine tuned" the force strengths and particle masses, or whether such matters instead vary in chance ways inside a gigantic cosmos, is of obvious importance to physics and cosmology.

20
The Origin of Consciousness
· · · · · · · · · ·
Richard G. Swinburne

Richard G. Swinburne is Nolloth Professor of the Philosophy of the Christian Religion at Oxford University and one of the most influential philosophers of religion writing today. Professor Swinburne delivered the prestigious Gifford Lectures in 1982–83 and 1983–84. His books include *Space and Time*, *Personal Identity*, *The Evolution of the Soul* and his well-known trilogy, *The Coherence of Theism*, *Faith and Reason*, and *The Existence of God*.

· · · · · · · · · ·

I

I begin by analysing my datum: I am concerned to explain the occurrence of conscious events. Events consist in the instantiation of properties in substances (that is, things) at times. My tie (substance) being red (property) now (time) is an event; so am I (substance) writing (property) today (time). (As I shall use the term, events include both continuing states and changes of state.)

Properties and events may be physical or mental. I understand by a physical property one such that no one subject is necessarily better placed to know that it is instantiated than is any other subject. Physical properties are public; there is no privileged access to them. Thus having a mass of ten pounds, being eight feet tall, and being square are all physical properties. So too are the typical properties of neurons in the brain—being in such-and-such an electrical state or releasing a transmitter substance. Anyone who chooses can find out as surely as anyone else whether something is eight feet tall or in a certain electrical state. Physical events, as I shall use the term, are those that involve the instantiation of physical properties alone. Mental properties, as I shall understand the term, are ones to which one subject has privileged access, about which he or she is necessarily in a better position to know about than is anyone else. Properties such as being in pain or having a red afterimage are mental, for any person in whom they are instantiated is necessarily better placed to know about them than is anyone else. For whatever ways you have of finding out whether I have a red afterimage (by inspecting my brain state or studying my behavior, for example) I can share; and yet I have an additional way of finding this out—by my own awareness of my own experience (an awareness that may or may not be fallible). Mental events are events that involve the instantiation of (one or more) mental properties (for instance, John being in pain at midday yesterday).

There are properties, and so events, that are mental on this definition and that can be analyzed in terms of a physical component and a mental component. These properties and events we may call mixed mental properties and events. Thus "saying 'hello'" is a mixed property, for my saying "hello" consists in my intentionally seeking to bring about the sound "hello" (a mental event) causing the occurrence of the sound "hello" (a physical event). It is the property of the instantiation of a certain mental property, causing the instantiation of a certain physical property, that is possessed by the substances that are people who say "hello." Those mental properties that cannot be analyzed in part in terms of a physical component I term pure mental properties. "Being in pain" and "desiring to eat" are such pure mental properties. In talking henceforward of mental properties I shall understand thereby (unless I specify otherwise) pure mental properties; and I shall understand by mental events the instantiations of pure mental properties.

Among pure mental events are conscious events, events of which the subject is to some extent aware while he is having them. Sensations are an important class of conscious events. Sensations include the sensory content of perception—by experiencing patterns of colour in my visual field, hearing noises, feeling pressure (minus any beliefs about how things are in the outside world—that there is a table present, say—that are mediated by the patterns of sensation in perception). They include also experiences similar in content to those had in perception, such as those of dreams and hallucinations, and the pale imitations of perception in memory images and imagined images. They include also sensations of taste or smell and pains and sensations of hot or cold in parts of the body.

Thoughts are another class of conscious events. By thoughts I mean those datable conscious occurrences of particular thoughts that can be expressed in the form of a proposition. Often these are thoughts that occur to a subject, flit through his mind, or strike him without the subject in any way actively conjuring them up. It may occur to me that today is Tuesday, or that I have a receptive audience, or that the weather is cold. A subject's awareness of his or her beliefs, and views of how the world is, come as thoughts. Perception involves, as well as sensations, the acquisition of belief (of which the subject is sometimes conscious) about how the world is surrounding the subject. (In so far as beliefs are states that continue while the subject is unaware of them, they are mental— because of the privileged access to them—but not conscious events.)

A further class of conscious events are what I shall call "purposings." By a subject's purposings I mean his endeavourings to bring about some events, meaning so to do. Every intentional action, everything that an agent does, meaning to do it, consists of the agent's bringing about some effect or trying but failing to do so. Yet when the agent brings about some effect, the active contribution may be just the same as when, unexpectedly, he tries but fails to bring about the effect. When I move my hand, I bring about the motion of my hand. Normally this action involves no effort and is entirely within my control. But on some occasion, I may find myself unexpectedly paralysed. My active contribution is the same as when I move my hand successfully, yet because I fail, we say that what I did was to "try" to move my hand. Normally we speak of "trying" only when effort or failure is involved. Yet we do need a word that covers both the trying that involves effort or failure and an agent's own intentional contribution to an action, when the performance is easy and successful. For this intentional contribution, for an agent's setting himself or herself to bring about some effect (even when effort or failure is not involved), I shall use the word "purposing."

A person's conscious life also includes from time to time awareness of desires, those in-built inclinations to do certain actions (or, in my terminology, to have certain purposings). (In so far as desires continue while the subject is unaware of them, they are like beliefs, mental states but not conscious events.)

All the conscious events that I have described, apart from sensations, are intrinsically propositional in character; that is, they consist in an attitude towards a state of affairs under a certain description. A thought is a thought that so-and-so (e.g., "today is Thursday"); a purposing is a purposing that so-and-so occur; and so on. Sensations by contrast are unconceptualized experiences; though normally, in perception, they accompany the acquisition of beliefs about the external world. When I see a table, I have a colored visual field (sensation), and I acquire thereby the belief that, causing it, is a table.

It seems to me evident that mental events, and especially conscious events, are distinct events from brain events or other physical events. To have a red sensation is not the same event as to have one's C-fibres fire or any other going-on in the brain. For each consists in the instantiation of a different property (redness; a certain distribution of electric charge) in the same subject at the same time. One event may cause the other, but there are two distinct goings-on. A Martian visitor who discovered everything physical that was happening in the human brain (in the way of redistribution of chemical matter and electric charge) would want to know whether or not humans felt anything when you kicked them and they screamed, whether they purposed their arms to move, whether they had thoughts about the world, and so on. A full history of a human being would list mental events as well as physical events. Much philosophical ink has been spent in trying to construct arguments to deny what seems to stare us in the face—that conscious events are distinct events from brain events.[1] Unfortunately, I do not have the space here to marshal counter-arguments, though I have done so elsewhere.[2] I shall therefore assume what I hope will be apparent—that consciousness is something distinct from what goes on in the brain, albeit closely connected causally to it. The conscious life, unlike the life of the brain, is rich in color, feeling, and meaning.

That we ourselves are in the above respects conscious is immediately evident. It is not much less evident that other humans besides ourselves are conscious. It is fairly evident that the higher mammals are conscious. It is quite evident that inanimate matter is not conscious. At some stage in evolutionary history consciousness first appeared; I shall not speculate when that was. No doubt the various facets of consciousness arrived on the evolutionary scene at different moments of history.

Many of our sensations are evidently caused by brain events, and the latter are normally caused fairly directly by more remote bodily events (such as light rays impinging on eyes). Plausibly, too, many thoughts (especially thoughts that express the content of beliefs acquired in perception) are caused directly by brain events. We do, however, believe some of our thoughts to be caused by other of our thoughts (as when we do a piece of mental arithmetic). We also believe that our purposings are often efficacious—that my purposing to move my arm, say, causes my arm to move, and it can only do that by causing a brain event that causes the arm to move. The epiphenomenalist denies that there is any "downward" efficacy; he claims that when purposing appears to cause bodily events, what is really happening is that the two have a common cause, a brain event that causes a purposing to move an arm and, slightly later, the arm movement; it is this, he claims, that produces the illusion of purposive efficacy. It does not seem that way. And no one can be a consistent epiphenomenalist and live. For to purpose to do something is to do what one believes to be likely to bring about the event purposed. To try to move one's hand is to do what one believes is likely to be causally efficacious in bringing about the hand motion. An epiphenomenalist, however, believes that nothing mental has effects in the physical world, and hence cannot perform any mental act that is believed to have such an effect. So the epiphenomenalist cannot try to move a hand or do any other intentional public action; the consistent epiphenomenalist must cease to try. But no one will do that, and that is because everyone really believes that their purposes are efficacious. I appeal to consensus in making the assumption that purposings affect brain states.

So we get the following picture of mind-body interaction (in the sense of the interaction of the conscious events and brain events of an agent; I am not assuming here that minds are substances): brain states cause many sensations and some thoughts; many purposings cause brain events; and perhaps some conscious events cause (in part) other conscious events. Can we have a scientific explanation of how the evolution of physical systems gave rise to conscious events that began to interact with physical events and direct the development of those systems?

• • • • • • • • •

II

The first thing we would need is an explanation of how in the present in humans and many other animals certain brain states give rise to certain conscious states, and conversely. For this purpose I shall make the normal (though very ill-evidenced) simplifying assumption of one-many simultaneous mind-brain correlation. That is, for each kind of conscious event there are one or more kinds of brain event, such that whenever one of the latter occurs, the former occurs simultaneously and conversely. Thus, given a specific kind of sensation, a round red image of a certain hue and size against a black background, say, there will be one or more kinds of brain events such that whenever one of the latter occurs, the image occurs; but the image never occurs without one of the latter occurring. In principle it will then be possible for scientists to compile a very, very long list of the correlations between brain events and conscious events, stating which conscious event occurs (a blue elliptical image, for another example) when a given brain event occurs. The correlations would be generalizations, stating that all brain events of this kind occur at the same time as conscious events of that kind (that is, correlations of the form "always whenever this brain event, that conscious event"). The correlations would be established by noting which brain states occurred when observers reported having some conscious event and not otherwise. To get exceptionless lists scientists would probably need to suppose that on some few occasions, to mislead the scientist or through inadequate grasp of sensory vocabulary or through misobservation, observers misreported their sensations.

But why do certain brain events give rise to conscious events and others do not, and why do brain events give rise to the conscious events that they do rather than to other events? Why does a certain brain event give rise to a pink image rather than to a smell of roses or to a thought that $2 + 2 = 4$? Physics and chemistry cannot possibly explain these things, since pink looks, rosy smells, and mathematical thoughts are not the sort of thing physics and chemistry deal in. These sciences deal in the physical (public) properties of small physical objects and of the large physical objects that they come to form—in mass and charge, volume, and spin.

But could not physics and chemistry be enlarged so as to become a superscience dealing with both physical and mental properties and providing explanations of their interactions? I do not think so, for the following reason. To give a scientific explanation of why some event occurred, you have to show that, given the previous state of affairs, the laws of nature are such that it had to occur. You explain why the planet today is in this position by stating where it and other heavenly bodies were last month (the initial conditions) and how it follows from Newton's laws of motion and gravitational attraction that those initial conditions would be followed a month later by the planet being where it is today. To provide a scientific explanation you need laws of nature. Laws state what must happen of natural necessity to all objects with certain properties; that is, they claim that some generalization "all As are B" (for example, As have certain properties or do so-and-so) holds of natural necessity. And what will be the evidence that some such generalization does hold of natural necessity? First, of course, no As must have been observed to be not-B; and secondly, normally many As must have been observed to be B. But that is not enough. All ravens so far observed have been observed to be black. But that is quite inadequate evidence for supposing that "all ravens are black" is a law of nature. We need evidence to suppose that all ravens so far observed being black is no mere accident of local conditions (caused by the chance that there has not actually occurred any mutation to produce a gene for whiteness in the genotype of raven) but that there could not be a black raven (however molecules were arranged, they could not give rise to a black raven). To show this of some generalization "all As are B," we need to show not merely that the generalization holds universally but that it fits neatly into a scientific theory that is a simple theory with few simple purported laws, able to predict a vast range of phenomena. The grounds that people had in the eighteenth century for believing Newton's "law" of gravity—that all bodies attract each other in pairs with forces proportional to the product of the masses of each and inversely proportional to the square of their distances apart—to be indeed a law of nature was that it was a very simple law that fitted into a theory with four "laws" in all, the others being equally simple, that together were able to predict a vast range of phenomena. The law of gravity ($F = mm^1/r^2$) is simple because the distance is not raised to a complicated power (e.g., we do not have $r^{2.003}$), there is only one term (e.g., we do not have $mm^1/r^2 + mm^1/r^4 + mm^1/r^6$), and so on. The law is also simple for the reason that, given this law and only given this law, the total force exerted by a body on a hollow sphere of given uniform thickness and density centred on the body remains the same, whatever the inner radius of the sphere. The theory, with four such simple laws, was able to predict with great accuracy the behavior of bodies of very different kinds in very different circumstances—the motions of planets, the rise and fall of tides, the interactions of colliding bodies, the movements of pendula, and so forth. Einstein's laws of General Relativity are, of course, more complicated than Newton's, but Einstein claimed for them that they had great coherence and great mathematical simplicity and elegance, at any rate in comparison with the complexity of the data they were able to explain. I conclude that the evidence that some generalization is a law, as opposed to a mere generalization (holding only perhaps in a limited spatio-temporal realm or by accident or coincidence), is that it fits into a simple coherent theory that predicts successfully a vast range of diverse data.

Now a scientist, I have assumed, could compile a long list of correlations between brain events and conscious events. But to explain those correlations we need by our principles to establish a much smaller set of purported laws, from which it follows that this kind of brain event has to be correlated with a red sensation, that one with a blue sensation, this one with a purposing to sing a high note, and that one with a purposing to sing a low note. The purported laws would need to fit together into a theory from which we could derive new correlations (predict, for instance, some totally new sensation to which some hitherto unexemplified brain state would give rise). If our purported laws could do all that, that would be grounds for believing them to be indeed laws, and so for believing that we had got a scientific explanation of the occurrence of sensations. Then we would be able to say why sodium chloride tastes salty rather than sweet in terms of the brain event that tasting sodium chloride normally causes, having a natural connection (stated by our theory) with a salty tang. Mere correlation does not explain, and because it does not explain, you never know when your correlations will cease to hold. Because you have no explanation of why all ravens are black, you may reasonably suspect that tomorrow someone will find a white raven.

The list of correlations is like a list of sentences of a foreign language that, under certain circumstances, translate sentences of English, without any grammar or word dictionary to explain why those sentences are under those conditions correct translations. In the absence of a grammar and dictionary you do not know when those translations will cease to be accurate (maybe "blah blah" only refers to the Sovereign when the Sovereign is male). Nor can you translate any sentence other than the ones listed.

But why should not the scientist devise a theory showing the kinds of correlation discussed to be natural ones? Why should the scientist not postulate entities and properties from whose interactions, the laws of which are simple, it would follow that you get the correlations that you do between brain events and conscious events? Although it is theoretically possible that a scientific theory of this kind should be created, the creation of such a theory does not look a very likely prospect. Brain events are such different things qualitatively from pains, smells, and tastes, thoughts and purposings, that a natural connection between them seems almost impossible. For how could brain states vary except in their chemical composition and the speed and direction of their electro-chemical interactions, and how could there be a natural connection between variations in these respects and variations in the kind of respects in which tastes differ—say the difference between a taste of pineapple, a taste of roast beef, and a taste of chocolate —as well as the respects in which tastes differ from smells and smells from visual sensations and sensations from thoughts and purposings. There does not seem the beginning of a prospect of a simple scientific theory of this kind and so of having established laws of mind-body interaction as opposed to lots of diverse correlations, which, just because they are unconnected in an overall theory, are for that reason not necessarily of universal application. If we cannot have scientific laws we cannot have scientific explanation. The scientist's task of giving a full explanation of the occurrence of a subject's conscious events seems doomed to failure. For a scientific theory with detailed laws could not be simple enough for us to have reasonable confidence in its truth (and so its universal applicability).

The history of science is, it is true, punctuated with many great "reductions," of one whole branch of science to another apparently totally different, or "integration" of apparently very disparate sciences into a superscience. Thermodynamics, dealing with heat, was reduced to statistical mechanics; the temperature of a gas proved to be the mean kinetic energy of its molecules. Optics was reduced to electromagnetism; light proved to be an electro-magnetic wave. And the separate sciences of electricity and magnetism came together to form a superscience of electromagne-tism. How is it that such integrations can be achieved if my argument that there cannot be a superscience that explains both mental events and brain events is correct?

There is a crucial difference between the two cases. All other integrations into a superscience, of sciences dealing with entities and properties apparently qualitatively very distinct, were achieved by saying that really some of those entities and proper-ties were not as they appeared to be, by making a distinction between the underlying (not immediately observable) entities and properties and the sensory properties to which they gave rise. Thermodynamics was originally concerned with the laws of temperature exchange, and temperature was supposed to be a property inherent in an object, that you felt when you touched the object. The felt hotness of a hot body is indeed qualitatively distinct from particle velocities and collisions. The reduction was achieved by distinguishing between the underlying cause of the hotness (the motion of molecules) and the sensations that the motions of molecules cause in observers. The former falls naturally within the scope of statistical mechanics—for molecules are particles; the entities and properties are not of distinct kinds. But this reduction has been achieved at the price of separating off the sensory from its causes and only explaining the latter. All "reduction" of one science to another dealing with apparently very disparate properties has been achieved by this device of denying that the apparent properties (such as the "secondary qualities" of color, heat, sound, taste) with which one science dealt belonged to the physical world at all. It siphoned them off to the world of the mental. But then when you come to face the problem of the sensations themselves, you cannot do this. If you are to explain the sensations themselves, you cannot distinguish between them and their underlying causes and only explain the latter. In fact the enormous success of science in producing an integrated physicochemistry has been achieved at the expense of separating off from the physical world colors, smells, and tastes, and regarding them as purely private sensory phenomena. The very success of science in achieving its vast integrations in physics and chemistry is the very thing that has made apparently impossible any final success in integrating the world of the mind and the world of physics.

There is little prospect for a scientific theory of the origin of sensations. And what goes for sensations goes for conscious events of other types. There is not the ghost of a natural connection between this brain event and that thought, so that we could understand how a change of this electrochemical kind would give rise to a thought that $2 + 2 = 5$ as opposed to a thought that $2 + 2 = 4$, the thought that there is a table here rather than the thought that there is no solid object here. There is a vast qualitative difference between thoughts with their in-built meanings (their intrinsic propositional content) and mere electrochemical events, so that it seems impossible to construct a theory in terms of which the various correlations between brain states and thoughts follow naturally, that was simple enough for us to expect to make successful predictions about which new thoughts would be correlated with hitherto unexemplified brain states. Only if this were done would the theory be one that we would be justified in believing to provide true explanations of the occurrence of thoughts. And what goes for thoughts goes also for purposes and other conscious events with intrinsic propositional content. There is no prospect of a scientific theory of why a purpose to move my hand should cause this neuron to fire rather than that one.

· · · · · · · · · ·

III

Let us, however, take it as given that by some means or other it comes about that brain events of certain kinds give rise to conscious events of certain kinds and, conversely, that the long list of correlations is operative. There are two remaining issues that science may have some prospect of explaining. First, how did it come about that there were organisms with brains with a repertoire of states of a kind to cause conscious events and be caused by them?

It is possible that there is a scientific explanation of this fact, though it is not easy to see how it would run. An orthodox Darwinian account would claim that genetic mutations or rearrangements caused the existence of genes that caused the growth of brains capable of mental interactions of certain kinds; organisms with such brains survived either because there was a selective advantage in having a conscious life or because there was a selective advantage in other characteristics also brought about by the same genetic material as gave rise to a conscious life. It is not easy to see what the selective advantage of having a mental life is. Just consider sensations. This system of ours in which sensations are causally intermediate between stimulus and response seems to have no evolutionary advantage over a mechanism that produces the same behavioural modifications without going through sensations to produce them. It looks as if there can be mechanisms of the latter kind—are not the light-sensitive, air-vibration-sensitive machines that we are now building just such machines? Maybe there is a discoverable physicochemical explanation of why there cannot be (or is not very likely to be produced) a set of genes that will give rise to such a machine; or perhaps an organism with sensations has a less cumbersome process for modifying its behaviour (in response to bodily damage, say) than such a non-conscious machine, and for that reason has an evolutionary advantage. The former, if true, would be far easier to show than the latter. However, along one of these lines there are possibilities for a Darwinian account of why organisms with a capacity to have sensations have an advantage in the struggle for survival.

The same point applies to conscious events of other kinds. There is no apparent advantage possessed by an organism who has a belief articulated in conscious thought that there is a table here, as opposed to a mere disposition to avoid bumping into the table and to put things on it (such as presumably is possessed by robots). What advantage is there in the mental awareness as opposed to the unconscious disposition? As with sensations, we can sketch a possible answer—perhaps organisms with conscious beliefs and so on will have less cumbersome processes for reacting to their environment than organisms without a mental life who react in the same way, and for that reason the former have greater survival value. (Robots perhaps need more bits and take up more space.) Or maybe it is not possible to have a set of genes produced by recombination of DNA molecules (as opposed to a silicon chip) that will give rise to an organism with complicated abilities to react to the environment, without that organism having beliefs about it and other mental attitudes towards it.

There are prospects for a Darwinian explanation of how animals have evolved with brains of the sort to give rise (by an inexplicable process) to consciousness, though the prospects are not very bright ones. In the absence of a Darwinian explanation, there might be a fairly ordinary scientific explanation of some other kind. Maybe DNA has got an in-built propensity to give rise to genes of the requisite type during the course of millions of years of recombination; maybe there is an orthogenetic tendency to evolve in this direction.

· · · · · · · · · ·
IV

We have noted, then, one crucial all-important question that is utterly beyond the powers of Darwinism or apparently science itself to answer—why do certain brain events give rise to certain mental events, and conversely?—and one question on which there are some possibilities for a Darwinian or other scientific answer. There is a third question, to which Darwinism can provide a clear and obviously correct answer as regards conscious beliefs, purposes, and desires. This is the question: given the existence of mind-brain correlations, and given that organisms with a conscious life will be favored in the struggle for survival, why are the brain events that cause and are caused by conscious events connected with other bodily events and extra-bodily events in the way in which they are? Take beliefs (of which the subject is aware in consciousness). Why is the brain connected via the optic nerve to the eye in such a way that the brain event that gives rise to the belief that there is a table present is normally caused to occur when and only when there is a table present? The answer is evident: animals with beliefs are more likely to survive if their beliefs are largely true. False beliefs, such as those about the location of food or predators, will lead to rapid elimination in the struggle for survival. If you believe that there is no table present, when there is one, you will fall over it, and so on. Those in whom the brain events that give rise to beliefs are connected by causal chains to the states of affairs believed are much better adapted for survival than those whose belief brain states are not so connected and who in consequence tend to have false beliefs. Many animals have a built-in mechanism for correcting in the light of experience any tendency to acquire false beliefs by a certain route—finding frequently that an object of a certain kind that looks like food is really not food, for example, they cease to acquire the belief that there is food in front of them when they receive visual stimuli from an object of that kind. Such animals are more likely to survive and produce offspring. A similar account can be given of why the brain events produced by purposes give rise to the movements of body purposed. If, when I tried to move my foot, my hand moved instead, predators would soon overtake me. Similarly, given that I am going to have desires caused by brain events, there are evolutionary advantages in my having some under some circumstances rather than others under other circumstances—desire for food when I am hungry rather than when I am satiated, say. I do, however, have some doubt as to whether there can be a satisfactory explanation of why the brain events that give rise to sensations (as opposed to thoughts and purposes) are connected to bodily and extra-bodily events in the way that they are. What is the selective advantage in ripe tomatoes and other objects normally called "red" giving rise to red sensations, and unripe tomatoes and other objects normally called "green" giving rise to green sensations rather than conversely?

In summary, then, the evolution of consciousness in animals is a matter of: 1) there existing certain physical/mental correlations (brain events of certain kinds being correlated with conscious events of certain kinds); 2) there having evolved animals with brains, having a repertoire of events of the kinds correlated with conscious events; and 3) those animals having their brains "wired into" their bodies so that peripheral and extra-bodily events are causally connected with consciousness in certain familiar ways. Darwinian or other scientific mechanisms can explain quite a lot of 3), and possibly some of 2), but neither Darwinism nor any other science has much prospect of explaining 1). Hence to explain adequately the origin of the most novel and striking features of animals (their conscious life of feeling, choice, and reason) probably lies utterly beyond the range of science.

I conclude that the process of animal evolution, apparently so regular and predictable, is yet in the respect of those all-important properties of animals (their mental life that makes them, like humans, deserving of kindness and reverence, and that makes them also interact with ourselves) not fully explicable scientifically and not likely ever to be.

· · · · · · · · · ·

V

I have argued that science cannot fully explain the evolution of a mental life. This is because, so far as we can see, there is no law of nature stating that physical events of certain kinds will give rise to correlated mental events and, conversely; there is nothing in the nature of certain physical events or of mental events to give rise to the correlations. Yet there are so many evident regular correlations between consciousness and the brain that their orderliness cries out for explanation. Is there any other way of explaining them?

There are two basic and very different ways of explaining phenomena. There is the scientific way of explaining an event by a preceding initial set-up and laws of nature, such that the description of the latter two entails the description of the event to be explained; laws themselves are explained by being deducible from higher-level laws (and perhaps also some general description of a pervasive feature of the universe on the small or large scale). By contrast there is personal explanation, whereby we explain an event as brought about intentionally by some agent, for its own sake or for the sake of some further purpose. Much human behavior is explained in the latter way, and such "explanation" is recognized as explanation, as showing what it was that brought about the event in question.[3] But personal explanation shows an event occurring because an agent sought to bring about a goal, rather than because prior blind forces brought it about.

A possible personal explanation in this case is that God, the power behind nature, brings it about that the brains of men and some animals are connected with a conscious life in regular and predictable ways. God, an omnipotent, omniscient, perfectly free, and perfectly good source of all, would need to be postulated as an explanation of many diverse phenomena (including the operation of laws of nature themselves) to make his existence probable. But the ability of God's actions to explain the otherwise mysterious mind-body connection is just one more reason for postulating God's existence.

The suggestion is that God has given to each human brain and some animal brains a limited nature, as it were; a limited nature such that in the circumstances of normal embodiment it keeps a conscious life functioning and interacting with the brain in predictable ways without the brain having that nature deriving from any general law of brain/mind connection, and determining in general under what circumstances there occur conscious events of different kinds.[4] God, being omnipotent, would have the power to give to the brain such a limited nature, to produce intentionally those connections which, we have seen, have no natural connection. And God would have a reason for so doing: to give to human beings beliefs, thoughts, desires, and sensations caused in regular ways by brain states, and purposes that cause brain states in regular ways, would allow them to acquire knowledge of the world and to make a difference to it by conscious choice—to allow them to share in the creative work of God himself. That there are animals who also acquire some true beliefs and make some choices, and interact with each other and with men in so doing, is also a good thing that an omnipotent God would have reason for bringing about.

A God would have the ability and a reason for bringing about such connections. The occurrence of the conscious life and its mode of functioning (under the limited conditions of embodiment in bodies with brains), which otherwise are likely to remain totally mysterious, can be explained in terms of divine action.

• • • • • • • • •

Notes

This paper is based on material contained in my book, *The Evolution of the Soul* (Oxford: Clarendon Press, 1986), particularly ch. 10.

1. See, for example, most of the papers in *The Mind-Brain Identity Theory*, edited by C. V. Borst (London: Macmillan, 1970); D. M. Armstrong, *A Materialist Theory of Mind* (London: Routledge and Kegan Paul, 1968); H. Putnam, "Minds and Machines" and "The Mental Life of Some Machines," in his *Philosophical Papers*, Vol. 2: *Mind, Language and Reality* (Cambridge: Cambridge University Press, 1975); and D. Davidson, "Mental Events," in his *Essays on Actions and Events* (Oxford: Clarendon Press, 1980), 207–25.
2. *The Evolution of the Soul*, ch. 3; and "Are Mental Events Identical with Brain Events?", *American Philosophical Quarterly* 19 (1982): 173–81.
3. Personal explanation is entirely different in pattern and cannot be reduced to scientific explanation. On this see *The Evolution of the Soul*, ch. 5; or my *The Existence of God* (Oxford: Clarendon Press, 1979), ch. 2. The next few paragraphs summarize the argument for the existence of God from consciousness given in *The Existence of God*, ch. 9.
4. My account leaves it open whether God confers this limited nature on evolved animal brains, once they have them; or, as it were, determines in advance that brains with a certain repertoire of states will be the ones that give rise to consciousness, leaving it to Darwinian or other scientific processes to bring it about that animals and humans have brains of that kind.

· · · · · · · · · ·

The Universe and the Existence of God

Many worthwhile arguments for the existence of God seem to me to have a common pattern. Some phenomenon E, which we can all observe, is considered. It is claimed that E is puzzling, strange, not to be expected in the ordinary course of things; but that E is to be expected if there is a God; for God has the power to bring about E and He might well choose to do so. Hence the occurrence of E is reason for supposing that there is a God. E may be a large phenomenon, such as the existence of the universe, or something a lot smaller, such as our own individual religious experiences.

This pattern of argument is one much used in science, history, and all other fields of human inquiry. A detective, for example, finds various clues—John's fingerprints on a burgled safe, John having a lot of money hidden in his house, John being seen near the scene of the burglary at the time when it was committed. He then suggests that these various clues, although they just *might* have other explanations, are not in general to be expected unless John had robbed the safe. Each clue is some evidence that he did rob the safe, confirms the hypothesis that John robbed the safe; and the evidence is cumulative—when put together it makes the hypothesis probable.

Let us call arguments of this kind arguments to a good

explanation. Scientists use this pattern of argument to argue to the existence of unobservable entities as causes of the phenomena which they observe. For example, at the beginning of the nineteenth century, scientists observed many varied phenomena of chemical interaction, such as that substances combine in fixed ratios by weight to form new substances (for example, hydrogen and oxygen always form water in a ratio by weight of 1:8). They then claimed that these phenomena would be expected if there existed a hundred or so different kinds of atom, particles far too small to be seen, which combined and recombined in certain simple ways. In their turn physicists postulated electrons, protons, and neutrons and other particles in order to account for the behavior of the atoms, as well as for larger-scale observable phenomena; and now postulate quarks in order to explain the behavior of protons, neutrons, and most other particles.

To be good arguments (that is, to provide evidence for their hypothesis), arguments of this kind must satisfy three criteria. First, the phenomena which they cite as evidence must not be very likely to occur in the normal course of things. We saw in the burglary example how the various clues, such as John's fingerprints on the safe, were not much to be expected in the normal course of things. Secondly, the phenomena must be much more to be expected if the hypothesis is true. If John did rob the safe, it is quite likely that his fingerprints would be found on it. Thirdly, the hypothesis must be simple. That is, it must postulate the existence and operation of few entities, few kinds of entities, with few easily describable properties behaving in mathematically simple kinds of ways. We could always postulate many new entities with complicated properties to explain anything which we find. But our hypothesis will only be supported by the evidence if it postulates few entities, which lead us to expect the diverse phenomena which form the evidence. Thus in the detective story example, we could suggest that Brown planted John's fingerprints on the safe, Smith dressed up to look like John at the scene of the crime, and without any collusion with the others, Robinson hid the money in John's flat. This new hypothesis would lead us to expect the phenomena which we find just as well as does the hypothesis that John robbed the safe. But the latter hypothesis is supported by the evidence whereas the former is not. And this is because the hypothesis that John robbed the safe postulates *one* object—John —doing *one* deed—robbing the safe—which leads us to expect the several phenomena which we find. Scientists always postulate as few new entities (for example, subatomic particles) as are needed to lead us to expect to find the phenomena which we observe; and they postulate that those entities do not behave erratically (behave one way one day, and a different way the next day) but that they behave in accordance with as simple and smooth a mathematical law as is compatible with what is observed. There is an old Latin saying, *simplex sigillum veri*, "the simple is the sign of the true." To be rendered probable by evidence, hypotheses must be simple.

Arguments from the Existence and Order of the Universe

My first phenomenon which provides evidence for the existence of God is the existence of the universe for so long as it has existed (whether a finite time or, if it has no beginning, an infinite time). This is something evidently inexplicable by science. For a scientific explanation as such explains the occurrence of one state of affairs S1 in terms of a previous state of affairs S2 and some law of nature which makes states like S2 bring about states like S1. Thus it may explain the planets being in their present positions by a previous state of the system (the Sun and planets being where they were last year) and the operation of Kepler's laws which state that states like the latter are followed a year later by states like the former. But what science by its very nature cannot explain is why there are any states of affairs at all.

My next phenomenon is the operation of the most general laws of nature, that is, the orderliness of nature in conforming to very general laws. What exactly these laws are, science may not yet have discovered—perhaps they are the field equations of Einstein's General Theory of Relativity, or perhaps there are some yet more fundamental laws. Now science can explain why one law operates in some narrow area, in terms of the operation of a wider law. Thus it can explain why Galileo's law of fall holds—that small objects near the surface of the Earth fall with a constant acceleration towards the Earth. Galileo's law follows from Newton's laws, given that the Earth is a massive body far from other massive bodies and the objects on its surface are close to it and small in mass in comparison. But what science by its very nature cannot explain is why there are the most general laws of nature that there are; for, *ex hypothesi*, no wider law can explain their operation.

That there is a universe and that there are laws of nature are phenomena so general and pervasive that we tend to ignore them. But there might so easily not have been a universe at all, ever. Or the universe might so easily have been a chaotic mess. That there is an *orderly* universe is something very striking, yet beyond the capacity of science ever to explain. Science's inability to explain these things is not a temporary phenomenon, caused by the backwardness of Twentieth Century science. Rather, because of what a scientific explanation is, these things will ever be beyond its capacity to explain. For *scientific* explanations by their very nature terminate with some ultimate natural law and ultimate arrangement of physical things, and the questions which I am raising are why there are natural laws and physical things at all.

However, there is another kind of explanation of phenomena which we use all the time and which we see as a proper way of explaining phenomena. This is what I call personal explanation. We often explain some phenomenon E as brought about by a person P in order to achieve some purpose or goal G. The present motion of my hand is explained as brought about by me for the purpose of writing a philosophical paper. The cup being on the table is explained by a man having put it there for the purpose of drinking out of it. Yet this is a different way of explaining things from the scientific. Scientific explanation involves laws of nature and previous states of affairs. Personal explanation involves persons and purposes. If we cannot give a scientific explanation of the existence and orderliness of the universe, perhaps we can give a personal explanation.

But why should we think that the existence and orderliness of the universe has an explanation at all? We seek for an explanation of all things; but we have seen that we have only reason for supposing that we have found one if the purported explanation is simple and leads us to expect what we find when that is otherwise not to be expected. The history of science shows that we judge that the complex, miscellaneous, coincidental, and diverse needs explaining and that it is to be explained in terms of something simpler. The motions of the planets (subject to Kepler's laws), the mechanical interactions of bodies on Earth, the behavior of comets, and so forth formed a pretty miscellaneous set of phenomena. Newton's laws of motion constituted a simple theory which led us to expect these phenomena and so was judged a true explanation of them. The existence of thousands of different chemical substances combining in different ratios to make other substances was complex. The hypothesis that there were only a hundred or so chemical elements of which the thousands of substances were made was a simple hypothesis which led us to expect the complex phenomenon.

Our universe is a complex thing. There are lots and lots of separate chunks of it. The chunks have each a different finite and not very natural volume, shape, mass, and so forth—consider the vast diversity of the galaxies, stars and planets, and pebbles on the sea shore. Matter is inert and has no powers which it can choose to exert; it does what it has to do. There is a limited amount of it in any region and it has a limited amount of energy and velocity. There is a complexity, particularity, and finitude about the universe.

The conformity of objects throughout endless time and space to simple laws is likewise something which cries out for explanation. For let us consider what this amounts to. Laws are not things, independent of material objects. To say that all objects conform to laws is simply to say that they all behave in exactly the same way. To say, for example, that the planets obey Kepler's laws is just to say that each planet at each moment of time has the property of moving in the ways that Kepler's laws state. There is therefore this vast coincidence in the behavioral properties of objects at all times and in all places. If all the coins of some region have the same markings, or all the papers in a room are written in the same handwriting, we seek an explanation in terms of a common source of these coincidences. We should seek a similar explanation for that vast coincidence which we describe as the conformity of objects to laws of nature—for example, the fact that all electrons are produced, attract, and repel other particles and combine with them in exactly the same way at each point of endless time and space.

The hypothesis of theism is that the universe exists because there is a God who keeps it in being and that laws of nature operate because there is a God who brings it about that they do. He brings it about that the laws of nature operate by sustaining in every object in the universe its liability to behave in accord with those laws. He keeps the universe in being by making the laws such as to conserve the matter of the universe, that is, by making it the case at each moment that what there was before continues to exist. The hypothesis is a hypothesis that a person brings about these things for some purpose. He acts directly on the universe, as we act directly on our brains, guiding them to move our limbs (but the universe is not his body—for he could at any moment destroy it and act on another universe, or do without a universe). As we have seen, personal explanation and scientific explanation are the two ways we have of explaining the occurrence of phenomena. Since there cannot be a scientific explanation of the existence of the universe, either there is a personal explanation or there is no explanation at all. The hypothesis that there is a God is the hypothesis of the existence of the simplest kind of person which there could be. A Person is a being with power to bring about effects, knowledge of how to do so, and freedom to make choices of which effects to bring about. God is by definition an omnipotent (that is, infinitely powerful), omniscient (that is, all-knowing), and perfectly free person. He is a person of infinite power, knowledge, and freedom; a person to whose power, knowledge, and freedom there are no limits except those of logic. The hypothesis that there exists a being with infinite degrees of the qualities essential to a being of that kind is the postulation of a very simple being. The hypothesis that there is such a God is a much simpler hypothesis than the hypothesis that there is a god who has such and such a limited power. It is simpler in just the same way that the hypothesis that some particle has zero mass or infinite velocity, is simpler than the hypothesis that it has 0.32147 of some unit of mass or a velocity of 221,000 km/sec. A finite limitation cries out for an explanation of why there is just that particular limit, in a way that limitlessness does not.

That there should exist anything at all, let alone a universe as complex and as orderly as ours, is exceedingly strange. But if there is a God, it is not vastly unlikely that he should create such a universe. A universe such as ours is a thing of beauty and a theater in which men and other creatures can grow and work out their destiny. The orderliness of the universe makes it a beautiful universe, but, even more importantly, it makes it a universe which men can learn to control and change. For only if there are simple laws of nature can men predict what will follow from what—and unless they can do that, they can never change anything. Only if men know that by sowing certain seeds, weeding and watering them, they will get corn, can they develop an agriculture. And men can only acquire that knowledge if there are easily graspable regularities of behavior in nature. So God has good reason to make an orderly universe and, *ex hypothesi*, being omnipotent, he has the power to do so. So the hypothesis that there is a God makes the existence of the universe much more to be expected than it would otherwise be, and it is a very simple hypothesis.

Hence the arguments from the existence of the universe and its conformity to simple natural laws are good arguments to an explanation of the phenomena and provide substantial evidence for the existence of God.

The Argument from the Evolution of Animals and Men

A third phenomenon best explained by postulating the existence and creative activity of God, and so adding to the cumulative case for his existence, is the evolution of animals and humans. In the middle of the last century Darwin set out his impressive theory of evolution by natural selection to account for the existence of animals and humans. Animals varied in numerous ways from their parents (some were taller, some shorter, some fatter, some thinner, some had beginnings of a wing, others did not; and so on). Those animals with characteristics which made them best fitted to survive, survived and handed on their characteristics to the next generation. But, although in general resembling their parents, their offspring varied from them, and those variations which best fitted the animal to survive were again the ones most likely to be handed on to another generation. This process went on for millions of years, producing the whole range of animals which we have today, each adapted to survive in a different environment. Among the characteristics giving advantage in the struggle for survival was intelligence, and the selections for this characteristic eventually led to the evolution of man. Such is Darwin's account of why we have today animals and men.

As far as it goes, his account is surely right. But there are two crucial matters beyond its scope. First, the evolutionary mechanism which Darwin describes only works because there are certain laws of biochemistry (animals produce many offspring, these vary in different ways from the parents, and so forth) and certain features of the environment (there is a limited amount of food, drink, space, and so on). But why are there these laws rather than other laws? Perhaps because they follow from the most fundamental laws of physics. But the question then arises as to why the fundamental laws of physics are such as to give rise to laws of evolution. If we can answer this question we should do so. There is again available the same simple answer—that there is a God who makes matter behave in accord with such laws in order to produce a world with animals and men. To develop my earlier point—God has an obvious reason for producing men. He wants there to be creatures who can share in His creative work by making choices which affect the world they live in and the other creatures who live in that world. By the way we treat our environment and our bodies, bring up our children and influence our governments, we can make this world beautiful and its other inhabitants happy and knowledgeable; or we can make it ugly and its other inhabitants miserable and ignorant. A good God will seek other beings with whom to share in his activity of creation, of forming, moulding, and changing the world. The fact of a mechanism to produce men is evidence of God behind that mechanism.

Secondly, Darwinian theory is concerned only with the physical characteristics of animals and men. Yet men have thoughts and feelings, beliefs and desires, and they make choices. These are events totally different from publicly observable physical events. Physical objects are, physicists tell us, interacting colorless centers of forces; but they act on our senses, which set up electrical circuits in our brains, and these brain events cause us to have sensations (of pain or color, sound or smell), thoughts, desires, and beliefs. Mental events such as these are no doubt largely caused by brain events (and vice-versa); but mental events are distinct from brain events—sensations are quite different from electrochemical disturbances. They are in fact so different—private, colored, or noisy, and felt—from public events that it is very, very unlikely indeed that science will ever explain how brain events give rise to mental events (why this brain event causes a red sensation, and that one a blue sensation). Yet brain events do cause mental events; no doubt there are regular correlations between this type of brain event and that type of mental event, and yet no scientific theory can say why there are the particular correlations there are, or indeed any correlations at all (why did not evolution just throw up unfeeling robots?). Yet these correlations which science cannot explain cry out for explanation of another kind. That is available. God brings it about that brain events of certain kinds give rise to mental events of certain kinds in order that animals and men may learn about the physical world, see it as imbued with color and smell making it beautiful, and learn to control it. Brain events caused by different sights, sounds, and smells give rise to different and characteristic sensations and beliefs in order that men may have knowledge of a beautiful physical world and thus have power over it. Darwinism can only explain why some animals are eliminated in the struggle for survival, not why there are animals and men at all with mental lives of sensation and belief; and in so far as it can explain anything, the question inevitably arises why the laws of evolution are as they are. All this theism can explain.

Each phenomenon which the simple hypothesis of theism can explain adds to the cumulative case for the existence of God. My claim is that the phenomena which I have just described provide very substantial support for that case; and when added to the support provided by other phenomena within the universe, the history of the human race, and individual religious experience, makes that case a strong one.

21

Religious Responses to the Big Bang

● ● ● ● ● ● ● ● ● ●

Ian Barbour

Ian Barbour is Professor of Religion and Professor of Science, Technology and Society, Emeritus at Carleton College. With degrees in Physics from Duke University (M.S., 1946) and the University of Chicago (Ph.D., 1950), and in Theology from Yale University (B.D., 1956), he became an influential teacher and writer of seminal articles and books such as *Issues in Science and Religion* and *Myths, Models and Paradigms*. His Gifford Lectures (1989–1991) have recently been published in two volumes as *Religion in an Age of Science* and *Ethics in an Age of Technology*.

● ● ● ● ● ● ● ● ● ●

Abstract

The presentation will first consider three responses to Big Bang cosmology that seem dubious, the claims that there are, respectively, 1) agreement, 2) conflict, or 3) total independence in comparing Western religious ideas of creation with recent scientific theories of cosmology. Then we examine some philosophical implications of cosmology concerning design, chance, and necessity. Finally we will look at theological implications of cosmology: the intelligibility and contingency of the cosmos; "creation out of nothing" versus "continuing creation"; and the significance of humanity.

Let me briefly summarize the current scientific understanding of the Big Bang before examining a variety of religious responses to it. In 1929, Hubble discovered the "red shift" of light from distant nebulae, which was evidence for an expanding universe. Extrapolating backward in time, the universe seemed to be expanding from a common origin about fifteen billion years ago. In 1965, Penzias and Wilson discovered a faint background of microwaves coming from all directions in space. The spectrum of those waves corresponded very closely to the residual radiation which had been predicted from relativity theory. In April 1992, data obtained by NASA's Cosmic Background Explorer (COBE) satellite showed very small variations in this microwave background among different regions of space. The existence of such variations early in cosmic history would account for the clumping of matter in galaxies.[1]

Theories relevant to the very early moments of the Big Bang have come from high-energy physics. Physicists have sought theories that would integrate the electromagnetic force, the weak nuclear force, the strong nuclear force, and gravity. In 1967, Weinberg and Salam showed that the electromagnetic and weak forces could be unified within an Electro-weak Theory. The theory predicted the existence of two massive particles, the W and Z bosons, which mediate between the two kinds of force. In 1983, Rubbia and co-workers found particles with the predicted properties of W bosons among the products of high-energy collisions in the CERN accelerator in Geneva.

There has been some progress in attempts to unite the electro-weak and strong forces in a Grand Unified Theory. The unification would be mediated by very massive X-particles which could only exist at energies higher than those in any existing accelerator.[2] The unification of gravity with the other three forces within one Supersymmetry Theory has appeared more difficult because there has been no successful quantum theory of gravity. But there has been great interest in Superstring Theory, which postulates the production of very long, thin, massive strings when symmetry is broken during the cooling-off process.[3]

Putting together the evidence from astronomy and high-energy physics, a plausible reconstruction of cosmic history can be made. Imagine a trip backwards in time. Ten billion years after the Bang, our planet was formed. One billion years from the beginning, the galaxies and stars were coming into being. At $t=500,000$ years, the constituent atoms appeared. A mere three minutes from the beginning, the nuclei were starting to form out of protons and neutrons. Protons and neutrons were probably forming from their constituent quarks at 10^{-4} seconds, when the temperature had cooled to 10^{12} (a thousand billion) degrees. This fantastically dense sea of hot quarks had been formed at about 10^{-10} seconds when the fireball had expanded and cooled enough for the electro-weak forces to be distinguishable from the strong and gravitational forces.[4] Before 10^{-35} seconds, the temperature was so high that all the forces except gravity were of comparable strength. This is the period to which a Grand Unified Theory would apply. We have almost no idea of events before 10^{-43} seconds, when the temperature was 10^{32} degrees. The whole universe was smaller than the size of an atom today, and all four forces were united. This would have been the era of Supersymmetry.

Time	Temperature	Transition
15 billion years		(today)
10 billion years		Planets formed
1 billion years		Galaxies formed (heavy elements)
500,000 years	2000°	Atoms formed (light elements)
3 minutes	10^9	Nuclei formed (hydrogen, helium)
10^{-4} seconds	10^{12}	Quarks to protons and neutrons
10^{-10} seconds	10^{15}	Weak and electromagnetic forces separate
10^{-35} seconds	10^{28}	Strong nuclear force separates
10^{-43} seconds	10^{32}	Gravitational force separates
(0	Infinite	Singularity ?)

But what happened before that? At the time $t=0$, was there a dimensionless point of pure radiation of infinite density? And how is that point to be accounted for? To the scientist, $t=0$ is inaccessible. It appears as a "singularity" to which the laws of physics do not apply, though Stephen Hawking and others have proposed a theory in which time is finite but unbounded. I will return later to examine some of these theories of quantum cosmology.

How might this Big Bang cosmology be related to religious ideas of creation? I will first summarize three responses that seem to me inadequate, and then examine in more detail what I take to be the valid philosophical and theological implications of cosmology.

· · · · · · · · ·

Three Dubious Responses

Three common views present creation and cosmology as being 1) in agreement, or 2) in direct conflict, or 3) as completely independent kinds of assertions. All three of these claims seem to me dubious.

Agreement of Creation and Cosmology

In the 1950s and 1960s some astronomers were defending the Steady State Theory, which postulated hydrogen atoms coming into being slowly throughout space during an infinite span of time. Fred Hoyle argued that the steady state was more compatible with his own atheistic beliefs than Big Bang theories that postulated a finite time span.[5] Some theologians were therefore delighted when astronomers abandoned the Steady State Theory and endorsed the Big Bang Theory. After centuries of conflict between theologians and astronomers, there seemed to be a common ground in the idea that the universe had a beginning which science could not explain. Pope Pius XII said in 1952 that astronomical evidence for the Big Bang confirmed the idea of creation out of nothing.[6]

More recently, the astrophysicist Robert Jastrow has argued that "the astronomical evidence leads to a biblical view of the origin of the world." He ends his book, *God and the Astronomers*, with this striking passage:

> At this moment it seems as though science will never be able to raise the curtain on the mystery of creation. For the scientist who has lived by his faith in the power of reason, the story ends like a bad dream. He has scaled the mountains of ignorance; he is about to conquer the highest peak; as he pulls himself over the final rock, he is greeted by a band of theologians who have been sitting there for centuries.[7]

At a press conference in 1992 announcing the findings from the COBE satellite program, the team leader George Smoot said, "If you're religious, it's like seeing God." Smoot later said: "Science can never answer the religious questions. You still have 'what came before?' and you can ask 'who designed it all?'" The NASA team leader, John Mather, told *The Washington Post* that he saw a parallel between the biblical version of creation and the scientific version. The media picked up on these comments, and one paper ran a headline "The Grand Unification of Religion and Science."[8]

I am dubious about all of these attempts to identify religious ideas of creation with scientific ideas of cosmology. One reason for caution is that in the past God has often been invoked to explain gaps in the prevailing scientific account. This has been a losing proposition as one gap after another has been filled by the advance of science—first in seventeenth-century astronomy and physics, then in nineteenth-century geology and biology, and now by twentieth-century cosmology. The present case appears different because events at the time t=0 seem to be in principle inaccessible to science. Yet this situation might conceivably change, for much of contemporary cosmology is tentative and speculative.

For example, it is possible to combine the Big Bang and infinite time if one assumes an oscillating cosmos. Before the present era of expansion there could have been an era of contraction—a Big Crunch before the Big Bang. Concerning the future of the cosmos, observations suggest that the velocity of expansion is very close to the critical threshold between expanding forever (an *open* universe) and expanding a very long time before contracting again (a *closed* universe). Evidence announced recently suggests that black holes may provide sufficient mass at least to slow the expansion, and additional mass may be present in neutrinos or interstellar dark matter.

Some atheistic or agnostic astronomers feel more comfortable with the idea of an infinite series of oscillations, just as there are some theists who welcome a beginning of time. But I would say it is equally difficult to imagine a beginning of time or an infinite span of time. Both are unlike anything we have experienced. Both start with an unexplained universe. I do not think there are major theological issues at stake, as has often been assumed. If a single, unique Big Bang continues to be the most convincing scientific theory, the theist can indeed see it as an instant of divine origination. But I will suggest later that this is not the main concern expressed in the religious notion of creation.

Conflict between Creation and Cosmology

A second view sees creation and Big Bang theory as incompatible. Biblical literalists insist on a literal interpretation of the seven days of Genesis, and they reject the idea that the cosmos is billions of years old. They point out that there are disputes among cosmologists, just as there are disagreements among evolutionary biologists, and they claim that both cosmic and biological evolution are "theories and not facts." I believe this is a serious misunderstanding of the nature of scientific theories and the way they are supported by observational data. To be sure, there are disagreements among scientists about the details of many of the transitions in the history of the universe. But virtually all scientists acknowledge a long process of historical development, which is supported by overwhelming evidence from many fields of science, including geology, paleontology, biochemistry, and several branches of biology, as well as astronomy.

From the other side, there are some scientific materialists who hold that cosmology excludes all ideas of creation and not just literalist interpretations. Carl Sagan has maintained that we should only believe what can be ascertained by the scientific method, and he asserts that "the Cosmos is all that is or ever was or ever will be."[9] In his introduction to Hawking's *A Brief History of Time* he writes:

> This is also a book about God, or perhaps about the absence of God. The word God fills these pages. Hawking embarks on a quest to answer Einstein's famous question about whether God had any choice in creating the universe. Hawking is attempting, as he explicitly states, to understand the mind of God. And this makes all the more unexpected the conclusion of the effort, at least so far: a universe with no edge in space, no beginning or end in time, and nothing for a Creator to do.[10]

There are other cosmologists who look to the future and conclude that the universe will either expand until it is too cold to sustain life, or it will collapse in the Big Crunch and become too hot for life. Thus Steven Weinberg says that life is the accidental result of chance and it will eventually be wiped out. He holds that scientific activity is the only source of consolation in a meaningless world:

> The more the universe seems comprehensible, the more it seems pointless. But if there is no solace in the fruits of research, there is at least some consolation in the research itself. . . . The effort to understand the universe is one of the very few things that lifts human life above the level of farce, and gives it some of the grace of tragedy.[11]

I would argue that both religious fundamentalists and scientific materialists fail to observe the boundaries of their disciplines. Biblical literalists move from religious writings to make claims about scientific matters which they are incompetent to judge. Scientific materialists start from science, but end by making broad philosophical claims which go far beyond what is reported in any scientific journal. They are offering philosophical reflections and not scientific conclusions. In both cases, the differences between the disciplines are ignored.

Independence of Creation and Cosmology

There can be no conflict between science and religion if they are independent and autonomous enterprises. According to this view, each has its own distinctive domain and its characteristic methods. Each mode of inquiry is selective and has its limitations. This separation into watertight compartments is motivated not simply by the desire to avoid conflicts, but also by the attempt to be faithful to the distinctive character of each area of life and thought. It is sometimes said that science asks how-questions about regularities in impersonal processes, while religion asks why-questions about meaning in personal life. The goal of science is to understand and control nature; the goal of religion is personal reorientation and a way of life within a framework of meaning. The language of science and the language of religion serve very different functions in human life.

Anthropologists and historians have looked at a variety of creation stories, studying their function in the ordering of human experience. These stories provide patterns for human behavior, archetypes of authentic human life in accord with a universal order. They portray basic relationships between human life and the world of nature. Religious interest in creation is mainly directed toward implications for life today.[12]

The opening verse of Genesis says that in the beginning "the earth was without form and void, and darkness was upon the face of the deep, and the spirit of God was moving over the face of the waters." Historians of religion see here an echo of the Babylonian creation story, which also starts with a primeval watery chaos. Throughout the Hebrew scriptures there are references to a continuing struggle between order and chaos. But clearly the biblical story differs from other ancient creation stories in its assertion of the sovereignty and transcendence of God and the dignity of humanity. Creation is orderly and deliberate, resulting in a harmonious and interdependent whole.[13]

The biblical creation story was later developed into a formal theological doctrine as part of the self-definition of the Christian community in relation to rival philosophies, especially in response to the challenge of Hellenistic dualism. The idea of *creatio ex nihilo,* creation out of nothing, which does not appear in the Bible itself, was elaborated to exclude the gnostic teaching that matter is evil, the work of a lesser being, not the work of the God who redeems. Against claims that pre-existing matter limited God's creativity, *ex nihilo* asserted that God is the source of matter as well as of form. Against pantheism, it asserted that the world is not divine or part of God, but is distinct from God. It was such theological assertions, and not any specific references to a temporal beginning, which were of importance to the early church.[14]

By the fourth century, Augustine was willing to accept a metaphorical and figurative interpretation of Genesis and said that it was not the intent of scripture to instruct us about such things as the form and shape of the heavens. "God did not wish to teach men things not relevant to their salvation." Augustine held that creation was not an event in time, if time was created along with the world. Creation is the timeless act through which time comes to be, and the continuous act by which God preserves the world. He said that we cannot ask what God was doing before creating the world, for there was no time without the created world.[15]

Thomas Aquinas accepted a beginning of time as part of scripture and tradition and said that such a beginning helps to make God's power evident. But he argued that a universe which had always existed would equally require God as creator and sustainer. What is essential theologically could be stated without reference to a beginning or a singular event. In one version of the cosmological argument, Aquinas asks: Why is there anything at all? He replies that the whole causal chain, whether finite or infinite, is dependent on God. God's priority is ontological rather than temporal. Moreover, God as primary cause continues to work through the secondary causes which science describes.

We must note also that there has been a subordinate theme of continuing creation from biblical times to the present. Edmund Jacob has said that while there are many biblical texts which refer to a primordial creation in the beginning, "other texts, generally more ancient, draw much less distinction between the creation and conservation of the world, and make it possible for us to speak of a *creatio continua*."[16] There is a recurring witness that God is still creating through natural processes. Some of the psalms use the present tense: "Thou dost cause the grass to grow for cattle and the plants for man to cultivate. . . . When thou sendest forth thy Spirit, they are created" (Ps. 104: 14 and 30).

What are the human experiences that lie behind the idea of creation? I would list the following: 1) a sense of dependence, finitude, and contingency; 2) a response of wonder, trust, gratitude for life, and affirmation of the world; and 3) a recognition of the interdependence, order, and beauty of the world. The religious idea of creation starts from wonder and gratitude for life as a gift.

The basic theological affirmations in the first chapter of Genesis are: 1) the world is essentially good, orderly, coherent, and intelligible; 2) the world is dependent on God; and 3) God is sovereign, free, transcendent, and characterized by purpose and will. Creation is an enduring relationship rather than an event in the past. The biblical writers expressed these religious convictions poetically and imaginatively in terms of the view of the cosmos current in their day. But the basic convictions can be affirmed independent of ancient cosmology and independent of current cosmology.[17] Reform and Conservative Judaism, the Catholic church, and most of the mainline Protestant denominations today maintain that we do not have to choose between theism and science. We can look on the Big Bang and subsequent evolution, or whatever science discovers, as God's way of creating.

Such separation of science and religion as two distinct and independent languages seems to me a good first approximation. For most people, religious beliefs are based on religious experience interpreted in the conceptual categories of a historical tradition, not on arguments from the world of nature. Nevertheless some of these categories of interpretation may need to be modified by the findings of science. In particular, beliefs about God's relation to nature must take into account the scientific understanding of nature, especially the idea of a dynamic and evolving rather than a static universe. Moreover, if we imagine God as related only to personal life and not to nature, we will have less respect for other forms of life and less motivation to challenge environmentally destructive attitudes. Having acknowledged the distinctiveness of both scientific and religious language, we must go on to explore some relationships between them that are more subtle than simple agreement or conflict.

. . . .

Philosophical Implications of Cosmology

I suggest that Big Bang cosmology has three philosophical implications, dealing respectively with Design, Chance, and Necessity. I will suggest that all three are compatible with theistic belief.

Design: The Anthropic Principle

A striking feature of the new cosmological theories is that even a small change in the physical constants would have resulted in an uninhabitable universe. Among the many possible universes consistent with Einstein's equations, ours is one of the few in which the arbitrary parameters are right for the existence of anything resembling organic life. Thus Carr and Rees conclude that the possibility of life as we know it "depends on the value of a few basic constants" and is "remarkably sensitive to them."[18] Among these fine-tuned phenomena are the following:

1 *The Expansion Rate.* Stephen Hawking writes: "If the rate of expansion one second after the big bang had been smaller by even one part in a hundred thousand million million it would have recollapsed before it reached its present size."[19] On the other hand, if it had been greater by a part in a million, the universe would have expanded too rapidly for stars and planets to form. The expansion rate itself depends on many factors, such as the initial explosive energy, the mass of the universe, and the strength of gravitational forces. A very delicate and precise balance is required.

2 *The Formation of the Elements.* If the strong nuclear force were even slightly weaker, we would have only hydrogen in the universe. If the force were even slightly stronger, all the hydrogen would have been converted to helium. In either case, stable stars and compounds such as water could not have been formed. Again, the nuclear force is only barely sufficient for carbon to form; yet if it had been slightly stronger, the carbon would all have been converted into oxygen.[20]

3 *The Particle/antiparticle Ratio.* For every billion antiprotons in the early universe, there were one-billion-and-one protons. The billion pairs annihilated each other to produce radiation, with just one proton left over. A greater or smaller number of survivors—or no survivors at all if they had been evenly matched—would have made our kind of material world impossible. The laws of physics seem to be symmetrical between particles and antiparticles; why was there a tiny asymmetry?[21]

One could list other unexplained "remarkable coincidences." The simultaneous occurrence of many independent improbable features appears wildly improbable. Reflection on the way the universe seems to be fine-tuned for intelligent life led the cosmologists Dicke and Carter to formulate the Anthropic Principle: "What we can expect to observe must be restricted by the conditions necessary for our presence as observers."[22]

Some physicists see evidence of design in the early universe. Stephen Hawking, for example, writes: "The odds against a universe like ours emerging out of something like the Big Bang are enormous. I think there are clearly religious implications."[23] And Freeman Dyson, in a chapter entitled "The Argument from Design," gives a number of examples of "numerical accidents that seem to conspire to make the universe habitable." He concludes:

"The more I examine the universe and the details of its architecture, the more evidence I find that the universe in some sense must have known we were coming."[24]

Chance: Many-worlds Theories

One way of explaining the apparent design in these "remarkable coincidences" is to suggest that there were many worlds existing either successively or simultaneously. If there were billions of worlds with differing constants, it would not be surprising if by chance one of them happened to have constants just right for our forms of life. That which is highly improbable in one world might be probable among a large enough set of worlds. There are several ways in which many worlds could occur:

1 *Successive Cycles of an Oscillating Universe.* Wheeler and others suggest that the universe is reprocessed in each Big Crunch before the next Big Bang. The universe and all its structures are completely melted down and make a new start as it expands and cools again. In the quantum uncertainties entailed by those very small dimensions there are indeterminate possibilities. If the constants vary at random in successive cycles, our particular combination will eventually come up by chance, like the winning combination on a Las Vegas slot machine. Present evidence does not favor cyclic theories, but they cannot be ruled out.

2 *Multiple Isolated Domains.* Instead of multiple bangs in successive cycles, a single Big Bang might have produced multiple domains existing simultaneously. The domains would be like separately expanding bubbles isolated from each other because their velocity of separation prevents communication even at the speed of light. The universe might have split into many domains with differing constants or even differing laws. Some of the new inflationary models of the universe allow for regions very unlike ours, beyond our horizon of possible observation. Perhaps this just happens to be one of the few regions in which life could be present.

3 *Quantum Vacuum Fluctuations.* A strange feature of quantum theory is that it permits very brief violations of the law of conservation of energy. It is permissible for a system's energy to go into debt, if the debt is rapidly paid back—so rapidly that it could never be detected within the limits of the uncertainty principle. This means that empty space, a vacuum, is really a sea of activity in which pairs of virtual particles are produced and almost immediately annihilate each other again. The energy needed to create a universe might be small or even zero if the negative gravitational energy is taken into account.

All three of these theories would allow us to explain the combination of constants favorable to life as a chance occurrence among a set of worlds most of which would be lifeless. The philosopher John Leslie has argued that the God-hypothesis is simpler and more plausible as an explanation of the fine-tuning than these various many-worlds hypotheses.[25] These theories, he says, are all very *ad hoc* and unsupported by any independent evidence, whereas there are other kinds of evidence to which one can appeal in support of belief in God.

These theories are highly speculative. It is simpler, from the viewpoint of both science and theology, to assume that there has been only one world. The vacuum fluctuation theory is consistent with the fact that the creation of virtual particles occurs in the laboratory. It has sometimes been viewed as a secular version of *creatio ex nihilo*, because it starts with a vacuum, which might be thought of as "nothing." However, all our experiments with a vacuum are within an already existing spacetime framework, in which a "vacuum" is the quiescent state of the ever-present quantum field. Most theories of an initial vacuum fluctuation assume the existence of such a field. How do we account for the situation in which a gigantic quantum fluctuation could have occurred?

Necessity: A Theory of Everything

Perhaps the values of the constants, which appear arbitrary, are in fact dictated by a more basic structure of relationships. Perhaps there is a more fundamental theory which will show that the constants can only have the values that they have. Some proposals for a Grand Unified Theory (GUT) suggest that the slight imbalance between particles and anti-particles may have arisen from a slight asymmetry in the decay processes of the X and the anti-X bosons.

There are also promising new inflationary theories which may explain why the present expansion rate is so close to the critical balance between an open and a closed universe (the so-called "flatness problem"). Inflationary theories could also explain why the microwave radiation is very nearly uniform in all directions. These theories entail a very rapid expansion at about 10^{-35} seconds, due to the tremendous energy released in the breaking of symmetry when the strong force separated out.[26] Before inflation, the universe would have been so small that its parts would have been in communication and thus could have achieved thermal equilibrium, which would account for the fact that the background radiation is nearly homogeneous over vast distances, as seen in the COBE experiments.

Current theories are quite inadequate to deal with the even earlier period before 10^{-43} seconds when the fourth force, gravity, would have been united with the other three. The hope is to develop theories of Supersymmetry which would provide a quantum theory of gravity. Because it would unite all the basic physical forces, it has been referred to as a Theory of Everything (TOE). Perhaps the whole cosmos can be derived from one simple and all-inclusive equation. Such a theory has been called the Holy Grail of the current quest in physics.

Would successful GUT and TOE theories undermine the argument for design in the early universe? Perhaps self-consistency and fundamental laws will show that there is only one possible universe, *i.e.*, that it is necessary and not contingent. I would reply that such theories would only push the argument back a stage. For it is all the more remarkable if a highly abstract physical theory, which itself has absolutely nothing to say about life, turns out to describe structures which have the potential for developing into life. The theist could welcome this as part of God's design. A theory that starts with a superlaw and a singularity would leave unanswered the question: Why that superlaw and that singularity? Can a TOE ever explain itself, or how it comes to be instantiated in the real world?

In physics, moreover, predictions are ordinarily made from a combination of universal laws and particular initial conditions. From universal premises alone one cannot derive conclusions about particulars. There would be contingent boundary conditions even if it turned out that time is infinite and there was no "beginning." At any point, however far back, there was a particular "given" situation which, along with laws and chance, affected the subsequent course of history.

Stephen Hawking, working with J. B. Hartle, has developed a theory of quantum gravity in which there is no initial singularity.

In their theory, time is finite but it has no beginning. The two-dimensional surface of the earth is finite but unbounded, and three-dimensional relativistic ("curved") space is finite but unbounded; similarly, Hawking's spatial and temporal dimensions are both finite but unbounded. The equations are relationships involving imaginary time, which is indistinguishable from the three spatial dimensions. In that imaginary time frame, real time gradually emerges.[27] Hawking grants that the interpretation of events in imaginary time is not clear. It seems to me inconsistent to speak of time as emerging, since emergence refers to changes in real time.

Hawking makes some interesting comments on the theological implications of a self-contained universe without boundaries or initial conditions. Earlier Big Bang theory assumed a singularity at which the laws of physics break down. At the singularity, God would have had freedom to choose both the initial conditions and the laws of the universe. But in Hawking's universe there are no initial conditions, and the choice of laws is restricted by self-consistency and by the Anthropic Principle: the early universe must provide the conditions for the later existence of humanity. He concludes:

> [God] would, of course, still have had the freedom to choose the laws that the universe obeyed. This, however, may not really have been all that much of a choice; there may well be only one, or a small number, of complete unified theories, such as the heterotic string theory, that are self-consistent and allow the existence of structures as complicated as human beings who can investigate the laws of the universe and ask about the nature of God.
>
> Even if there is only one possible unified theory, it is just a set of rules and equations. What is it that breathes fire into the equations and makes a universe for them to describe? The usual approach of science of constructing a mathematical model cannot answer the questions of why there should be a universe for the model to describe.[28]

My own conclusion is that both *chance* and *necessity* are compatible with *design*. Chance does of course exclude the idea of a pre-determined universe in which every detail is providentially ordained in the initial design. But it does not exclude the idea that a variety of creative possibilities are built into the design. We can still stand in awe of a universe in which galaxies and life and consciousness and self-consciousness came into being. Evidence from cosmology does not provide a proof for the existence of God, but it is consistent with belief in a cosmic design that is not pre-determined in all its details.

• • • • • • • • • •

Theological Implications of Cosmology

I suggest that the Big Bang cosmology has several theological implications that can be affirmed, regardless of which particular cosmological theory comes to be accepted in the scientific community.

Intelligibility and Contingency

The search for a unified theory is motivated by the conviction that the cosmos is rationally intelligible. Physicists must of course check their theories against experimental evidence, but they are convinced that a valid general theory will be conceptually simple and aesthetically beautiful. Einstein said that the only thing that is incomprehensible about the world is that it is comprehensible.

Historically, the conviction that the cosmos is intelligible had both Greek and biblical roots. The Greeks saw the universe as a single system. They had great confidence in the power of reason, and it is not surprising that they made significant progress in mathematics and geometry. But historians have claimed that the biblical doctrine of creation made a distinctive contribution to the rise of experimental science because it combined the ideas of *rationality* and *contingency*. If God is rational, the world is orderly; but if God is also free, the world did not have to have the particular order that it has. The world can then only be understood by observing it—rather than by deducing its order from necessary first principles, as the Greeks tried to do.[29]

The theologian Thomas Torrance has written extensively on the theme of "contingent order." He stresses God's freedom in creating as an act of voluntary choice. Both the existence and the structure of the world are contingent in the sense that they might not have been. The world might have been differently ordered. We can discover its order only by observation. Moreover, the world can be studied on its own because in being created it has its own independent reality, distinct from the transcendent God. Science can legitimately assume a "methodological secularism" in its work, while the theologian can still assert that the world is ultimately dependent on God.[30]

Einstein, on the other hand, saw any contingency as a threat to belief in the rationality of the world, which he said is central in science. "A conviction, akin to religious feeling, of the rationality or intelligibility of the world lies behind all scientific work of a high order."[31] He spoke of a "cosmic religious sense" and "a deep faith in the rationality of the world." He rejected the idea of a personal God whose acts arbitrarily interfere in the course of events; he subscribed to a form of pantheism, identifying God with the orderly structure itself. When asked if he believed in God, he replied: "I believe in Spinoza's God, who reveals himself in the orderly harmony of what exists."[32] Einstein equated rationality with orderliness and determinism; he never abandoned his conviction that the uncertainties of quantum theory only reflect temporary human ignorance which will be left behind when deterministic underlying mechanisms are discovered.

John Polkinghorne, physicist and theologian, discusses the intelligibility of the world in a theistic framework. The key to understanding the physical world is mathematics, an invention of the human mind. The fit between reason in our minds and in the world would be expected if the world is the creation of mind. Polkinghorne holds that God is the common ground of rationality, both in our minds and in the world. Orderliness can also be understood as God's faithfulness, but it does not exclude an important role for chance. He maintains that the theist can account for the intelligibility which the scientist assumes.[33]

I suggest that four forms of contingency can be distinguished in cosmology:[34]

1 *Contingent Existence.* Why is there anything at all? This is the question of greatest interest to theologians. The existence of the cosmos as a whole is not self-explanatory, regardless of whether it is finite or infinite in time. The details of particular scientific cosmologies are irrelevant to the contingency of the existence of the world. Even if a theory were to show that there is only one possible universe, the universe would still only remain possible; nothing in the theory provides that a universe actually exists, or that the theory is instantiated.

2 *Contingent Boundary Conditions.* If there was a beginning, it was a singularity to which the laws of physics do not apply, and as such it cannot be scientifically explained. If time is infinite, there would be no beginning, but at any point in time, no matter how far back, one would have to postulate a particular state of affairs, treating it as a "given." Hawking's theory avoids initial conditions, but the interpretation of imaginary time in his scheme remains problematic. His theory also assumes pre-existing laws and quantum operators as well as Hilbert spaces.

3 *Contingent Laws.* Many of the laws of cosmology appear to be arbitrary. But some of them may turn out to be necessary implications of more fundamental theories. If a unified theory is found, however, it will itself be contingent. It is implausible that the universe is necessary in the sense that its history could be deduced from the laws of logic alone, for then experiments and observations would be superfluous, contrary to all we know about the methods of science. Moreover, I suggest that the laws applicable to higher emergent levels of life and mind are not derivable from or reducible to the laws of physics. It is misleading to refer to a unified theory in physics as a "Theory of Everything," for its unity would be achieved only by a high degree of abstraction which leaves out all of the diversity and particularity of events in the world and the emergence of more complex levels of organization from simpler ones. We could hardly expect a TOE to tell us very much about an amoeba, much less about Shakespeare, Beethoven, Newton, or Hawking.

4 *Contingent Events.* We have seen that quantum phenomena influenced the very early history of the Big Bang. To the critical realist, uncertainty in quantum physics reflects indeterminacy and chance in the world and not simply the limitations of our knowledge. Similar unpredictability is present in non-equilibrium thermodynamics, chaos theory, mutations in evolution, and freedom in human life. Evolution must be described by an historical account of unique and unpredictable events, not by predictive laws alone.

"Creation out of Nothing" and "Continuing Creation"

I argued earlier that the doctrine of creation expresses the experience of wonder, dependence on God, gratitude for life as a gift, and recognition of interdependence, order, and novelty in the world. In the Christian tradition the formal doctrine of creation was developed historically as *creatio ex nihilo* and *creatio continua*. I propose that these ideas parallel the four meanings of contingency above:

1 *The contingency of existence* corresponds to the central religious meaning of *creatio ex nihilo*. In both the scientific and the theological contexts, the basic assertions can be detached from the assumption of an absolute beginning. On the scientific side, it now appears likely that the Big Bang was indeed an absolute beginning, a singular event, but if there is new evidence for a cyclic universe or infinite time or unbounded finite time, the contingency of existence would remain. On the theological side, we have seen that the *ex nihilo* doctrine was formulated by the church fathers to defend theism against an ultimate dualism or a monistic pantheism. We still need to defend theism against alternative philosophies, but we can do so without reference to an absolute beginning.[35] With respect to the central meaning of *creatio ex nihilo*, I agree with the authors who say that it is the sheer existence of the universe which is the datum of theology and that the details of scientific cosmology are irrelevant here. The message of *creatio ex nihilo* applies to the whole of the cosmos at every moment, regardless of questions about its beginning or its detailed structure and history. It is an ontological and not an historical assertion.

2 *The contingency of boundary conditions* also expresses the message of *ex nihilo* without requiring an absolute beginning. It may turn out that past time was finite and that there was a singularity at the beginning, inaccessible to science. Such a beginning was assumed by the church fathers in the classical *ex nihilo* doctrine, even though it was not their chief concern. As Aquinas said, such a beginning would provide an impressive example of dependence on God. On the other hand, if time were infinite, we would still have contingent boundary conditions; scientists could not avoid dealing with situations or states which they would have to treat as givens.

3 *The contingency of laws* can be identified with the orderly aspect of continuing creation. Traditionally, creation has been identified with the provision of order. Such order, it was assumed, was introduced at the beginning, though it had to be continually sustained by God. By the eighteenth century, the order of nature seemed to be all-embracing, mechanical, and self-sustaining. In deism, God's role was simply to design and start the mechanism. But now we know that the history of the cosmos involves both law and chance, both structure and novelty. Here the findings of science are indeed relevant. The laws applicable to emergent higher levels of reality are not reducible to laws governing lower levels. New and more complex forms of order have emerged in successive eras. Life and mind would not be possible without these underlying structures which go back to the early cosmos, but they cannot be explained by the laws of physics.

4 *The contingency of events* corresponds to the novel aspect of continuing creation. We can no longer assume the static universe of the Middle Ages, in which the basic forms of all beings were thought to be unchanging. Coming-to-be is a continuing process throughout time, and it continues today. Nature in all its forms must be viewed historically. Here astrophysics adds its testimony to that of evolutionary biology and other fields of science. Genuine novelty appears in cosmic history. It is a dynamic world with a long story of change and development.

On the theological side, continuing creation expresses the theme of God's immanence and participation in the ongoing world. God builds on what is already there, and each successive level of reality requires the structures of lower levels. Here I find the insights of process philosophy particularly helpful. For Whitehead and his followers, God is the source of both order and novelty. This is one of the few schools of thought which takes seriously the contingency of events, from indeterminacy in physics to the freedom of human beings. In this "dipolar" view, God is both eternal and temporal: eternal in character and purpose, but temporal in being affected by interaction with the world.[36] I would argue that in talking about continuing creation and God's ongoing relation to the world, the theologian must indeed take the findings of science into account.

The Significance of Humanity

We noted earlier that the function of creation stories is not primarily to explain events in the distant past but to locate present human experience in a larger framework of significance. Does modern cosmology contradict the biblical message concerning humanity?

1 *The Immensity of Space and Time.* Humanity seems insignificant in the midst of such vast stretches of time and space. But today those immensities do not seem inappropriate. We now know that it takes about fifteen billion years for heavy elements to be cooked in the interior of stars and then scattered to form a second generation of stars with planets, followed by the evolution of life and consciousness. A very old expanding universe has to be a huge universe—on the order of fifteen billion light years. Moreover, as Teilhard de Chardin pointed out, we should not measure significance by size and duration, but by such criteria as complexity and consciousness.[37] The greatest complexity has apparently been achieved in the middle range of size, not at atomic dimensions or galactic dimensions. There are one hundred trillion synapses in a human brain; the number of possible ways of connecting them is greater than the number of atoms in the universe. There is a higher level of organization and a greater richness of experience in a human being than in a thousand lifeless galaxies. It is human beings, after all, that reach out to understand that cosmic immensity.

2 *Interdependence.* Cosmology joins evolutionary biology, molecular biology, and ecology in showing the interdependence of all things. We are part of an ongoing community of being; we are kin to all creatures, past and present. From astrophysics we know about our indebtedness to a common legacy of physical events. The chemical elements in your hand and in your brain were forged in the furnaces of stars. The cosmos is all of a piece. It is multi-leveled; each new higher level was built on lower levels from the past. Humanity is the most advanced form of life of which we know, but it is fully a part of a wider process in space and time. The new view may undercut anthropocentric claims that set humanity completely apart from the rest of nature, but it by no means makes human life insignificant.

3 *Chance and Purpose.* Traditionally, God's purpose in creation was identified with order. An emphasis on God's sovereignty led to a determinism in which everything was thought to happen in accordance with a detailed divine plan. Any element of chance was viewed as a threat to God's total control. It is not surprising, then, that some scientists and philosophers who are impressed by the role of chance are led to reject theism. (Bertrand Russell, Jacques Monod, Stephen Jay Gould, and Steven Weinberg, for example, view life as the accidental result of chance and assume that chance and theism are incompatible.)

One possible answer is to say that God really controls all the events that appear to us to be chance—whether in quantum uncertainties, evolutionary mutations, or the accidents of human history. This would preserve divine determinism at a subtle level undetectable to science. But I maintain that the presence of genuine chance is not incompatible with theism. We can see design in the whole process by which life came into being, with whatever combination of probabilistic and deterministic features the process had. Natural laws and chance may equally be instruments of God's intentions. There can be purpose without an exact predetermined plan.[38]

. . . .

Conclusion

The astronauts were neither cosmologists nor theologians, but some of them combined respect for science with respect for the idea of creation. As the first astronauts in orbit around the moon appeared live on television, Frank Borman responded to the beauty of the earth, spinning in the vastness of space, by reading the opening verses of Genesis. I think we can join the astronauts in celebrating the beauty of our amazing planet and in expressing gratitude for the gift of life.

Now we know the cosmos has included stretches of space and time which we can hardly imagine. What sort of world is it in which those strange early states of matter and energy could be the forerunners of intelligent life? Within a theistic framework it is not surprising that there is intelligent life on earth; we can see here the work of a purposeful Creator. Theistic belief makes sense of this datum and a variety of other kinds of human experience, even if it offers no conclusive proof. We still ask: Why is there anything at all? Why are things the way they are? With the psalmist of old, we can say: "O Lord, how manifest are thy works! In wisdom thou hast made them all. . . . When thou sendest forth thy Spirit, they are created" (Ps. 104:30).

. . . .

Notes

1. Carey Powell, "The Golden Age of Cosmology," *Scientific American*, July 1992, 17–22.
2. James Trefil, *The Moment of Creation* (New York: Collier, 1983); John Barrow and Joseph Silk, *The Left Hand of Creation* (New York: Basic Books, 1983).
3. Michael Green, "Superstrings," *Scientific American*, September 1986, 48–60; Mitchell Waldrop, "Strings as a Theory of Everything," *Science* 229 (1985), 226–28.
4. Steven Weinberg, *The First Three Minutes* (New York: Basic Books, 1977).

5. Fred Hoyle, *The Creation of the Universe* (New York: Harper and Brothers, 1950), and *The Ten Faces of the Universe* (San Francisco: W. H. Freeman, 1977).

6. Pope Pius XII, "Modern Science and the Existence of God," *The Catholic Mind*, March 1952, 182–92.

7. Robert Jastrow, *God and the Astronomers* (New York: W. W. Norton, 1978), 116.

8. "Cosmic God Squad Under Fire," *Science* 257 (1992), 29.

9. Carl Sagan, *Cosmos* (New York: Random House, 1980), 4.

10. Carl Sagan, introduction to Stephen Hawking, *A Brief History of Time* (New York: Bantam Books, 1988), x.

11. Weinberg, op. cit., 144.

12. Mircea Eliade, *Myth and Reality* (New York: Harper and Row, 1963).

13. Joan O'Brien and Wilfred Major, *In the Beginning: Creation Myths from Ancient Mesopotamia, Israel and Greece* (Chico, CA: Scholars Press, 1982); Bernhard Anderson, ed., *Creation in the Old Testament* (Philadelphia: Fortress Press, 1984).

14. David Kelsey, "Creatio ex Nihilo," in Ernan McMullin, ed., *Evolution and Creation* (Notre Dame: University of Notre Dame Press, 1985).

15. See Ernan McMullin, "How Should Cosmology Relate to Theology," in A. R. Peacocke, ed., *Science and Theology in the Twentieth Century* (Notre Dame: University of Notre Dame, 1981), 19–21.

16. Edmund Jacob, *Theology of the Old Testament* (New York: Harper and Brothers, 1958), 139.

17. Langdon Gilkey, *Maker of Heaven and Earth* (Garden City, NY: Doubleday, 1959), and *Creationism on Trial* (Minneapolis: Winston Press, 1985).

18. B. J. Carr and M. J. Rees, "The Anthropic Principle and the Structure of the Physical World," *Nature* 278 (1979), 605–12; John Barrow and Frank Tipler, *The Anthropic Cosmological Principle* (Oxford: Oxford University Press, 1986).

19. Hawking, *A Brief History of Time*, 121; also his "The Anisotropy of the Universe at Large Times," in M. S. Longair, ed., *Confrontation of Cosmological Theories with Observational Data* (Dordrecht, Holland: Reidel, 1974).

20. Carr and Rees, loc. cit.

21. Barrow and Silk, op. cit., 91; Paul Davies, *God and the New Physics* (New York: Simon & Schuster), 30.

22. B. Carter, "Large Number Coincidences and the Anthropic Principle in Cosmology," in Longair, ed., op. cit. See also Davies, op. cit., Chapter 12.

23. Hawking, quoted in John Boslough, *Stephen Hawking's Universe* (New York: William Morrow & Co., 1985), 121.

24. Freeman Dyson, *Disturbing the Universe* (New York: Harper and Row, 1979), 250.

25. John Leslie, *Universes* (London: Routledge, 1989).

26. Alan Guth and Paul Steinhardt, "The Inflationary Universe," *Scientific American,* May 1984, 116–28.

27. J. B. Hartle and S. W. Hawking, "Wave Function of the Universe," *Physical Review D* 28 (1983), 2960–75. See also C. J. Isham, "Creation of the Universe as a Quantum Process," in J. R. Russell, W. Stoeger, and G. Coyne, eds., *Physics, Philosophy and Theology* (The Vatican: Vatican Observatory, 1988).

28. Hawking, *A Brief History of Time,* 174.

29. See Michael Foster, "The Christian Doctrine of Creation and the Rise of Modern Science," in Daniel O'Connor and Francis Oakley, *Creation: The Impact of an Idea* (New York: Charles Scribner's Sons, 1969).

30. Thomas F. Torrance, *Divine and Contingent Order* (Oxford: Oxford University Press, 1981).

31. Albert Einstein, *Ideas and Opinions* (London: Souvenir Press, 1973), 262.

32. Quoted in Robert Jastrow, op. cit., 28.

33. John Polkinghorne, *One World* (Princeton: Princeton University Press, 1987), 45, 63, and 98.

34. Robert John Russell, "Contingency in Physics and Cosmology: A Critique of the Theology of Wolfhart Pannenberg," *Zygon* 23 (1988), 23–43.

35. W. Norris Clarke, "Is Natural Theology Possible Today?" in Russell, Stoeger, and Coyne, op. cit.

36. John Cobb and David Griffin, *Process Theology: An Introduction* (Philadelphia: Westminster Press, 1976).

37. Pierre Teilhard de Chardin, *The Phenomenon of Man* (New York: Harper and Row, 1959), 226–28.

38. Ian G. Barbour, *Religion in an Age of Science* (San Francisco: Harper and Row, 1990), 172–76.

• • • • • • • • •
A Theology of Nature

1 What are your views on cosmic beginnings, particularly with reference to the origin of the universe, of life, and of Homo sapiens?

I have discussed my views of "cosmic beginnings" in "Religious Responses to the Big Bang."

2 What are your views on human ends, especially as this relates to the framework of cosmic beginnings?

I take "human ends" to refer to normative goals of human life, rather than to human endings or destiny. I believe we should seek the broad goal of the fulfillment of human potentialities in harmony with the flourishing of nonhuman life. These goals can be clarified by the scientific understanding of human nature and our evolutionary and ecological interdependence. But after reflection on the given structures and wider context of human existence as understood by science, there are still choices of alternative patterns of life in accordance with differing visions of the good life. The biblical vision emphasizes the values of interpersonal love and social justice. Our task today is to combine these values with sustainability and the preservation of the nonhuman environment.

3 What do you think should be the relationship between religion and science?

In relating science and religion, I see a limited role for a "natural theology" based only on science. The intelligibility and contingency of the cosmos, the fine-tuned physical constants that make life possible, the directionality of evolution, and the emergence of self-consciousness are all suggestive of intelligent design, as indicated in my essay. The cosmic story and the processes and structures of nature do evoke our responses of wonder and gratitude. But the prevalence of chance, waste, suffering, and evil suggest an overall direction rather than a detailed preordained plan carried out by an omnipotent creator.

I see religion as arising primarily from other distinctive kinds of human experience: numinous experience of the holy; mystical experience of unity; personal transformation and renewal; moral obligation; and courage in facing death and suffering. Each of these experiences has been interpreted in the conceptual frameworks of particular historical communities and has been expressed in their myths and rituals. Today the concepts of all religious communities, based on such experiences, must be reformulated in the light of scientific knowledge. In Christian thought, the doctrines of creation, providence, and human nature must be revised to take into account the evolutionary and ecological character of the world. Such a "theology of nature" will draw from both scientific knowledge and the historical experience of a particular religious community, enriched by the insights of other religious traditions.

22

From Cosmic Beginnings to Human Ends
· · · · · · · · · ·
Roy Abraham Varghese

Roy Abraham Varghese is a co-founder of two high-technology companies in Dallas, Texas, who is currently working with scientists on systems software and telecommunications. As a journalist he has organized several international conferences on the interface of science, philosophy, and religion, as well as a conference at Yale University on Artificial Intelligence and the human mind. He co-edited (with Henry Margenau) the book *Cosmos, Bios, Theos.*

· · · · · · · · · ·
Abstract

This essay considers the significance of cosmic beginnings and human ends in the frameworks of both the atheistic and the religious views of reality. The atheistic framework of ultimate randomness allows purposes *in* life but not a purpose *of* life. The religious view—whether theistic or monistic—sees an Ultimate Reality as Cosmic Beginning and Human End and is therefore a framework of ultimate rationality. The theistic world-vision sees the Ultimate Reality as personal, recognizes the irreducible nature of consciousness, affirms the ultimacy of distinct personal identity, and views the meaning and purpose of human existence in terms of union with the Ultimate Reality.

Well, our friend Dirac, too, has a religion, and its guiding principle is: 'There is no God and Dirac is His prophet.'

—Wolfgang Pauli on Paul Dirac[1]

That man is the product of causes which had no prevision of the end they were achieving; that his origin, his growth, his hopes and fears, his loves and his beliefs, are but the outcome of accidental collocations of atoms; that no fire, no heroism, no intensity of thought and feeling, can preserve an individual life beyond the grave; that all the labors of the ages, all the devotion, all the inspiration, all the noonday brightness of human genius, are destined to extinction in the vast death of the solar system, and the whole temple of man's achievement must inevitably be buried beneath the debris of a universe in ruins—all these things, if not quite beyond dispute, are yet so nearly certain that no philosophy which rejects them can hope to stand.

Only within the scaffolding of these truths, only on the firm foundation of unyielding despair, can the soul's habitation henceforth be safely built.

—Bertrand Russell[2]

It is not enough to live. Man needs a destiny . . .

—Albert Camus[3]

"In my beginning is my end . . . In my end is my beginning," wrote the poet T. S. Eliot in his famous *Four Quartets*.[4] That one's conception of cosmic beginnings will shape one's conception of human ends seems a glimpse of the obvious. Equally clearly the intractable debates in philosophy and religion—the existence of God and the soul, the freedom of the will, the basis of morality, the purpose and meaning of human life—simply bear witness to the multitude of available options when it comes to conceptions of beginnings and ends.

Questions of cosmic beginnings and human ends cannot simply be answered by appealing to "science" or by dignifying one's assertion with the adjective "scientific." "The scientific view" of cosmic beginnings and human ends is sometimes set against "the religious view." This contrast is misleading and springs from what can best be described as a "category mistake." Science concerns itself with the observable and the quantifiable. To ask "What physical processes led to the formation of the universe?" is to ask a scientific question. To ask "Why does the universe exist?" is to ask a non-scientific question, one which falls entirely outside the realm of telescopes and supercolliders, fields and strings, equations and information superhighways. Any answer to this question is necessarily philosophical or theological. Philosophical affirmations masquerading as "scientific views" are simply a variety of pseudoscience.[5]

Another variety of pseudoscience, it must be said, is the attempt to import theological concepts into scientific discourse. The empirical realm in its entirety is the province of science and any quantitative claim concerning the empirical must conform with the canons and norms of the scientific method. The age of the earth must be determined by science and not theology. In his recent *Genesis One Through the Ages*[6] Stanley Jaki shows both the importance of sound exegesis and the peril of concordism, the assumption that cosmological theory can be based on biblical texts. These dangers lurk in the East as much as in the West, as shown in "Eastern Mysticism and the Alleged Parallels with Physics"[7], a careful analysis of attempts to establish parallels between discoveries in modern physics and Eastern mystical philosophies. (The distinctions between science and pseudo-science are usefully dissected by Professor Ian Barbour in this anthology.)

Having issued all these caveats and qualifications we must admit that the questions considered or addressed by world religions continue to fascinate scientists. A recent extended exchange of letters in the pages of *Nature* on the relation of science to religion makes this only too clear, as does the September 1993 Dublin symposium of distinguished scientists held to discuss the question "What Is Life?"

In the final analysis, it seems to me, there are two ways of viewing the world: it is simply here, a brute fact that defies explanation, or it owes its origin and meaning to an ultimate reality that transcends it. The first option is presupposed by most varieties of atheism and the second option lies at the heart of a religious view of reality, whether theistic or monistic. It is our object here to consider the significance of cosmic beginnings and human ends in the frameworks of both the atheistic and the religious views of reality. It is not my purpose to argue for the truth of any particular conception of cosmic beginnings and human ends. I seek simply to compare the relevance of the two major world-conceptions—theism and atheism—for one's understanding of cosmic beginnings and for the meaning and significance of human existence. In other words, what difference does being a theist or an atheist entail in terms of "beginning" and "end"?

· · · · · · · · · ·

Cosmic Beginnings and Human Ends in the Framework of Ultimate Randomness

Atheism is an assertion of ultimate randomness: in sum, the existence of anything at all is an inherently inexplicable state of affairs and ultimately everything is uncaused and unpurposed. In this framework there is an ultimate randomness about reality because there is no ultimate aim or purpose "behind" the cosmos or human existence.[8]

No assertion of cosmic beginnings in the framework of ultimate randomness really starts from scratch: even within a Big Bang framework—perhaps by reference to multiplying "bubble" universes and the like—it is simply assumed that the cosmos in some form or another has always existed (of course a given atheist could argue that the universe arbitrarily sprang out of a void; but this hypothesis is so wildly speculative that it precludes any possibility of verification and as such it is simply a god-of-the-gaps argument in reverse). The scientific data, however, have no bearing on the affirmation of ultimate randomness. Scientific theories in the eras of Lucretius and the Carvaka materialists of India differed dramatically from scientific theories prevalent in the lifetimes of Feuerbach, Nietzsche, Sartre, and Bertrand Russell. Nonetheless, they were all atheistic.

There are no ultimate cosmic beginnings in the framework of ultimate randomness. But does the affirmation that reality is random, that there is no ultimate cosmic beginning or purpose, admit the possibility of human ends? The answer to this question is more ambiguous. On the face of it there seems no way to salvage meaning or significance for human existence in the context of a cosmos unrelated to any Ultimate Reality. The anguish, angoisse, angst of life in a universe without God has been chronicled by atheists themselves, most poignantly perhaps by the modern existentialists who have equated atheism with absurdity for the world and human existence. Said Jean-Paul Sartre, "Death is never that which gives life its meaning; it is on the contrary that which on principle removes all meaning from life."[9]

Death is the dark shadow hanging over every human thought, choice, plan, and action, robbing them of ultimate meaning and value. T. S. Eliot again:

> O dark dark dark. They all go into the dark,
> The vacant interstellar spaces, the vacant into the vacant,
> The captains, merchant bankers, eminent men of letters,
> The generous patrons of art, the statesmen and the rulers,
> Distinguished civil servants, chairmen of many committees,
> Industrial lords and petty contractors, all go into the dark,
> And dark the Sun and Moon, and the Almanach de Gotha
> And the Stock Exchange Gazette, the Directory of Directors,
> And cold the sense and lost the motive of action.
> And we all go with them, into the silent funeral,
> Nobody's funeral, for there is no one to bury.[10]

On the random view of reality, we humans have come from nowhere and from nothing and are likewise destined to return nowhere, become nothing. In a cosmos with hundreds of billions of galaxies human society and history are merely activities of specks on a speck. And in relation to cosmic time scales in the billions of years, human history is a mere second, individual human lives mere milliseconds. Whether we kill ourselves in thermonuclear warfare or perish ultimately in the heat death of the universe, all that we have achieved and become will finally be forgotten forever: it will be as if we humans had never been. Randomness marks even the existence of each human person, for each person is the result of countless chance occurrences, the first of which happens to be the chance meeting of one's parents; and for each of us our own death is tantamount to the annihilation of all that exists. From this line of thought the inference that we have "lost the motive of action" seems plausible. The atheist Albert Camus for one saw the question of suicide in the face of an absurd universe as the most important issue to be addressed by philosophy.

I have said that the answer to the question of human ends in a random universe is ambiguous. In the last few decades a number of atheist thinkers have vigorously resisted the idea that the randomness of reality entails the meaninglessness of human existence. The most influential defense of this view is Kurt Baier's essay "The Meaning of Life: Christianity Versus Science."

Baier's arguments include the following:

> There are many things that a man may do, such as buying and selling, hiring labourers, ploughing, felling trees, and the like, which are foolish, pointless, silly, perhaps crazy, to do if one has no purpose in doing them. A man who does these things without a purpose is engaging in inane, futile pursuits. Lives crammed full with such activities devoid of purpose are pointless, futile, worthless. Such lives may indeed be dismissed as meaningless. But it should also be perfectly clear that acceptance of the scientific world picture does not force us to regard our lives as being without a purpose in this sense. Science has not only not robbed us of any purpose which we had before, but it has furnished us with enormously greater power to achieve these purposes. Instead of praying for rain or a good harvest or offspring, we now use ice pellets, artificial manure, or artificial insemination.
>
> By contrast, having or not having a purpose, in the other sense, is value neutral. We do not think more or less highly of a thing for having or not having a purpose. "Having a purpose," in this

sense, confers no kudos, "being purposeless" carries no stigma. A row of trees growing near a farm may or may not have a purpose: it may or may not be a windbreak, may or may not have been planted or deliberately left standing there in order to prevent the wind from sweeping across the fields . . .

People mistakenly conclude that there can be no purpose *in* life because there is no purpose *of* life; that *men* cannot themselves adopt and achieve purposes because *man*, unlike a robot or a watchdog, is not a creature with a purpose.[11]

On the question of death and the meaning of life Baier says,

It is now quite clear that death is simply irrelevant. If life can be worthwhile at all, then it can be so even though it be short. And if it is not worthwhile at all, then an eternity of it is simply a nightmare. It may be sad that we have to leave this beautiful world, but it is so only if and because it is beautiful. And it is no less beautiful for coming to an end . . .

It will perhaps be objected now that I have not really demonstrated that life has a meaning, but merely that it can be worthwhile or have value. It must be admitted that there is a perfectly natural interpretation of the question, "What is the meaning of life?" on which my view actually proves that life has no meaning . . .

People are disconcerted by the thought that *life as such* has no meaning in that sense only because they very naturally think that it entails that no individual life can have meaning either. They naturally assume that *this* life or *that* can have meaning only if *life as such* has meaning. But it should by now be clear that your life and mine may or may not have meaning (in one sense) even if life as such has none (in the other). Of course, it follows from this that your life may have meaning while mine has not.[12]

Baier's views are developed further in the works of Kai Nielsen who argues that:

The claim that man's life will lack purpose without God trades on a crucial ambiguity about 'purpose.' When it is claimed that without God life would have no purpose, the religious apologist is talking about a purpose for man qua man. He is trying to talk about man qua man having a purpose in the sense that an artifact, plumber, merchant, doctor or policeman has a purpose. But it is far from clear that man has a purpose in that sense. It is also entirely unclear that man must remain estranged, sensing to the full that his life in the world is absurd, if he does not have such a purpose.

Many people feel that if man were not made for a purpose, his life must be without purpose. But here a spiritual malaise is being engendered by conceptual confusion. Sometimes 'purpose' is used to mean function or role; but sometimes 'purpose' is used to indicate that an action was deliberately or intentionally done, that it was the carrying out of someone's aim or wish.

The second use of 'purpose'—the use that Dostoyevsky was talking about in our initial example—is such that we would say that only people and perhaps some animals could have it. When we use 'purpose' in this sense, we are speaking of people's goals, aims, intentions, motives and the like. 'Purpose' has this sense when we speak of our purpose in doing something specific: "What was your purpose in bringing home that dog?" and "I wonder what his purpose was in coming here?" Now this is one major way in which 'purpose' is used in which the theist and non-theist alike are in complete accord that there is purpose in our lives—God or no God. And it is true that a life devoid of purpose in that sense would, without doubt, be a dreadful, senseless affair.

By contrast, we use 'purpose' in the first sense when we ask: "What is the purpose of that gadget in the kitchen?" or "What is the purpose of that fence along the road?" Here we imply that someone did something, in the doing of which he had some purpose; namely, to bring about the thing with the purpose. Of course, *his* purpose is not identical with *its* purpose. . . .

More importantly still, when we say "life must have a purpose or there is no point of going on," we are usually using 'purpose' in the second sense. It is in this sense that we so desperately want life to have a purpose. But life can have a purpose in that sense in the twilight, or even in the complete absence, of the Gods. And whether or not something has or does not have a purpose in the first sense of 'purpose' does not matter at all, for having or lacking a purpose in this first sense carries neither *kudos* nor stigma.[13]

Taken as they stand the distinctions made by Baier and Nielsen between "purpose *of* life" and "purpose *in* life" are unexceptionable, even trite. Of course we can give our own purpose to our activities: in this sense there is purpose *in* life even if there is no purpose *of* life. But this is hardly the issue. The question is not whether there can be purpose *in* life even if there is no purpose *of* life. The question, rather, is, "What difference does the fact that there is no purpose *of* life make to our lives here and now and to the various purposes *in* life that we give to our activities?" If there is no ultimate purpose, do proximate purposes have any real value? If we find ourselves on the highway headed nowhere in particular, is it any consolation to say that we can try to enjoy the ride while it lasts and stop at scenic spots and restaurants on the way until we finally run out of gas? True, we have to make the best of a bad situation. Nonetheless let's not pretend that the final futility of all human striving is not a "bad situation."

It is all very well to say that we should not be "disconcerted" by the absence of a "purpose of life" and of a life after death. But such counsel can only seem preposterous to a daughter mourning the loss of her father or to the reflective person facing the fact that everything we become and achieve will disappear forever. It is no doubt possible to make merry in the brief span between womb and tomb while trying to shut out all thought of one's mortality. Nevertheless there is a morbid quality about happiness obsessively pursued in the shadow of the Grim Reaper; and in any case all such hopes and joys and dreams are doomed to disappear almost instantly in "death's dateless night."

One can take a more noble, even heroic stance in the face of ultimate randomness by holding that life is precious because it is short and that we should try to enrich our lives and those of our fellow beings during our "nasty, brutish, short" spans of existence. This is a commendable plan of action indeed, but it does not slow down or alter the impact of the inexorable march of death. And if death is total extinction, then the degree to which you enriched your own life and those of your friends is ultimately irrelevant: first there is nothing, then there is your life, and finally there is nothing again, nothing forever and ever. In a section labelled "Atheism, Zeal, and Gloom" in the *Encyclopedia of Philosophy*, another atheist philosopher, Paul Edwards, argues that atheists can be attached to goals that give direction to their lives but concedes that "it cannot be denied that the thought of annihilation can be quite unendurable."[14] The idea that we come from nothing and return to nothing is disconcerting even to those thinkers who have sought refuge in the purpose and meaning we create for ourselves. Take Bertrand Russell. In *The Conquest of Happiness* this well-known skeptic prescribed a formula designed to produce happiness and to eliminate all factors conducive to unhappiness. In theory his program sounded both viable and attractive, but in practice it could not help even its progenitor. In *My Father Bertrand Russell* Russell's daughter Katherine Tait reports that "he [Russell] had had to struggle to keep despair at bay, and the optimistic visions of his popular books had not come easily to him; they were products of the will, maintained by determined effort against the sense of desolation that was always lying in wait for him. In moments of grief or weariness, it could overcome his ordinary hopefulness, and from the mountaintops of his vision of heaven he would plunge to the depths of hell."[15]

We see that it is possible to create our own "human ends" in the framework of ultimate randomness but that there is no preordained "end" to which the human enterprise is headed. Creating our own "ends" cannot take the sting out of the constant awareness that there is no ultimate "end" and therefore no ultimate meaning or significance. The idea of a purpose *of* life is derided by Nielsen and Baier because it implies for them that we are artifacts or gadgets in the hands of a master puppeteer. Such anthropomorphic concepts of God as artisan are foreign to traditional theism. And the purpose *of* life in at least some versions of theism is simply that of finding fulfillment in loving God and one another. About this vision of human existence, Bertrand Russell said, "Nothing can penetrate the loneliness of the human heart except the highest intensity of the sort of love the religious teachers have preached. Whatever does not spring from this motive is harmful and at best useless."[16]

. . . .

Cosmic Beginnings and Human Ends in the Framework of Ultimate Rationality

In contrasting the atheistic and the religious views of the world, we noted that the latter portrays the world as owing its origin and meaning to an ultimate reality that transcends it. In making this affirmation the religious view affirms thereby the ultimate rationality of reality. It is our object now to consider cosmic beginnings and human ends in the framework of ultimate rationality.

In the first place it is necessary to clarify what is meant here by the "religious view." Obviously there is no single view of reality held in common by the adherents of all religions. With respect to the existence of God, religions tend to adopt one of three positions: theistic, monistic, or agnostic (this classification is by no means comprehensive but is sufficient for the limited purpose of comparing the most influential views). In a nutshell, theism holds that the world (meaning all that exists) is the creation of an infinite, omnipotent, omniscient, omnipresent, personal Being. Monism holds that empirical phenomena and the multiplicity of selves are illusory and that the Ultimate Reality is all that exists. Presumably those who take an agnostic position on the existence of God will also take an agnostic view on the relation of cosmic beginnings and human ends to God; that being the case the agnostic position will not be considered here.

On cosmic beginnings it is clear that almost all the major religions have sought to relate the Many to the One (this theme is developed in great detail by Frederick Copleston, the historian of philosophy, in his Gifford Lectures published as *Religion and the One*). The existence of the world is the datum that has to be explained. The various religions explain the world either as a creation of the One or as an illusory manifestation of the One. In some cases the world itself is seen to be the self-transforming One.

Theism and monism both accept the existence of an Ultimate Reality. In addition both appear to agree that the world must be related to the Ultimate Reality. The differences between these two world-visions lie in their respective depictions of the nature of both the Ultimate Reality and the world and in their respective descriptions of the relation of the Ultimate Reality to the world.

It is a common error to identify theism strictly with the religions of the Book (Judaism, Christianity, Islam). Some of the most eloquent expositions of theism have come to us from Hindu thinkers like Madhva. It is equally erroneous to identify Hinduism and Eastern religions exclusively with monism or pantheism. As a matter of fact the majority of the Vedic and the non-Vedic schools affirmed the ultimacy of a plurality of souls that could not be identified with an Ultimate Reality. Pluralism was affirmed not just by the Nyaya, Vaisesika, Sankya, Yoga, and Mimamsa Vedic schools but also by prominent thinkers in the Vedanta tradition.

The most influential presentation of monism comes to us from the founder of the Advaita (non-dualistic) Vedanta school of thought in Hinduism, Sankara. In Sankara's view Ultimate Reality is Nirguna Brahman, wholly impersonal and without attributes, beyond human thought and conceptualization. Nirguna Brahman as the object of human thought and devotion is manifested as Saguna Brahman, as God, Who is personal and possesses all the attributes of deity. Sankara's distinctive claim was that the inner soul of each human being—atman—is one with Nirguna Brahman and with all other souls. It is ignorance—avidya—that prevents us from realizing that we are at one with Nirguna Brahman. Whether Sankara meant that all souls are identical with Nirguna Brahman when he said they are not different from Brahman is a matter of disputed interpretation. Ultimately Sankara based his exposition of monism on his interpretation of the Upanishads—particularly the famous "That thou art" passage. Although he believed that monism as a philosophy was internally coherent and could even be approached through mystical experience, the primary basis for his monism was his interpretation of the Upanishads.

Sankara's monism was by no means the only influential philosophy in Hinduism. Madhva's interpretation of the Upanishads called for a theistic understanding (see, for instance, "Madhva, Sankara, and the Ghost of the Buddha in the History of Vedanta" by Daniel Sheridan, *Religious Traditions*, volume 17, 1994). He criticized the Advaita philosophy because it contradicted the everyday experience of plurality. He also rejected the notion that the human soul is identical with Brahman, pointing out that one cannot be conscious of being identical with something else since this presupposes the "otherness" of the something else. His commentaries on the Hindu scriptures drew attention to the distinction between human imperfection and the perfection of God. Several other Hindu thinkers also insisted on the personal nature of Ultimate Reality, including Sorikantha, Nimbarka, and Vallabha.

The basis of theism is the affirmation that the only explanation for the existence of the world, or of anything at all, is the existence of a transcendent self-explanatory being that brought all things into being. This claim—that a transcendent self-explanatory being, God, brought all things into being—lies outside all possibility of scientific analysis or verification because science can only deal with things already in being, not with nothingness itself nor with things coming into being from nothingness.

The notion of "nothing" giving rise to "something" is today almost a commonplace in cosmological discussions of vacuum fluctuations and the like. Over the centuries philosophers and theologians who have considered the concept of "nothing" have been careful to emphasize the point that "nothing" is not a kind of something. Absolute nothingness can never be the object of

scientific inquiry because all such inquiry presupposes the existence of the object of study and of some order governing the
behavior of the object. William Stoeger notes that

> physics and cosmology, when they do deal with the origin of the
> universe, rarely do so directly, and always in terms of the origin
> of certain pervasive features of the universe, like space and time,
> or space-time, matter, or rather mass-energy, and so on. And in
> investigating their origin they must inevitably do so in terms of
> some pre-existing entities or structures or some pre-existing set
> of laws which these obey. Even the vacuum in physics is such a
> structure and obeys certain laws. It is not absolutely nothing.
> Neither is geometry—nor the principles of mathematics and
> logic. The origins with which science can deal are always what
> we might call "relative origins", which are indeed very impor-
> tant, absolutely crucial, for us to understand. But they are not
> absolute, or ultimate, origins.[17]

The "nothing" discussed by contemporary cosmologists often
turns out to be "something" in disguise. The use and misuse of
"nothing" in contemporary cosmology is usefully chronicled by
the philosopher Richard Swinburne (a contributor to this anthology):

> All these models have the consequence that you cannot explain
> states of affairs except in terms which involve other states of
> affairs. Laws cannot explain states of affairs by themselves; if they
> are to explain states of affairs, they can only do so in virtue of
> their operation on prior states of affairs. From time to time
> including very recently, cosmologists have suggested that a law
> by itself could explain the beginning of the universe ex nihilo.
> The suggestion (to caricature it a bit) is that the law might have
> the form "nothing necessarily gives rise to something" or (a bit
> more precisely) "there is a high probability that a zero energy
> vacuum lead to a space-time of negative or positive energy." The
> first thing wrong with a suggestion of this sort is that under close
> examination 'nothing' never turns out to be nothing; it is some
> sort of empty space in a quiescent state. If 'nothing' was really
> nothing, and the law really was "nothing necessarily gives rise to
> something", then since there are an infinite number of possible
> universes (each nonexistent at some past moment of time), not
> spatially related to each other, then by the law they must all have
> come into existence. In fact an infinite number of universes must
> come into existence at each moment of time. But that is to
> multiply entities beyond plausibility. A plausible law to explain

the beginning of the universe would at least have to have the form "empty space necessarily gives rise to matter-energy", where "empty space" is not just "nothing", but an identifiable particular. In an important sense there must have been something there already. The other thing wrong with the laws-can-do-it-alone suggestion is, granted that laws could explain why empty space at time t_0 produced matter-energy at time t_1, that does not explain why there is a universe of matter-energy unless we have an explanation of why the laws took over at t_0 rather than earlier. Some cosmologists would deny that there is any sense in requesting an explanation for the latter, and hold with Augustine (nullum tempus sine creatura) that if the Universe began, time began at that time as well. But the only content I can give to "the universe began 15,000 million years ago", entails that at a time before 15,000 million years ago there was nothing and then there was a universe. How can something begin to exist if it has existed at all moments of past time (i.e. always)? So if there was empty time before the universe, we need to explain why it began at the moment it did rather than earlier, and laws alone will not explain that. To put it another way—give a name which rigidly designates the actual present moment, call it T, and suppose that name to name it even when it is past. Then the question arises—why did the Universe begin 15,000 million years before T, and rather than 16,000 million years? We need states of affairs as well as laws to explain things; and if we do not have them for the beginning of the universe, because there are no earlier states, then we cannot explain the beginning of the universe.[18]

Another influential idea of our day on the origin of the universe is the Hawking-Hartle theory. In his consideration of theistic and atheistic pictures of creation, John Leslie, a leading authority on the anthropic principle, writes in this volume,

> Cosmologists now often try to avoid believing in infinite past time. In particular, many of them admire the Hartle-Hawking theory that time becomes more and more spacelike at ever earlier moments; the result is that, despite not stretching backwards for infinitely many years, the cosmos has no instant at which it began. Asking what existed before it began, to cause it, is like asking what Earth is like to the north of the North Pole. The cosmos has no cause. It just *is*. Yet even this can sound very unsatisfactory. Cannot we ask why there is this system with its laws which fuse space with time in this particular manner? Cannot we ask such a question even if those laws leave no room

for the system to be caused by something at a previous time? Philosophers often work with a concept of cause, or at least of responsibility, which is non-temporal. Augustine's God was creatively responsible for the universe although he had not existed before it: he created time and the world together. Believing that God was self-explaining, Descartes was correspondingly willing to speak of God as "self-causing", although he agreed that this would be nonsense if causation necessarily involved temporal priority.[19]

It has also been said that a theory of this kind is essentially based on an arbitrary aesthetic preference:

> To say, in Hawking's phrase, that the boundary condition for quantum cosmology is that there should be no boundary makes it sound as if the need for boundary conditions has been obviated. In truth, however, the decision to restrict attention to boundary-less universes is, in its own way, a boundary condition—a way of getting rid of unwanted solutions to the equations. For the hydrogen atom, we are justified in throwing away the bad wavefunctions, because we know in advance what hydrogen atoms look like, but for quantum cosmology there is no comparable independent check on the choice of boundary condition. If we were able to survey a great number of universes, as we can hydrogen atoms, we could figure out the correct conditions empirically. We have only one universe to examine, however, and the whole point of doing quantum cosmology was to find out from first principles what the universe ought to look like. This does not work: only by making an additional assumption, in the form of the no-boundary condition, does a sensible answer emerge, but the reason that the particular assumption was made was because we wanted to get a sensible answer. Clearly, this is circular reasoning. Hawking throws away "bad" universes because his quantum-cosmological formulation would go awry if they were included. But deciding that certain phenomena do not exist because the available theory cannot cope with them is a back-to-front strategy in any kind of science.
>
> Hawking's preference for closed universes mirrors the view of Einstein, who always found the idea of a closed universe, a finite construction with no boundary, more appealing to his sensibilities. At the bottom of all this, there seems to be little more than a vague feeling that finiteness is nicer than infiniteness. By contrast, there have always been some physicists and cosmologists who have found the endless stretch of space and time in an

infinite universe more comfortable, precisely because of the limitless possibilities it seems to allow. For all of quantum cosmology's sophistication, it ends up being a technically complicated piece of machinery that does little more than offer an incomplete physical justification for what remains an essentially aesthetic preference.[20]

Hawking himself acknowledges in his most recent book that his latest theory still leaves open the question of God's existence:

> SUE: To oversimplify your theories hugely, and I hope you'll forgive me for this, Stephen, you once believed, as I understand it, that there was a point of creation, a big bang, but you no longer believe that to be the case. You believe that there was no beginning and there is no end, that the universe is self-contained. Does that mean that there was no act of creation and therefore that there's no place for God?
>
> STEPHEN: Yes, you have oversimplified. I still believe the universe has a beginning in real time, at a big bang. But there's another kind of time, imaginary time, at right angles to real time, in which the universe has no beginning or end. This would mean that the way the universe began would be determined by the laws of physics. One wouldn't have to say that God chose to set the universe going in some arbitary way that we couldn't understand. It says nothing about whether or not God exists—just that He is not arbitrary.[21]

In my introduction to the anthology *Cosmos, Bios, Theos,* I tried to outline the path that leads from the scientific enterprise to a religious view of reality. On the question of cosmic beginnings, both theism and monism affirm the need for explaining the Many in terms of the One. Where these world-visions differ is on the reality of the world and on the question of a radical distinction between the world and the Ultimate Reality.

It would be a grave error to identify the subtle monism of Sankara with the naive pantheism of currently popular New Age philosophies. Pantheism taken as the identification of God with the world is simply tantamount to atheism. As Schopenhauer said, the term "God" is a superfluous label if God is identified with the world. The philosophy of Sankara, on the other hand, leaves room for interpretations that do not insist on the identity of the human soul with the Absolute. The notion that the Absolute is impersonal, however, is simply incoherent, as pointed out by H. P. Owen:

> It may be said that God is really supra-personal, and that personal symbols of him are merely finite attempts to express the

inexpressible; they are only modes in which a wholly supra-personal reality appears to untutored minds. This view is conceptually incoherent because the idea of a non-personal form of being that is not sub-personal is meaningless; for it is one to which we cannot give any content.[22]

One could ask two further questions concerning the first (the objective) interpretation of personal theistic terms. First, is not the idea of a wholly supra-personal, qualityless Absolute meaningless? How can we distinguish it from the idea of, simply, 'nothing'? Secondly, how could an impersonal Absolute assume personal properties? The only answer is the one given by Huxley—that it already contains them 'supereminently'. But to give the answer is to endorse the classical theist's view that the Godhead is, essentially and throughout its being, both infinite and personal.[23]

On the question of human ends there is a dramatic difference between the frameworks of ultimate randomness and ultimate rationality. The same question facing the random view must be addressed by the perspective of ultimate rationality: does human life have any ultimate purpose, meaning, and significance? All the major religions hold that the true "end" of *Homo sapiens*—the raison d'etre of human existence—is union with the Ultimate Reality. We do not come from nowhere and nothing and return to nowhere, to nothing. We come from God and our fulfillment comes in union with God. There are, of course, significant differences among the world religions on the nature of this union with the Ultimate Reality and on what it takes to attain union.

It is not our concern here to delve into the details of the systems of salvation—of union with the Ultimate Reality—embodied in the various religions, but it would be helpful to compare the monistic and the theistic views of "human ends." On the monistic view, salvation comes in dissolution of one's identity in the Absolute. On most theistic views, salvation comes from everlasting union with God—a union in which each creature retains its identity.

The nature of the human person, as understood in the influential schools of monism and theism, is clearly relevant in considering the idea of union with the Ultimate Reality and in the overall context of cosmic beginnings and human ends. On the monistic side Sankara saw the existence of a substantial, spiritual soul separate from the body to be a truth that cannot be denied without contradiction. Most theistic systems also hold that the human person is a union of body and soul. Prescinding qualifications of soul, spirit, and mind, we shall focus here on the claim that the human mind is intrinsically incorporeal and irreducible to the physical.

In modern times the scientific environment has been for the most part severely critical of non-physical notions of "soul" and "mind." Advancements in neuroscience and artificial intelligence (AI) have been cited as evidence for the purely material nature of mind and consciousness. But the debate is far from over. Noted scientists, most recently the Oxford mathematician Roger Penrose, have launched frontal assaults on the hardcore materialists; distinguished philosophers of science like Sir Karl Popper and Thomas Nagel have been long-time critics of naive materialism. In the world of artificial intelligence, the philosopher John Searle has emerged as a prominent critic of AI models of the mind.

For cosmologists who consider philosophical problems, the datum of departure is the existence of the world: how, ultimately, did it come into being? For neuroscientists and AI theorists, the datum of departure is the mystery of consciousness: how do we explain our very real experience of consciousness as a phenomenon radically different from the physical world? An article in a special issue of *Scientific American* devoted to mind and brain outlines the nature of the datum demanding explanation. Consciousness

> is quite rightly regarded as the most difficult problem in nature, more puzzling perhaps than the one which worried Einstein. And yet there are scientists prepared to insist that consciousness itself will yield to analysis, just as the problem of life has yielded. But there's the rub!—or rather the double bind. Although consciousness exists by virtue of some physical property of the brain, just as bioluminescence exists by virtue of some chemical property of certain specialized cells, it is *not*, as bioluminescence is, an observable property of living matter. It isn't a brain glow. Nor is it, on the other hand an *invisible* property, less readily detectable than other biological processes. It is detectable to anyone who has it. The difficulty is that the method by which consciousness is detected is logically different from the method by which bioluminescence is detected. To put it bluntly, consciousness is not *detected* at all, because that would imply that it could pass *un*detected, and that doesn't make sense. *Your* consciousness may pass undetected by me, but my consciousness, if I have it at all, is self-evidently self-evident to me.[24]

In the view of most materialist thinkers the problem of consciousness has already been solved by modern science. Two recent books have sought to demolish traditional conceptions, *Consciousness Explained* by Daniel Dennett and *The Astonishing Hypothesis: The Scientific Search for the Soul* by Francis Crick. Searle, who is a materialist himself, is not convinced that such demolition attempts will work. About Dennett he says, "It's not consciousness explained; it's consciousness explained away."[25] In his recent *The Rediscovery of the Mind* Searle takes many counterintuitive defenses of materialism to task by pointing out that "no sane person can deny its [consciousness's] existence, though many pretend to do so." About some rejections of consciousness he writes that these "are too insane to merit serious consideration."[26] It must be said here that some thinkers who take consciousness seriously up to a point—such as the Nobel Laureate Roger Sperry (a contributor to this volume) and the mathematician Roger Penrose—ultimately revert to reductionism: their attempts to "reengineer" common physicalist conceptions of consciousness remain rooted exclusively and entirely in physical processes (microtubules for Penrose, upper-level brain processing for Sperry). Professor Crick, who is similarly a reductionist with an "electrophysiological" explanation of consciousness, has generated considerable interest in consciousness in the scientific community—his exhortations on the matter have reportedly "helped incite an intellectual stampede" (*Scientific American*, July 1994, "Can Science Explain Consciousness?", 88). His essay on the soul, however, is really just a study of consciousness and simply visual consciousness for that matter. He is concerned with the brain activities accompanying visual awareness, not with the myriad mysteries of human thought. It is our experience of identity, intention, insight, and the like that we must attempt to explain if we really wish to engage in a "search for the soul"—but these territories are not explored or charted in *The Astonishing Hypothesis*.

The importance of remaining true to our experience is emphasized by Lynne Rudder Baker in *Saving Belief: A Critique of Physicalism*:

> To deny the common-sense conception of the mental is to abandon all our familiar resources for making sense of any claim, including the denial of the common-sense conception. If the thesis denying the common-sense conception is true, then the

concepts of rational acceptability, of assertion, of cognitive error, even of truth and falsity, are called into question.[27]

If consciousness is to be described and explained, it must be taken on its own terms, not on terms that are presupposed and superimposed by one's philosophical agenda. The idea that human consciousness can be adequately and entirely described in physical terms is a philosophical idea: it cannot be proved or disproved by science since *our experience* of subjectivity, intentionality, thought, and the like—unlike the physiological transactions that accompany the experience—cannot be quantitatively measured or tested. Richard Swinburne examines the scientific and the philosophical issues involved in his book *The Evolution of the Soul*. In his essay here he notes that

> It seems to me evident that mental events, and especially conscious events, are distinct events from brain events or other physical events. To have a red sensation is not the same event as to have one's C-fibres fire or any other going-on in the brain. For each consists in the instantiation of a different property (redness; a certain distribution of electric charge) in the same subject at the same time. One event may cause the other, but there are two distinct goings-on. A Martian visitor who discovered everything physical that was happening in the human brain (in the way of redistribution of chemical matter and electric charge) would want to know whether or not humans felt anything when you kicked them and they screamed, whether they purposed their arms to move, whether they had thoughts about the world, and so on. A full history of a human being would list mental events as well as physical events. Much philosophical ink has been spent in trying to construct arguments to deny what seems to stare us in the face—that conscious events are distinct from brain events. Unfortunately, I do not have the space here to marshal counter-arguments, though I have done so elsewhere. I shall therefore assume what I hope will be apparent—that consciousness is something distinct from what goes on in the brain, albeit closely connected causally to it. The conscious life, unlike the life of the brain, is rich in color, feeling, and meaning.[28]

Assuming the existence of an incorporeal mind or soul, we are led to the next question of what happens to the soul upon the death of the body. In monism it is assumed that each soul successively "occupies" various bodies in the process of liberating itself from the phenomenal world as it realizes its identity with

Brahman, the Absolute (the Buddhist theory of rebirth is different from Hindu theories of reincarnation because Buddhists do not recognize the continued existence of a substantial self: rebirths in Buddhism affirm the transmission of dispositional traits, not of a single soul). For the monist the culmination of the soul's journey of liberation from ignorance to enlightenment is its dissolution in the Absolute (we have seen, however, that most Vedic schools were pluralist and not monist in this fashion). The notion of dissolution in the Absolute has been criticized by Eastern and Western philosophers for not taking our experience of self-consciousness and the ultimacy and immediacy of our distinct personal identity seriously. H. P. Owen pursues this line of analysis:

> Pantheism fails to explain our awareness of distinctness and autonomy in things and persons. Our total experience of both personal and sub-personal entities is pervaded by the conviction that each is an independent form of existence. This conviction is immediately and uniquely present in each person's self-consciousness, whereby each is aware of himself as distinct from (and *therefore* capable of relating himself to) other persons. Pantheists can give one of two accounts of selfhood and thinghood. Both accounts are wholly unconvincing. According to the first account (available to those who adopt a rational form of pantheism), although each person is a mode of God each possesses a form of selfhood appropriate to this modality; each is a *self-conscious* mode. But this is absurd for three reasons. First, to speak of a self-conscious mode, or aspect, is a self-contradiction; it is like saying that 'a side of a large house' is equivalent to 'a small house'. Secondly, if we are self-conscious modes, why are we not conscious of being so? How did this metaphysical amnesia arise and (yet more seriously) come to pervade and dominate our whole experience? Thirdly, it is inconceivable how the Universal Self could include finite selves. A's thought, simply because it is A's, *cannot* include, though it may coincide with, B's thought. Their mutual exclusion belongs (ontologically) to the nature, and so (logically) to the definition, of selfhood. Yet if we say (with Bradley) that finite selves are mere 'appearances', or *a fortiori* (with Sankara) that they are illusory, we must face two unanswerable objections. First, how could such an appearance or illusion of multiplicity be created by a unitary Absolute? Secondly, if our selfhood is illusory, or even if it is only semi-real, none of our individual statements can be true—least of all our statements concerning a supposed Absolute.[29]

It can be argued that monists and pantheists who talk of the soul dissolving in the Absolute are really describing the soul's total dependence on God in dramatic metaphors. This might be true in some cases. For the theist of any religion, at any rate, true fulfillment for the human person comes from a union of love with the infinite plenitude of perfections Who is both Beginning and End, the Alpha and the Omega.

In concluding these reflections I confess to being one who has made the journey from a random view of reality to the view that there is an Ultimate Reality and that this Reality is Trinitarian: and that all humans are called to share (if they consent to do so) in the beginningless endless Love Act of the Three Persons. In *The Marriage of East and West* my late friend Dom Bede Griffiths, a living link between the wisdom of two worlds of thought and life, draws on the Trinitarian mystery in relating East to West:

> But the question arises, does the individual soul or consciousness survive in this ultimate state of being? Of this it must be said that every individual soul is a centre of consciousness itself. In its final fulfillment it participates in the consciousness of the supreme being and reflects the other centres of consciousness in itself, but it does not cease to be a unique centre of consciousness. The very purpose of creation was that the One should be able to communicate himself to the many, that finite and temporal beings should come to participate in the infinite and eternal being and consciousness of the One and experience the bliss—Saccidananda—of the Supreme. And this bliss is a bliss of love. Love seeks to communicate itself, and the purpose of love would not be satisfied if there were no one to share that love.
>
> But does this mean that there is duality in the godhead? It is here that the concept of relationship and 'co-inherence' which was developed in the Christian doctrine of the Trinity comes into play. Though there is no duality in the godhead, there is relationship—relationship of knowledge and love. By knowledge we receive the form of another being into ourselves, we become that other being, by a mutual 'co-inherence'. This is seen above all in personal relationship. By love we communicate ourselves to other persons and they communicate themselves to us. There is a mutual self-giving which is enjoyed in sexual union, but this takes place at a deeper level of consciousness, where there is a complete indwelling, I in you and you in me. In human life this communion is never fully realized but in the divine life this is realized in its fullness. This is what is revealed in St. John's Gospel when Jesus says, 'I am in the Father and the

Father in me'. This is not a simple identity—he does not say, 'I am the Father'—but a relationship of knowledge and love. But at the same time, there is perfect co-inherence. The Father is in the Son and the Son in the Father in such a way that they have but one nature which is totally in each without any duality. There is no difference between the Father and the Son except that of relationship. Their nature or essence is one 'without duality', without any difference whatsoever.

It would seem that this doctrine helps us to see how there can be knowledge and love in the godhead, that is in ultimate reality, while it remains for ever 'without duality.' But it also shows how created beings can come to share in this non-dual mode of being and consciousness . . .

When human nature is taken up by the Spirit into the knowledge and love of the Father and the Son, the human consciousness is opened up to the divine mode of consciousness . . . This is the vision of ultimate reality which is given us in the perennial philosophy. It is common to Greece and to India, China and Arabia, and is found in the Christian doctrine of the Mystical Body of Christ, where each creature participates through the indwelling presence of the Spirit in the inner life of the godhead and each reflects the glory in the other, 'being changed from the glory into glory as by the Spirit of the Lord.'[30]

"The Knight of Faith," wrote Saul Bellow, ". . . having set its relations with the infinite, was entirely at home in the finite."[31] Herein lies the relation of cosmic beginnings to human ends in the framework of ultimate rationality.

• • • • • • • • •

Notes

1. Werner Heisenberg, *Physics and Beyond: Encounters and Conversations* (New York: Harper and Row, 1971), 87.
2. Bertrand Russell, *Why I Am Not a Christian* (New York: Simon and Schuster, 1957), 107.
3. Albert Camus, *The Rebel: An Essay on Man in Revolt*, trans. Anthony Bower (New York: Random House, 1956).
4. T. S. Eliot, *Four Quartets* (New York: Harcourt, Brace and World, 1943), 11, 17.
5. Of course influential contemporary philosophers like Richard Rorty hold that philosophical questions themselves are pseudo-questions, but the notorious difficulties of such positions have been amply documented in systematic treatments of nihilism.
6. Stanley Jaki, *Genesis One Through the Ages* (London: Thomas More Press, 1992).

7. Eric R. Scerri, "Eastern Mysticism and the Alleged Parallels with Physics", *American Journal of Physics*, 57 (August 1989), 8.
8. "Random" is discussed here in the sense of absence of purpose and not in the specialized sense of probability theory.
9. Jean-Paul Sartre, *Being and Nothingness* (London: Methuen, 1957), 539–40.
10. T. S. Eliot, *Four Quartets*, 14.
11. Kurt Baier, "The Meaning of Life: Christianity Versus Science" in *Philosophy for a New Generation*, A. K. Bierman and James A. Gould, eds. (New York: Macmillan, 1973), 681–82.
12. Ibid., 686.
13. Kai Nielsen, *Ethics Without God* (New York: Prometheus Press, 1973), 38–40. Nielsen's claims about morality without God are trenchantly analyzed in R. Z. Friedman's "Does the Death of God Really Matter? Kai Nielsen's Humanistic Ethics," *International Philosophical Quarterly* 23 (1983): 321–32.
14. Paul Edwards, ed., *The Encyclopedia of Philosophy*, vol. 1 (New York: Macmillan, 1967), 188.
15. Katherine Tait, *My Father Bertrand Russell* (New York: Harcourt Brace Jovanovich, 1975), 182–83.
16. Bertrand Russell, *The Autobiography of Bertrand Russell*. Vol. 1 (Boston: Little, Brown, 1967).
17. William Stoeger, "The Origin of the Universe in Science and Religion," in *Cosmos, Bios, Theos*, Henry Margenau and Roy Abraham Varghese eds. (La Salle: Open Court, 1992), 263
18. Richard Swinburne, "The Limits of Explanation," in *Explanation and its Limits*, Dudley Knowles, ed. (Cambridge: Cambridge University Press, 1990), 178.
19. John Leslie, "Creation Stories, Religious and Atheistic," 344f.
20. David Lindley, *The End of Physics* (New York: Basic Books, 1993), 243–44.
21. Stephen Hawking, *Black Holes and Baby Universes* (New York: Bantam Books, 1993), 172.
22. H. P. Owen, *Concepts of Deity* (London: Macmillan, 1971), 42.
23. Ibid., 123.
24. Jonathan Miller, "Trouble in Mind", *Scientific American*, September 1992, 180.
25. Quoted in Robert K. J. Killheffer, "The Consciousness Wars," *Omni*, October 1993, 54. Dennett admits that explanations of consciousness rely on plausible metaphors, but his metaphors of "Joycean machines" and "multiple drafts" have been criticized on the grounds of implausibility. About Crick's book one reviewer writes, "Could two things so apparently dissimilar as a thought and neural firing really be identical? Brushing aside this philosophical question with the insouciance of a great scientist, Mr. Crick instead takes the reader on an absorbing tour of the experimental efforts aimed at discovering how brain processes give rise to our visual consciousness. . . . Near the end of *The Astonishing Hypothesis*, the always genial author con-

cedes that there may be aspects of consciousness that lie beyond the reach of science. Yet so stalwart is his faith in the scientific method that he urges it even on those who believe that the soul is something more that the purely material firing of neurons." Jim Holt, "Decoding Our Ancient Genetic Text", *Wall Street Journal,* January 24, 1994.

26. John R. Searle, *The Rediscovery of the Mind* (Cambridge: MIT

27. Lynne Rudder Baker, *Saving Belief: A Critique of Physicalism* (Princeton, New Jersey: Princeton University Press, 1987), 134. The reductionists have not been left unchallenged. For instance, the Rutgers philosopher Colin McGinn in *The Problem of Consciousness* writes "that no strictly physical theory—whether based on quantum mechanisms or neural ones—can explain consciousness." This theme was pursued by David J. Chalmers of Washington University at a recent conference of neuroscientists, "Toward a Scientific Basis for Consciousness": "All physical theories, Chalmers claims, can describe only specific mental *functions*—such as memory, attention, intention, introspection—correlating to specific physical processes in the brain. According to Chalmers, none of these theories addresses the really 'hard' question posed by the existence of the mind: Why is the performance of these functions accompanied by subjective experience? After all, one can certainly imagine a world of androids that resemble humans in every respect—except that they do not have a conscious experience of the world. Science alone cannot supply an answer to this question, Chalmers declares" ("Can Science Explain Consciousness?," *Scientific American,* July 1994, 94). See also "The Emergence of Intelligence" in the *Scientific American* special edition "Life in the Universe" (October 1994), where William Calvin acknowledges the startling nature of language and intelligence while (implausibly) straining to explain their emergence in reductionist terms.

28. Richard G. Swinburne, "The Origin of Consciousness," 358.

29. H. P. Owen, *Concepts of Deity,* 71–72.

30. Dom Bede Griffiths, *The Marriage of East and West* (London: Collins, 1982), 98–100. H.-T. Huang's paper in this collection notes that Taoist thought includes a concept of the Trinity. Also, the Oxford New Testament scholar N. T. Wright has shown that early Judaism came to think of Wisdom and Torah almost as distinct beings without compromising monotheism.

31. Saul Bellow, *Mr. Sammler's Planet* (New York: Penguin, 1971), 52.

. . . .

From Rationality and Intelligibility to an Ultimate Explanation

1 What are your views on cosmic beginnings, particularly with reference to the origin of the universe, of life, and of *Homo sapiens?*

In my view the ultimate explanation for the existence of the world, or of anything at all, is the existence of a transcendent self-explanatory being that brought all things into being. This claim—that a transcendent self-explanatory being, God, brought all things into being—lies outside all possibility of scientific analysis or verification because science can only deal with things already in being, not with nothingness or with things coming into being from nothingness. It is a philosophical claim rooted in the insight that the world is rational and intelligible (Einstein said that "a conviction of the rationality or intelligibility of the world lies behind all scientific work of a higher order"), and that this very rationality and intelligibility calls for an ultimate explanation of the Many in terms of the One.

I hold also that we experience consciousness as a phenomenon qualitatively different from the physical world and that the postulation of an incorporeal mind "makes sense" of the phenomenon of human consciousness. On the origin of consciousness I share the view articulated by Professor Swinburne in this anthology: "The occurrence of the conscious life and its mode of functioning (under the limited conditions of embodiment in bodies with brains), which otherwise are likely to remain totally mysterious, can be explained in terms of divine action."

2 What are your views on human ends, especially as this relates to the framework of cosmic beginnings?

For the theist of any religion, true fulfillment for the human person comes from a union of love with the infinite plenitude of perfections Who is both Beginning and End, the Alpha and the Omega.

3 What do you think should be the relationship between religion and science?

Regarding the relationship between science and religion, it must be understood that the empirical realm in its entirety is the province of science and any quantitative claim concerning the empirical must conform with the canons and norms of the scientific method. To ask "What physical processes led to the formation of the universe?" is to ask a scientific question; to ask "Why does the universe exist?", however, is to ask a non-scientific question, one which falls entirely outside the realm of telescopes and supercolliders, fields and strings, equations and information superhighways. Any answer to this question is necessarily philosophical or theological.

INDEX
· · · · · · · · · ·